THE DIALECTIC IS IN THE SEA

The Dialectic Is in the Sea

THE BLACK RADICAL THOUGHT
OF BEATRIZ NASCIMENTO

BEATRIZ NASCIMENTO

EDITED AND TRANSLATED BY
CHRISTEN A. SMITH, BETHÂNIA N. F.
GOMES, & ARCHIE DAVIES

PRINCETON UNIVERSITY PRESS

PRINCETON & OXFORD

Published by Princeton University Press
41 William Street, Princeton, New Jersey 08540
99 Banbury Road, Oxford OX2 6JX

press.princeton.edu

All Rights Reserved

Library of Congress Cataloging-in-Publication Data

Names: Nascimento, Maria Beatriz, author. | Smith, Christen A., 1977– editor, translator. | Gomes, Bethânia, editor, translator. | Davies, Archie, editor, translator.
Title: The dialectic is in the sea : the Black radical thought of Beatriz Nascimento / Beatriz Nascimento ; edited and translated by Christen A. Smith, Bethânia N. F. Gomes, and Archie Davis.
Other titles: Black radical thought of Beatriz Nascimento
Description: Princeton : Princeton University Press, [2023] | Includes bibliographical references.
Identifiers: LCCN 2023021221 (print) | LCCN 2023021222 (ebook) | ISBN 9780691241227 | ISBN 9780691241203 (pbk.) | ISBN 9780691241210 (ebook)
Subjects: LCSH: Movimento Negro Unificado (Brazil) | Black people—Race identity—Brazil. | Black people—Brazil—Social conditions—20th century. | Women, Black—Brazil—Social conditions—20th century. | Social movements—Brazil—History—20th century. | Brazil—Race relations. | Brazil—Social conditions. | Nascimento, Maria Beatriz. | Women intellectuals—Brazil—Biography. | BISAC: HISTORY / Latin America / South America | POLITICAL SCIENCE / Essays
Classification: LCC F2659.B53 N384 2023 (print) | LCC F2659.B53 (ebook) | DDC 305.896/081—dc23/eng/20230602
LC record available at https://lccn.loc.gov/2023021221
LC ebook record available at https://lccn.loc.gov/2023021222

British Library Cataloging-in-Publication Data is available

Editorial: Priya Nelson, Emma Wagh, and Morgan Spehar
Production Editorial: Nathan Carr
Jacket/Cover Design: Heather Hansen
Production: Lauren Reese
Publicity: Jodi Price, Carmen Jimenez, and Alyssa Sanford
Copyeditor: Natalie Jones

Jacket/Cover Credit: Roman Melnychuk / Unsplash

This book has been composed in Arno

10 9 8 7 6 5 4 3 2 1

Bethânia:

To Isabel Nascimento, Francisco and Rubina,
and the Nascimento family.

Christen:

To Hoji and Kayô, and in memory of
Annie Viola Williams Wiggins.

Archie:

To Christen and Bethânia.

CONTENTS

Preface: Dear Mamãe

Bethânia N. F. Gomes

I FIRST KNEW Beatriz Nascimento as my mother, *Mamãe*. Simply a beautiful Black woman with whom I identified.

When I talk about Beatriz, it returns me to my childhood, my teens, and my early adulthood: those moments that shape who we later become, when we create our earliest dreams. The world that Beatriz presented to me was diverse, yet very Afrocentric. When I was growing up, my everyday life was full of talk of Blackness. The word *negro* was everywhere in my mother's presence. I believed my mother was born saying that word. *O negro, o negro brasileiro, o negro americano*, and, of course, *a mulher negra*—the Black woman. The words *África* and *diáspora*, too. As I was growing up, I asked myself why she talked about us— *negros*—all the time. As a lower-middle-class Black girl, in Rio de Janeiro, my answer was all around me. Yes, we had *samba* and *carnaval*, but I would hear Beatriz talking about "something else": social injustice, and the monster of racism.

She taught me so much about being a Black girl born in Brazil. She shaped me to be positive, to love my skin, my people, my culture, and to love the African diaspora. I came to understand the African continent as the mother of diversity, and my homeland, Brazil, as one of its children. As the African continent was to Brazil, so was my mother to me. My father was African, from Cape Verde, and my mother made me a proud and assured Black, Brazilian, African woman. She traveled to

Africa and the Caribbean, and she never let me doubt my identity: my African heritage and the strength passed to me from my ancestors, including her.

She wrote night and day. In my teens she began to write more and more poetry. Sometimes I would sneak in and read her beautiful words. I asked her to write a book of poetry so I could enjoy the art and music of our journey. I came to love those poems with all my heart and soul. There, the Black person was not just someone suffering pain and injustice. Her poems confronted racism and told a beautiful history straight from the heart of a strong African descendent—my mother.

One day, near the anniversary of the abolition of slavery (May 13), a phrase she wrote came to my mind: *É preciso saber de onde se vem para saber a onde se vai* (We must know where we have come from to know where we are going). That was the first time I learned that activism had its own poetry.

I was constantly seeking people who were like me but had a different geographical or linguistic background. I was in awe when my Cape Verdean family came to visit. Today, I can still feel my little heart jumping at hearing their accents and their Criollo language—even more so at the English-speaking people who came into my life: first musicians like Bob Marley, Michael Jackson, Tina Turner, and Diana Ross, and then my mother's friends from overseas, who came to our home and spoke in English. And that's when one of my dreams began.

My dream was to travel the world and see many different cultures and faces. My dream was also to live in the United States and practice classical ballet: I was and still am a professional dancer. With the support of my mother and my family, I became more self-confident and resilient. I believed that I would fulfill my dream of moving across the borders of body, culture, and language. In my late teens, I took the first big step on this journey when I joined the Dance Theatre of Harlem (DTH) Professional Program and then the company itself. Arthur Mitchel became my director, mentor, and second father. When I received my first contract, another dream crystallized in my mind and soul: to bring my mother to live with me in the United States and become a soloist with DTH.

On January 28, 1995, however, that dream was cut short. Beatriz no longer walked this earth. She was no longer able to move her body, speak her languages, and communicate her genius. She transitioned into another dimension, where her Ôrí kept on speaking and reaching out to some of us. When she passed away, the road was hard. In many moments, for many years, I felt that I had lost the ground beneath my feet. After years of recovering from such a tragedy in my life, finding myself again and again without her, through the pain, anger, and solitude, I was blessed with an extended family. And the people who gave me that are the very four people who are part of this book, as well as other studies, panels, classes, and symposia on Beatriz Nascimento.

First, thank you to Alex Ratts, my mother's biographer and my cosmic brother, with whom for years I have shared my wish to enable my mother's work to touch others' hearts like it touched mine. It was when I met him, in his own search for Beatriz and working on his book *Eu sou Atlântica* (2006), that I felt a reunion with my mother and felt she was coming to me. Christen A. Smith, an anthropologist who through her research on anti-Black racism in Brazil and the United States found Mamãe, became my soul sister from Washington, DC. Archie Davies, who, with bravery, translated my mother's work with so much patience and care, and witnessed my moments of emotional struggle. And, finally, thank you to my beloved godfather Muniz Sodré, who held me at my mother's funeral and who holds me, spiritually, every time I ask him, to this day, for his blessings through Father Xango.

I would also like to acknowledge and honor the strength of my aunt Maria Isabel Nascimento, who, in a moment of great sorrow, was able to save her sister's legacy, holding my hand and Ôrí to donate the Beatriz Nascimento Archives to the Brazilian National Archives. Without Tia Bebé all of this wouldn't be possible.

Today, I translate my mother's work and legacy to fulfill my dream of bringing her to the World and to the African diaspora. Through the work on this book, I have reunited with my mother, and I have found myself. But I also believe that others can find in it the beauty of our history, our soul, and our activism. It's not just because she is my mother: I believe the work of this amazing woman can show us part of our history. I fulfill, too, the wishes from her Ôrí, that never cease to enlighten us to a better understanding of who we are as Africans, who were labeled as products in the market that I, Bethânia, will always call a holocaust. We are the living bodies of Quilombo. We will shape the African diaspora, and the World, into a new chapter, into a better human life and a better future, in the cosmic hands of Beatriz Nascimento.

   Beatriz Nascimento vive.

Beatriz Nascimento lives.

Axé!

ACKNOWLEDGMENTS

IN PROJECTS like this, which reflect the summation of years of thought and multiple research trajectories, it is difficult to thank everyone who helped us through the journey. Nevertheless, we try to do our best. One of the most enjoyable and challenging elements of this project has been fact-checking in the archives. Although we were able to visit the National Archives in Rio de Janeiro prior to the coronavirus pandemic, during the pandemic we were limited in our ability to travel to conduct research. During this time and just following the period when public spaces reopened, we were privileged to have access to the LLILAS Benson Library at the University of Texas at Austin. Librarian Ryan Lynch, senior library specialist Alejandro Lopez, and library specialist Gab Alderete-Cruz were invaluable partners during this time, performing great feats of archival sleuthing in order to help us locate Beatriz Nascimento's original publications, which were often miscited in previous publications, or difficult to find. They were also extremely warm and generous in allowing us the flexibility to access and scan rare materials and share a warm cup of coffee. Words cannot express our gratitude to them and all the fantastic library staff at the Benson, whose collection of historical material related to Brazil's Black Movement is unmatched. We would also like to thank the archivists at the National Archives in Rio de Janeiro for their assistance in 2019 and 2023.

Negotiating distance between collaborators when writing and researching is always a keen challenge. We were privileged to have the support of Christen's doctoral candidate Daisy Guzman, who was able to offer research assistance on this project and liaise with Bethânia to scan much-needed photographs from New York City. We would like to thank the editors of *Antipode*, Andy Kent, and the Antipode Foundation for their support for this work in an earlier iteration. Some reworked elements of the text from the introduction to these essays in *Antipode* appear in the introductory essays in this book. We would like to thank Alissa Trotz, Pat Noxolo, and Alex Ratts for their early comments on that work during the Feminist Futures / Feminist Pasts Symposium hosted by the Center for Women's and Gender Studies on April 28, 2021 (a video of the event, "In Front of the World: Translating Beatriz Nascimento," can be viewed on YouTube).

We are very grateful to Emma Wagh, Natalie Jones, Priya Nelson, and Nathan Carr at Princeton University Press for their professionalism and patience.

Bethânia would like to thank Josiane Nascimento, Luena Nascimento Nunes Pereira, Arjan Adjani N. Gomes, Djosa Gomes, Maria do Carmo Nascimento, Maria Zelia Nascimento, Vitor Manuel Nascimento, Evorah Nascimento, and Isolda Nascimento Bustillo Z. Bastos.

Christen would like to thank her family—Hojidiamazy, Olukayô, Clayton, Elaine and Wallace Smith—for giving her the space, time, and energy to research and write this book with Archie and Bethânia. They allowed her to spend mornings and weekends collaborating over Zoom and squirreling away in her office and in the archives, and for that she is immensely grateful. She would also especially thank Clayton for introducing her to the film *Ôrí* when he invited her to its relaunch at the Livraria Cultura in 2009—that experience made her fall in love with Beatriz Nascimento, and inspired her to take a deep dive into Nascimento's work.

Key to writing is feedback, and Christen would like to thank the colleagues who have read versions of this work over the years and have commented on portions of what we present here. Special thanks to Bryce Henson and Melissa Stuckey for feedback on parts of the introductory texts.

Archie would like to thank Jenny Pickerill, for sage counsel and calm words during the project, and Nadia Mosquera Muriel, who offered encouragement and friendship in its early days in an office at the Institute of Latin American Studies in London. Alexandra Reza accompanied the project from the beginning and advised on myriad points of translation and interpretation. She overheard the laughter of a hundred Zoom calls.

As unconventional as this may be, the three of us would like to thank each other. As we compiled our individual acknowledgments, we each included one another unwittingly. We think this is a testament to the friendship and trust we have cultivated over the years. So, in the spirit of collaboration, we thank each other for one another's brilliance, dedication, patience, and friendship. Arriving to this book has been a long journey, and we cannot think of better collaborators to be our companions. It has truly been a pleasure being in dialogue together, and we are eternally grateful for our partnership. We all, in some way, have welcomed one another into the world of Beatriz Nascimento. Our mutual trust and friendship continue to be a source of great joy.

Introductory Section

Introduction

Christen A. Smith, Bethânia N. F. Gomes,
& Archie Davies

The earth is round; the sun is a disc. Where is the dialectic? In the sea.
—"PORTUGAL"

General Introduction

Beatriz Nascimento was one of the most innovative Black intellectuals of the twentieth century in the Americas. During the twenty-five-year period in which she wrote, she produced compelling, avant-garde, and foundational ideas about the Black condition and the Atlantic world. A working-class Black woman who grew up in the peripheries of Sergipe and Rio de Janeiro, she was a radical public intellectual, and an organizer in Brazil's Black Movement from the 1970s through the 1990s. She critiqued white supremacy, patriarchy, sexism, racial capitalism, white paternalism, and racial democracy at the height of Brazil's military dictatorship, making her a critical voice on the Left during one of the most repressive periods in Latin American modern history. She was also one of only a few women to become a leading intellectual voice on the national stage for Brazil's Black Movement in that time of intense political struggle. She was transnational in her thinking, passionate in her critiques, and decisive in her analytics. In 1995, her life was cut short when she was tragically murdered, leaving behind unfinished essays, unrealized dreams, and our own speculations about the global impact she could have had, should she have lived longer. In the spirit of expanding her reach and her legacy, this book is the first to collect and translate her work into English.

Beatriz Nascimento engaged in topics from Brazilian history, culture, and politics, to race, gender, and sexuality. She wrote academic scholarship, public opinion pieces, essays, and poetry. Her primary theoretical contributions focused on the past and present life of *quilombos*—communities of runaway enslaved Africans that formed in Brazil beginning in the sixteenth century (roughly translated as *maroon communities*). However, despite her deep and richly insightful work, to date her oeuvre has been understudied. Like many intellectuals from the Global South writing and researching in languages other than English—especially Black and Indigenous scholars—Beatriz Nascimento has not received the global academic attention she deserves. The fields to which she contributed most—history, human geography, anthropology, sociology, communications, Black Studies, and gender and sexuality studies—can learn much from her writings. This book hopes to partly redress her marginalization by putting her into her rightful place in the global Black radical tradition.

A Short Biography

Beatriz Nascimento was born in Aracaju, Sergipe, Brazil, on July 12, 1942. Her parents, Rubina Pereira Nascimento and Francisco Xavier do Nascimento, had ten children, of whom Beatriz was the eighth. Her mother cared for the family and the home, and her father worked as a stonemason. When she was seven, the family moved from the northeast to Rio de Janeiro, and settled in the suburb of Cordovil.

After excelling at school, Beatriz Nascimento briefly worked in a textile workshop. In 1967 she married José do Rosário Freitas Gomes, an artist and architect from Cape Verde, with whom she had one child, Bethânia Gomes. That same year, she began her undergraduate studies, and completed her bachelor's degree in history from the Federal

FIGURE 0.1. Beatriz Nascimento, private collection of Bethânia
Gomes.

University of Rio de Janeiro (UFRJ) in 1971. Afterward, she interned at
the National Archives in Rio de Janeiro, working with the historian of Rio
de Janeiro, José Honório Rodrigues (1913–1987). She completed graduate work at the Fluminense Federal University (UFF) in 1981. In 1994
she began a master's in communication from the UFRJ under the direction of renowned Black Brazilian intellectual Muniz Sodré.

Beatriz Nascimento's most sustained academic and political concern
was "to rewrite and reinterpret the history of black people in Brazil"—a
task that she connected directly to the question of Black liberation, freedom, and peace.[1] For Nascimento, writing history was a fiercely political
act. She used historical analysis to mount an affront against the racism
of the Brazilian academy and the Brazilian state. She relentlessly insisted
on documenting the intrinsic and intimate relationship between living
Black people, African history in Africa and the Americas, and Black cultural practices and forms. Her research on quilombos was key to this life
project. Quilombos became the representation of Black continuity for
Beatriz Nascimento. While pursuing her thesis at UFF (in the 1970s),
she conducted ethnography on surviving quilombo communities in the

state of Minas Gerais. Between 1976 and 1979 she investigated this topic, often working with Black anthropologist Marlene de Oliveira Cunha (1950–1988). Cunha was the first president of the Grupo de Trabalho André Rebouças (GTAR) and collaborated with Nascimento, undertaking oral history and archival research in a quilombo near Carmo da Mata in Minas Gerais. The most important elements of this work were published and became part of Nascimento's master's thesis. A large portion of this work is gathered in part III of this book.

Nascimento carefully crafted a theory of quilombo that argued for a continuous sociocultural-political relationship between the historical practice of quilombo and Brazil's Black culture today—particularly as it manifests in *favelas*. She developed this perspective through her ethnographic interactions with quilombo communities, her close analysis of urban Black culture in Rio de Janeiro and São Paulo, and her archival research on quilombos in Angola, Brazil, and Portugal. Nascimento always saw this research as intimately connected to her political work. And, as her writing in this collection shows, she also connected this work to her personal experience.

Beatriz Nascimento's political and intellectual trajectory can be traced back to her work as a student organizer in Rio de Janeiro in the 1960s and 1970s. As the global student protest movement reached its apex in May 1968, students on the Left in Brazil protested the military dictatorship, marched in the streets, and occupied universities. These actions were met with police repression, torture, and disappearances.[2] During this period, Nascimento participated in, and helped found, several Black student groups at UFF. She took part in important public events and debates around Blackness and contemporary racial politics, contributing to the resurgence of Black activism in the context of Brazil's military dictatorship (1964–85). While the stories of student and leftist organizing during the dictatorship have become central to political discourse in Brazil in the four decades since the end of the period, histories of the Black experience under the dictatorship remain silenced and marginalized.[3] The dictatorship was a dangerous time for anyone to be politically active, and to be a young Black woman leading student and Black political movements was highly risky work.

Nevertheless, Nascimento remained outspoken and active throughout the most intense periods of political repression.

Beatriz Nascimento was an early member of the Movimento Negro Unificado (MNU, the Unified Black Movement).[4] In the early 1970s she began to organize student groups in Rio de Janeiro and Niterói, and at the newly created the Centro de Estudos Afro-Asiáticos (CEAA, Centre for Afro-Asiatic Studies), founded in 1973. With others, including Eduardo de Oliveira e Oliveira (1924–1980) and Marlene Cunha, she founded and ran the Grupo Trabalho André Rebouças (GTAR, The André Rebouças Working Group).[5] The group was both academic and activist, made up of Black students and scholars. It was named, by Beatriz Nascimento herself,[6] after the Black Brazilian engineer and abolitionist André Pinto Rebouças (1798–1880). Under Nascimento's intellectual leadership, the GTAR had the strategy of taking their meetings outside the university, and they organized events at the CEAA as well as at the Teatro Opinião (The Opinion Theater) in Copacabana. For instance, in 1976 they organized the Week of Study on the Contribution of Black People in the Brazilian Social Formation, and they continued to organize events for two decades.[7]

In 1977 Nascimento was one of only a few women who took part in the Quinzena do Negro (Black Fortnight) at the University of São Paulo. This was a vitally important event in the history of Black Brazilian thought, bringing together activists and scholars, and setting out new directions for the movement. At the Quinzena, Nascimento was in dialogue with other important Black scholar activists, like Hamilton Cardoso (1953–1999) and Eduardo de Oliveira e Oliveira. It was during the Quinzena that Nascimento introduced her early theoretical ideas about quilombos as not just historical occurrences but also cultural and political practices that can be traced back to Bantu-Congo (Angolan) cultural practices. She also expounded her reflections on the intersectional political realities of Black women in Brazil and articulated a critique of racism in the Brazilian academy. In various capacities she worked with, or was in dialogue with, other important Black women intellectuals and activists, such as Thereza Santos and Lélia Gonzalez.[8] Nascimento maintained a wide and deep network of relationships

FIGURE O.2. Beatriz Nascimento (*left*) with Abdias do Nascimento (*center*) and Lélia Gonzalez (*right*), photograph by Elisa Larkin Nascimento, archive of Instituto de Pesquisas e Estudos Afro-Brasileiros (IPEAFRO, Afro-Brazilian Studies and Research Institute).

with Black activists not just in Brazil but increasingly across the Atlantic world.

In September–October 1979 Nascimento made an important trip to Angola, via Portugal, to conduct research on quilombos and write on newly emerging social and national formations in the recently independent African nation.[9] In 1987–88 she traveled to Dakar with a Brazilian delegation to attend the Festival Pan-Africaine des Arts et Cultures (FESPAC, The Pan-African Festival of Art and Culture). Her archive attests to a growing international network in this period,[10] and in the early 1990s she traveled to the Caribbean, to Martinique and Haiti. Following the success of her film *Ôrí* (1989), which won international prizes from Ouagadougou to Portugal and San Francisco, Nascimento was invited, alongside her collaborator, the film director Raquel Gerber, to present the film outside Brazil, including in Germany.

Nascimento's activism is indissociable from her writing and research, and she writes explicitly about her activist work in texts published here, such as "The Slaves Seen by the Masters: Merchandise and Counterculture

FIGURE 0.3. Beatriz during screenings of *Ôrí*, private collection of Bethânia Gomes.

in National Cinema," and "Maria Beatriz Nascimento: Researcher." The most poetic source, however, for her activist work, is perhaps the film *Ôrí*, which she worked on between 1977 and 1988 with its director, Raquel Gerber. The film, which was released in 1989, draws on her research, writing, and political practice, and constitutes one of Nascimento's most significant intellectual offerings.

Nascimento continued to write and research while teaching in the early 1990s, particularly in publications linked to the Black Movement.[11] Beatriz Nascimento's life ended tragically on January 28, 1995. She was murdered while defending a friend, Áurea Gurgel Calvet da Silveira, against an abusive partner. Upon her death, the secretary of the antiracist

FIGURE 0.4. Beatriz Nascimento at book signing, private collection of
Bethânia Gomes.

organization the Centro de Articulação de Populações Marginalizadas
(Centre for the Articulation of Marginalized Populations), Ivanir dos
Santos, placed her death in a long line of murders of Black political
activists.[12] She was in a relationship with Roberto Rosemburg at the
time of her death. She was buried in the São João Batista cemetery in
Botafogo, Rio de Janeiro.

In addition to her published articles and essays, Nascimento left a
substantial archive of unpublished academic and nonacademic work. It
is clear that if she had continued living, she would have published pro-
lifically. Her research incorporated a broad range of topics, including
but not limited to African and Afro-Brazilian history, the Black condition, gendered racism, and Black love. Her work helped build the intellectual foundation for Brazil's Black Movement at a key moment in its
history by forging a new Brazilian thought and politics.

Since her death, Beatriz Nascimento has been increasingly recognized as a vital figure in Black Brazilian intellectual and political history.
In 1997 the Afro-bloco Ilê Aiyê paid homage to her in their carnival
presentation. In 2016 the National Archive in Rio de Janeiro named its

main library after her. In October 2021 the UFRJ, her alma mater, bestowed her an honorary doctorate.

In the rest of this introduction, we first place Beatriz Nascimento's work in the context of the Black radical tradition in Brazil. We then introduce how her work might be read in relation to contemporary English-language Black Studies, Black feminism, and critical geography, articulating how her theorizations of the quilombo and transatlantic Black history and experience can extend and challenge our understandings of Blackness, race, space, and nature in the anglophone world. Finally, we discuss the spirit of collaboration that lies behind this book, as well as some of the challenges and nuances of translating Beatriz Nascimento into English.

The Black Movement in Brazil

Brazil's Black radical tradition must be understood within the context of the broader transnational Black liberation movement of the 1970s. The Black Movement in Brazil—which was indeed a resurgence of national Black organizing against anti-Black racism—is the milieu of Beatriz Nascimento's *militáncia*—radical Black political action—and the intellectual context in which she developed her most influential ideas. Yet, it is the broader historical arc of Black radical politics in Brazil that comes to shape Beatriz Nascimento's thinking about Black history, quilombos, and Black resistance.

The history of the Black Movement in Brazil is punctuated by various key junctures that mark paradigm shifts in the approach to Black politics. Since the first enslaved Africans were brought to Brazil, Black Brazilians have struggled for equality and justice within Brazil's system of racial oppression. Throughout the legal slavery period (ca. 1541–1888), enslaved Africans fought against their forced servitude by organizing successful and unsuccessful revolts and escapes. This fight continued after the legal end of slavery as de facto conditions of slavery persisted. Before 1888, this fight included, most notably, the establishment of quilombos as autonomous Black/African societies outside of and against Portuguese colonial rule.[13] As historian João Reis notes, the practice of quilombo was everything from stealing away from plantation work to attend candomblé ceremonies (African-Brazilian religious practices), to periodic escapes and the establishment of autonomous societies that lived independently from Portuguese rule and refused enslavement. From the notable quilombo kingdom of Palmares, to the Malê Revolt in Bahia in 1835, African people fought Portuguese oppression directly, often at great cost. The threat of slave revolts was a real and present danger in the minds of the ruling classes within slave society. The most famous of these was arguably the Malê Revolt, which was ultimately unsuccessful but which set the stage for the repression of Black people in Brazil for generations to come. Many of the laws resulting from this crackdown led to the increased victimization of Black people by the courts and heightened restrictions on the movement of Blacks both free and enslaved. The revolt also inspired a spirit of refusal and subversion among enslaved Africans and their descendants for generations. In many ways, the practice of quilombo is the inaugural expression of Black anti-colonial, anti-slavery political articulation in Brazil and even in the Americas.

The quilombo kingdom of Palmares became one of the more important historical symbols of the Black Movement beginning in the 1970s. Palmares was a cluster of quilombos self-governed by enslaved Africans who escaped servitude and inhabited by a diverse population (including a few white and some Indigenous people). The kingdom was founded in approximately 1605 when enslaved Africans on a large plantation in the captaincy of Pernambuco, in the present-day state of Alagoas, revolted.[14] Preferring to take their chances in the wilderness than remain on the plantation and wait to be discovered, they fled. Their community grew, and they established a system of government, army, and society while periodically fending off invasion attempts by the Portuguese. Palmares managed to remain independent until 1694, when the quilombo was overtaken. The king of Palmares, Zumbi, evaded capture until 1695, when on November 20 Portuguese colonizers captured, hanged, and quartered him, gruesomely displaying his body. The colonizers stuck his head on a pole and put it in the town square as a threat to all enslaved Africans. The death of Zumbi became more than a warning sign,

however. For generations of Black Brazilians, the death of Zumbi be-
came a symbol of African resistance and a sign of Black agency. In Porto
Alegre in 1971, a Black Movement group named Palmares suggested that
the Black community declare November 20 the annual day of Black
consciousness in Brazil. As we discuss in the introduction to part I,
May 13 (the date of legal abolition) became an insult to many Black
Brazilians because of its focus on the alleged benevolence of Princess
Isabel, who was responsible for signing the law of abolition in 1888 (Lei
Áurea, Golden Law), rather than the agency of the enslaved. As a counter
to this narrative, the Black Movement came to embrace November 20
as the true day of Black consciousness.[15] This date became nationally
recognized as the Day of Black Consciousness in 2003 and was official-
ized as a commemorative date in 2011, although it has yet to become a
national holiday.[16]

After slavery legally ended, the descendants of Africans continued to
organize against racialized oppression. Two Black political expressions
reflected this moment: the emergence of the Black press and the 1931
founding of the Frente Negra Brasileira (FNB, The Black Brazilian
Front), Brazil's first national Black political party, to combat racism on
the state and federal political levels.[17] The organization addressed issues
pertinent to the Black community like unemployment, a phenomenon
the FNB linked (and rightfully so) to the state's immigration policies at
the time.[18] It also became a defender of Far-Right political tendencies—a
counterpoint to the later leftist trajectory of the Black Movement in the
1970s onward. The Black Brazilian Front was never successful in promoting its political agenda, but its legacy of political activism would
reverberate through the years.

More sustainable was the Black press. While social movement
organizations and Black political mobilizations waxed and waned from
the nineteenth century through the twenty-first century, the Black
press has been a relatively stable and continuous voice of Black politics.
From *Clarim d'Alvorada* and *A Voz da Raça* in the nineteenth century
to *Maioria Falante* in the 1980s and 1990s and *Jornal Ìrohìn* in the 1990s
and 2000s, Black newspapers and magazines have historically been a
key way for Black Brazilians to express their political thoughts and

frustrations.[19] As we will see, these venues became a critical outlet for Beatriz Nascimento's writing. Many of her most widely read essays were published in and by the Black Press.

Ultimately, President Getúlio Vargas dissolved FNB for being a separatist organization, shifting, once again, the national paradigm of Black politics in the country. In 1944 actor, *militante* (literally *militant* but widely used by the Black Movement to self-identify as radical Black organizers), scholar and artist Abdias do Nascimento founded the Black Experimental Theater (O Teatro Experimental do Negro [TEN]) in Rio de Janeiro.[20] The organization won a place in the national spotlight from 1944 to the early 1960s by radically questioning how the Brazilian stage should and would represent Black people, and by using the theater as a political base for organizing the Black community around issues of social change. The fact that the theater became such a vital voice against racism and for the valorization of Black culture and heritage was and still is significant. The Black Experimental Theater not only set the tone for Black politics in the 1940s, 1950s, and early 1960s; the company also set the stage for the resurgence of Black radical politics in the 1970s through the medium of the arts. TEN would become the precedent for cultural groups like the Black carnival group Ilê Aiyê, which we discuss below. These groups would use cultural spaces and expressions as a method of radically refusing the myth of racial democracy—the utopic and erroneous notion that race does not exist in Brazil, only color gradations of a unified, national people.[21]

In 1964 the military dictatorship began in Brazil. Intense censorship started in December 1968 with the enactment of Institutional Act Number Five, "which gave juridical sanction to the institutions of repression and 'internal security.'"[22] Criticisms of Brazilian society and, in particular, attention to racial discrimination, became subversive acts punishable by law.[23] During the most intense period of the military dictatorship's censorship (1969–75), Black communities across Brazil politically stirred. In 1974 two Black men, Apolônio de Jesus and Antônio Carlos "Vovô," exasperated by the racism of Bahian carnival and Brazilian society established Ilê Aiyê, an Afrocentric carnival group (Afro-bloco) designed to valorize Black aesthetics and Black culture. Ilê Aiyê would become a critical moment in the shift in Black politics during the dictator-ship period. The Afro-bloco movement would come to have a tremen-dous impact on the country, particularly in the case of Salvador, Bahia. Ilê Aiyê became a catalyst for a new generation of Black politics in Brazil under the shadow of the repressive regime.[24]

In 1978, motivated by de facto segregation and police violence, Black community leaders in São Paulo organized the Movimento Negro Unificado Contra Discriminação Racial (MNUCDR, later just MNU), the first nationwide Black political organization since the FNB. When the MNUCDR organized in 1978, it also revived the memory of Zumbi. The group's manifesto used Zumbi as the symbol of pride that empow-ered them to fight for justice against discrimination and for full citizenship rights for Black people. The words that the MNUCDR used in their 1978 manifesto draw directly on this historical connection: "We, Black Brazil-ians, proud descendants of Zumbi, leader of the Black Republic of Pal-mares, that existed in the State of Alagoas from 1595 to 1695, are today united in a fight to reconstruct Brazilian society, directing it toward a new order, where there will be a real and just participation of Black people, who are the most oppressed of the oppressed; not just here, but everywhere we live."[25] In addition to invoking Zumbi, the MNUCDR also took care to acknowledge the transnational connections between the plight of Black people in Brazil and the plight of Black people every-where around the globe. This reminds us that Pan-Africanism has played an important role in defining Black Movement politics in Brazil, and we see this clearly in Beatriz Nascimento's writings.

Throughout the 1970s and 1980s, cultural and political organizing around Black identity issues intensified, and Black/Afro-identity be-came a symbol of cultural as well as political resistance. This politicized aesthetic was exemplified by the Afro-funk movement in the periphery of Rio de Janeiro. Black poets and actors across the country also actively engaged the theater and performance as a means of both cultural and political expression. This engagement was tied closely to the broader Black Movement happening around the country. For example, in books and at public events, the poetry collective Quilombhoje of São Paulo talked openly about racism and issues facing the Black community.

Black arts politics constituted the soul of Black political fervor. It was amid this political context of Black expression that Beatriz Nascimento emerged as a Black radical thinker.

The Black Radical Tradition

Beatriz Nascimento's ideas on Black liberation made an indelible impact on Black politics in Brazil during the military dictatorship. As Bethânia recalls in our conversation that closes this volume, Nascimento was arrested by military police in the 1970s while she was a university student. During that time, one of the questions the police asked those they arrested was "What are you reading?" Ironically, what may have saved Nascimento from disappearance and torture is the racist state assumption that Black people from the favela could not possibly be reading, because they could not possibly be intellectuals. They did not even come to her house to look through her books, despite the fact that her family, in their concern, rushed to get rid of them. In the Brazilian social imagination, the dominant image of the university student was (and still is) a white person. Black people and especially working-class Black people living in the periphery were not imagined to be intellectual subjects. Although Black people from the peripheries were indubitably criminalized by the military and its repressive rule, the idea that these same people could be intellectual threats to the state was counterintuitive . . . or was it?[26] This assumption, of course, was wrong.

Beatriz Nascimento was, in every sense, an intellectual militante—an intellectual whose research and thinking were accompanied by a fierce commitment to organizing and dismantling oppressive social structures. Each word that Nascimento wrote was also part of a larger political project of Black liberation and antiracism. When she conducted in-depth ethnographic research in the surviving quilombo communities of Maranhão, spent time in the archives, and completed major academic research projects that were both individual and collaborative, she was doing so not only to satisfy her intellectual curiosity but also to contribute to the larger project of Black liberation in Brazil.

Nascimento's academic research anchored her in the practice of radical Black organizing: protest, contestation, confrontation, and deconstruction. For this reason, much of her writing is public writing—she wrote to shape public discourse, not to satisfy the arbitrary benchmarks of the academy. She was politically active from her days as a university student until her death. In each of her texts, we see the same goals: dismantling and demystifying anti-Black racism and sexism in Brazil, and delegitimizing the repressive, anti-Black state and its correspondent discourses of racial democracy.

In using the phrase "the Black radical tradition" to define Beatriz Nascimento's thinking, we deliberately locate her intellectual legacy within a particular global discourse. The term *radical* is not one that she used to describe herself (at least not to our knowledge). The word *radical* in English translates literally into *radical* in Portuguese, but carries a negative and even pejorative connotation in the Brazilian cultural context. Our decision to employ it is not, therefore, a linguistic one. Rather, it is a genealogical mapping that recognizes the resonance between her ideas and those whom anglophone Black Studies scholars have traditionally considered part of the Black radical tradition: for example, Andaiye, Amílcar Cabral, Angela Davis, Frantz Fanon, W.E.B. Du-Bois, C.L.R. James, Claudia Jones, Audre Lorde, Eric Williams, Huey Newton, Kwame Nkrumah, Cedric Robinson, Walter Rodney, Thomas Sankara, Aimé Césaire, Suzanne Césaire, Richard Wright, and Sylvia Wynter, among others.[27]

Black women's place within the Black radical tradition has often been erased or undervalued. Carole Boyce Davies engages the work of Robin D. G. Kelley when reflecting on where and how Black women fit into the Black radical tradition.[28] Specifically, Davies notes that Kelley argues that Black intellectuals writing about the "global implications of black revolt" is in part what defines Black radical thought.[29] Indeed, anti-colonialism, anti-racism, anti-imperialism, anti-capitalism, the deconstruction of anti-Blackness and the insistence on the right to Black self-determination might all be characterized as aspects of the Black radical tradition. In addition, writings and musings on Black freedom and autonomy, particularly when tied to aspirations for Black revolution, are also dimensions of the Black radical tradition. Beatriz Nascimento and her contemporaries fit squarely into this rubric. Her writings take direct aim at the repressive, racist/sexist regime of the Brazilian state and Brazilian society. Many of these critiques are via a historical lens, which is both a brilliant and savvy way to critique the state without referring to contemporary politics during dangerous political times. For example, in speaking of slavery, she often uses the present tense despite referring to the past. This allows her to imply the perpetuation of the conditions of slavery into the present without directly (and dangerously) critiquing the Brazilian military state's dictatorial investment racial democracy. It is interesting to note, too, that her research on quilombos was funded by not only the Léopold Sédar Senghor Foundation but also by the Ford Foundation.[30] However, as she notes in the unpublished text "Alternative Social Systems Organized by Black People: From Quilombos to Favelas (b)," translated here, the Ford Foundation, while willing to fund her historical research, refused to fund the extension of that work into the contemporary world of favelas. Though one of the more progressive funding bodies working in Brazil at that time, the Ford Foundation balked at the revolutionary potential of her move to see the quilombo in the favela.[31]

Beatriz Nascimento is a Black radical intellectual precisely because her writings helped buttress the Black Movement's efforts to confront the white supremacy of the Brazilian state by delegitimizing racial democracy and celebrating a diachronic Black history—the existence of a Black past, a Black present, and a Black future. It was her writing—along with that of other Black intellectuals like Clóvis Moura and Abdias do Nascimento—that helped create a narrative around the history of Black insurrection, fugitivity/flight, and autonomous community-building that became the backdrop to the fight against racism and anti-Blackness in the 1970s through the 1990s, which included the ratification of the new constitution in 1988 after the end of the dictatorship. By researching and writing about quilombos, Black everyday resistance, Black psychology, Black cultural expressions, Black solidarity, Black trauma, and Black life

more generally, Beatriz Nascimento effectively argued that Black Brazilians have a revolutionary, anti-colonial genealogy of struggle that continues to shape the culture and mindset of Black people in Brazil today. This
deceptively simple concept became the principle historical and intellectual battle cry of the Black Movement during the military dictatorship
and continues to define present-day Black radical politics in Brazil.

Another fundamental element of Beatriz Nascimento's work that locates her squarely within the Black radical tradition is her focus on the
African diaspora through her theorization of the Atlantic. For Nascimento, the Atlantic Ocean is not only a physical geographic zone but also
a metaphysical space of Blackness.[32] This thinking comes out clearly in
the film Ôrí, which was based largely on her master's thesis. This beautiful film, primarily narrated by Nascimento, traces the historiography of
the practice of quilombo as a Black cultural legacy intimately connecting
Brazil with Angola/the Americas and Africa. Ôrí builds on her research
on quilombos, as well as her autobiography and her philosophical and
cultural interpretation of transatlantic Black space. It traverses the ocean,
and brings into critical and creative juxtaposition Black dance, philosophy, history, and politics. It is also a powerful archive of Brazil's Black
Movement in the 1970s and 1980s. In making the film, Raquel Gerber
created invaluable footage of Black Movement debates at the height of
the Black struggle in the 1970s and 1980s, footage that demonstrates the
important contribution that Beatriz Nascimento's theorizations of
Black politics and culture made to those discussions. Ôrí displays Nascimento's diasporic sensibility, which is at once grounded in contemporary Brazilian urban space and connected to global African histories of the transatlantic slave trade and colonial economy. Nascimento's
conscious refashioning of elements of the politics and discourse of a
global Black radical tradition were particularly palpable toward the end
of her life. We can read this engagement, for instance, in the discussion
of Steve Biko, and the allusions to Frantz Fanon, in "For a (New) Existential and Physical Territory."

Seriously engaging the work of Black intellectuals from Latin America in the discourse of the Black radical tradition is long overdue. Beatriz

Nascimento is a key thinker who deserves a place in the Black radical pantheon.

Black Studies

Beatriz Nascimento played a fundamental role in forming what Alex Ratts calls "the academic Black Movement" in Brazil in the 1970s, 1980s, and 1990s. Like many of her Black Movement contemporaries, Nascimento began organizing while she was studying at the university—a place that was fertile ground for leftist political formation at this time. Black students interested in Black organizing, the majority of whom were working class, developed a parallel political articulation that was both academic and community engaged. Thus, the Black Movement emerged in the classroom and in the streets in parallel. Nascimento's university organizing played a fundamental role in shaping the academic Black Movement. As she notes in "Letter from Santa Catarina," her work was read at one of the early meetings that led to the founding of the Centro de Estudos Afro-Asiáticos by students from the Fluminense Federal University. This influence is in addition to her founding the GTAR. Beatriz Nascimento can quite easily be described as one of the founders of Black Studies in Brazil.

During the late 1960s, close to the time that Nascimento and her contemporaries were organizing, the academic field of Black Studies (in African American/Black Studies departments and programs at universities) in the United States emerged in the wake of the student uprisings of the Black Power movement. Efforts to create the first Black Studies program (which would become a department) began at San Francisco State University in 1968 after a series of successful student protests that insisted on the institutionalization of Black Studies. This moment was part of a larger wave of student protests for the creation of Black and ethnic studies that reverberated across the country over the next decade. As Robin D. G. Kelley observes in *The Black Scholar* (2020), in his retrospective on the fiftieth anniversary of Black Studies, "The interdisciplinary project we have come to call 'Black studies' has always been about Black lives, the structures that produce premature death, the ideologies that render us less than human, and the struggle to secure our future as a people and for humanity. It emerged as an intellectual and political project rooted in a Black radical tradition without national boundaries and borders." The project of Black Studies has historically been an activist-intellectual project grounded in the insistence on the preservation and proliferation of Black life and the upturning of all social systems of oppression ideologically anchored in anti-Blackness.

In Brazil, Black Studies as an intellectual-political project was defined by the organic intellectualism of the Black Movement. We distinguish Black Studies from Afro-Brazilian studies, which, within the context of Brazil, have historically been programs established *within* (not against or despite of) universities to research Black people not as subjects but as objects of study. This disciplinary area has historically been dominated by white-mestizo liberal intellectuals who study race and Blackness rather than Black intellectuals who come from Black Movement political spaces.[33] This is significant for understanding many of the critiques that Beatriz Nascimento registers here in her writings, particularly in part I of this book. Black Brazilian intellectuals have developed a unique Black Brazilian radical tradition in direct conversation with grassroots political organizing for Black liberation, and often in tension if not in direct conflict with the white-mestizo university system.[34]

Space, Time, and Spirituality

Nascimento's writing reminds us of the need to expand our knowledge of Black women's unique experiences and theorization of space, time, and spirituality (including embodiment, ontology, and subjectivity) in the Americas. It is her symbolic interpretation of quilombos that has left its most lasting legacy, as her biographer, Alex Ratts, discusses in this volume. Connected to this work are deep reflections on history, geography, and spirituality that demonstrate her epistemological groundings and philosophical approach to the world.

Beatriz Nascimento's work can be put fruitfully into dialogue with the field of Black geographies and Black feminist geographies, which have emerged as rich spheres of work in the last two decades.[35] Her contribution, here, is to be found in the interconnections between territory, embodiment, liberation, and the transoceanic space of the Black diaspora. Katherine McKittrick, following Dionne Brand, observes, "humanness is always geographic—blood, bones, hands, lips, wrists, this is your land, your planet, your road, your sea."[36] For Nascimento, Blackness, the body, the earth, and the sea are also similarly interconnected and profoundly geographic. The sea, the body, and the land constitute physical and metaphysical spaces of grounding for Blackness in the Americas. The term *grounding* here is both energetic and physical. It is also historical cultural, political, and spiritual. It gels people of the African diaspora together across time and space, even in the absence of physical exchange and connection. In other words, quilombo—as praxis, territory, and space—is a political manifestation as well as an embodied and metaphysical search for freedom. This conceptual background provides the mapping necessary to understand the conceptual impetus behind much of Nascimento's work.

Beatriz Nascimento's interest in the body as a political site is deeply connected with her interpretation of the practices of trance in candomblé. The transcendental possibilities of trance and Black spirituality, and their concrete transoceanic histories, are vital for her poetic/political vision of liberation.[37] In the Afro-Atlantic experience of trance, emerging from African religious practices across the Americas, the Black body can exceed its geographic and territorial boundaries.[38] In elaborating these ideas, Nascimento draws on candomblé cosmology. The *orixás*, *minkisi*, and *voduns* (African gods from different African religious traditions variously practiced in Brazil today in candomblé) traveled with enslaved people across the Atlantic—rooting displaced Africans to both American and African earth. Thus, the body, as flesh, is a space of relative freedom tied to an ancestral home-space mediated through the natural world, and the orixás, voduns, and minkisi of candomblé spirituality. Across Nascimento's work—and in particular in her later, exploratory thinking on sound and the cosmic (see figure 0.5)—these spiritual practices are also linked to the spatial history of quilombo. She notes, for instance, that African religions were practiced in quilombos in Brazil (see, for instance, "Black People, Seen by Themselves" and "Kilombo and Community Memory: A Case Study"). This means that, in Nascimento's hands, Black geographies are anchored in both liberated territory and spiritual embodiment—an embodiment located within a history of oppression but also a history of flight (*fuga*) in pursuit of freedom.

Nascimento was not a trained geographer, and her work has not, with the vital exception of Alex Ratts's framing of her as a cultural geographer in *Eu sou Atlântica* (2006), been systematically engaged by geographers, whether Brazilian or otherwise. She framed her work, in academic terms, generally in relation to the discipline of history, and as a critique of its methods, conclusions, and politics in Brazil. Yet her writing is profoundly spatial, from the scale of the body to the scale of the ocean. When read alongside her political practice, and the history of the Black Movement in Brazil, her work offers another string to the bow of the analysis of diverse Black spatial imaginaries.[39] Her writing on territory, quilombo, and land can contribute, for instance, to the burgeoning field of work that addresses what Sharlene Mollett calls "land-body entanglements in the Americas."[40] Considering Beatriz Nascimento as part of an open, global, always expanding tradition of thinking about space and nature aims to suggest that her writing offers a great deal to movements to challenge and reassess the history of geographical thought. More open (multilingual, transnational) intellectual histories can be important tools for critical engagements with the history of disciplines such as geography. Powerful new forms of anti-colonial, anti-racist geographies are emerging, under banners including the decolonial,[41] Black geographies,[42] and abolition geographies.[43] We hope that Nascimento's work finds readerships in these fields. That said, this is not to try to fit Nascimento into these categories, and we should be very cautious about co-opting her radical voice into confected schools, which can gather enormous variety under anaesthetizing categories.[44] Rather, her work challenges categorization while offering new points of reference, new coordinates, and new ideas, to geographical thinking about space and liberation.

NAME: MARIA BEATRIZ NASCIMENTO
DATE OF BIRTH: 17/07/1942
NATIONALITY: BRAZILIAN

I - Professor attached to The Secretary of Education - RJ - 1984
  until now
II - Post-Graduate in Social Comunication and Information in Brazil,
  ECO/UFRJ - Comunication School/Federal University Rio de Janeiro,
  1992.
III - Post-Graduate and Specialist in History of Brazil - ICHF/UFF
  (Federal University Fluminense) 1979-1981
IV - Graduated and Licensed in Universal History - IFCS/UFRJ, 1971
V - Itinerary, Long Text and Narrative on Long Documentary Film,
  ORI of Raquel Gerber Director:
  - Costa Azul Prize (The Man and the Nature section) 5º Cine Tróia
    Festival - Portugal. 15 Best Documentaries in the World-Centenn-
    ial of the City of Yamagata International Documentary Film Fest-
    ival, 89. - Japan. Honorable Mention for Documentary - Prized
    Pieces 89 - National Black Programming Consortium, Columbus -
    Ohio - USA. Special Jury Award Film and Video Sociology Cate-
    gory in the gold Gate Awards Competition - San Francisco Interna
    tional Film Festival - California, USA. 11º Paul Robenson Prix
    in the Pan African Festival Cine and Television, Ougadogou, Bor
    kinafaso - Africa. 1989
VI - Research on the Theatrical Play "THE LIBERTY CAUSE" - Black mos-
  vement from Slavery Abolition, 1988.
VII - Speaker in meetings concerning Afro-american culture andthe
  Hero Zumbi de Palmares - since 1974 until now.

FIGURE 0.5. Beatriz Nascimento's resumé, early 1990s. The context of this document is unclear in her archive, but it shows that she was expanding her anglophone intellectual interests at this time. Fundo Maria Beatriz Nascimento, National Archives of Brazil, Rio de Janeiro.

```
VIII -  Many International Journeys to Africa (RPDE Angola, Senegal,
        Mali, Nigeria, Côte D'Ivoir) and Caribean Islands (Martinique,
        Guadalupe) - 1979, 1987, 1991.
XIX -   Research of the Kilombos movement in History at the Ford Foun
        dation, also at the Leopold Senghor Foundation, 1978 - 1980.
X -     At present doing research on sounds emitted in Holography spa-
        ce by Afro-Brasilian and Afro-Latin entities (Placed in Candom
        ble's Ecological Heap).
```

Rio de Janeiro, 17 october 1992

Maria Beatriz Nascimento

FIGURE 0.5. (*continued*)

Writing, Text, and Style

"African knowledge" is put in museums, libraries, and academic and religious temples. Our knowledge is canonized. What does this mean? The protected archives of the West will guide our future, loaded with stigmas and preconceived marks. In the next generations we will have to live with this, and to live well with it. In the end, these are the true records of the inter-relations between Europeans, Africans, and Americans, and they are preserved by the hegemonic hemisphere.

—"ARUANDA!"

This book, like others in Portuguese publishing Beatriz Nascimento's work after her death, has to work with an archive of published and un-published writing that is highly various in form, state of completion, intent, and style. In her lifetime, Beatriz Nascimento published articles in mainstream newspapers including the *Folha de São Paulo* and *Jornal do Brasil*, as well as cultural magazines such as *Revista de Cultura Vozes* and *Revista do Patrimônio Histórico*. She also published in specialist academic journals including *Estudos Afro-Asiáticos* and was a member of the editorial board of *Boletim do Centenário da Abolição e República*. She coauthored a book, *Negro e cultura no Brasil* (Black people and culture in Brazil) (1987), with José Jorge Siqueiro and Helena Theodoro. In the last two decades, a number of projects have emerged in Brazil to publish her writing. These include three books edited by Alex Ratts—*Eu sou Atlântica* (2007), *Uma história feita por mãos negras* (2021), and *Beatriz Nascimento: O negro visto por ele mesmo* (2022)—and *Beatriz Nascimento: Quilombola e Intelectual* (2018), organized by the Union of Pan-Africanist Collectives and edited by Editora Filhos de Africa with Abisogun Olatunji Oduduwa, Jéferson Jomo, Raquel Barreto, and Lucimara Barbosa. These books have been invaluable to putting together this edition. Two essays, "A mulher negra no mercado de trabalho" and "A mulher negra e o amor," have been reprinted in the edition *Pensamento feminista brasileira: formação e contexto* (Brazilian feminist thought: Formation and context) (2009), edited by Heloisa Buarque de Hollanda.

The major source for this book, as for those described above, is Nascimento's archive, which is housed in the Brazilian National Archives in Rio de Janeiro. Following in the steps of Alex Ratts, important intellectual work has recently begun to emerge drawing on this archive—notably two doctoral theses. Wagner Vinhas Batista both offers an interpretation of Beatriz Nascimento's intellectual trajectory and does vital archeological work on the archive itself, in producing a schematic index;[45] and Diego de Matos Gondim has combined ethnographic, philosophical, and historical work to develop the relationship between land, meaning, and the notion of quilombo.[46] More work remains to be done on that rich collection of documents, which offers great insights not only into the development of her thought and practice but also into late-twentieth-century networks of Black and Third Worldist movements in Brazil as well as the wider Atlantic world.

Nascimento's poetry was largely unpublished in her lifetime, though in the early 1990s she was seeking funding to organize and publish this body of work.[47] This work has now been completed, with the publication in Portuguese in *Todas (as) distâncias: poemas, aforismos e ensaios de Beatriz Nascimento* (2015), edited by Bethânia Gomes and Alex Ratts.

We have included a single poem to introduce each section of texts, but a full English edition of her verse will have to wait for another book.

Her prose style has at least three modes. These are, first, an academic and studious mode, which conforms to Brazilian norms of scholarly writing, with quite careful referencing and a social scientific tenor in the construction of argument. This style predominates in, for instance, part III of this book, in her writing on quilombos. The second mode is more hawkish, but still academic and social scientific. This style is found in public texts that intervene into debates about Brazilian politics, society, and historiography, such as those in part I, like "For a History of Black People" and "Our Racial Democracy." Here, her writing often adopts a sardonic texture, in particular when dealing with mainstream white and Luso-tropicalist Brazilian social science, and with co-optations and distortions of Black culture and politics. This style is always tightly bound to her political projects of the moment; these texts, interviews, and reflections, and Nascimento's modulations of her voice within them, are fruitfully read alongside the development of the Black Movement in the moment of their publication. The final mode is more personal, private, and existential. This tone is steeped in her poetic and artistic vision and practice. It often predominates in texts that were not published in her lifetime, such as "The First Great Loss" and "An Aside to Feminism." Here, her style is allusive and spiritual.

The most intricate and enduring moments of Beatriz Nascimento's style, perhaps, emerge when these two latter modes coincide. We can find this in texts like "For a (New) Existential and Physical Territory" and "Toward Racial Consciousness." These pieces combine the confessional, personal, forthright writing of her poetic side with the trenchant, uncompromising clarity of her political demands for justice and truth.

There are different difficulties associated with translating these three modes. The academic prose presents relatively familiar challenges for translating Brazilian academic discourse: what to do with the long sentences that are a hallmark of Brazilian scholarly style but lose their focus in English. Transposing those sentences into English requires a disaggregation of singular, complex arguments, whose grammar and syntax face inward, into a series of phases and phrases of an argument that are

separate from one another at the level of the sentence, but whose interaction is marked by conjunction and explicit interconnection. This is
one practical way in which translation is interpretation: the building
blocks of arguments are often implicit to the Portuguese syntax but
made explicit in the English translation. In the second mode, in which
the sardonic is a political tool, an attentive ear for tone is necessary, and
here the collaborative process of our translation, discussed further
below, was vital, as we each picked up on particular cues of humor and
irony. Translating these moments of critique is always delicate, but we
have tried to be clear without being heavy-handed. It is worth noting,
too, that of the translation collective members, one is British (Archie),
another is US American (Christen), and another is Brazilian and has
also mainly lived in the United States since her teenage years (Bethânia). For each of us the sound of irony is slightly different, so we might
each translate it slightly differently. It's not just a cliché that British
humor is dry; it's also a translation challenge. The third, more personal
mode raises other questions of translation and editing. Here, in particular, Bethânia's role has been vital, not only in terms of her intimacy
with her mother but also through her detailed knowledge of her
mother's poetry.

In a project like this, translation involves any number of difficult
choices. Terminology for race and ethnicity in Brazil poses a particular
problem, however. There are two main words for *Black* in Portuguese:
preto and *negro*. Both of these terms have historically been used since
the slavery era to describe people of African descent in Brazil, and each
term has had a different political charge at different social and political
moments in Brazilian history. For example, the Black Movement in Brazil is known as *o movimento negro*, whereas Black people in Brazil have
been denoted by the term *pretos* on the census, in demographic studies
and on official government documents (like birth certificates).[48] We
have translated *negro* throughout as either "black people," "black," or
"black man." This decision follows the colloquial toggling between these
multiple definitions in everyday parlance. At times, the masculine form
(*negro*) means a collective, ungendered reference to a Black person or
Black people (as in the case of *o negro*). At other times, however, *negro*

literally refers to a Black man or *the* Black man. This usage parallels similar uses of the term *man* in English during the same time period. The most acute instance of this problem is the title of "For a History of Black People." The original title, "Por uma História do Homem Negro," translates literally as "For a History of the Black Man," and the text directly confronts the universalizing project of the History of Man. In the text itself, she predominately uses the phrase "uma História do negro," omitting the word *Homem* but using a capital *H* and a lowercase *N*, while making the argument that Black history must be part of universal History. Although it would be a legitimate translation to retain the gendered term *Man* in the title, we have decided that in this case her underpinning project is more accurately translated by a shift toward the gender-neutral term in the title. Such translation choices remain hard, and open to interpretation.

In our own texts, we have chosen to capitalize *Black* when referring to Black people. This is a deliberate, collective, political decision that also follows a widespread paradigm shift in the capitalization of the term in North America in the wake of the murder of George Floyd by police officers in Minneapolis, Minnesota, in 2020.[49] To capitalize the term *Black* is to recognize that this color term also has social and political significance when it is associated with people of African descent who have historically been racialized by the term. Capitalization acknowledges that Black is not simply a color marker but also an ethnic classification that indicates the shared culture and history of people of African descent globally and locally within specific geographic zones, like Brazil.[50] It is clear that as an outspoken political voice in Brazil's Black Movement, Beatriz Nascimento uses the term *Black* in a diasporic, political, and sociocultural sense. However, we have decided to use the term in lowercase in our translations, to reflect her own usage of the lowercase, and to avoid anachronism. Her use of the term *black* moves between the color term and the racial marker—a slippage that she intentionally reflects on and plays with. Imposing a capitalization would risk losing her nuance in the use of the term. She uses the word *negro, also,* to refer to the unique cultural experiences and perspectives of people of African descent with brown[51] skin is also a consistent reminder of the political convictions of her diasporic politics. In addition, she consistently and deliberately inserted herself into the diasporic discourses of Blackness bubbling across the hemisphere during her time. We can see this in her references to Black Brazilians as a people with a collective past, present, and experiences. It also comes out in her theorization of the Atlantic and quilombo.

The vocabulary of racial classification, racism, anti-Blackness, and ethnicity in Brazil is manifold. Some of these terms translate more easily than others. Terms that are more difficult include *preto, pardo, mestiço, caboclo, sertanejo*, and others. Within the colorist logics of Brazilian racial hierarchy, these terms operate in various ways: *preto* refers to dark-skinned people, *pardo* to lighter, brown-skinned people; *mestiço* is a more general (though highly contested) term for *mixed* that tends to refer to someone who is of white and Indigenous heritage and corresponds with the word *mestizo* in Spanish, but can also refer to someone who may have remote African heritage that is barely perceptible. *Caboclo* refers to people of mixed Indigenous ancestry whose Indigenous heritage is clearly identifiable, but it is also used at times as a general term to refer to any brown or Black person, particularly a man of brown skin (as in "hey, man"—in this way *caboclo* corresponds with a term like *dude* in North American English). *Sertanejo* is another ambiguous, racialized term that refers to people from the *sertão*, or the backlands of the northeast and the center of Brazil. These terms have differently loaded discriminatory and offensive weight depending on their context and their speaker; *preto* can be a racial slur but can also be (historically, not unrelatedly, of course) a general reference to a Black person (used widely in southern Brazil specifically) or a demographic, census category.

Beatriz Nascimento uses terms of race and ethnicity in a variety of ways, whether by ventriloquizing racism in society, citing demographic research, or conducting her own historical and sociological critique of racial politics and ethnic groups. This is further complicated by the fact that she also discusses ethnic differentiations in the United States and sub-Saharan Africa, and their interconnection with forms of racial and ethnic identification in Brazil. All of this means that we have taken a contextual approach to translating these terms. We have chosen to leave the terms *preto* and *pardo* untranslated when these distinctions are vital to the argument she is making, for instance in her essay on the Antônio Conselheiro movement. These are subjective choices, requiring a balance between rendering her thought as lucid as possible to contemporary readers and retaining the historical and political specificity of her ideas within the context in which they developed and intervened.

On Collaboration

This project began in its current form in August 2018, when the three of us initiated conversations regarding our first translation project. Archie Davies reached out to Christen A. Smith to float the idea of doing a collaborative publication on Beatriz Nascimento for the radical geography journal *Antipode*. The idea at the time was simple: to translate Beatriz Nascimento's 1985 essay "O conceito de quilombo e a resistência cultural negra" and "Por uma História do Homem Negro" from 1974. Archie would do the translation and Christen would write the introductory essay to the text. Since 2014 Christen had been collaborating with Bethânia Gomes and Alex Ratts on Nascimento's legacy, particularly in terms of bringing it into dialogue with the academy in the United States. This resulted in their collaboration on the book project *Todas [as] distâncias: poemas, aforismos e ensaios de Beatriz Nascimento*[52] in addition to other academic panels and presentations. When Archie contacted Christen about the *Antipode* idea, Christen invited Bethânia to join the project as well, and our collaborative relationship began. The first fruits of that collaboration were, indeed, published in *Antipode* in 2021,[53] albeit not precisely in the original form envisaged, and the shape of our collaboration has developed and deepened.

Each of us comes to this project from different positionalities. Bethânia is the primary arbiter of Beatriz Nascimento's legacy, holding all copyright to her image and her archives as her only heir. However, it is not just legal status that drives Bethânia's work on behalf of her mother. Since her mother's death, she has fought passionately to preserve and proliferate her legacy. This has included her long-term friendship and collaboration with Alex Ratts, the first scholar in Brazil to deeply analyze and popularize Beatriz Nascimento's intellectual contributions in book form with the publishing of *Eu sou Atlântica* in 2007. This book catapulted Beatriz Nascimento to the forefront of the Black Brazilian imagination and solidified her place as a key intellectual figure in the Black Movement and an important symbol of the Black feminist movement in Brazil.

It is Ratts's work that inspired both Archie and Christen to read Beatriz Nascimento more deeply. Christen became enchanted by the work of Nascimento in 2007, when she purchased *Eu sou Atlântica* from the Kitabu bookstore in the Lapa neighborhood in Rio de Janeiro while she was co-teaching a course on Black radical thought at the Universidade Estadual do Rio de Janeiro (UERJ). However, it was not until the film *Ôrí* was relaunched in 2009, and Christen attended the relaunch event in São Paulo at the Livraria Cultura, that she became enamored with Beatriz Nascimento not only as a scholar but also as a poet-philosopher. Seeing her image and hearing her speak brought her theories of quilombo and their relationship to Black women and the Black female body to life in new ways, inspiring her to start to research and write about Nascimento.

Archie, as he discusses further below, came to Nascimento's work through a dual interest in the history of radical Brazilian thought and anti-colonial understandings of space and nature. It was as a geographical thinker that he first read Nascimento, alongside other major figures of an undervalued Brazilian tradition of critical geography that includes geographers like Milton Santos and Josué de Castro, as well as writers such as Marilena Chauí, Francisco de Oliveira, and Lélia Gonzalez, who may never have identified as geographers but whose work takes forward rich, global debates on the production of space and nature.

The Structure of the Book

This introductory section is completed by a translator's note and an essay by Alex Ratts. We then turn to Nascimento's writings. We have organized the texts into four sections: "Race and Brazilian Society";

"The Black Woman"; "Quilombo: Thoughts on Black Freedom and Liberation"; and "Black Aesthetics, Spirituality, Subjectivity, and the Cosmic." Some texts could belong in multiple sections, but we hope this proves to be a structure that clarifies the distinct parts of Nascimento's achievements and gives readers various ways through her oeuvre. At the beginning of each section is an essay by Christen, placing the texts in an interpretative, intellectual, and historical context. Each section is also introduced by a single poem.

The process of selecting and organizing the texts in this book has been long and iterative. Some of Beatriz Nascimento's best-known published essays, such as "The Black Woman and Love" and "The Black Woman in the Labor Market," obviously had to be part of this collection. We note the original place of publication of all published texts, and the majority of what she published in her lifetime included here (with the notable exception of her coauthored book *Negro e cultura no Brasil: pequena enciclopédia da cultura brasileira* (1987) [Black people and culture in Brazil: Short encyclopedia of Brazilian culture]). We consulted the original publications in order to check our translations and get much-needed context for the writing. Many publications, when taken out of their original context, lose some meaning. For example, "The Black Woman and Love" is part of a larger multiauthored article, "The Left That the Black Person Wants," which encircles it. For unpublished texts we provide a date where it is available, and its location in the archive. The majority of the texts translated here have also been published (sometimes more than once) in Portuguese in one of the collections mentioned in this introduction, and we warmly acknowledge the crucial editorial and intellectual work of the Brazilian editors of her writing, who we reference throughout the text.

Some of Nascimento's unpublished texts, such as "Toward Racial Consciousness" and "The First Great Loss," stand out so markedly in her oeuvre that it was obvious to us that they too had to be included. Not least because of their provisionary, unedited quality, some of these texts have echoes of one another, but we have included them to allow readers to pick their own paths through how her ideas developed.

Where texts overlap (for instance, the two versions of "Alternative Social Systems" and "'Quilombos': Social Change or Conservatism?") we have included these either because we think they offer an important genealogy for the development of her ideas (for example, her texts on the history of quilombo rework one another), or because they possess unique aesthetic or political qualities. In order to include a breadth of her work, we have therefore had to exclude some significant texts, including, for instance, a long reflection on "the historiography of the quilombo," a transcription of a 1977 conference that, while including fascinating sections, also repeats much of what she wrote in the texts published here.[54]

The final section reflects on Beatriz Nascimento's life. We include this at the end so readers can come to it having already read her words. It contains a chronology and a very selective set of biographical notes on key interlocutors among Black Brazilian intellectuals and activists mentioned in the book. The section also includes a postface by Muniz Sodré. As Bethânia noted in the preface, Muniz Sodré is her godfather and a close personal friend of Beatriz Nascimento and her family. He was also supervising Nascimento's research at the time of her death. He is, today, one of the foremost Black intellectuals in contemporary Brazil, and professor emeritus at the Federal University of Rio de Janeiro.[55] He is uniquely placed, therefore, to draw both personal and intellectual conclusions to this collection, and we are honored to have his participation.

The book closes with a selection from a conversation between the three members of the editorial and translation collective. Beatriz Nascimento's legacy is to be found not only in her creative and intellectual outputs but also in the lives of those she knew. We draw out some of her personal qualities and relationships in the conversation that concludes this book. This exchange picks up personal and political themes from Nascimento's life through the words of her daughter, and is intended to give readers a sense of the personal journeys that lie behind the texts collected here. In this conversation we reflect on the stakes and dilemmas of translating Beatriz Nascimento today, and how her work speaks to the contemporary moment. As an intimate and informal conclusion, we hope it encourages readers to explore Nascimento's own life and work further, opening up connections between this book and the wider worlds of African diasporic politics, culture, and thought.

Notes

1. "Black People, Seen by Themselves."

2. See, for instance, "For a (New) Existential and Physical Territory."

3. For an important conversation of state surveillance of Black people under the repressive era, see Marcelo Domingos and Seth Garfield, "The Modernist City, Racial Repression and Political Resistance: Recovering Narratives of National Security and Black Activism in Brasilia, Brazil (1978–1988)" (University of Texas, 2022).

4. David Covin, *The Unified Black Movement in Brazil, 1978–2002* (Jefferson, NC: McFarland & Co., 2006).

5. For more on the life of Marlene Cunha, see João Alipio Cunha, "Em busca de um espaço: a linguagem gestual no candomblé de Angola À memória de Marlene de Oliveira Cunha," Cadernos de Campo, São Paulo 26, no. 1 (2017): 15–41.

6. See the rich materials on Cultne.TV recorded at a 2019 exhibition and series of seminars on the "Grupo de Trabalho André Rebouças," available at https://tinyurl.com/2p94nw3t (accessed June 16, 2022). Sebastião Soares, one of the few original members of the group from the 1970s, discusses the first years of the group's activist work as guided above all by Beatriz Nascimento.

7. On the history of the GTAR, see Sandra Martins Da Silva, "O GTAR (Group de Trabalhos André Rebouças) na Universidade Federal Fluminense: Memória social, intelectuais negros e a universidade pública" (The GTAR in the Federal University of Fluminense: Social memory, Black intellectuals and the public university, 1975–95) (master's thesis, UFRJ, 2018).

8. Her archive, for instance, includes a transcript of a conversation (not translated here), seemingly organized by Raquel Gerber in relation to the film *Ôrí*, between Beatriz Nascimento and Thereza Santos (1938–2012). Santos was an actor, communist activist, teacher, and writer who wrote for and produced theater with the Black Experimental Theater of Rio de Janeiro and in São Paulo. She also traveled to Angola and Guinea and played an active role in the liberation struggles there. See Flavia Rios, "A trajetória de Thereza Santos: comunismo, raça e gênero durante o regime militar" (The trajectory of Thereza Santos: Communism, race and gender during the military regime), *Plural* 21, no. 1 (2014): 73–96. The archive also includes letters between her and Lélia Gonzalez. For example, Nascimento wrote to Gonzalez on January 30, 1988, to vigorously defend her and collaborators against mainstream, white theater critics. She addresses Gonzalez as "A Ilustríssima Diretora do Planetário, Professora Lélia Gonzalez" (The most illustrious director of the Planetário), the name of the theater Gonzalez directed between 1987 and 1989. Fundo Maria Beatriz Nascimento (MBN—National Archives Collection, Brazil) 13.2.27.

9. See "Post-revolutionary Angolan Nativism."

10. See, for instance, documents from DAWN, "Development Alternatives with Women for a New Era," a global network of Black women and women of color pursuing a new vision of

environment and development; a book dedicated by hand to her from the important Afro-Venezuelan writer José Marcial Ramos Guédez (both in Fundo MBN 3.3); and invitations received from the Black anthropologist from UCLA, Claudia Mitchell-Kernan, about the creation of a network, "Women and the Future of the Black World."

11. For example, "A luta dos quilombos: ontem, hoje e amanhã" (The struggle of the quilombos: Yesterday, today and tomorrow), *Mergulho* (January 1990): 3 (not published here), and "A mulher negra e o amor" (The Black woman and love), *Maioria Falante* 17 (February/March 1990): 3.

12. Wagner Vinhas Batista, "Palavras sobre uma historiadora transatlântica: estudo da trajetória intelectual de Maria Beatriz Nascimento" (Words on a transatlantic historian: A study of the intellectual trajectory of Maria Beatriz Nascimento) (Doctoral thesis, Universidade Federal da Bahia, 2018), 22.

13. João José Reis, *Slave Rebellion in Brazil: The Muslim Uprising of 1835 in Bahia*, trans. Arthur Brakel (Baltimore: Johns Hopkins University Press, 1995); João José Reis and Flávio dos Santos Gomes, *Freedom by a Thread: The History of Quilombos in Brazil* (New York: Diasporic Africa Press, 2016).

14. Flávio dos Santos Gomes, *Palmares: escravidão e liberdade no Atlântico Sul* (São Paulo: Contexto, 2005).

15. Lélia Gonzalez, "The Unified Black Movement: A New Stage in Black Political Mobilization," in *Race, Class and Power in Brazil*, ed. P.-M. Fontaine (Los Angeles: University of California, Los Angeles, 1985), 123.

16. In November 2011 the federal government passed LEI N° 12.519, de 10 de Novembro de 2011, officializing the commemoration of the anniversary of the death of Zumbi dos Palmares as the National Day of Black Consciousness. http://www.planalto.gov.br/ccivil_03/_ato2011-2014/2011/lei/l12519.htm.

17. The Frente Negra Brasileira was founded on September 16, 1931, under the leadership of Arlindo Veiga dos Santos. The FNB promoted and supported various newspapers and publications like *A Voz da Raça* and *Clarim d'Alvorada*. Marcio Barbosa and Barbosa Aristides, *Frente Negra Brasileira: depoimentos: projeto de dinamização de espaços literários afro-brasileiros* (São Paulo: Quilombhoje, 1998).

18. The FNB's anti-immigrant political platform was partly responsible for the group's eventual dismantling. The FNB's stance on immigration facilitated an alignment with fascist movements. The association between these two groups as well as other factors like the separatist nature of race-based politics led President Getúlio Vargas to outlaw the FNB along with all other exclusive political groups.

19. Ana Flávia Magalhães Pinto, *Imprensa negra no Brasil do século XIX* (São Paulo: Selo Negro, 2010); Ariovaldo Lima Junior, "Jornal Irohin: Estudo de caso sobre a relevância educativa do papel da imprensa negra no combate ao racismo (1996–2006)" (Dissertação, Programa de Pós-Graduação em Educação, Universidade Federal de São Paulo, 2009); Flavio Thales Ribeiro Francisco, "Um novo abolicionismo para a ascensão na nação da Mãe Preta: discursos sobre a fraternidade racial no jornal O Clarim da Alvorada (1924–1932)," *Antíteses* 10, no. 19 (2017): 376–96.

20. Abdias do Nascimento, ed., *Teatro Experimental do Negro: Testemunhos* (Rio de Janeiro: Edições GRD, 1966).

21. For a more robust discussion of the myth of racial democracy and the Black Movement's deconstruction of it, see, for example, Lélia Gonzalez's prolific writing on the topic, and also of course Beatriz Nascimento's writings in this volume. Lélia Gonzalez, *Primavera para as rosas negras: Lélia Gonzalez em primeira pessoa*, União dos Coletivos Pan-Africanistas (São Paulo: Diáspora Africana, 2018). In English, see also Pierre-Michel Fontaine, ed., *Race, Class, and Power in Brazil* (Los Angeles: Center for Afro-American Studies, University of California, 1985).

22. Before this intense time of censorship began, political expression was still tolerated. Social protest through art manifested in the theater (O Teatro de Arena e o Teatro Oficina), music (samba, for example), and culture centers (Os Centros Populares de Cultura (CPCs). Marcelo Ridenti, *O Fantasma da Revolução Brasileira* (São Paulo: Editora UNESP, 1993), 75. Harsh cultural repression began officially under Act Number Five, which established strict censorship in December 1968 by "[giving] juridical sanction to the institutions of repression and 'internal security.'" See Mitchell in Fontaine, *Race, Class, and Power in Brazil*, 85, 95.

23. See Turner in Fontaine, *Race, Class, and Power in Brazil*, 79. The military regime enforced unprecedented repression of state social analysis. In 1969 the University of São Paulo Sociology Department was "purged" and some of its members (like the members of the São Paulo School associated with the UNESCO reports of the 1950s) were forced into exile. Thomas E. Skidmore, *The Politics of Military Rule in Brazil, 1964–85* (New York: Oxford University Press, 1988).

24. In Salvador, the development of Afro-blocos was a response to the racist policies of many of the carnival blocos that refused to allow Black people to parade with their groups. The Afro-bloco movement was inspired by the similar phenomenon of Black samba schools in Rio de Janeiro, which Beatriz Nascimento mentions in several essays. Ilê Aiyê took the controversial stance that no white people would be allowed to parade with them, inverting the long-term de facto racist policies of mainstream elite carnival blocos that found subtle yet effective ways to bar working-class Black people from participating in their carnival groups. This controversy pushed Ilê Aiyê into the national spotlight. People from around the country accused the bloco of racism. The attention, not surprisingly, won the carnival organization considerable ridicule. However, ironically, this polemic also allowed Ilê Aiyê to draw attention to the close relationship between the valorization of Black culture, cultural appropriation, and symbolic genocide (a concept Abdias do Nascimento would outline in *Brazil, Mixture or Massacre?*). This conversation is important when we read Beatriz Nascimento's critiques of cultural appropriation, racial democracy, and white supremacy in Brazil. The Afro-bloco movement was inspired by the similar phenomenon of Black samba schools in Rio de Janeiro.

25. Translated from the original Portuguese.

26. Many poor and working-class Black people were killed, tortured, and disappeared during the military dictatorship as part of the state's political repression. However, the narrative that the state used to justify these killings was not focused on intellectual censorship. When the state targeted university students, the image in its imaginary was not a Black student from the favela. Christen A. Smith explores the history of the state's torture and killing of Black people in her book *Afro-Paradise: Blackness, Violence, and Performance in Brazil* (Urbana: University of Illinois Press, 2016). For a more in-depth discussion of the history of policing, torture, and repression in Brazil, see, for example, R. S. Rose, *The Unpast: Elite Violence and Social Control in Brazil* (Athens: Ohio University Press, 2005). For reflections on the military dictatorship and Black

intellectuals, see Paulina L. Alberto, *Terms of Inclusion: Black Intellectuals in Twentieth-Century Brazil* (Chapel Hill: University of North Carolina Press, 2011).

27. Cedric Robinson's *Black Marxism* delineates "the historical archeology of the Black Radical Tradition," drawing on W.E.B. DuBois, C.L.R. James, and Richard Wright as primary examples. The discourse around the Black radical tradition has traditionally been dominated by Black men from anglophone nations, despite its anti-colonialist and anti-imperialist positioning. Carole Boyce Davies, *Left of Karl Marx: The Political Life of Black Communist Claudia Jones* (Durham, NC: Duke University Press, 2008), 121–22; Carole Boyce Davies, "Sisters Outside," *Small Axe* 28:13, no. 1 (2009): 217–29; Cedric J. Robinson, *Black Marxism: The Making of the Black Radical Tradition* (Chapel Hill: University of North Carolina Press, 2000).

28. Boyce Davies, "Sisters Outside."

29. Boyce Davies, "Sisters Outside," 218; Robin D. G. Kelley, "'But a Local Phase of a World Problem': Black History's Global Vision, 1883–1950," *Journal of American History* (1999): 1045–77.

30. For more on the fraught history of the Ford Foundation, see, for example, Noliwe M. Rooks, *White Money/Black Power: The Surprising History of African American Studies and the Crisis of Race in Higher Education* (Boston: Beacon Press, 2006).

31. See Rooks, *White Money/Black Power*. See also C. Suprinyak and R. Fernández, "Funding Policy Research under 'Distasteful Regimes': The Ford Foundation and the Social Sciences in Brazil, 1964–71," *Journal of Latin American Studies* (2022): 1–26; and L. Canêdo, "The Ford Foundation and the Institutionalization of Political Science in Brazil," in *The Social and Human Sciences in Global Power Relations. Socio-Historical Studies of the Social and Human Sciences*, eds. J. Heilbron, G. Sorá, and T. Boncourt (Cham: Palgrave Macmillan, 2018), 243–66.

32. Christen Smith argues this in her reading of Beatriz Nascimento. Her analysis of Nascimento's understanding of the Atlantic as a physical and metaphorical space is also inspired by Alex Ratts. See Alex Ratts, *Eu sou Atlântica: sobre a trajetória de Beatriz Nascimento* (São Paulo: Imprensa Oficial [SP] e Instituto Kuanza, 2006); Christen Smith, "Towards a Black Feminist Model of Black Atlantic Liberation: Remembering Beatriz Nascimento," *Meridians* 14, no. 2 (September 1, 2016): 71–87.

33. For more on whiteness and race in the university system, see, for example, Sales Augusto dos Santos, *O sistema de cotas para negros da UNB : um balanço da primeira geração* (Jundiaí, SP: Paco Editorial, 2015); and Flavia Rios, "Movimento negro brasileiro nas Ciências Sociais (1950–2000)," *Sociedade e Cultura* 12, no. 2 (2009): 263–74.

34. This reality is starkly reflected in the debate over affirmative action in the 2000s. See, for example, Ana Flávia Magalhães Pinto, Braga Maria Lúcia de Santana, and Sales Augusto dos Santos, *Ações afirmativas e combate ao racismo nas Américas* (Brasília: Ministério da Educação, 2005); Dalila Noleto Torres and Juliet Hooker, "Affirmative Action in Brazil: Affirmation or Denial?" (master's thesis, University of Texas, 2012).

35. Katherine McKittrick's theorizations of Black feminist geography are fundamental to this conceptualization. See, for example, Katherine McKittrick, *Demonic Grounds: Black Women and the Cartographies of Struggle* (Minneapolis: University of Minnesota Press, 2006).

36. McKittrick, *Demonic Grounds*, ix.

37. See M. Jacqui Alexander, *Pedagogies of Crossing: Meditations on Feminism, Sexual Politics, Memory, and the Sacred* (London: Duke University Press, 2005).

38. For an interesting discussion of trance as co-presence in Afro-Atlantic religious traditions, see Aisha Beliso-De Jesús, *Electric Santería: Racial and Sexual Assemblages of Transnational Religion* (New York: Columbia University Press, 2015).

39. A. Bledsoe and W. J. Wright, "The Pluralities of Black Geographies," *Antipode* 51 (2019): 419–37.

40. Sharlene Mollett, "Hemispheric, Relational, and Intersectional Political Ecologies of Race: Centring Land-Body Entanglements in the Americas," *Antipode* 53 (2021): 810–30.

41. Michelle Daigle and Margaret Marietta Ramírez, "Decolonial Geographies," *Keywords in Radical Geography: Antipode at 50* (2019): 78–84.

42. C. Hawthorne, "Black Matters Are Spatial Matters: Black Geographies for the Twenty-First Century," *Geography Compass* 13 (2019): e12468.

43. Ruth Wilson Gilmore, *Abolition Geography: Essays Towards Liberation* (London: Verso Books, 2022); Nik Heynen, "Toward an Abolition Ecology," *Abolition: A Journal of Insurgent Politics* 1 (2018): 240–47.

44. We are thinking in particular of the institutional co-optation and defanging of the terms *decolonial* and *decolonizing*, but other academic-political imperatives, including *abolition*, face the same risk.

45. Wagner Vinhas Batista, "Palavras sobre uma historiadora transatlântica: estudo da trajetória intelectual de Maria Beatriz Nascimento" (Words on a transatlantic historian: A study of the intellectual trajectory of Maria Beatriz Nascimento) (Doctoral thesis, Universidade Federal da Bahia, 2018).

46. Diego de Matos Gondim, "Manifestos Quilombolas: desta terra, nesta terra, para esta terra" (Quilombo manifests: From this land, on this land, for this land) (Doctoral thesis, Universidade Estadual Paulista, 2021).

47. She successfully applied for a grant to this end in February 1991 to the organization. See document in Fundo MBN, 21.3.3, dated February 12, 1991.

48. Melissa Nobles, *Shades of Citizenship: Race and the Census in Modern Politics* (Stanford, CA: Stanford University Press, 2000).

49. The *New York Times*, for example, decided to begin capitalizing the term *Black* in 2020.

50. In this context, there is an important debate to be had about the capitalization of the term *w/White*, recognizing that whiteness is, of course, a racial formation. We have chosen not to capitalize *white* in this book in order to work with the grain of current norms in Black thought and best editorial practice in the United States, which avoids capitalization in order to avoid reifying white supremacy.

51. We also keep *brown* lowercase because of its alignment with the word *pardo*. It is important to note, however, that *Brown* has also been historically capitalized to refer to the Latinx and Chicanx movements in the United States and at times to also refer to darker-skinned people who are not of African descent. By leaving the term lowercase, we specifically refer to racialization through color rather than these political configurations.

52. Alex Ratts and Bethânia Gomes organized *Todas [as] distâncias*—the first published collection of Beatriz Nascimento's poetry with the inclusion of a few of her essays. Alex and Bethânia invited Christen to contribute an essay to the collection. The other three collaborators on this project were Conceição Evaristo, Lúcia Gato, and Arnaldo Xavier. In addition, in 2014

Christen organized a panel for the Latin American Studies Association on our collaborative work on Beatriz Nascimento's life and legacy with the participation of Bethânia Gomes, Alex Ratts, and Keisha-Khan Perry. Alex Ratts and Bethânia Gomes, *Todas [as] distâncias: poemas, aforismos e ensaios de Beatriz Nascimento* (Editora Ogum's Toques: Salvador, Bahia, 2015).

53. C. Smith, A. Davies, and B. Gomes, "'In Front of the World': Translating Beatriz Nascimento," *Antipode* 53 (2021): 279–316.

54. This piece has also been published in *Beatriz Nascimento, Quilombola e Intelectual: Possibilidade nos dias da destruição* (São Paulo: Editora Filhos da África, 2018), 125–65.

55. See the Biographical Glossary for further details.

A Note on Translation

Archie Davies

THE WHOLE of this project has been collaborative, but it is worth stepping outside the collective voice to reflect briefly on the structure and process of that collaboration in relation to translation itself, and in relation to the politics of translating Beatriz Nascimento. In particular, this involves explicitly reflecting on my role. The position of the translator is never straightforward, and the position of being a white man translating Beatriz Nascimento's words is delicate. This is, in part, why we chose to make our translation process a dialogic and collaborative one. Here I want to briefly articulate my own position within our collective, not only intellectually, but also personally.

The status of Bethânia and Christen in relation to Beatriz Nascimento is clear: Bethânia is not only her mother's daughter but also the protector of Nascimento's legacy in archival, public, and practical terms; Christen is a leading scholar of Black Brazil, and an anthropologist with years of experience working in close collaboration with Black feminist and Black liberation movements in the Americas. Both are Black women. I am a white British man whose relationships with Brazil, Black Brazilian thought, and intersectional feminist politics are quite different. My meeting with Beatriz Nascimento has taken place on the page, within the context of a broader scholarly project exploring the intellectual history of Brazilian geographical thought. I came to Beatriz Nascimento out of a concern to challenge, destabilize, and radically reopen powerful, Northern, settled, settler categories of geographical knowledge. In the creative force of Nascimento's thinking about territory and liberation is the kind of antiracist, anticolonial, spatial thought and practice that can counter hegemonic knowledge about space, time, and society. Christen's groundbreaking interpretation of her work, and Alex Ratts's pathfinding editorial, theoretical, and historical interventions both accompanied my first reading of it. As a translator, it was clear to me that Nascimento's writings should be made available in English, though equally clear that it was not up to me to do that translation alone. This collaboration was the result, and it has grown to be more personally enriching, educational, and joyful than I could ever have hoped.

Translating radical thought from Latin America has an important role to play in challenging the ideas that shore up and perpetuate uneven structures of epistemological power. Translating into English, in particular, requires us to engage both with the fraught qualities of English as a globally dominant language of knowledge production, and to recognize that bringing ideas into English from a less widely read language such as Portuguese opens them up to being read by speakers of many languages, who can also read English. Translation, then, can operate to amplify, multiply, and diversify ideas. It can take up and support subordinated knowledges as a technique of solidarity. This is not to mystify translation, nor is it monolithically true; translation can be a colonial, expropriating act too: context, intent, and process are vital. I want to reflect here on these three dimensions of any translation project.

By *context*, I want to draw attention not only to the moment and manner in which translations are produced, by whom and when, but also to the ways in which the "originals" become available to be translated. This involves reflecting on historical questions of publication and the lack of publication; the survival or destruction of manuscripts and other documents; the processes of archiving; the political economy of publication, republication, and translation; and the political and intellectual circumstances of translation. I have reflected on this process as a historical geographer in writing about the life and work of Josué de Castro (1908–73). Castro, a Brazilian intellectual from Recife,

Pernambuco, in the Brazilian Northeast, was a radical geographer, a public intellectual and a tireless political campaigner against hunger. In his case, the anglophone reception of his life's work can be said to rotate around a set of mis- and missed translations. Castro's most important work—as was well known in Brazil, France and elsewhere—was his detailed, coruscating critique of endemic hunger in Brazil, *Geografia da Fome* (Geography of hunger), published in 1946 in Brazil, and, for instance, in France in 1950 as *Géographie de la Faim*, as well as in many other languages. For a set of historical and political reasons to do with publishing power and anglophone supremacy, that book was never translated. Rather, a very different book, called *The Geography of Hunger*, but not in fact a translation of *Geografia da Fome*, was translated into English in the United Kingdom and the United States in 1952. *Geografia da Fome*, the 1946 book, has never been published in English. The impact of this mis-/missed translation was profound on the way in which Castro came to be mis/understood in the anglophone world.

I briefly tell this story to illustrate that my own concern with translation is not only as a practitioner but also as a researcher. I want to emphasize that the act, or lack, of translation is important for how knowledge itself moves and transforms. The story of Josué de Castro and the geography of hunger is one of accident and contingency, which draws attention to the power relations embedded in how texts circulate. In the case of Beatriz Nascimento, the historical circumstances by which this body of texts have come to be translated by this group of people, by Princeton University Press, in 2023, is relevant not only to the details of how the texts appear in English (see, for instance, our discussion of linguistic choices), but also to how they will be read and interpreted. We discuss, elsewhere in this introduction, the process by which Beatriz Nascimento's texts have been archived. Our work on this book has spanned the COVID-19 pandemic, and our access to that archive was affected by that context.

Two further points will illustrate the question of context. The first is to draw attention to the fact that some of the texts are not only translated here but significantly restaged in this context. Many of the articles published in magazines like *Maioria Falante* were in close dialogue with other essays published alongside them, as well as artworks and political debates. Translation, in this context, is just the latest in a series of transformations that affect the interpretation and meaning of Nascimento's words. We note this here to emphasize that our translations are necessarily interpretative.

This brings me to the question of *intent*. It is important to be as explicit as possible about the intent that has driven our translation, to give readers more tools to construct their own interpretations. The introductory texts here lay out how and why we see this body of texts as important to ongoing intellectual and political debates around the Atlantic and beyond. We do not translate innocently and do not want to dissolve or gainsay our role: clearly our political and intellectual commitments have shaped how these texts are presented. The fact that the sections are also introduced by interpretative essays by Christen consciously frames these translations, not least to allow readers to reinterpret and contest Beatriz Nascimento's meaning.

This brings me to *process*. There are many ways to go about translation. In other projects I have worked on my own. For instance, I recently translated the Black Brazilian geographer Milton Santos's 1978 book *For a New Geography*. That book, published and republished by the most high-profile Brazilian university press, of São Paulo—the *Editora da Universidade de São Paulo*—has a very stable textual history, being reissued many times in Brazil over four decades. Milton Santos—though a Black intellectual in a white supremacist society—was endowed, particularly by the end of his career, with significant institutional power, and engaged prominently in institutionalized national and international circles of professionalized knowledge production. Translating his monograph on the history of geography and the theory of space for a North American university press was a very different kind of political and intellectual task to this project, and I completed it largely unaided and alone. (To the extent, that is, that any intellectual project is solitary; I accrued many intellectual and personal debts and interchanges along the way, and developed a deep affection, through the written page and across history, for Milton Santos and his many interlocutors). For historical, political, and practical reasons, the process and practice of translation for this project had to be different.

Reflecting on our own translation process brings me to a different, more personal dimension of my practice of translation. For me, translation is a kind of relief. Specifically, it helps me process, and quieten, two cacophonies that ring in my head as a white man writing in the academic knowledge-production complex. Working in the neoliberal university, the need to publish is incessant, even when you don't have anything to say. The sheer volume of stuff that is written, the endless journal articles and books constantly flowing out of laptops, are a slippery and unstable kind of commodity, but no less of a commodity for that. To be an academic requires that you build a little pile of your own knowledge production, as quickly as you can. Whether people *actually read* what you write is often secondary, and whether what you write *actually needs to be said* is tertiary. The academic is forced to function as a little enterprise whose primary commodity for sale into the market is their own words. This first cacophony is the sound of neoliberal knowledge production.

As a researcher, I have become interested in concrete things: space, nature, race, and hunger. I am interested in how these have come to be known and voiced, and the injustices embedded in the histories of that knowing and voicing, whose historical and contemporary inequalities track and reproduce the shifting hegemonies of colonial and racial capitalism. Writing about space, nature, and race—and writing about writing about them—is still dominated by particular voices: white, male voices, like mine. Confronting the geographies of knowledge production—what Doreen Massey might call knowledge's geometries of power[1]—therefore calls into question whose voices need to be heard. This second cacophony is the sound of the whiteness of knowledge production.

I have turned to translation as a way to hear my own voice differently. It is critical, then, that in this context our translation process has been collaborative. The power relations between translator and author are always specific and contextual. In the case of Beatriz Nascimento, it is vital to think through the ways in which she was not—in important ways, at least—a professional academic. She was not endowed with institutional power, but was a *militante*, an activist, and a Black woman writing in a patriarchal and white supremacist society. It is important, therefore, to explain how we have collectively worked with Beatriz Nascimento's words. Over a number of years, Christen, Bethânia, and I have spoken every week. The sheer weekly delight of those transatlantic conversations is hard to express, but I can only hope readers might hear its traces in our translations. I wrote a first draft of the texts we selected, flagging difficult areas or points of uncertainty. I sent this to Christen, who rewrote and reworked the text. I returned to her edits and addressed what I could. Together we highlighted areas that required Bethânia's intervention: to select the right words, to provide more context, to adjust the tone, or to solve some other linguistic, intellectual, or political question. The final coherence of the voice, therefore, is a collective attempt to get to what we think Beatriz would like her words, as she wrote them then, to say, now, in English. The open, dialogic, and collective process of translation—which has much in common, certainly, with many other processes of collective writing, not least, of course, those developed by Black feminists—takes a great deal of time, but it is a methodology for translation that has, in this particular context, offered me a way to speak through the white noise.

Note

1. D. Massey, *Space, Place and Gender* (Minneapolis: University of Minnesota Press, 1994).

Remembering the Great Atlantic: Beatriz Nascimento and Diasporic Black Thought

Alex Ratts

BETWEEN 1974 AND 1994, or, rather, between the ages of thirty-two and fifty-two, the activist-intellectual, historian, researcher, and poet Beatriz Nascimento produced a significant body of essays, articles, interviews, and poems about Black, African, racial, ethnic, spatial, and gender questions. They all bear on the diaspora between Africa (the Congo-Angola region), Portugal, and Brazil, the geopolitical and geocultural complex that she refers to as "transatlanticity." One part of this output (1974–85) was produced in parallel with the formation of Black Movements under military governments that monitored and repressed social groupings and social movements. The other (1985–94) emerged in the period of redemocratization and alongside some of the victories of the Federal Constitution of 1988: the criminalization of racism, the recognition of the role of Afro-Brazilians in the formation of the nation, and the provision of rights to quilombola communities.

Brazil in the 1970s was characterized by a particular juxtaposition of ideas and images: the myth of racial democracy was defended by both intellectuals and scholars of Brazilian history and culture and by the military who used it to inhibit the discourse of the Black Movements.

From the hegemonic perspective, to question racial democracy was to foment racism and separatism. Since the 1930s, when this image took shape in Brazilian social thought, particular forms of Black cultural expression—such as samba and capoeira—were selected and presented as national symbols. During the period in question, the image of the Black body was connected with corporeal dexterity (as in both capoeira and football), hypersexualization, extreme happiness (samba and carnival), and exoticism combined with Africanism (candomblé, music, and Afro-Brazilian food). These were the images constructed and broadcast in the worlds of politics, culture (radio, cinema, and television), and intellectual life (universities and artistic movements). The Black corporeality that could be seen and heard in various Brazilian cities, speaking with a public voice of denunciation, demand, and intention, did not fit in those worlds.

From her earliest essays, reviews, and interviews, Beatriz Nascimento chose to write about racism in everyday life, and, more precisely, racism in the academy and the world of images and representation. Regarding the politics of space, Beatriz Nascimento studied quilombos, (Black communities that, throughout the whole colonial period, existed and continue to exist in the Americas under various names). She also studied gender/race inequality, and the ways that Black women's affective lives had been strained and restricted since slavery.

Beatriz Nascimento took part in a political and cultural turn in the trajectory of Black Movements and communities in the Americas and in Africa. This took the form of an aesthetic of the body-space that emerged in corporeality, voice, the occupation of spaces, the appearance of collective subjects (student-militants, Black women, activist-intellectuals), and in the arts (visual arts, literature, *blocos* Afro and Afoxé, connections with so-called traditional cultural expressions such as samba).

The process of translating Nascimento's work into English prompts us to turn our attention to the elaboration of her thought, expressed in written texts, but also in audiovisual records. She not only addressed political and cultural processes in Brazil but also the United States (the civil rights movement and Third Worldist Women's movements),

Angola (independence and decolonization), and South Africa (Black consciousness and the struggle against apartheid).

Race, Sex, and Class: Black Women
of the Diaspora and Some Points in Common

Beatriz Nascimento began her course in history at the Federal University of Rio de Janeiro in 1968. It was an agitated time marked by mobilizations on the national and international stage: the recent formation of the Black Panthers and the assassination of Martin Luther King Jr.; the student movements in France and Brazil (for example, the March of the Hundred Thousand in Rio de Janeiro, triggered by the killing of a student by government agents); and the protest of the African American athletes John Carlos and Tommie Smith, during the Olympics in Mexico, against racism and segregation in sports. These events and processes, seen at a transnational scale, mark the position Nascimento takes: "At that moment I became conscious of my blackness and the extent to which I could really start all over again. My political activism began then, with the militancy of the Black Movement. In truth, these were the first stirrings toward a social change that was beginning to crystallize in every continent of the world, no longer in the *Imaginary*, but in the *Real*."

She finished her course in 1972 and dedicated herself to archival research. In the archives, she began to identify the sources with which to compose Black history and the history of quilombos. In 1974 she published two essays, "For a History of Black People" and "Black People and Racism," and drafted another manuscript. In these three texts, she dealt with racism in Brazilian society, particularly in intellectual, critical, and historical circles, and in historiography, as well as in modern and colonialist science. Her third article of 1976—"My Internal Blackness"—is an essay that sits between the biographical and the fictional, in which a therapist interpolates the narrator. When the subject mentions forms of racism, the therapist asks whether her "inner black person" is not exaggerating, often, in perceiving the issue, and making themselves uncomfortable. Published some years after in the newspaper *Village Voice* with the title "The Negro Inside," and published in Brazil only in 2015, the text is an exercise in perception and reaction, in which the protagonist recalls her displacements across class and race:

> I left the consultation reflecting on my internal blackness, "the negress inside"; thinking of her natural conflicts with the petit-bourgeois woman I had become, ex-factory worker who was today a graduated professor, married and divorced from a black architect, and mother of a black child. That woman, for various reasons, was not adjusting herself to all this; to the social ascension, the cultural broadening. She found herself perceiving things dually, with two separate minds. The most troublesome, perhaps, was the recognition that the majority of my people continue in the misery and vicissitudes imposed by poverty, ignorance and social confinement.

The character, always seeing herself in this hall of mirrors, amplifies the weight of the observation and returns to the subalternization of the Black population. In this same sense, Beatriz Nascimento formulates critiques of social thought that start from economic questions as the key to explaining social processes. For her, a central question is the recognition of Black people as subjects and not only as "slaves," as she affirms in the transcript of the conference on the Historiography of Quilombo, recorded in the film *Ôrí*: "The economic question is not the great drama, you see? It is a drama, but it is not the great drama. The great drama is the recognition of black people who have never before been recognized in Brazil."

In dealing, for instance, with Black women in the labor market, Nascimento points out triple domination (race, gender, and class) and reflects on the ideological mechanisms of their perpetuation: "The black woman—the element in which the structure of domination is most profoundly crystallized, as black and as woman—thus finds herself occupying the spaces and roles that have been attributed to her since slavery. . . . We might add to the above, however, that contemporary mechanisms for the maintenance of privilege by the dominant group are superimposed onto these cultural survivals or residues of slavery." Here, always in a reflexive mode, she raises a preoccupation with Black people from the working classes who, in ascending socially, particularly through graduating from university, move away from the popular sections of society. In this way, in the essay "The Black Woman and Love," she throws light on the affective situation of Black Women: "In the context in which she finds herself, the demystification of the concept of love falls to this woman. She must transform it into a culturally and socially dynamic force (by involvement in political activity for example), more often seeking greater parity between the sexes than 'enlightenment equality.'"

There is no evidence that Beatriz Nascimento took part in feminist organizations, but we can see her in a Black feminist context. Her archive is full of bibliographical references about women. In Brazil, along with Lélia Gonzalez, her contemporary, and author of articles on the "triple domination" of race, sex, and class, I argue that Nascimento's essays allow us to connect her to the work of Black authors in the United States, particularly her contemporaries such as Audre Lorde and Alice Walker. All began to write their articles and essays in the 1970s, which were only collected later (as single authors in the case of Walker and Lorde, and as coauthors in the case of Gonzalez and Nascimento). The different scale of international visibility of the first two is clear, but it is worth emphasizing that *Living by the Word* (1988) was translated and read in Brazil, and the contemporary publication in Brazil of Nascimento, Gonzalez, Angela Davis, and Lorde indicates, at the least, a common thread. Some of their concerns and positions can be connected: the relationship between race, class, space, and sex (or gender), before the existence of the term *intersectionality*; the "writing of the self"; essays about the body, image, love, and language; and, finally, distinct and varied approximations with feminism and academia.

Race, Ethnicity, and Space:
Transmigration and Transatlanticity

The studies on quilombos by Beatriz Nascimento range from preliminary observations (1976–78), research papers (1978–81), essays (1982–94), and annals of events that were published in journals, and one text that remained unpublished until recently. With few sources from the time, but with the example of David Birmingham's studies on the Portuguese intervention in Angola in mind, and having done research in the interior of Minas Gerais (1978/79) and in some Angolan provinces along the Cuanza river (1979), Beatriz Nascimento traces the African Kilombo, a military grouping of the second half of the seventeenth century, formed by the Jaga and Imbangala, associated with Queen Njinga Mbandi and linked to the kings of Ndongo and Matamba. She correlates these with the quilombo of Palmares, a group of settlements that repeatedly came into conflict with plantation owners.

One part of her formulations is contained in the documentary *Ôrí* (1989), directed by the filmmaker and sociologist Raquel Gerber, which covers more than a decade in the Brazilian Black Movement, from 1977 to 1988, in juxtaposition with the trajectory of the historian and activist herself. In the film, Beatriz Nascimento, as a historian, uses the term *transmigration*, her own concept, that corresponds to a spatial, cultural, and racial dislocation at multiple scales, for example from the plantation and the slave quarters to the quilombo, from the countryside to the city, from the Northeast to the Southeast of Brazil (from Sergipe to São Paulo), from Africa to America: "What is African and American civilization? It is a great transatlantic. It is not Atlantic civilization, it is Transatlantic. An African form of life was transported to America. It is the transmigration of a culture and an attitude in the world, of one continent to another, of Africa to America."

She elaborates on the notion of "transatlanticity" that also covers many scales, from the individual, to the body, to international connections: "to be able to make ties of connection in a fragmented history. Africa and America and again Europe and Africa. Angolas, Jagas. . . . I am Atlantic." Her perspective is sharply critical of the hegemonic white and Eurocentric vision of history.

In this context, Beatriz Nascimento's thought is based on two Black African epistemological formations that mark out her Brazilian political, cultural, artistic, and intellectual training: that of Congo-Angola, so-called Bantu, with a focus on the societies of Congo, Loango, Ndongo, Matamba, and Benguela, bordered by the rivers Congo and Cuanza, colonized by

the Portuguese; and that of Nigeria-Benin, taking as its seed the societies of Dahomey, Ilê-Ifé, Oyó, and others of the Niger Delta, colonized
by the French and the English.

Black Voice, Writing, and Corporeality

The 1970s and 1980s were a time of "assuming the risk of speaking," in
the words of Lélia Gonzalez, and of "speaking from your own ethnicity"
or racial group, as Beatriz Nascimento said. Across Brazil, Black people
young and old went to university, founded political-cultural groups, and
held study events and debates that helped constitute the Black Movements, including that known as the academic Black Movement. Up until
the first years of the redemocratization of the country, they published in
outlets of the Black, feminist, and leftist press, as well as in academic
journals and newspapers with wide circulations. Beatriz Nascimento recalls the discursive victories of the movement: "In the 1970s we were
mute. And the others were deaf to us. And this logic was embedded in
the process of the History of Brazil itself. And suddenly this Black Movement spills over the whole nation that was blocked in its own discourse,
in its *logos*, in its own logic. Ours was a necessary logic, a necessary
human discourse, because we were being harshly repressed by censorship." As she indicates, it was a process that moved from the individual
to the collective, from personal subjectivity to political organization in
the face of the barriers imposed by the military governments.

Since the end of slavery and the diffusion of racism, white society's
vision of Black people and Black communities became filled with
stereotypes, and with barriers to social mobility. At most, Black people
were granted some influence over cultural and corporeal expression.
Black people were denied the forms of knowledge that were considered
most complex. Discursive conquests also meant occupying the spaces
of speech, writing, and protest, as Nascimento said in an interview with
a national magazine, *Revista Manchete*:

Black people do not only have spaces to conquer, they have things to
reclaim. Things that are theirs and that are not recognized as theirs.

Thought, for example. I am shocked when white brains are endowed, for example, with rationality, and black people are given the body, intuition, and instinct. black people have emotion and intellectualism, they have thought, like any other human. They need to recover knowledge—that is theirs too. It was merely stolen by domination. And there we get to the discussion about the possession of knowledge.

—"BLACK PEOPLE, SEEN BY THEMSELVES"

After the reorganization of the Black Movements, their composition and perspectives were quite plural, bringing together many people from the suburbs, some from the popular neighborhoods, and a few from the middle class. They came from different generations but above all were young people from various educational backgrounds. There were great cultural events like the so-called *bailes black* (Black dances) of the Soul Movement, and meetings to discuss the struggle against segregation in the United States and the decolonization of African countries: "The majority, however, were young people who knew about African independences and the Civil Rights Movement in North America (Social Integration and 'Black Power,' the Vietnam War and Soul Music). They watched the fall of colonialism in Portugal (and its Overseas Empire) and in the Lusophone African countries: Guinea-Bissau, Angola, and Mozambique."

The Black Movement proposed the decolonization of the body, of ideas, and of practices. Black voices and the conquest of spaces took place in parallel with processes in other social segments. In the texts narrated in the film *Ôrí*, it is clear that Beatriz Nascimento is making an initial proposition to learn the Black body as a map, document, and territory.

It is important to emphasize that activist-intellectuals formed social movements that also formed them. Some intersectional subjects, for example Black women, intervened in more than one movement or social organization. However, the movements—Black, feminist, "homosexual"—had different and unequal formations in the conquest of the voice and the written word, which led to mismatches. One of the ideas of the Black Movements is that the racial question is a structural question in Brazil, which does not exclude the coming together of differences:

The racial question runs through the whole edifice of our society. More and more, the solution depends on the push to solidify the Black Movement (in associations of all types, in political parties, churches, and the State)... Today we move into a different phase. The Black Movement has exhaustively discussed the questions of the oppressed, generically called minorities: black people, women, homosexuals, children, and old people. This is how the Black Movement is organizing itself.

Black speech and writing are also internally differentiated: feminine, masculine, nonbinary, and LGBTQIA+; academic, political, and artistic; rural and urban; traditional and contemporary. Sometimes, we activists crave the ability to represent the whole of the movement, the entirety of collectives, the Black community, and the Black population, but there are many limits and mediations. Multiple transpositions of languages are needed for this to be possible.

Looking back at the trajectory and work of those who were student-militants and became activist-intellectuals, like Beatriz Nascimento, we can watch them going through processes of illness, early death, and erasure in academic and media spaces. Yet it is also important to observe that their names continue to be remembered in the memory of activists, and their ideas put in practice in contemporary epistemological disputes over the recognition of Black people as the subjects of knowledge.

Black-African Spatial Poetics

In the 1980s, without dropping her other activitiesd, Beatriz Nascimento dedicated herself to poetry. She was a schoolteacher, a member of the teaching staff on courses about Black history and Africa, a participant in panels and debates with Black and white intellectuals—often as the only woman—and was also making the film *Ôrí*, as well as publishing essays and giving interviews.

The themes worked through in her poems often drawn on the experience of being a transmigrated, transatlantic Black-African woman. It is important to remember that Beatriz Nascimento made the journey referred to above to Luanda, Angola, in 1979. She was interested in the records of the kilombos of the seventeenth century and in the independence process of Angola, which included transformations in the frameworks of power and in artistic circles. As an activist and artist, she took part in various international events, including FESPAC in Dakar, Senegal, in 1989.

Her poems are both poetic and political work. More than once she paints the meeting/confrontation that took place with the arrival of the navigators and the colonial occupiers from the sixteenth century on, by juxtaposing the two hemispheres (Western and Eastern). She created a cartography that is rare in academic spaces:

> The time of the great discoveries was a moment of hemispheric relation. Two hemispheres, Western and Eastern, entering into relation. . . . black Africa, unknown Africa, she seeks to know herself through the meeting with those who are arriving. It was the meeting of the West with the East, with Africa, and the possibility of reaching the Indies. What is African and American civilization? It is a great transatlantic. It is not Atlantic civilization, it is Transatlantic.

A significant part of what I discuss here, in terms of the trajectory of her work, above all the outlines of a diasporic African perspective, can be seen in her poem "Mais uma vez saudade" (Once again, missing), written in 1988.

> Dakar vivid memory,
> Cap Vert poured hope
> On a sunny afternoon
> Dimension of the World!
> From East to West
> The meaning of directions
>   From the balcony facing the sea
>
> Dakar, black city,
> You bleed my heart
> From sense to return
> Always urgent, because it is urgent to turn

From East to West
And to shut up emotions . . .
   from the dining hall

Dakar luminous space
Of invisible disquiet
Of turbulent silences, of explosive calms.
Marks my heart
From West to East
Reversing the direction
   of the waters of the fountain

Dream my dream with me
Transport to any future
The saga that you hid
In your curved streets
In your naked fever, like an indifferent woman!
From East to West
   Or in any other direction

Dakar vivid memory
One afternoon, a man
Who knows an ancient ascendant
Maybe a recent sailor
In the waves of my emotion
Bleeding my heart
   Stagnant in the west

You made my heart sail
In waves that imprison it
Without supplying the laws that can set it free
From the perplexity of love
Dakar, soothe my soul
With a splash of hot sand
   You, who like History, set me into the World again

The whole poem boils over not only with the feeling of the Black Movement in Rio de Janeiro, but with the idea of decolonization that situates her in the first ranks of Black thought, that passes through Césaire and Fanon, and that finds an inflection in the ideas of Black women, chicanas, quilombolas, and Indigenous peoples. The stamp of this thought is found in the realization of stagnation, and the urgent necessity for reorientation at a variety of scales, from the house to the map of the African diaspora.

To finish, in the symbolic geometry of transmigration and transatlanticity, Beatriz Nascimento signals points in a circle that mark returns and remembrances: "The process does not end. It is a sphere, it is the Earth." Her work, itself part of the diaspora that she tries to understand, is at once political and poetic. The poem "Aeroporto" (Airport), written in 1988, inscribes what I am trying to translate as I see her work arriving on the North American shores of the ocean:

> I remember you, great Atlantic
> That skirts me
> That rejects me
> Forgetting our initial alliance
> I was born of you
> I want to return to you

PART I

Race and Brazilian Society

On Race, Racism, and Racial Democracy

Christen A. Smith

No one will make me racist
Rotted dry stem
Without veins, without warm blood
Without rhythm, hard body?
They will never make exist in me
That lacerated cancer

—"ANTIRACISM"

Being black is to confront a history of almost five hundred years of painful resistance, of physical and moral suffering, the feeling of not existing, the practice of still not belonging to the society to which you gave everything you had, and to which still, today, you give what is left of yourself.

—"FOR A HISTORY OF BLACK PEOPLE"

BEATRIZ NASCIMENTO'S WRITINGS on race are the cornerstone of her intellectual oeuvre. Always thinking on the sharp edge of public national debates, her work provides a glimpse into racial politics in Brazil from the 1970s to the 1990s. Nascimento contributes to public discourse and weighs in on bitter controversies. To fully appreciate her contributions, we should understand the sociopolitical landscape of race in Brazil during her time, and the social, political, and historical context that produced it.

As Alex Ratts notes in his introductory essay, Beatriz Nascimento's writings can be divided into two phases. The first phase (1974–1985) was during Brazil's military dictatorship. The second phase (1985–1994) encompassed Brazil's redemocratization era. This twenty-year time frame covers some of the most decisive moments in the history of racial politics in Brazil. The first period witnessed the emergence of a new Black Movement that would become the catalyst for a radical pushback against the myth of Brazilian racial democracy and the solidification of Black cultural and political rights under the 1988 constitution. The second period witnessed the consolidation of a Black left politics and the Black Movement (Movimento Negro, MN)—which Black organizers would come to define as a conglomeration of Black organizations that encompassed social, cultural, and religious groups and individuals who sought to redress the violence of anti-Blackness in Brazil.[1] Black radical intellectuals like Beatriz Nascimento engaged in passionate debates regarding the nature and future of the Black Movement, as well as its political role in Brazilian society. They also grappled with how to situate themselves and the needs of Black Brazilians in this intense political period. We get a sense for the spirit of Black political debate quite clearly, for example, in the Black newspaper *Maioria Falante*, where Beatriz Nascimento published at least two of her essays. The redemocratization period would also lay the groundwork for the most significant race-based public policy in Brazil's history: affirmative action. Beatriz Nascimento's writings are set against the backdrop of national debates regarding race—dialogues that Black radical intellectuals like Nascimento passionately proliferated.

The Black Brazilian Condition

There is one project that sums up Nascimento's raison d'être as a public intellectual: the "ambitious project" "to write and reinterpret the history of black people in Brazil."[2] In 1974 she sketched out this radical idea in a series of two essays outlining her treatise on the diachronic identity of Black Brazilians ("For a History of Black People" and "Black People and Racism"). In these essays she fervently asserts that there exists a tangible relationship between lived Black experiences, the feeling of being Black, Black Brazilian culture, and Black Brazilian identity. This assemblage of what it means to be Black and Brazilian—embedded in the milieu of Brazilian racism—is encapsulated in a diachronic, identifiable Black identity enfleshed in the Black body. "We are the Living History of black People, not numbers," she writes.[3] She goes on to say, "We have to make our History by finding ourselves, shaking off our unconsciousness, our frustrations, our complexes, and studying them, not evading them." Yet why was this claim—the insistence on a Black History intimately connected to *lived Black experiences* so radical, emotionally charged, and intimately personal for Beatriz Nascimento?

A Hundred Years without Abolition

On May 13, 1888, Princess Isabel of Brazil signed the Golden Law (Lei Áurea), legally freeing all enslaved Africans in Brazil. One hundred years later, the same year as the ratification of the new constitution following the end of the military dictatorship, Brazil celebrated the hundredth anniversary of the Golden Law. However, while the newly democratic nation hoped to use the hundredth anniversary to validate the myth of Brazil's racial democracy, the Black Movement took to the streets to protest the government's celebration of the anniversary of abolition, choosing instead to take up the slogan "cem anos sem abolição" (a hundred years without abolition).[4] While the country was poised to celebrate, Black people protested having lived for a hundred years under the false pretenses of liberation. They boldly rejected the image of the kindly princess having graciously and morally freed the enslaved out of the goodness of her heart. Instead, they asserted that while legalized slavery ended in Brazil in 1888, the conditions of Black Brazilians had not changed. Since the time of slavery, a state-endorsed system of racial discrimination, veiled in the rhetoric of racial democracy, had endured, ensuring a de facto, post facto state of slavery.[5]

Although Brazil symbolically embraced its Black and African roots as part of its national identity (illustrated by the enthusiasm surrounding the commemoration), Black people had been systematically denied full civil rights. The Black Movement found the state's celebration hypocritical. Princess Isabel had not freed the enslaved; the enslaved had freed themselves. Moreover, the social conditions of slavery had never truly been abolished. Black Brazilians were still economically and socially disenfranchised. Racial democracy was a farce.[6] Indeed, Black radical thinkers often framed Black Brazilians as internally colonized denizens within Brazil.[7] The radical Black politics that Beatriz Nascimento espoused in the 1970s and 1980s were part of this chorus. Nascimento's writings on race, racism, and racial democracy contributed substantively to these conversations.

The Myth of Racial Democracy

The national, ideological investment in the myth of racial democracy from the 1970s to the 1990s produced a utopic image of Brazil that denied the existence of distinct and isolatable racial identities in the country, and instead affirmed the theory of a multiracial continuum: a racial spectrum or racial democracy. Alongside this idea came the presumption that race relations are generally amicable and racial tensions mild to nonexistent. Within this political context, mainstream Brazilian society (especially white Brazilians) perceived Black Brazilians' decrying of racism, marginalization, and exclusion as anti-nationalist. More pointedly, they interpreted the idea that racism is alive and well in Brazil as nothing short of blasphemous. This was one reason why Black intellectuals like Nascimento often found themselves under state surveillance during the military dictatorship period and even later.[8]

The assumption that Brazil is a society of infinite color gradations was well documented by scholars of Brazil throughout the 1960s, 1970s, and 1980s.[9] At times, the Brazilian Institute of Statistics and Geography (IBGE)—the government unit responsible for national censuses— removed the color question from the census in an attempt to underscore the racial unity of the country.[10] At other times, the state used the plethora of color classifications to argue that race does not matter in Brazil. For example, a 1976 survey conducted by *A Pesquisa Nacional por Amostra de Domicílios* (PNAD)[11] received a hundred thirty-five different responses for the category of race when the group allowed respondents to write in their racial classification.[12] However, despite this proliferation of color categories, researchers as far back as the 1950s have demonstrated that Brazil is an unequal nation with stark, dichotomous racial divides.

Statistics on racial inequality from just a few years after Beatriz Nascimento's death, give further context for the Brazil of her era. Starting in the early 2000s, state and national governments began to implement affirmative action policies in response to Black Movement debates and grassroots organizing. As a result, statistics regarding racial inequality begin to shift in the early 2000s.[13] However, 1998 statistics reveal the world that Beatriz Nascimento knew. In that census year, the population of Brazil was 169,806,557. Fifty-five percent of the population was classified as white (*branco*), 38 percent was classified as *pardo* (brown/light-skinned person of African descent), 6 percent Black (*preto*/dark-skinned person of African descent), and 1 percent other (primarily Asian and Arab descent).[14] Of this number, approximately 69 percent of the poorest Brazilians were Black. Afro-Brazilians were earning at least 40 percent less than white Brazilians. In addition, Black Brazilians were less formally educated than white Brazilians. Approximately 65 percent of the population was living in poverty and only 2.2 percent of all university students were Black, 1 percent of whom would graduate. Furthermore, 25 percent of white Brazilians were illiterate while 40 percent of Black people were illiterate.[15] The level of education among Black Brazilians is particularly alarming given the fact that illiterate Brazilians did not have the right to vote until the new constitution in 1988.[16]

The 1998 statistics mirror similar patterns in the 1970s and 1980s that fueled political debate among Black intellectuals and helped build the Black Movement's political platform against racism and racial democracy. Black people consistently lived in a state of economic and social marginalization that was disproportionately more precarious than their white peers.[17] Economic status and educational attainment limited a Black person's ability to fully participate in the nation as an equal with her white counterparts.[18]

Like her contemporaries, Beatriz Nascimento insisted on demonstrating the insidious, pervasive nature of anti-Black racism in Brazil. She leveled damning critiques of racial democracy, taking on the sardonic tone that Archie Davies mentions in our introduction. She writes, "Interracial relations in Brazil are mild if we consider the apparent conduct between all the races and peoples who live in Brazil. We know, however, that with Black people they take on a different aspect. We feel, as black people, that tolerance toward us camouflages a profound racial prejudice that blooms in the most trivial of interactions, even among those that appear affectionate." In other words, the alleged mildness of Brazilian race relations is a faintly veiled charade that obfuscates the everyday lived realities of racism for Black people. While this statement may not seem revolutionary or radical now, it was decidedly subversive when Nascimento published these words in 1974 at the height of the repressive regime. Indeed, as mentioned previously, one of the ideological tenets of the military dictatorship was Brazilian racial democracy—a point of national pride that the state forcibly defended by punishing and labeling those who dared suggest that racism existed in Brazil. Beatriz Nascimento, like other Black Movement intellectuals, risked threats and persecution when speaking out boldly against Brazil's refusal to acknowledge the latent and explicit racism rampant within Brazilian society. She expressed this boldness through her critiques of Brazilian history.

From Whitening to Racial Democracy

Brazil has hotly debated racial politics since the nineteenth-century abolition period. One of the major projects of the First Republic, declared November 15, 1889, was the modernization of the nation. This project included, among other things, "cleaning up" the "unwanted" parts of the national population.[19] Frequently, "unwanted" people were racialized as Black, Indigenous, or some combination thereof, and debates regarding the need to "whiten" the Brazilian population soon turned into the public policy of whitening (*embranquecimento*). Embranquecimento encouraged European migration to Brazil to balance out and gradually eliminate Brazil's Black and Indigenous populations—eugenics thinking that was both raced and classed.[20] Not surprisingly, the majority of poor and disenfranchised people of both the urban and rural areas were of African, Indigenous, or mixed ancestry.[21] Many of the modernizing projects of the state included the "clean-up" of primarily poor neighborhoods and communities.[22] Projects such as the Vaccine Project of Rio de Janeiro were spatially and socially located. Race and class marked places that needed to be modernized, as much of the poor, non-white population lived in the rural areas of the country or the poor urban "slums," also known as favelas, which Beatriz Nascimento would come to write about in her theorizations on quilombo.[23]

The 1900s–1930s were a period of national identity consolidation.[24] Beatriz Nascimento's work on racism addresses this critical period of abolition, whitening and building the New Republic (see also part III of this book). This period played a significant role in the consolidation of the myth of racial democracy and its hegemonic rise to national prominence. The national discourse of race shifted away from whitening to racial democracy in the 1930s, but the residual effects of the whitening ideology were never fully eliminated. The 1930 revolution of Getúlio Vargas brought the First Republic to an end. Vargas's election as president shifted the power structure from an oligarchy led by coffee-planters to the more bourgeois power base of the Liberal Alliance, whose primary platform was "defense of individual freedom, amnesty (this was a gesture toward the lieutenants), and political reform, which would guarantee what they called electoral truth."[25] The Liberal Alliance sought to create a unified, centralized nation. This project included centralizing economic and political power. The need to create a unified national identity was a natural consequence, and industrialization played an important role in Vargas-era politics. The Brazilian nation-state coupled an emphasis on industrialization with the production of Brazilian national goods. Again, this moment brings us back to Beatriz Nascimento's writings. Nascimento references the national historical project of industrialization in her discussions of racialized gender roles in "The Black Woman in the Labor Market" (part II of this volume). This historical analysis also brings us back to the rise of racial democracy as a national ideology.

The Rise of Racial Democracy

In 1933 Gilberto Freyre, arguably the most famous intellectual in Brazilian history, wrote his most influential book, *Casa Grande e Senzala*.[26] Freyre's writing is important context for reading Beatriz Nascimento. She critiques him explicitly and with good reason: he is, in many ways, the intellectual father of racial democracy.

Casa Grande e Senzala sought to debunk the idea that Brazil was inferior to other nations because of its long history of miscegenation. Rejecting this eugenicist narrative (championed by French eugenicist Arthur de Gobineau, among others), Freyre instead celebrated Brazil's mixed heritage.[27] He touted racial mixture as one of the "successful" results of Portuguese colonization. Brazil allegedly succeeded as a colonial project because the Portuguese were adaptable to the tropical climate, and had a natural "attraction" to Black women, which "proliferated" racial mixture between Portuguese masters and enslaved African women.[28] This colonial environment created a racially mixed population uniquely combining "the best qualities" of both the African and Portuguese people.[29] Freyre's theory became known as Luso-tropicalism, and despite his exile and disillusionment with the 1930 Vargas Revolution, his work became an acclaimed element of the modern nationalist project. The notion that Brazil was a hybrid culture—encompassing the best parts of its three ancestors: the Indigenous, the African, and the Portuguese—fell in line with the efforts by the Vargas regime to unify the national identity. Thus the theory of Luso-tropicalism had an enormous impact on the myth of racial democracy and the course of Brazilian racial politics.

There is no doubt that Freyre's theories were both racist and sexist. Black feminists like Lélia Gonzalez, Sueli Carneiro, and Edna Roland have crafted harsh critiques of Freyre's theses, instead noting that

miscegenation was part of a pattern of patriarchal, anti-Black, white supremacist sexual violence.[30] These explicit critiques of Freyre's racism and
sexism emerge in Beatriz Nascimento's writings here and in part II, in her
work on Black women. Nascimento invested much of her intellectual energy debunking racial democracy. In these critiques, she explicitly names
Freyre to draw attention to the fallacy of his arguments. For example, in
"For a History of Black People," Nascimento writes of an incident that she
suffered in school when Freyre's theories were used to argue for the eventual disappearance of Black people (worth quoting at length):

> One of the things that most defined my time in school, and my train-
> ing afterward, was when a Geography teacher, talking about Brazilian
> ethnicity, based on the Luso-tropicalism of Gilberto Freyre, said, "At
> the beginning of the century, it was impossible to live in the society
> of Rio de Janeiro, there were only Blacks." He added, comparing the
> racial question in the United States with that in Brazil, "In Brazil there
> is no racism, because miscegenation always existed, and continues to
> exist. We will not have conflicts, because *black people are going to
> disappear.*"
>
> The impact was powerful. At the same time that I felt racism blos-
> som bitterly, I thought that perhaps this really was the solution to
> feeling equal to white people. Yet I felt a great sadness, and I didn't
> know where it came from.
>
> Later, I was able to totally reject this theory, but I did not feel at
> peace, because I found this miscegenation to be ever more present,
> ever more sought after by black people. Miscegenation will take its
> course, but it is ideologically based on whitening—that emerged in
> the Pombaline era of the History of Brazil.[31] It was not as immediate
> as they hoped it would be, but it goes on.

Nascimento's visceral, painful reaction to her teacher's words sears
the deeply upsetting and traumatic effects of Freyre's theories onto
our imaginations. Freyre and racial democracy are at the disquieting
heart of Beatriz Nascimento's zeal for speaking out against racism. Indeed, one of Beatriz Nascimento's most decisive interventions is her
writing against Brazilian whitening and racial democracy through her

articulation of a Black History. She believed that while Brazilian historiography failed to address the history of Black people in Brazil, a new History of Black people would be possible through the demystification of racial democracy and its insidious, racist roots. Nascimento interweaves this scathing exposition of racial democracy with her rejection of white paternalism (another hallmark of Freyre) and a passionate call for a total History of Black people.

Appropriating Black Culture

The discourse of racial democracy, buttressed by Freyre's theories, promoted the appropriation of Black culture as well. In the 1930s, those aspects of Brazilian society that were once ridiculed as expressions of the subordinate lower/Black classes were suddenly incorporated into the national identity.[32] This is significant within the context of Nascimento's reflections on race because her work delimits explicit and implicit arguments against the supposition that Black culture is the cultural patrimony of all Brazilians. Indeed, as Black activist Abdias do Nascimento argued, cultural appropriation is one dimension of anti-Black genocide in Brazil: the social lynching of Blacks.[33] To fight against this genocide, Beatriz Nascimento insisted on the existence and importance of Black culture and its undeniable connection to *lived Black experience*. Returning again to "For a History of Black People," she writes,

> How then can we unmake our complexes? ... When we believe in Brazilian racial democracy? When we accept phrases like "am I the blackest white man in Brasil?" (*Samba da Benção*, by Vinícius de Moraes). When we rise through the social classes? When the groups we socialize with are totally white? When we believe that in spite of everything "we contribute to the formation of the Brazilian ethnicity through food and music," as most of our History and Geography books would have it? Did we contribute, or were we forced to make this culture? Our "contribution" was as enslaved people. The majority of our race has no access to wealth, to well-being. But can it be that they only need this to feel equal?

Vargas nationalized multiple aspects of Black culture in his efforts to consolidate the nation: candomblé, feijoada, capoeira, carnival, and samba, for example.[34] This appropriation created a paradox: it dissociated Black culture from the *everyday life of Black people in Brazil*, effectively denying the existence of Blackness as a discreet racial identity by declaring that all Brazilians can claim ownership of Black Brazilian cultural expressions. Black culture became national patrimony trapped in a temporal vacuum—slavery's past. This denied Blackness a diachronic identity, rendering Black *people* (racialized Black subjects) nonexistent. In other words, the idea that there was no longer any racial identity except the Brazilian race, symbolically marked Black people as nonexistent. As Beatriz Nascimento notes, at one point race was removed from the census—a symptom of this shift in perspective. However, as she and others would observe, the concept of "hybridity" presupposes (and so, reinforces) the existence of separate and original races. Thus, the concepts of "white" and "Black" are never truly lost. Racial democracy simply obfuscated racial dichotomies within the nation.

Insisting on the reality of Black identity was one key element of Black Movement politics in Nascimento's time. She contributed to these radical discussions by emphasizing the actuality of Black cultural forms and their historical, social, and political importance for Black people. For example, in "Black People and Racism" she writes:

> in my opinion, there still exists in Brazil a black culture of its own, a black way of life, that can only be perceived to the extent that black people themselves identify as black. But this is another problem: is it certainly interesting for black people that black culture is known outside their own context, but do they run the risk of furnishing knowledge about themselves which will be used against them? We must be wary. And black people, at the moment, are wary.

Her arguments tie back to refusal of the narrative that Black people are a dying and disappearing race in Brazil. Defending Black culture is truly a matter of survival for Nascimento, not just an intellectual exercise.

The Academic Dismantling of Racial Democracy

Beatriz Nascimento's writing is part of the broader Brazilian intellectual debate on racial democracy in her time. Brazilian academics began to demystify the myth of racial democracy in the 1950s.[35] Brazil's efforts to consolidate national identity behind racial democracy had a global impact. In the 1930s, Brazil developed an international reputation for being a nation free of racial tensions (although that perception is traced by some to the nineteenth century).[36] It was thought that Brazil, unlike the United States and South Africa, had succeeded in becoming a racially harmonious nation. In the wake of World War II, this legend became particularly important on the world stage. The devastation of the Holocaust thrust race to the forefront of world politics. Nations wanted to know whether a racially harmonious nation could exist, and if so, how.

At the 1950 Fifth General Conference of UNESCO in Florence, Italy, Brazil was chosen as the subject of an upcoming report that would be "a comprehensive investigation of economic, social, political, cultural and psychological aspects that did or did not influence the emergence of cooperative relations between races and ethnic groups."[37] The 1950 conference set the stage for what would be a cataclysmic event in Brazilian nationalist politics. Rather than finding Brazil to be a racially harmonious country, the UNESCO reports found the country racially stratified and divided along class lines.

The most influential and famous contributors to these findings were the members of the Sociology Department at the University of São Paulo (USP), known as the São Paulo School. Florestan Fernandes, whom Beatriz Nascimento references in "For a History of Black People," coordinated this group, and their findings became a watershed moment in Brazilian social studies. The UNESCO reports undermined the notion of racial democracy, shifting it from an assumed reality to a verified myth. Fernandes and his students (Octavio Ianni, and later-president Fernando Henrique Cardoso) used sociological data and Marxist theory to reveal that Brazil was divided racially along class lines. The São Paulo School suggested that the remnants of racial inequality in Brazil were due to Brazilian society's failure to fully emerge from the legacy of racial capitalism inaugurated by slavery. The result of this failure was the residual placement of Black people in a relatively lower economic status in comparison to whites.

The findings of the UNESCO reports shocked Brazil as well as the rest of the world. The country was now confronted with the reality of race, and the Black population it had tried to erase and silence for so long. The UNESCO reports found that Black Brazilians consistently faced racial discrimination in trying to obtain employment and in educational status. Additionally, they revealed that Black Brazilians were generally economically and socially marginalized.[38] Florestan Fernandes had this to say about his findings in São Paulo:

> The white man does not have a clear picture of the city's racial situation. . . . He continues to hold to the errors and hypocrisy of racial ideology and racial utopia that developed in the past under slavery. . . . Thus he clings to the prejudice of having no prejudice, limiting himself to treating the Negro with tolerance, maintaining the old ceremonial politeness in interracial relationships, and excluding from this tolerance any truly egalitarian feeling or content.[39]

Fernandes asserted that white Brazilians were primarily oblivious to the incongruence of racial democracy. Beatriz Nascimento confirms this obliviousness in "Black People and Racism." She writes:

> They insist on not seeing that racial prejudice is a reflection of society as a whole, and that it is in every layer of society. Ideology, therefore, where prejudice lies, is not disassociated from the economic layer, or the legal-political layer. It is not before or after these two, nor above or below them. Ideology, in its many forms, is integral to a particular society, it accumulates within it, precisely alongside these other two structural layers.

Nascimento refers indirectly to racial democracy as an ideology—an argument that Howard Winant would later make in *The World Is a Ghetto* (2001).[40] The subtext of Fernandes's statement reveals another story as well. While white Brazilians were attached to a utopic notion of racial harmony, they were also engaging in a "ceremonial politeness in interracial relationships." This implies that public interactions between the races were mediated by a false cordiality and the true feelings behind interracial public encounters were hidden beyond the surface. This "ceremonial politeness" is a famous stamp of Brazilian society and is something to which Nascimento refers repeatedly in her essays on race. For her, there is hypocrisy and shallowness in the (white) Brazilian adoption of Black culture (and even, at times, Black identity) that mimics false cordiality. White Brazilians evacuated and denied the politics and history of the Brazilian racial regime while claiming to hold ownership over Black culture. It is this hypocrisy that led Nascimento to insist that Brazilian history must be reinterpreted and reanalyzed from the perspective of Black people to rectify the lies of the past. Although racial democracy hid the subtle yet decisive political, economic, and social debilitation of Black Brazilians within a complex system of institutionalized racial discrimination, it was time to unveil the true reality of structural racism in Brazil. This is the sociopolitical dilemma at the heart of Nascimento's writings on race.

Writing into the Moment

Throughout her intellectual life, Beatriz Nascimento wrote thoughtfully, provocatively, and poetically against Brazilian racism. Her prose takes on a didactic tone, arguing—at times passionately and at times in a tongue-and-cheek fashion—for the need to redefine Black history on Black people's terms. She is preoccupied with defining race, racism, and racial democracy as ideologies, defining an appropriate methodology for understanding the Black experience, arguing for a Black identity defined by Black people (Black lived experience), and diagnosing the veiled racism of Brazil.

This section begins with two essays that she published in *Revista de Cultura Vozes* in 1974 ("For a History of Black People" and "Black People and Racism"). It also contains public scholarship that she published in the popular press, like "Black People, Seen By Themselves," which was an interview published in *Revista Manchete* in 1976; "Realizing Consciousness," which appeared in *Maioria Falante* in 1990; and "Our Racial

Democracy," which was published in the famous Brazilian magazine *Revista IstoÉ* in 1977. Both *Revista Manchete* and *Revista IstoÉ* were national publications with a primarily, but not exclusively, white readership. Nascimento intentionally crafted her tone and assertion according to her audience. On the contrary, "Realizing Consciousness" appeared in a Black Movement periodical—intended for the Black, radical, and politicized audience of the Black Movement. "Realizing Consciousness" is also interesting because of its dialogic nature. As mentioned previously, the article itself has no title and is actually a short commentary within a text box inside a bigger article, "The Left That the Black Person Wants" (A Esquerda que o Negro Quer) by Togo Ioruba, another Black Movement intellectual and organizer of the time. That article is also accompanied by two satirical drawings of the racism of poverty in Brazil by the artist MANEI, whom Nascimento quotes at the beginning of her essay. This context is important for reading the piece, as it is in effect a thought essay meant to be in dialogue with the broader points raised in the larger article and the cartoon. That larger article by Ioruba argues that both the Left and the Right reinscribe white supremacy in their attitudes toward and treatment of Black people.

Nascimento's essays on race are part of a series of broader conversations: Does racism exist in Brazil? If racism exists in Brazil, is it milder and less harmful than racism elsewhere? Is there a Black culture? Isn't class the issue, not race? Are Black people naturally inclined to dysfunctional behaviors, like criminality, sexual licentiousness, and excess? Do Black people have a history (are Black people really a People?)? Can Black people exist within a racially hybrid nation? The list goes on.

The poem that opens this section, "Antiracism," encapsulates the marriage between the two dimensions of her thinking: the poetic and the analytical. As with much of her other writing, the texts included here are deeply personal and reflective. The argument is clear: racism not only exists in Brazil but also wreaks havoc on Black people's lives. Racism, like the lacerated cancer in her poem, is what threatens to take away the sweetness of Black life. It is the "rotted dry stem" of Brazilian society, its dying flesh.

Notes

1. In publications like *Maioria Falante*, Black Movement intellectuals use the phrase *Movimento Negro* (MN) (Black Movement [capitalized]) repeatedly to define the Black left social movement of the 1970s–1990s.

2. Quote taken from the epigraph to "Black People, Seen by Themselves."

3. "Black People and Racism."

4. Larry Crook and Randal Johnson, *Black Brazil: Culture, Identity, and Social Mobilization* (Los Angeles: UCLA Latin American Center Publications, University of California, Los Angeles, 1999), 9.

5. My reading of the de facto, post facto state of slavery is inspired by Esmeralda Ribeiro's 1988 poem "Fato" (Fact) in homage to protests against the hundredth-anniversary celebrations. A powerful political statement about the falsity of Brazilian abolition, "Fato" (Fact) represents the ambiguity surrounding the meaning of abolition that Black organizers shared at this time: slavery might have been legally abolished, but the conditions of slavery remained.

6. Abdias do Nascimento, renowned Black activist, scholar, and artist, wrote of the perpetuation of the condition of slavery post-abolition: "Throughout the era of slavery, from 1530 to 1888, Brazil carried out a policy of systematic liquidation of the African. From the legal abolition of slavery in 1888 to the present, this policy has been continued by means of various well-defined mechanisms of oppression and extermination, leaving white supremacy unthreatened in Brazil." Abdias do Nascimento, *Brazil, Mixture or Massacre?: Essays in the Genocide of a Black People*, trans. Elisa Larkin Nascimento. 2nd rev. ed. (Dover, MA: Majority Press, 1989), 1.

7. Building on the intellectual work of Beatriz Nascimento, Lélia Gonzalez, Clóvis Moura, and Abdias do Nascimento, I make this argument extensively in my book *Afro-Paradise: Blackness, Violence, and Performance in Brazil* (Urbana: University of Illinois Press, 2016). Clóvis Moura, *Dialética radical do Brasil negro* (São Paulo: Editora Anita, 1994); Nascimento, *Brazil, Mixture or Massacre?*.

8. For example, Abdias do Nascimento was forced into exile in the United States prior to the beginning of the military dictatorship primarily due to his ideas on race and his organizing against racism. Abdias do Nascimento and Elisa Larkin, *Africans in Brazil: A Pan-African Perspective* (Trenton, NJ: Africa World Press, 1992); Ollie Johnson, "Abdias Nascimento and Brazilian Politics," *Journal of Black Studies* 52, no. 6 (2021): 627–42.

9. Brazilian scholars and US Brazilianists often contrasted race relations in Brazil with that of the United States at this time. The widespread assumption was that the United States relied primarily on a system of racial classification based on hypodescent in contrast to Brazil, which had a more fluid understanding of racial classification and racial identity. The assumption that the United States operated on a bifurcated racial classification system (Black/white) contrasted with the Brazilian racial spectrum that contained an infinite number of racial possibilities. Today, this myth has been largely debunked by decades of research demonstrating systematic racial inequality in Brazil. Nevertheless, the ideological and cultural investment in Brazil's racial democracy remains salient. See, for example, Marvin Harris, *Patterns of Race in Latin America* (New York: Walker, 1964); Carl N. Degler, *Neither Black Nor White* (New York: The MacMillan Company, 1971); Anthony W. Marx, *Making Race and Nation: A Comparison of the United States,*

South Africa, and Brazil (Cambridge: Cambridge University Press, 1998). See also Hanchard, *Orpheus and Power* and Winant, *The World Is a Ghetto*.

10. For more on the history of the census in Brazil, see, for example, "Introdução," in IBGE, *Metodologia do Censo Demográfico 2000* (Rio de Janeiro: IBGE, 2003); Melissa Nobles, *Shades of Citizenship: Race and the Census in Modern Politics* (Stanford, CA: Stanford University Press, 2000).

11. National Household Sample Research, referenced in Pierre-Michel Fontaine, ed., *Race, Class, and Power in Brazil* (Los Angeles: Center for Afro-American Studies, University of California, 1985).

12. Dijaci David de Oliveira, *A cor do medo: homicídios e relações raciais no Brasil* (Brasília: Editora UnB, 1998), 42.

13. See Edward Telles and Tianna Paschel, "Who Is Black, White, or Mixed Race? How Skin Color, Status, and Nation Shape Racial Classification in Latin America," *American Journal of Sociology* 120, no. 3 (2014): 864–907. And see, for example, Santos, *O sistema de cotas para negros da UNB*.

14. These statistics were taken from the Minority Rights Group 1995 report. For this study, the Minority Rights Group followed the racial classification system that is widely used in Brazil, combining pardos and pretos under the classification "negro," which we translate here as "Black." Minority Rights Group, ed., *No Longer Invisible: Afro-Latin Americans Today* (London: Minority Rights Publications, 1995). For a historical statistical comparison of racial inequality between Brazil and the United States, see George Reid Andrews, "Racial Inequality in Brazil and the United States: A Statistical Comparison," *Journal of Social History* 26, no. 2 (1992): 229–63.

15. One of the drawbacks to these statistics is the lack of information regarding what tests were used to judge literacy. Were respondents asked to write their name, or read a passage? Given this lack of information, it is hard to assess the picture these statistics present. With that in mind, the proportions are what is important. Regardless of the standards used, a discrepancy between white and Black people exists.

16. For more discussion and elaboration of these statistics, see the proceedings of the World Conference against Racism in Durban, South Africa, 2001, statistics from the Minority Rights Group, and statistics from the Inter-American Trade Union Institute for Racial Equality.

17. Carlos Alfredo Hasenbalg, *Race Relations in Modern Brazil* (Latin American Institute, University of New Mexico, 1984); Carlos Alfredo Hasenbalg and Nelson do Valle Silva, *Estrutura social, mobilidade e raça* (Instituto Universitário de Pesquisas do Rio de Janeiro, 1988); Peggy A. Lovell and Charles H. Wood, "Skin Color, Racial Identity, and Life Chances in Brazil," *Latin American Perspectives* 25, no. 3 (1998): 90–109.

18. See also Edward E. Telles, *Race in Another America: The Significance of Skin Color in Brazil* (Princeton, NJ: Princeton University Press, 2014).

19. See, for example, Seth Garfield, *Indigenous Struggle at the Heart of Brazil: State Policy, Frontier Expansion, and the Xavante Indians, 1937–1988* (Durham, NC: Duke University Press, 2001).

20. One of the key texts on the history of whitening in Brazil, Thomas Skidmore's *Black into White*, was published in 1974 right as Beatriz Nascimento was also publishing on race.

Thomas E. Skidmore, *Black into White: Race and Nationality in Brazilian Thought* (New York: Oxford University Press, 1974); Sales Augusto dos Santos, "Historical Roots of the 'Whitening' of Brazil," *Latin American Perspectives* 29, no. 1 (2002): 61–82.

21. Lorraine Leu, *Defiant Geographies: Race & Urban Space in 1920s Rio de Janeiro* (Pittsburgh, PA: University of Pittsburgh Press, 2020); Archie Davies, "The Racial Division of Nature," *Transactions of the Institute of British Geographers* 46, no. 2 (2021): 270–83.

22. Skidmore, *Black into White*. See also Jerry Dávila, *Diploma of Whiteness: Race and Social Policy in Brazil, 1917–1945* (Durham, NC: Duke University Press, 2003).

23. Davila, *Diploma of Whiteness*. See also Leu, *Defiant Geographies*.

24. See Garfield, *Indigenous Struggle at the Heart of Brazil*.

25. Boris Fausto, *A Concise History of Brazil*, trans. Arthur Brakel (Cambridge: Cambridge University Press, 1999). The Vargas Revolution and the subsequent establishment of the Estado Novo (as it was called) incorporated a hodgepodge of supporters all united behind the desire to overthrow the old regime. In this respect, supporters of the revolution shared a diversity of opinions on how the new state should take form. The political elite shifted, but it is important to note that this did not mean the disappearance of the oligarchies altogether. The most important mark of the Vargas regime was the emphasis on national centralization. The states lost much of their autonomy as the central government took on more responsibility. Since the political base of the First Republic was primarily based on federalism and maintaining regional state power, this was a considerable change. Fausto, *A Concise History of Brazil*, 190–97.

26. Gilberto Freyre et al., *Casa-grande & senzala, edição crítica* (Madrid: Allca XX, 2002).

27. Gilberto Freyre's work falls into a genre of work on race and nation being done by Latin American scholars and activists during the "Latin American modern moment." The work of José Vasconcelos in *La Raza Cosmica* (1929) and Fernando Ortiz's *Contrapunteo Cubano de Tabaco y el Azucar* (1940) are two principal examples. Their work also made an argument for celebrating the mixed heritage inherent in the Latin American young nations. Freyre, along with other Latin American scholars, used the concept of miscegenation as the empowering (as opposed to weakening point) of the new Latin American identity.

28. Black Brazilian feminists like Lélia Gonzalez and indeed Beatriz Nascimento vehemently and relentlessly critiqued and ridiculed this element of Freyre's theories in their writings. Particularly, Gonzalez notes that sexual violence and coercion were the backdrop to this alleged "attraction" to Black women and should not be dissociated from the violent context of slavery. Lélia Gonzalez, *Primavera para as rosas negras: Lélia Gonzalez em primeira pessoa* (São Paulo: Diáspora Africana, 2018). See also Beatriz Nascimento's writings in part II.

29. Freyre's impact on Brazilian national discourse was in every way shaped by his personal background. Freyre grew up on a former plantation and became familiar with the legacies of slavery in Brazilian culture during his childhood. His fascination with race and race relations can be traced to the influence of his mentor, anthropologist Franz Boas, with whom he worked at Columbia University during his time in the United States. See Jeffery D. Needell, "Identity, Race, Gender and Modernity in the Origins of Gilberto Freyre's *Oeuvre*," *American Historical Review* 100, no. 1 (1995): 51–77.

30. Lélia Gonzalez, *Primavera para as rosas negras*; Sueli Carneiro and Conceição Evaristo, *Escritos de uma vida* (Belo Horizonte, MG: Letramento, 2018).

31. Referring to the early eighteenth century, the period of the domination of the Marquis of Pombal in Portugal and Brazil.

32. This is not to say that there were not visible elements of African culture being expressed within Brazilian society prior to this. Quite to the contrary, interracial participation in African cultural manifestations, particularly religious expression, can be traced back to the time of slavery. João José Reis, *Rebelião escrava no Brasil: a história do levante dos malês em 1835* (São Paulo: Companhia das Letras, 2003).

33. Nascimento, *Brazil, Mixture or Massacre?*.

34. Hermano Vianna, in his book *The Mystery of Samba* (1999), chronicles this appropriation of Black culture to the national identity as he follows the development of samba into the national dance of Brazil. Arguing against the conventional notion that the 1930s witnessed the sudden incorporation of Black culture into the national identity, Vianna demonstrates the gradual process of appropriation that started during slavery with the exchange of culture between the Portuguese and the Africans brought to Brazil. In particular, he traces the connections between the Brazilian intellectual elite and Black cultural trends, such as samba, of the time. He highlights the trend in denouncing "official Brazil" among these elite and in particular cites an article by Gilberto Freyre, a fan of the back-alley samba of Rio de Janeiro, published in a newspaper in 1926 entitled "On the Valorization of Things Black." Beatriz Nascimento engages in a similar debate in her reflections on cultural appropriation.

35. Here I am referring to the first UNESCO reports of the 1950s. A second UNESCO report reconfirming the existence of racial discrimination in Brazil was released in 1972 (Fontaine, *Race, Class and Power in Brazil,* 2).

36. Marcos Chor Maio, "The UNESCO Project: Social Sciences and Race Studies in Brazil in the 1950s," trans. José Augusto Drummond (2000).

37. Maio, "The UNESCO Project."

38. Florestan Fernandes, *O negro no mundo dos brancos* (São Paulo: Difusão Européia do Livro, 1972); Fernandes Florestan, *The Negro in Brazilian Society*, trans. Jacqueline D. Skiles, A. Brunel, and Arthur Rothwell (New York: Columbia University Press, 1969).

39. Fernandes, *The Negro in Brazilian Society*, xv.

40. Howard Winant, *The World Is a Ghetto: Race and Democracy since World War II*, 1st ed. (New York: Basic Books, 2001).

Antiracism

No one will make me lose tenderness
Like the four beetles
Generation of generation
Gestation of freedom
The heron's flight, sure
No one will make me lose sweetness
Palm sap, coconut plasma
Pendulum extended
In the extensive sea—open
Scaled mackerel in the sand's milk
No one will make me racist
Rotted dry stem
Without veins, without warm blood
Without rhythm, hard body?
They will never make exist in me
That lacerated cancer

Note

The original title of this poem was "Antiracismo." February 6, 1990.

For a History of Black People

Another general aspect of the deficiency in historical life [is that] individual life as yet has no history. . . . This individual experience of a disconnected everyday life remains without language, without concepts, and without critical access to its own past, which has nowhere been recorded. Uncommunicated, misunderstood and forgotten, it is smothered by the spectacle's false memory of the unmemorable.

—GUY DEBORD, *THE SOCIETY OF THE SPECTACLE* (1967)[1]

HOW CAN WE TAKE up, again, the true time of History, apparently lost with mechanization and the Industrial Revolution in the seventeenth and eighteenth centuries? How can we live a human history that has been depreciated in favor of a scientism and a technicism that endures precisely because it is part of that History? How can we make, how can we write History without being enslaved by its fragmentary approach?

Is it possible to reduce it to the History of Man, Total History, to specialisms? Is it possible to reduce it to a science that simply verifies what we seem to live? Can we limit History to a historically reductive time, and understand it only as it has been presented to us since the nineteenth century? As just another Science?

How should we approach, for example, the History of Black people in Brazil? Can we only do so through ethnographic, religious, or socio-economic approaches? That is, fragmentarily. These approaches have been brilliantly done, but what about the History of Black people? In the end, we are humans, individuals who must be studied as such.

One of the most serious works on black people in Brazil is Florestan Fernandes's *The Negro in Brazilian Society*.[2] It is one of the earliest sources for the study of black people in Brazil (São Paulo). Other similar approaches consider the problem of black people from the point of view of class, or social mobility. This type of approach, rich in data and statistics, leads some scholars (even those who only seek a greater understanding of our problematic) to only see black people from a social perspective.

This kind of approach is the primordial form of contemporary historical studies. I see this as a dangerous fragmentation for the History of Black people in Brazil, because in approaching only certain aspects, it pretends to explain the whole. Work that deals with a people such as us, must take into account not only socioeconomic but also racial aspects. We cannot implicate ourselves in the perpetuation of mystifications and stereotypes that go back to the origins of the historical life of a people who were uprooted from their habitat, enslaved, and raped in their *Real History*.

What would we be, as individuals, as the black Man, if there had been no Commercial Revolution in the West in the fifteenth century? I know that I ask a question that will startle the scientists, those who simply see science in History and those who are committed to nineteenth- and twentieth-century thought. Science is considered "Mater Mundi" today. We cannot go against its dogmas.

Returning to the problem of the History of Black people in Brazil: Who are we, in human terms? Can we accept that they study us as primitive beings? As artistic expressions of Brazilian society? As a social class, confounded with all of the other elements of the lower economic classes, as many would like? I ask in terms of scholarship. Can we, being studied, be confused with poor Northeasterners? With poor white people? With Indigenous people?

Can we even confuse our racial experience with that of Jewish people because we both suffer discrimination? Historically, I believe that the two are hardly comparable, even if we think in internationalist terms. In terms of Brazil, it would be beyond fanciful to think in such terms; in Brazil, a Jewish person is white, before Jewish. In other words, they are a powerful people, thanks to the mutual aid they have historically developed among themselves.

Is it not possible that we might have our own characteristics, not only in "cultural" terms, or social terms, but in human terms? Individually? I believe so. I am black, I think and feel black.

Interracial relations in Brazil are mild if we consider the apparent conduct between all the races and peoples who live in Brazil. We know, however, that with black people they take on a different aspect. We feel, as black people, that tolerance toward us camouflages a profound racial prejudice that blooms in the most trivial of interactions, even among those that appear affectionate.

We are shown racial prejudice constantly—we feel it. However, since it is dressed up as tolerance, it is not always possible for us to perceive to what extent there has been an intention to humiliate us. In a way, we have already incorporated some of these manifestations into ourselves. When aggression emerges, though, it manifests itself in an uncontainable violence on the part of white people. Yet, even on these occasions, we "think twice" before reacting, since, as I explained above, the mystifications worked well on our "historical ego." Racial prejudice against black people is violent and, at the same time, subtle: It is latent, and often comes to the fore in our relations among ourselves. We could say that we have an attitude of love and hate toward ourselves; and the presence of and confrontation with the other bothers us, too.

Perhaps Brazilian racial democracy exists, but in relation to black people, it does not.

The manifestations of prejudice are so strong that among our intellectuals, our literati, our poets—the national consciousness, so to speak—we are treated as if we still live under slavery. Our representation in literature, for example, is as house slaves or, in the case of women, as the concubine from the colonial period. The most important aspect of this scholarly negligence is that there has never been an attempt to study us as a race. The white Brazilian in general, and the intellectual in particular, refuses to approach the discussion of black people from the perspective of race. They decry racial reality out of complacency, fear, or indeed racism. In this way, they perpetuate theories that are completely disconnected from our racial reality. Even more seriously, they create new mystifying theories, profoundly distanced from that same reality.

One of the things that most defined my time in school, and my training afterward, was when a Geography teacher, talking about Brazilian ethnicity, based on the Luso-tropicalism of Gilberto Freyre, said, "At the beginning of the century, it was impossible to live in the society of Rio de Janeiro, there were only blacks." He added, comparing the racial question in the United States with that in Brazil, "In Brazil there is no racism, because miscegenation always existed, and continues to exist. We will not have conflicts, because *black people are going to disappear.*"

The impact was powerful. At the same time that I felt racism blossom bitterly, I thought that perhaps this really was the solution to feeling equal to white people. Yet, I felt a great sadness, and I didn't know where it came from.

Later, I was able to totally reject this theory, but I did not feel at peace, because I found this miscegenation to be ever more present, ever more sought after by black people. Miscegenation will take its course, but it is ideologically based on whitening—that emerged in the Pombaline era of the History of Brazil.[3] It was not as spontaneous as they hoped it would be, but it goes on.

There has been a new mystification, principally coming from intellectuals and artists. In theory, it is a contradiction of miscegenation, but it demonstrates a racial prejudice that is perhaps even more dangerous. One of the worst aggressions that I have suffered of this kind came from a white intellectual. He told me that he was blacker than I was because he had written a piece on Afro-Brazilian religion, and I didn't wear my hair in an Afro or follow candomblé.

It was one of the claims that I have found most difficult to situate. One of the most subtle of the racial prejudices that exists in Brazil. We suffer subtle aggressions in the street, at school, at work, even in the family. But this was truly the most violent. I do not know how best to describe it.

I believe that this is part of the newest mystification about prejudice against black people. Artists, intellectuals, and other white people, faced with the crisis of Western thought and culture, turn to us to soak up their historical frustrations yet again. Is it possible that now, on the terrain of ideas and of the arts, we will once again be the "hands and feet" of Western society? They think that by going to candomblé, making music that speaks of our happiness, our wisdom, and other stereotypes, they can even take away our racial identity. If a brilliant, young, blonde, bourgeois intellectual, after years of studying one of our cultural manifestations, reaches the conclusion that he is blacker than I am, what is it that I am?

In the streets people attack me in manifold ways. Inside me, I repress the simplest aspirations. When I come into contact with people, I have to recite my whole curriculum vitae in order to garner the slightest bit of respect. Eighty years ago, my race lived in the most degrading of conditions. I sometimes think that I might have been on my continent of origin had there not been a white economic revolution, with which, right up to today, I have had nothing to do. Most of my peers remain socially and economically oppressed and have no access to the riches of the country that they built. When I return to my daily life, I find that people see my color as the defining feature of my identity, and to this extent they treat me as an inferior being. I wonder, what absurd ideology is this, of people who want to strip my identity away from me?

Generally, when we are attacked in the street, and we react, the aggressors rush to assert what they know about racial integration, and how they get on great with black people—apart from me, obviously. They assert that I do not understand that it was a term of affection to call me, for example, *darky*, in a deprecating and aggressive tone, or to demand that I summon the homeowner when I answer the door of my own apartment. At other times violence manifests itself in plain sight through threats and physical aggression. At school, or at work, they always expect you to be either incapable, or a genius. In the first case, they say: "but he's black"; and in the second, "he's Black, but . . ." In other words, he knows and must continue to stay in his place, his role, his part.

In these moments, we don't always fight back. In fact, it is impossible to be prepared to consciously fight back twenty-four hours a day, against all these forms of prejudice, which often come from black people themselves.

Among us, there is a defensive attitude toward other black people that at times takes the form of aggression. This is where our repression blossoms most.

All these unresolved aggressions, all the repression of a History that has still to be written, still to be truly addressed, make us repressed, and give us complexes. I do not state this empirically. Psychology demonstrates theoretically that complexes exist in all people, that what is unresolved exists as repression. In these eighty years of "Abolition" in which we have barely participated, that did not emerge from our politico-ideological maturity either as a race, or as Brazilians, our frustrations have not been resolved. The slave quarters are still standing. In terms of Total History, eighty years is a matter of days.

How then can we unmake our complexes? By believing that we are whitening ourselves when we lighten our skin? When we straighten our hair? When we marry a white man, raising the possibility that the next generation will be lighter? When we believe in Brazilian racial democracy? When we accept phrases like "am I the blackest white man in Brasil?" (*Samba da Benção*, by Vinícius de Moraes). When we rise through the social classes? When the groups we socialize with are totally white? When we believe that in spite of everything "we contribute to the formation of the Brazilian ethnicity through food and music," as most of our History and Geography books would have it? Did we contribute, or were we forced to make this culture? Our "contribution" was as enslaved people. The majority of our race has no access to wealth, to well-being. But can it be that they only need this to feel equal? Can it be that we are not represented except through Afro-Brazilian cults, samba, football, happiness, and sex, as some famous writers want? The intellectuals say that we do not have our own ideology, because fundamentally we want to whiten ourselves. Could it be that this is it, exactly? Or should our ideology not come to the surface? The History of the black race is still to be written, within a History of Brazil that is still to be written.

This is a difficult project. It is a challenge. I fully accepted this challenge from the moment at which a white intellectual told me he was blacker than I was. It was, for me, the most baffling, the most specious and most challenging affirmation. He thinks that it is enough to understand and participate in some cultural events to be black: others think that those who study us under slavery understand us historically. As if History could be limited to "spectacular time," to represented time, and not the contrary: time is that which is inside History. You cannot study historical experience in living black people. *We are the Living History of Black People, not numbers.*

We cannot accept that the History of Black people in Brazil today be understood through ethnography or sociology. We have to make our History by finding ourselves, shaking off our unconsciousness, our frustrations, our complexes, and studying them, not evading them. Only thus will we be able to understand ourselves and force ourselves to accept ourselves as we are: black, Brazilian, before anything else—without confusing ourselves with Americans or Africans. Our history is different, as are the problems we face. In a country in which the concept of race is based on color, when a white man says that he is blacker than you, we are dealing with a racism that is very sophisticated and very destructive on a personal level. In that moment, in response to my reaction, when they asked me if I had a complex, I surprised myself by saying yes with a pride that I had never felt before.

I justify it this way: if my culture is considered as "a contribution to . . ."; if my race never had access, either jointly or representatively, to the wealth of this country; if the majority of us are dispersed by the force of a disarticulation that we must come to understand (black Brazilians, with rare exceptions, do not come together in groups); if our religious events are turned into folklore, or worse, are consumed as music on the TV (see the music of Vinícius de Moraes and Toquinho, singing the name of Omulu), then when a white man wants to take away my physical identity, the single real fact of my History in Brazil—all that remains to me is within me, all that remains to me is to take on my unresolved complex.

All that remains to us is our unconscious, that can be understood and resolved only through history.

I no longer accept any form of paternalism, especially intellectual paternalism. Like the young white man, I acquired the tools of my understanding through the study of history, in which I believe totally. They are tools acquired in white Western culture, so I owe nothing to him. However, as the person I love most told me—a black man, my husband—the things that I reflect now already existed in my mother's womb, in some quilombo in the Northeast, in Africa, where I no longer want to, or can, return. That is: in my race, in the History of Man.

Notes

This article was originally published as "Por uma História do Homem Negro." *Revista de Cultura Vozes* 68, no. 7 (1974): 41–45.

1. Guy Debord, *The Society of the Spectacle*, trans. Ken Knabb (Berkeley, CA: Critical Editions, 2021).

2. Translation of *A integração do negro na sociedade de classes*, trans. Jacqueline D. Skiles, A. Brunel, and Arthur Rothwell, ed. Phyllis B. Eveleth (New York: Atheneum, 1971).

3. Referring to the early eighteenth century, the period of the domination of the Marquis of Pombal in Portugal and Brazil.

Black People and Racism

THERE ARE MANY ECONOMIC and political studies on the historical-social formation of Brazil. However, the "theories" that attempt to explain the ideological aspects of Brazilian society always seem to be concepts imported from European or North American social science. This limits the talk of ideology to closed intellectual circles, or bars at the end of the night. Studying "national ideology" continues to be seen as an elite subject, at best. Or it is seen as purely subjective (while economics is objective), and as a kind of dishonorable speculation.

Yet, in order to understand our society, it is crucial to understand one particular, extremely important element in its historical formation. This element does not, generally, manifest itself to the higher strata of the population. It has limited access to so-called cultivated circles. It cannot take part in *snobbish* discussions. (In Brazil, it is considered snobbish to discuss or interpret the plural ideological aspects that make up the Brazilian social formation.) The element in question is the black Brazilian, who can only be understood through a profound study of *national ideology* and black people's part in the social whole. Yet the racial prejudice with which black people are endlessly provoked in everyday life in Brazil has marginalized Black people from national ideology. In historical terms, this racial prejudice can be seen in the lack of free thinking by Brazilians about themselves, and by black people about themselves.

When, in an essay published in the first issue of *Revista de Cultura Vozes* this year,[1] we said that we must be understood as Brazilians, without being confused with black North Americans or Africans, we wanted to say that there exists a bias, at the level of ideas, toward understanding us through the problems of other black people who live in a different social and racial reality from ours. Importing "ideologies" is typical of Brazilian intellectual thought, which is the whitest and most Europeanized of the whole so-called Third World. To put it another way, Brazil possesses the most complexed elites precisely because it has never managed to incorporate into the social whole, that degrading element which, by historical fact, was the most important feature of its process of formation. The black enslaved person, like the black person today, did not only take part in the social formation of Brazil through their work and through their suffering. They also took part in that social formation at the table, in the bed, in thought, and in the political struggles of the colonizer and their descendants. Everywhere that white people look they see the specter of those they enslaved and corrupted. It is precisely the fact of having corrupted us that eats away at the savior complexes of many of our "defenders." Now they want to redeem us by studying us in our socioeconomic aspects. They present themselves as "feeling" black, as if centuries of suffering and marginalization can be redeemed by a feeling of "being black." Being black is to confront a history of almost five hundred years of painful resistance, of physical and moral suffering, the feeling of not existing, the practice of still not belonging to the society to which you gave everything you had, and to which still, today, you give what is left of yourself. Being black cannot be summed up as a "state of mind," a "white or black soul," or aspects of behavior that certain white people call black and adopt for themselves.

Assuming blackness is as simple as it is deceitful. It hides an attempt to maintain the dominant racial framework. It is a sophisticated form of presenting, through paternalism, the prejudice of those who cannot deny an origin that they repudiate, and who owe the greater part of what they possess to the people they enslaved and dehumanized. It is too uncomfortable a paradox. The dominant have not accounted for the idea that the dominated would accrue not just suffering and poverty but also aspects of their culture, their vices, and their virtues.

Today, with the crises of western culture—in forms of thought, the arts, and institutions in general—the intellectual elites of countries with black populations are looking for ways out through what they imagine as forms of being and feeling black. They repeat—I do not know whether consciously or not—the eighteenth-century myth of the "good savage." Dozens of "Rousseaus" appear, running after us to ask which type of African we are, if we come from Africa, what tribe we are from, etc. . . . Or rather, based on their reading of black Americans and the "feeling" of "Black power," they want to raise our consciousness, a consciousness that, perhaps, is that of white people. It's just that they forget that it is no longer possible to survive on myths (created precisely to institutionalize domination and secure its moral foundations) of purity, beauty, etc., because western domination took care not only to physically use those it dominated, but also, through ideology, to impregnate them with western habits, objectives, and morality. They forget that they corrupted us and that it's no use now seeing us as beautiful. Because to us it is very clear that the white westerner dominates the world, with his money, his weapons, his science, his morals, and his aesthetics.

In Brazil, "good savages" do not exist. Nor do "pure blacks" who know their African roots. After exploiting us and taking the best from us, after repressing us, the dominant ideology now wants to "discover us" (as some of black people's knights in shining armor put it) "pure," our "culturally rich," "conscious of our race." They do not understand that the ideas of purity, beauty, virility, and strength that they want to inculcate us with are their own concepts, impregnated with their own culture. As for our own consciousness of ourselves, it can only emerge from us, and based on an awareness of the oppressor.

Forgive us if we do not correspond to the expectations of our former masters. It is no longer possible to find a "pure" black man, at least here in Brazil. For now, we only want to be "equal," to be "accepted." For now, the aesthetic ideals of white people still reign inside us. For now, we have to see ourselves with a "white soul," because we are part of a whole dominated by the ideology of the dominant. We are not "beautiful" like black Americans, and we do not want to be, we could not be. If some white intellectual wants to know, he could only understand us if he lost his inferiority complex in relation to Europe and the United States. (Indeed, the Brazilian has a complex in relation to the whole World; one of his great dreams is to be a foreigner, and to speak French.) He needs to confront us as we are: accept that he is mixed with us, that he has made use of all of our goods. He must accept himself as part of us, fed, loved, and defended by us. Accept that he has denied, in practice, his morals, his religion and his culture by sleeping in our beds. He has been fed at our breasts, been protected and taught by our men. Accept it without guilt, without prejudice. Accept himself to be as miserable as those he enslaved, as hungry as them, as "untaught" as them—or even more so. Perhaps, in this way, something of us might be used to understand his society in crisis.

Prejudice against the study of ideologies provokes a series of misunderstandings that perpetuate racism among the Brazilian educated classes. In spite of the apparent "acceptance" of the "cultural contribution" of black people, they fundamentally do not know who these "contributors" are. Worse, they don't want to know. They prefer that "theorists" repeat blindly that the origin of discrimination is the socioeconomic make-up of Brazilian society. They insist on not seeing that racial prejudice is a reflection of society as a whole, and that it is in every layer of society. Ideology, therefore, where prejudice lies, is not disassociated from the economic layer, or the legal-political layer. It is not before or after these two, nor above or below them. Ideology, in its many forms, is integral to a particular society, it accumulates within it, precisely alongside these other two structural layers. To confuse the schematization of concepts to better comprehend the problem, with the practice of concepts in concrete reality, is to demonstrate the ignorance of a bad student. Indeed, it would be to reiterate the very same prejudice again, but under the veil of a "(very) useful innocence." To repeat that racial prejudice has its origins in economics or is a result of the phenomenon of class struggle, means looking for explanations of a deeply complex situation only in the economic foundations. It does not clarify; it only raises new questions. It does not offer solutions for those who have a direct interest in finding them.

The ideology of racism has such deep roots in the Brazilian social formation that we must take into account a series of forms of behavior, habits, ways of being and acting inherent not only in white people (agents) but in black people (patients). Above all, we need to clarify the whole ideological product from the perspective of black people, after four centuries of nonexistence in a society in which the black person has participated at every level.

We propose for ourselves, and for black Brazilians, that through common effort we should try to understand and expose how the characteristics of racial prejudice are reflected in our behavior, in our way of being. We seek to characterize it not only through recounting the same situations again, but through an honest interpretation of the reflections of racism in ourselves, so that we can integrate ourselves into the "national consciousness" not as objects of study, mummified by the force of omission and dependency of thought that does nothing but perpetuate the "status quo" to which we have been historically subjected. It is time to speak for ourselves, not as "contributors," not as victims of but as participants in Brazil's historical and social formation.

When we proposed writing a History of Black People in Brazil, we knew the difficulty of the task. The initial challenge was to find an adequate methodology and a new conceptualization. This difficulty emerges not only in the research itself but in building concepts that go against those universalized by western domination, which serve to express the position of the dominant in the face of the dominated. In using particular terms like "acceptance," "integration," "equality" at the beginning of this exposition, I wanted to show how, in practice, the ideology of domination represents prejudice in language itself. Here, language is evidence of the actually existing conditions of racism and discrimination. "Acceptance," "integration," and "equality" are points of view of the dominator.

Taking these three concepts as examples, we can demonstrate the difficulty for black people in studying racial discrimination (and not only that but the whole history of black Brazilian people) and conceptualizing, from their own perspective, their situation, and aspirations within the dominant society. It is even more difficult to find a method for this study. Impregnated by a culture that is in every sense white and European, we must ask ourselves if certain terms correspond to our own perspective, or if they are just reflections of prejudice, repeated automatically, without any critical reflection. Are we only repeating the concepts of the dominator without asking ourselves if they correspond, or not, to our vision of things? Are these concepts a kind of practice, and if they are, is it adequate for black people? Accepted by whom? For what? What changes if we are accepted? What is it to be equal? Whom are we equal to? Is it possible to be equal? Why be equal?

The questions asked of the concepts used up to now in relation to black people and the study of discrimination, must, in my view, be interrogated, and their implications minutely deconstructed. Like those discussed here, almost everything that has been said about black people, everything that has been attributed to them, everything that up to now has been considered as being black, including black culture, must be reexamined not from the perspective of the dominant ideology, but from the point of view of our own aspirations and our own needs. This will only be possible if we stick close to History. Only a historical approach to the lived experience of black people in Brazil, put forward by their descendants—those who actually experience in practice this existential inheritance—will be able to eradicate the complexes of black people, and the racial prejudice of white people.

Notes

This article was originally published as "Negro & Racismo." *Revista de Cultura Vozes* 68 (1974): 65–68.

1. Nascimento is referring to "For a History of Black People."

Black People, Seen
by Themselves

Interview by Eloí Calage

MARIA BEATRIZ NASCIMENTO, thirty-four years old, graduated in History from the Institute of Philosophy and Social Sciences at the Federal University of Rio de Janeiro (UFRJ). She is currently a researcher at the Centre of Research and Documentation of Contemporary History at the Getúlio Vargas Foundation. For the last three years, she has been working on an ambitious project: to rewrite and reinterpret the history of black people in Brazil. Hers is not conventional immersion in the past. Rather, by starting from the past she aims to establish the relations of historical continuity that could lead to a new understanding of black people's role in the history of Brazil, right up to the present day. Maria Beatriz spoke to *Manchete* about her work.

> MANCHETE: Did professional or personal motivations lead you to writing this history of black people in Brazil?
>
> MARIA BEATRIZ: It's difficult to separate the two things. Even as a student I felt a great need to know and understand the role of black people in Brazilian history. There is a great void of knowledge in this field. More than that, I felt that it was not enough merely to have more information on the subject: history has to be rewritten from a new critical and revisionist perspective that

reevaluates everything in the history and sociology of black people. At the existential level, being a black woman, I believe that it is necessary for all of this to be analyzed from the perspective of black people as subjects of History.

MANCHETE: Will your work reveal new documents on the subject?

MARIA BEATRIZ: The sources that I am using are, at least in part, familiar. I use a lot of secondary literature from abroad, especially from North America. In terms of primary documents, very little remains, and the majority is in Portugal, in the archive of the *Torre do Tombo*. These documents, that I have consulted, are mainly from one specific source: the colonial police. In them, black people appear when they need to be punished. I also base my work on more recent historical facts. I don't just want to narrate the events of the past, but to establish the continuity between the past and the present of black people in Brazil.

MANCHETE: Where do you look for this continuity?

MARIA BEATRIZ: The theme of my work is the quilombo. In my opinion, contrary to what I was taught, and to what is still taught in schools today, the quilombo was not simply an attempt to rebel against the slavocratic system. It was also a form of social and political organization with very profound ideological implications in the life of black people in the past. After abolition, these were projected into the twentieth century.

MANCHETE: So, in your opinion, the quilombo still survives?

MARIA BEATRIZ: It survives—not in its original form, but as a tradition of life for black Brazilians. The key is that it is a form of life for black Brazilians in whatever period. To take an example: studying nineteenth-century police documents, we can see that some regions of Rio de Janeiro—such as Catumbi, the hills of São Carlos and Santa Marta and other contemporary favelas—were previously sites of quilombos. Or, in another context, during the drought in the Northeast in 1877, migrant groups who traveled to Amazônia set themselves up in settlements formed by ex-quilombolas. Historical continuity can also be seen at the level of geography.

MANCHETE: Though Rio de Janeiro's favelas house a large concentration of the black population, people from other racial origins also live there. How can you establish, therefore, this continuity in terms of quilombo?

MARIA BEATRIZ: The colonial quilombo itself was not only a stronghold for black people, although they represented the majority of quilombos' populations. However, quilombos' social origins meant that they included black people and other oppressed people: Indigenous people, for example, and white women. Traditionally we have been told that these women were brought there by force by quilombolas, but that is an interpretation that we need to revisit.

A Society That Created Its Own Values

MANCHETE: What about what you call the social and ideological organization of the quilombo?

MARIA BEATRIZ: For me this is the most important aspect. It is still insufficiently studied by historians. Clearly flight, suicide, abortion, and murder of white people did exist as forms of reaction and revenge for the suffering inflicted on enslaved people. But it was not only the need to escape that enabled the establishment of quilombola society. It was this: the capacity to create an alternative society, with its own values, different to the dominant values of the society in which black people were forcibly integrated. Flight, in this case, was essential, given that black people, as prisoners of the plantations, did not have the necessary conditions to confront their oppressors in military conflict. But it was upon organizing their own society that black people affirmed themselves and became autonomous. Therefore, I am more concerned with uncovering aspects of the little known quilombola peace, than with rebellion as such.

MANCHETE: What were the characteristics of this peace?

MARIA BEATRIZ: The moments of peace correspond, essentially, with the social and economic development of quilombos. Periods in which they developed agriculture, ranching, the production of instruments of labor and weapons for defense. In these periods, the quilombos were able to establish relations within the wider economic system, renting their pastures to small cattle ranchers and trading their products with their neighbors. Therefore, the repression they suffered cannot not be fully explained by the fact that black rebels damaged colonial society by diminishing the potential labor force. Society repressed them most aggressively during moments of economic crisis, when victorious quilombos came to represent a threat, as competitors within the system itself.

MANCHETE: How do you explain the existence of enslaved people within the quilombos?

MARIA BEATRIZ: The quilombo is far from being a place of happiness, an ideal society. It is not the utopia described by white intellectualism in spectacles like Arena Conta Zumbi. I think this is a genuinely reactionary conception, because it shows only one aspect: black people as fragile, persecuted, suffering, and kindly. The quilombo, like any human society, had its own contradictions. Slavery was among them, though this slavery was not identical to colonial slavery, and it did not reach the limits of the cruelty meted out in white society.

MANCHETE: In your opinion there is a void in knowledge about black people. Or rather, black people are represented in an idealized form. How and why are you trying to de-idealize this image?

MARIA BEATRIZ: I think it is important to de-idealize the quilombo, because this would mean de-idealizing black people, freeing them from their supposed fragility. North American historians, for example, are surprised by what they call the "docility of the black Brazilian." This is explained, in part, by their own obscurantism about the historical struggles in which black people have been submerged. When I was a black child I heard, in school, that Africans lived free, dancing and hunting in the forests. Then they were captured and transported in slave ships—that child was certainly revolted by the brutality of slavery, but, at the same time, as a black girl, she felt belittled: were black people really that fragile?

The Lucrative Enslavement of Africans

MANCHETE: And in reality they were not?

MARIA BEATRIZ: Everything becomes more comprehensible when you tell that child that there was an agreement, a deal, between the European kings and the African kings themselves, who saw in slavery a way to turn the African man into a source of profit. black people, then, were not only the *victims* of slavery; African sovereigns, as accomplices in the trade in enslaved people, were executioners too.

MANCHETE: And in what sense can it be good that black people were executioners too?

MARIA BEATRIZ: What I am going to say might seem reactionary. But for people in general to become dominant, to win, means being strong. And this is one of the key aspects of the problem: it is necessary to show black people the historical truth, to give them the opportunity to understand their own strength. They need to know that they *can* dominate, they can organize a society and emerge victorious. Whether they are to use their strength to dominate others or simply to liberate and affirm themselves: *that* is their problem. What is important, initially, is to recover consciousness of their own strength, to feel potent. That is to say: black people are not synonymous with defeat. To know, for example, that there was a whole military and ideological preparation put in place prior to the constitution of the quilombo. Although enslaved people did flee, they also prepared their escapes and discussed them in advance in the senzala. The proof is that the first to flee were the men. The women and children were only brought when the quilombo reached a stage of organization that enabled it to defend itself.

MANCHETE: They were not spontaneous movements?

MARIA BEATRIZ: In no sense. The typical quilombola, if we could put it that way, did not flee just from the ill treatment of slavery. A man in normal physical and psychological condition, though living under a vigorously oppressive system, can voluntarily imagine for himself institutions which are more in line with his own potential and aptitudes which were impossible to realize within the slavocratic social order. The quilombo was not a stronghold of escaped black people: it was the alternative society created by black people.

Indirect Maintenance of Racial Prejudice

MANCHETE: And you, personally, how do you feel today as a black Brazilian woman?

MARIA BEATRIZ: I am myself, and I am a black woman. And, as a black woman, I am a product of racial relations in Brazil. Relations that we could call chaotic. For example: in terms of the census of the Brazilian population, I am no longer black. The demographic census abolished the question of color. Black does not exist in Brazil anymore. We were declared, in absentia, to be integrated into a racial democracy. Leaving law to one side, let's observe life: does color prejudice exist in Brazil? In what way? If we are a country of equals, what motivates black people to struggle for better living conditions? On the other hand, in my opinion, there still exists in Brazil a black culture of its own, a black way of life, that can only be perceived to the extent that black people themselves identify as black. But this is another problem: is it certainly interesting for black people that black culture is known outside their own context, but do they run the risk of furnishing knowledge about themselves which will be used against them? We must be wary. And black people, at the moment, are wary.

MANCHETE: How do you experience this wariness?

MARIA BEATRIZ: See, for example, the discussion about samba schools: Can white people join? Can they not? Does white people joining the school distort it or not? Another aspect: Afro-Brazilian religions are not open like the dominant religion. To get into the true Afro-Brazilian religions it is necessary to overcome a whole resistance that is based precisely on the wariness of its members, who refuse to furnish the *keys* to understanding. This intimacy of black people is significant. And it has its counterpart: black people do not show themselves off—in large part they "keep to their place." They occupy social spaces that they are allowed to occupy. Indirectly, this maintains discrimination.

MANCHETE: What are the spaces that black people have still not conquered?

MARIA BEATRIZ: Black people do not only have spaces to conquer, they have things to reclaim. Things that are theirs and that are not recognized as theirs. Thought, for example. I am shocked when white brains are endowed, for example, with rationality, and black people are given the body, intuition, and instinct. Black people have emotion and intellectualism, they have thought, like any other human. They need to recover knowledge—that is theirs too. It was merely stolen by domination. And there we get to the discussion about the possession of knowledge: Bacon was right when he said that knowledge is power.

Note

This interview was originally published as "O negro visto por ele mesmo." *Revista Manchete* (August 21, 1976): 130–31.

Our Racial Democracy

ONE TIME, I was speaking with a young man in Salvador who was the head of a family. He wanted to convince me that Bahia was the greatest center of racial tolerance in the world. In trying to back up this pretense, he revealed that he was a passionate supporter of miscegenation. He took himself as an example. He showed me his two little children, both mulattos, but with different skin shades: "See?" he said, "this one came out almost like me (pointing to the darker child), but this one came out better; almost blond." As the first child and I looked at him, astonished, he concluded: "This way, black people will disappear, and we won't have racial conflict like in the United States."

Perhaps it is around this last point that the deepest misunderstandings of Brazilian racial tolerance abound; and not only among ordinary people like my Bahian interlocutor. It is a national belief that we are lucky possessors of racial system that is the envy of the world because our social experience has not recently included the virulent racism typical of North American society. What should we make of the strange conviction of the young Bahian father whose final objective would be the physical disappearance of a group: a man who believes we have total tolerance in Brazil?

The recent, largely foreign, bibliography on race relations in Brazil is full of examples like the one above; examples that demonstrate that the negation of racial prejudice—more than constituting a conscious reflection of our situation—reveals a certain sense of urgency to alleviate the potential conflicts that emerge from the confrontation of power between the ethnicities that form our society. This fear, in the words of a young sociologist from Rio de Janeiro, made "racial democracy" into the self-image of Brazilian racial relations.

Hell

The ideal of "racial democracy" did not emerge out of the simple logic of ordinary people. Nor did mass miscegenation emerge as a solution to the potential conflict. Its origin can be found in the first centuries of colonialism. Antonil,[1] Brazil's first ideologue, wrote what became a maxim here: "Brazil is the hell of black people, the purgatory of white people, and the paradise of mulattos." From him, from the Marquis of Pombal (who in the Carta Régia advised the Portuguese to mix with the natives and mulatto women to increase the population of Brazil), right up to our Bahian friend, we find the idea of transforming Brazil into a "paradise" in which the preferable thing would be the total disappearance of those who live in "hell." This logic is the crux of a national ideology that underpins the debasing social space in which the mass of black people in Brazil lives.

Gilberto Freyre, that other great ideologue, to whom the term "racial democracy" is attributed, has recently, vaingloriously, pronounced upon Brazil's increasing *brown*-ness. He is responsible not only for the pioneering work on this form of ideology, but for the widespread belief in Brazilian racial tolerance. His work has directly influenced scientific studies, particularly by foreign sociologists such as Tannenbaum.[2] Tannenbaum affirms, based on Freyre, that, in the period of slavery in Brazil, the slave-masters recognized the "moral personhood" of the slave. In Brazil, then, unlike in the United States, there is a tradition of valorizing the humanity of black people. The high point of this phenomenon is the respect for black civil rights after Abolition, which did not happen in North America.

It so happens that, after the Abolition of Slavery, there was not a single black person at the center of Brazilian decision-making, when, leading up to that event, there were at least three black people with significant power in the two houses of Congress. In the United States we see the opposite: today, there are more and more black people taking part in various sectors of society. What is the cause of this discrepancy? It would be pertinent to ask ourselves if contemporary Brazilian society recognizes the value of our moral personhood. I believe this because the attitude of complacency (when it is not aversion), with regard to our participation in the heart of national society (as evinced in Gilberto Freyre's work, and in the ideology of racial democracy), takes us back to the past, where the stain of slavery, as a national stain, was linked to our group destiny.

After the Abolition of Slavery, we were integrated into the national whole. But, without a doubt, with the simple-minded hope that, through marriage or concubinage, we would "improve the race" to the point that the nation would become browner and browner and, with the help of European immigration, whiter and whiter.

Skepticism

But prejudice and stark discrimination manifest as latent conflict in the fields of education and work. If you struggle for social advancement you're offered the chance to be a footballer or *sambista*.

Through specific, selective mechanisms, Brazilian society is reducing the space dedicated to black people across the social scale. Since this space is integral to black culture, there is nothing more convenient than combining the useful with the agreeable. When we question the absence of black people in positions of social distinction, the response is just to mention Pelé, or the one or two sambistas making a decent living. As for the vast, marginalized majority, the easiest thing is to resort to economic or class explanations, not forgetting the inheritance of slavery that, according to some eminent theoreticians, means that black people are still not prepared to integrate into a competitive society.

Meanwhile, we, black people, sink into this well of contradictions and tangle of subtleties with quite a skeptical view. It is going on ninety years since the Abolition of Slavery, and it does not appear that the immigrants who came to replace us on the coffee plantations were any more capable of entering capitalist society (that had still not been formed by 1930) than we were. By what miracle is their social position better than ours? If we are an integral part of a racial democracy, why are our social opportunities so minimal compared to white people's? The response seems clear to us. But talking about the factors that led us to this position is taboo, or worse (and more seriously), we come up against a total lack of preparation to confront the problems that arise from the practice of discrimination. The origins of this lack of preparedness are to be found principally in the lack of opportunities in the field of education, which reduces our capacity to organize around a common objective. This impotence seems to legitimate the belief in a peaceful system of racial relations and reinforce the ideology of "racial democracy."

Yet all is not lost, because we have already come by consciousness the hard way, particularly the new generations in the principal urban centers. We already understand that hasty and simple-minded solutions, such as more miscegenation, are false. Much more is needed. Marvin Harris, in *Patterns of Race in the Americas*, says something clarifying: "It is time that adults stopped talking about racial prejudice in accordance with sex."[3] It is statistically demonstrable that the United States and South Africa have as many, or more, *mestiços* than Brazil.

Clearly, we cannot put Brazilian and South African society on the same plane. We do not have the experience of the ghetto, or of lynchings, but our situation is hardly ideal. That said, we should remind the white and black consciences of Brazil of a phrase that only the genius of Lévi-Strauss could have produced: "Tolerance is not a contemplative position, dispensing indulgences to what was and to what is. It is a dynamic attitude consisting in the foresight, the understanding, and the promotion of what wants to be."[4]

Thus, all that remains is to begin to tolerate.

Notes

This article was originally published as "Nossa democracia racial." *Revista IstoÉ* (November 23, 1977): 48–49.

1. André João Antonil, *Cultura e Opulência no Brasil* (São Paulo: Ed. Melhoramentos/MEC, 1976).

2. Frank Tannenbaum, North American sociologist, author of *Slave and Citizen: The Negro in the Americas* (Boston: Beacon Press, 1992).

3. Marvin Harris, *Patterns of Race in the Americas* (New York: Praeger, 1964), 68–69. We have quoted the original English. The Portuguese version Nascimento uses reads "de acordo com a cama," which translates literally as "in accordance with the bed[room]."

4. Claude Lévi-Strauss, *Structural Anthropology*, vol. 2, trans. Monique Layton (Chicago: University of Chicago Press, 1976), 362.

Fragment
(Realizing Consciousness)

Would that the Left were less bookish and more objective, in the practical sense—to raise the consciousness of the base. For then, it would actually represent the base as a group, and not the image of the individuals who supposedly represent it.

—MANEI, VISUAL ARTIST AND
BLACK MOVEMENT ORGANIZER

THE RACIAL QUESTION runs through the whole edifice of our society. More and more, the solution depends on the push to solidify the Black Movement (in associations of all types, in political parties, churches, and the State).

The intrinsic relationships between the Black Movement and the lefts are based in this national mega-conflict. Between 1974 (the year that Black Movement discussions began) and 1977, our conversations were very frank. All of us wanted to fracture arbitrary power, and it was the Black Movement that first proposed dialectical materialism as a response. Our discourse and insights on the *real*[1] came with a Marxist baggage. This Marxist perspective, above all, was a particular attribute of black people (the most subalternized of social groups).

However, the intellectual left saw us as just workers. They insisted that we should rupture the process of subalternization through the discourse of hate. We, however, knew deep down that unless we joined forces, we did not have the weapons to take power. Thus, the watchword *quilombo*: "coming together, organization, distribution, and love." In 1978, the movement launched the struggle to protect our cultural inheritance (the religious and recreational organizations of our people). The profound respect that we had for ourselves in this process led to the *political opening* and we went through these years with *nonviolence*, offering an example of leftist behavior *for life*.

Today we move into a different phase.

The Black Movement has exhaustively discussed the questions of the oppressed, generically called minorities: black people, women, homosexuals, children, and old people. This is how the Black Movement is organizing itself. In this new stage, what we can offer to the lefts, in our relations with them, is our "know-how" of this struggle that we undertake, for the resumption of freedom.

Axé *Zumbi*.

Notes

This article was originally published as "Atualizando a consciência." *Maioria Falante* III.16 (December 1989—January 1990): 7. This fragment appears as a commentary on a text called "A Esquerda que o Negro Quer" (The Left that the Black Person wants), by Togo Ioruba. It is untitled, though the image of Beatriz Nascimento that accompanies it has the caption "atualizando a consciência." This context makes the piece read as a kind of call to arms and shows how her work was in close dialogue with other Black radicals debating the nature of leftist politics and the possibilities of intersectional solidarity and organizing.

1. Brazilian currency used at this time.

PART II

The Black Woman

The Black Woman: Reflections on Blackness, Gender, Sexuality, and Racial Capitalism

Christen A. Smith

I want a world of uteruses, ah, if I could write it in ink. The History that
I dream of is a continental history, like the walls of a uterus; only shedding
and scraping the walls can destroy its contents.

—"AN ASIDE TO FEMINISM"

THE HISTORY of Black people that Beatriz Nascimento imagined was
a decidedly feminine one. When she reflects on the "History that she
dreams of" (to paraphrase her words), in "An Aside to Feminism," she
likens it to a uterus—feminized[1] matter that is both malleable and re-
newable; indestructible in its ability to reform, reshape, and reconstitute
itself. To be female/uterus is to be able to give birth to possibilities that
cannot be easily taken away, to create the world, to destroy it, and to
recreate it again . . .

Nascimento never explicitly defined herself as a feminist. Indeed, she
shared many of the critiques of feminism that Black women and women
of color have voiced since the 1970s: that feminism is for white women.

Yet she paid deep, philosophical attention to gender, and particularly the feminine, in some of the most personal and reflective essays and poems she wrote. The pieces in this section represent that writing. Like her essays on race in Brazilian society, Nascimento's musings on the Black woman should be read within the political context of the moment.

An Intersectional Perspective

The Black Brazilian feminist movement emerged in the late 1970s during the first period of Beatriz Nascimento's intellectual career. This movement was part of a wave of Black feminism that swept across the Americas and included notable figures like Andaiye, Alice Walker, Angela Davis, Audre Lorde, Barbara Smith, bell hooks, and others. Lélia Gonzalez, Beatriz Nascimento's contemporary, interlocutor, and former friend, emerged as the leading voice of Black feminism at this time. Gonzalez, like Nascimento, was a member of the Unified Black Movement (MNU).[2] Along with Sueli Carneiro, Edna Roland, Thereza Santos, and others, Gonzalez coordinated a Black woman's response to the racism of the Brazilian (white) feminist movement, which they and others critiqued for ignoring Black women's issues in favor of a discourse of the "universal" woman that was based on white women's experiences.[3]

Although Beatriz Nascimento did not participate directly in shaping the early Black feminist movement in Brazil, she did become one of the radical Black intellectual voices to address the intersectionality of Black women's experiences in Brazil through her public writing. These essays reveal a deep understanding of the complexities of gender, race, sexuality, and interlocking forms oppression. They also indubitably approximate what we have come to call Black feminism today.[4]

Nascimento is quintessentially "intersectional" in her thinking; she recognizes that the plight of the Black woman has everything to do with our triple oppression—the oppression of race, gender, and class.[5] Moreover, she is—despite her sharp criticisms—keenly engaged in feminist critique throughout her writings. This dimension of Nascimento's oeuvre leads me to situate her within the radical Black feminist tradition.[6]

In 1976 Nascimento published her first stand-alone essay on the condition of Black women in the Americas, "A mulher negra no mercado de trabalho" (The Black Woman in the Labor Market). This essay presents a deft analysis of the ways that race, class, gender, and sexuality have come to shape Black women's lives in Brazil since colonialism/slavery. It is clearly political in tone and form. Nascimento chooses to toggle between present and past tense throughout to underscore the continuation of the conditions of slavery into the present. Like with "A History of Black People," this essay focuses on redefining Brazilian history. She argues that Black women's position as workers in Brazilian society is an outgrowth of the logics of slavery, which cast Black women as *mãos de obra* (workhands) in the fields and in the domestic sphere. This categorically differentiates Black women from both Black men and white women. Her value as a workhand was, therefore, threefold. The enslaved Black woman served at the pleasure of the white plantation owners in the house (both as domestic servant and as sexual toy); worked alongside Black men in the fields as manual labor; and functioned as the reproductive engine of slavery by producing enslaved offspring. In other words, Nascimento analyzes labor beyond pure economic transaction, recognizing the relationship between Black women's work, the exploitation of Black women's reproductive labor, and the destabilization of Black female subjectivity. Like many of her Black feminist contemporaries, Nascimento argues that the sociopolitical construction of work cannot be separated from the politics of race and gender, and more importantly that both race and gender must be understood in conversation with one another.

"The Black Woman in the Labor Market" also relates to other contemporary Black feminist reflections on Black womanhood, race, and class, written in the 1970s and 1980s, inside and outside of Brazil. For example, five years after Nascimento's essay was published, Angela Davis published *Women, Race and Class* in 1981. That same year, Lélia Gonzalez published the essay "A mulher negra na sociedade brasileira" (The Black woman in Brazilian society). Six years after Davis's and Gonzalez's publications, Hortense Spillers published "Mama's Baby, Papa's Maybe" in *Diacritics* in 1987. These three pieces, like Nascimento's essay, present a historical exegesis of the uniquely raced and gendered positionality of Black women in the schema of slavery.[7] The resonance between the four texts puts Nascimento into dialogue with three of the leading Black feminist thinkers of this time.

Nascimento repeatedly deconstructs the politics of patriarchy and paternalism, particularly as they manifest in the lives of Black women as expressions of the dual projects of anti-Blackness and white supremacy. For her, the oppressive nature of whiteness has its roots in both patriarchy and colonialism/slavery. For example, she writes of Black women's relegation to menial jobs in the workforce: "The black woman—the element in which the structure of domination is most profoundly crystallized, as black and as woman—thus finds herself occupying the spaces and roles that have been attributed to her since slavery." For Nascimento, the devaluing of Black women during slavery—as women and as Black people—thus leads to the continued devaluation of Black women in the modern workforce.

"The Black Woman in the Labor Market" was written during the repressive military dictatorship (1974–85). Ideas about race and gender inequality were not only censured at this time but also politically treacherous, as we note in our introduction. As Lélia Gonzalez observes, the military dictatorship disarticulated Black intellectuals from mainstream Brazilian society.[8] The state's harsh repression was later focused on the production and circulation of subversive ideas; students and intellectuals found themselves to be the targets of abuse because of what they were reading, thinking, and theorizing. These ideas also included Black women's interventions into racialized, gendered, and sexualized violence of race relations in Brazil.

Race, Gender, and Trauma

Nascimento clearly identifies the ways that racism and sexism converge to produce unique forms of violence that affect Black women's lives. She describes how racism and sexism affect Black women's lives from childhood, scarring many, like herself, for life. Thus, she posits that embodied experiences of gender, sexuality, and Blackness define Black women's condition in Brazilian society. She also identifies both the joys and pains of being a Black woman and embraces this complexity. Nowhere is this complex thinking more evident than in her essays "Toward Racial Consciousness" and "Maria Beatriz Nascimento: Researcher."

The childhood trauma that often comes with Black girlhood is a deeply unsettling yet revealing element of Nascimento's reflections on the gendered Black experience in Brazil. She uses storytelling to relate painful, emotional memories and traumas, theorize them, and articulate their sociopolitical consequences.[9] This act of storytelling is particularly significant within the context of Brazil, where Black women's stories have been traditionally told, at least in scholarship and public discourse, by white men. These white men, like Gilberto Freyre, cast Black women as accessories to white male narratives of the birth of the patriarchal nation.[10] Retelling Black women's stories from the perspective of lived experience thus becomes a key gesture by Black women writing against patriarchal white supremacy in Brazil. For example, in 1979 Lélia Gonzalez published "The Black Woman: A Portrait," which, like Beatriz Nascimento, presents a personal reflection on Black women's lives using a mixture of ethnography and autoethnography.[11] For Nascimento and her contemporaries, telling Black women's stories is a foundational step in writing a History of Black People.

We open this section with one of the most powerful essays that she wrote during her lifetime, "Toward Racial Consciousness." This piece gives us insight into Nascimento's thoughts on not only race and racism but also gender, sexuality, mental health, trauma, and many of the other themes that emerge elsewhere in her poetry and prose. This essay is a microcosm of her thinking writ large and is a bridge to the themes of the other sections of this book.

In both "Toward Racial Consciousness" and "Maria Beatriz Nascimento: Researcher," Nascimento discusses her childhood growing up as a Black girl in Brazil, and how these experiences molded her in later life. Deceptively simple and straightforward in her articulations, Nascimento's reflections seem at first to be mere trips down memory lane. However, she presents an intimate account of Black Brazilian girlhood that bitterly critiques the myth of racial democracy. This engagement taps into her preoccupations with mental health by engaging with the question of childhood trauma. It also chronicles the difficulties that Black girls face in Brazil, recognizing that these difficulties typically arise first at school—a story that resonates transnationally. Familiar themes of Black girlhood in the Americas emerge: stigmatization and criminalization; being stereotyped as angry and confrontational; negotiating violence at home and at school; sexual abuse and teen pregnancy; poverty; beauty standards; perceived intelligence and self-worth.[12] Her memories are a glimpse into the insidiousness of coming of age in a sexist, patriarchal, anti-Black, and white supremacist society.

"Toward Racial Consciousness" speaks of the schoolhouse gazing onto a deeply painful and soul-stirring scenario: a young Beatriz Nascimento confronting her own race/gender identity through the refracted mirror of her schoolmate Jurema. Nascimento writes:

> She looked like me, physically. We were both slim, and the same height, though she was two years older than me. I met her while returning from secondary school, where I was in the second year. She was wearing a dirty, threadbare dress, and she had a child in her arms. It was dirty too, and she was heavily pregnant. At first, she smiled shyly at me, and studied her feet. Then she approached me very strangely, as if she was afraid of sullying me. She asked which class I was in. I said to her, also awkwardly, as if I ought to apologize to her for something, that I was in the second year of secondary school.

She goes on to describe the social-psychological toll that gendered and sexualized racism wrought on her and Jurema. Her words are both raw and fresh, revealing deeply painful unresolved feelings. Indeed, the essay is a letter to Jurema, so to speak. It is filled with wonder: "Wherever you are, I am making your words my own: 'Don't let them do this to us!'" Again, like her work on race in Brazilian society, the focus of this essay is a critique of racial democracy, a demystification of Brazilian racism, and an insistence on the intimate connection between lived Black experience and understanding the Black condition. "Toward Racial Consciousness" adds an important dimension to Nascimento's previous conversations, however. Brazil's national identity depends not only on racism but a racism that is sexualized and gendered by its attention to beauty standards, policing gender binaries and boundaries, measuring intelligence, and determining human worth.

"Maria Beatriz Nascimento: Researcher" continues this reflection on the Black Brazilian woman's condition through the lens of Black girlhood. It was originally published in a collection of "testimonies" (*depoimentos*) about being Black in Brazil by Haroldo Costa, *Fala, Crioulo* (1982).[13] It is striking then that Nascimento chooses to focus on race, gender, sexuality, and trauma in her autobiographical reflection. I draw attention to the passage where Nascimento discusses being sexually harassed as a girl because she had short hair. It begins with a discussion of a popular, racist and sexist song that parodies Black women's hair and sexuality, "Nega do Cabelo Duro" (Black girl with the nappy hair). Hair has historically been and continues to be a symbolic site for negotiating gender and racial politics, beauty, and status in Brazil. In her ethnography of Black women in Brazil, Kia Lilly Caldwell chronicles how the "nappy-haired Black woman" has historically circulated in Brazil as a familiar trope. This trope is the source of many sociopolitical critiques of Black women's experiences with violence.[14] Yet Nascimento's analysis begs us to move beyond the familiar interpretation of Black women's hair as a site of trauma and beauty standards toward a more nuanced and complicated critique of the racialized nature of gender itself. In this simple illustration, Nascimento eloquently demonstrates how the dehumanization of Black women and girls anchors itself in gendered discourses of beauty and ontological worth by associating Black women with masculinity. Nascimento tells a similar story in "Toward Racial Consciousness." Here, she also recounts being called a "João" and once again cites the song that gives birth to this association. The song goes, "Paletó sem manga é blusão, negra sem cabelo é João," which we translate to mean "A jacket with no sleeves is a vest, a black woman with no hair is a guy [John/João]."[15]

The use of the term "João" to derogate Black women and girls with short hair replays the historical process that Hortense Spillers calls "ungendering"—a process of dissociating and distancing Black women and girls from womanhood/femininity that began with the Middle

Passage. Black girls and women in the Americas are ungendered female at the violent convergence of anti-Blackness, misogyny, capitalism, and patriarchy.[16] The enslaved African was a malleable, dehumanized commodity whose gender was stripped then reinscribed as multiply violable. The dehumanization of enslaved Black people relied heavily on the erasure of gender on the one hand and the exploitation of gendered flesh (genitalia, sexual organs, copulation) on the other, to perpetuate the slave economy. The dual process of the masculinization and hyper-sexualization of Black women and girls is a perpetuation of this political, historical process of "ungendering," and, to follow Nascimento's thinking, is very much a part of the reality of Brazil. To strip Black girls and women of gender is to tailor racialized oppression by exacting hyper-focus on gender, specifically sexuality.

"Maria Beatriz Nascimento: Researcher" is a meditation on the violence and trauma that Black women specifically and Black people generally face in Brazil. After beginning with a reflection on Nascimento's childhood, the essay then moves into a critical assessment of the psychological and social impact of racism on Black Brazilian society. She writes,

> Looking closely, we come to the conclusion that we live in a dual, or triple, society. Society imposes the idea that it is a white society, and that your behavior has to be standardized according to white dictates. To that extent, as a black person you cancel yourself out and start to live another life, floating with nowhere to land, without references and without parameters for what your peculiar shape should be.

This sense of floating—which in both essays is exemplified by the experiences of Black children in schools—is also her entryway into a discussion of Blackness and mental health. The multiple traumas that she experiences as a Black girl and as a Black woman return us to her relationship with psychoanalysis. She writes, "I am currently seeing three psychoanalysts." She goes on to note how much mental illness has impacted Black Movement leaders in Brazil, citing the death of one prominent scholar-activist, Eduardo de Oliveira e Oliveira, who participated in the Quinzena do Negro at the University of São Paulo in 1977. Patriarchal white supremacy is, for Nascimento, a kind of violence that produces Black psychosis. As Audre Lorde notes, "If I didn't define my-self for myself, I would be crunched into other people's fantasies for me and eaten alive."[17] For Nascimento, isolation, alienation, and gaslighting all create the conditions necessary for Black madness.

Race, Sex, and Politics

Black women's passages through affective and erotic love in Brazilian society are an extension of the racialized and gendered exploitation meted out against them during slavery, and the racialized and gendered violence Black women experience from girlhood onward. "A mulher negra e o amor" is arguably one of Nascimento's most widely read essays on race, gender and sexuality. It is, as its title reflects, a meditation on Black women's travails with love, but also the relationship between sexuality and economics in a capitalist, heterosexist society. Notably, this essay, published in 1990, focuses exclusively on heterosexual relation-ships between men and women. It deconstructs, yet again, the complex relationship between gender, race, sexuality, class, desire, and social position. What distinguishes this essay from "The Black Woman in the Labor Market" is its focus on power and desire as aspects of race/gender/sexuality relationships. Here, Nascimento critiques eighteenth-century Enlightenment thinking and considers the western dissociation between women and reason. She writes of this Enlightenment concept of woman, "According to this way of thinking, a woman is a man, but incomplete. She can be a man cyclically, according to her natural cycle (puberty and motherhood). Outside of these states, her ability to work responds to the needs of economic development (called upon or ex-cluded as labor depending on economic fluctuations). Beyond these spaces, and even in them, she *is not*. She will be reason out of place, or she will exercise reason outside of the productive field."

Here, Nascimento takes on the illogical thesis that woman is woman because she is not man, which is most recognizably developed in Freud's writings on negation.[18] She also takes on the epistemological construc-tion of woman/the feminine as the opposite of reason (and by exten-sion, progress, science, and diachrony).[19]

Two of Nascimento's key contributions in this essay are her analysis of the matriarchal, collective structure of the Black family in Brazil and her deconstruction of the economic dimensions of affective relationships. Black women's access to the labor force shapes their sexual relationships. Again, here, Nascimento is in indirect dialogue with Black feminist critiques. In this case, she critiques the white supremacist, patriarchal demonization of the Black family. Senator Daniel Patrick Moynihan's 1965 report to the United States Congress, in which he argued that the dysfunctionality of the Black family in the United States could be traced back to its matriarchal structure, reverberated transnationally. Between the 1970s and 1990s, US Black feminists (including Angela Davis, bell hooks, Patricia Hill Collins, Barbara Smith, Hortense Spillers, and others) heavily critiqued the Moynihan Report for its racism and sexism.[20] Similar critiques also emerged in Black feminist debates in Brazil at this time, and Nascimento's attention to the similar Black family structure in Brazil and the need to disrupt hegemonic, patriarchal white supremacist devaluation of the Black family is in dialogue with this broader transnational conversation.[21]

Uteruses and Moons

Everything that Beatriz Nascimento wrote and thought about Black women's lived experiences was not focused on violence, trauma, and negativity. She also wrote poetically about the beauty of the feminine, its transcendence, its relationship to the metaphysical world and the universe; in short, the spiritual feminine. The final essay in this section returns us to this spiritual feminine and the epigraph to this introduction.

"Um aparte ao feminismo" (An aside to feminism) is strikingly different in tone from the other essays we include here. It is a poetic, playful, and dreamy essay that we found unedited in Nascimento's archives at the National Archives of Rio de Janeiro, with no date attached. Her references to childbearing and pregnancy imply that she must have written this sometime during or just after her pregnancy with Bethânia, however. Ironically, the title of this essay grates against its content. Far from a contraposition to feminism, it is arguably the most feminist essay she ever wrote. Here, Nascimento unabashedly reflects on, among other topics, the moon as the celestial embodiment of the feminine, menstruation, the political importance of the uterus, the need for women to run the world, the sacredness of childbirth and its spiritual dimensions . . . the list goes on. In short, this is a love letter to the feminine. It is also a glimpse into Nascimento's poetic voice, which we see also in the poem we include here, "Sonho" (Dream).

Despite the brevity of this section (only five short essays and one poem), Beatriz Nascimento's thinking on Black womanhood resonates throughout her life's work—especially in her poetic voice. Her theorizations of quilombo (which we discuss later) are, as Bethânia Gomes intimates in our conversation at the end of this book, a reflection of how she incorporated her physical body on this earth and imagined herself as a diasporic subject. Nascimento radiates this thinking in her narration of *Ôrí*, for example. This notion of "body-territory" is the gendered Blackness woven throughout her poetry and prose.[22] Indeed, based on her understanding of herself as a Black woman, and what that means within the context of the African diaspora, the Americas, and Brazil, the feminine—the Mother Atlantic—is what shapes the world.

Notes

1. By noting the historical, symbolic association between "female"/"feminized" and "uterus," we do not dismiss the fact that some people who identify as male also have uteruses. Rather, we note that there is a deep cognitive and conceptual association with the uterus and femaleness that Beatriz Nascimento intentionally invokes here.

2. Lélia Gonzalez (org. União dos Coletivos Pan-Africanistas), *Primavera para Rosas Negras* (Diáspora Africana, Editora Filhos da África, 2018).

3. In 1983 Sueli Carneiro, Marta Arruda, Thereza Santos, Sônia Nascimento, Solimar Carneiro, Edna Roland, Vera Saraiva, and several other Black women from São Paulo created the Black Women's Collective, the first Black women's organization with the express purpose of focusing on Black women's issues in São Paulo. The group emerged, in part, from the creation of the State Council on Female Affairs (Conselho Estadual da Condição Femina), an initiative that São Paulo's governor inaugurated in response to the United Nation's Council on the Status of Women's call for countries to create commissions to explore women's issues. São Paulo's council was the first in Brazil and had no Black women. This controversy led Carneiro and her counterparts to create the Black Women's Collective and become part of the Conselho Estadual da Condição Feminina in 1983. For more discussion of this early formation of Brazilian Black

feminism, see Christen A. Smith, "A Feminism So Complex and So Radical," in *Black Feminist Constellations*, eds. Christen A. Smith and Lorraine Leu (Austin: The University of Texas Press, 2023).

4. I borrow the phrase "interlocking forms of oppression" from The Combahee River Collective Statement of 1977. The Combahee River Collective used this phrase to describe the uniqueness of Black women's experiences at the crossroads of racism, heterosexism, classism, misogyny, and patriarchy. This statement and concept are widely recognized as foundational elements of Black feminist thought.

5. In 1949 Trinidadian communist thinker Claudia Jones argued that "Negro women—as workers, as Negroes, and as women—are the most oppressed stratum of the whole population." Carole Boyce-Davies notes that in making this assertion, Jones foreshadows the emergency of the Black feminist tenet of interlocking forms of oppression, theorized by The Combahee River Collective in 1977, which gives way to the theory of intersectionality, articulated by Kimberlé Crenshaw in 1991. Carole Boyce Davies, *Left of Karl Marx: The Political Life of Black Communist Claudia Jones* (Durham, NC: Duke University Press, 2007); Kimberlé Crenshaw, "Mapping the Margins: Intersectionality, Identity Politics, and Violence Against Women of Color," *Stanford Law Review* 43, no. 6 (1991): 1241–99; "The Combahee River Collective Statement," in Barbara Smith, *Home Girls: A Black Feminist Anthology*, ed. Barbara Smith (New Brunswick, NJ: Rutgers University Press, 2000).

6. Carole Boyce Davies writes extensively about radical Black feminism and its possibilities. See, for example, Boyce Davies, *Left of Karl Marx*.

7. Lélia Gonzalez, "A mulher Negra na sociedade brasileira," in *Lugar da mulher: estudos sobre a condição feminina na sociedade atual* (Rio de Janeiro: Graal Editora, 1981). (Also reprinted in *Primavera para Rosas Negras*.)

8. See Lélia Gonzalez's discussion of the repression of Black intellectuals during the military dictatorship; Lélia Gonzalez and Carlos Hasenbalg, *O Lugar do Negro* (Rio de Janeiro: Editora Marca Zero Limitada, 1982). See also Paulina L. Alberto, *Terms of Inclusion: Black Intellectuals in Twentieth-Century Brazil* (Chapel Hill: University of North Carolina Press, 2011).

9. Sociologist Patricia Hill Collins identifies storytelling as a Black feminist methodology. The articulation of storytelling as a method for relating Black women's experiences also emerges saliently in the work of Black Brazilian feminist author Conceição Evaristo. Patricia Hill Collins, *Black Feminist Thought: Knowledge, Consciousness, and the Politics of Empowerment*, 2nd ed. (New York: Routledge, 2000); Conceição Evaristo, *Becos da memória* (Rio de Janeiro: Pallas, 2017).

10. Key Black feminists in Brazil, like Lélia Gonzalez, Sueli Carneiro, Cida Bento, and Luiza Bairros, have long critiqued Gilberto Freyre—recognized as the father of Luso-tropicalism and progenitor of racial democracy—for his racist, sexist, patriarchal interpretation of Black women's role in Brazilian history. Luiza Bairros, "Mulher Negra: O Reforço da Subordinação," in *Desigualdade Racial no Brasil Contemporâneo*, ed. P. Lovell (Belo Horizonte: MGSP Editores, Ltda., 1991); Maria Aparecida Silva Bento, "A mulher negra no mercado de trabalho," *Estudos Feministas* 95, no. 2 (1995): 479–88; Sueli Carneiro, "Mulheres em movimento," *Estudos Avançados* 17, no. 49 (2003): 117–32; Sueli Carneiro, "As Viúvas de Gilberto Freyre," *Correio Braziliense*, March 14, 2005; Lélia Gonzalez, "Racismo e Sexismo na Cultura Brasileira," in *Movimentos Sociais Urbanos, Minorias Étnicas e Outros Estudos*, eds. P.F. Carlos Benedito da Silva, Carlos Vogt, Maurizio Gnerre, Bernardo Sorj, and Anthony Seeger (Brasilia: ANPOCS, 1983).

11. Taís Machado and Keisha-Khan Y. Perry, "Translation of 'The Black Woman: A Portrait,'" *Feminist Anthropology* 2, no. 1 (2021): 38–49.

12. For comparison, on Black girls' experiences with criminalization in schools in the United States, see Monique W. Morris, *Pushout: The Criminalization of Black Girls in Schools* (New York: The New Press, 2016).

13. Haroldo Costa, ed., *Fala, Crioulo* (Rio de Janeiro: Editora Record, 1982). It is important to note that Beatriz Nascimento's essay appears in the first edition (1982) of this book and not in the expanded edition (2009).

14. Kia Lilly Caldwell, *Negras in Brazil: Re-envisioning Black Women, Citizenship, and the Politics of Identity* (New Brunswick, NJ: Rutgers University Press, 2007).

15. We do not translate the name "João" to mean "John" (its literal translation) because of the cultural confusion that might arise. In American English, a John is also a man who solicits prostitution. To avoid confusion, we therefore choose to translate the name "João" to just signify "a guy."

16. Spillers argues that the enterprise of slavery stripped the enslaved African body of gender while at the same time reinscribing gender as a marker of difference and exploitation. "Male" or "female" identifications in the western, domestic understandings of the terms are an impossibility for Black people. Yet the ungendered female is distinguished by her overdetermination as a violable object. Spillers writes, "Since the gendered female exists for the male, we might suggest that the ungendered female—in an amazing stroke of pansexual potential—might be invaded/raided by another woman or man." Hortense Spillers, "Mama's Baby, Papa's Maybe: An American Grammar Book," *Diacritics* 7, no. 2 (1987): 77.

17. This quote is from Audre Lorde's 1982 speech "Learning from the 60s."

18. Sigmund Freud, *General Psychological Theory: Papers on Metapsychology* (New York: Touchstone, 1997).

19. Michel Foucault's critique of the construction of knowledge and power during the Enlightenment period gives further context for this conversation, as does Johannes Fabian's writing on time. Michel Foucault, *The Order of Things*, 2nd ed. (Boca Raton, FL: Routledge, 2018); Johannes Fabian, *Time and the Other: How Anthropology Makes Its Object* (New York: Columbia University Press, 1983).

20. See, for example, Hill Collins, *Black Feminist Thought.*

21. See, for example, Gonzalez, *Primavera para rosas negras.*

22. Alex Ratts uses the phrase "body-territory" (*corpo-territorio*) to describe Nascimento's geographical thinking on quilombo in *O negro visto por ele mesmo* (São Paulo: Ubu Editora, 2022).

Dream

Her name was pain
Her smile laceration
Her arms and legs, wings
Her sex her shield
Her mind freedom
Nothing satisfies her drive
To plunge into pleasure
Against all the currents
In one stream
Who makes you who you are?
Woman! . . .
Solitary, solid
Engaging and defying
Who stops you from screaming
From the back of your throat
The only cry that reaches
That delimits you
Woman!
Mark of a blunt myth
A mystery that announces all of its secrets
And exposes itself, daily
When you should be protected
Your rites of joy
Your veins crisscrossed with old trinkets

Of the strange radiant tradition
Woman!
There are cuts and deep cuts
On your skin and in your hair
And furrows on your face
They are the ways of the world
They are unreadable maps
In ancient cartography
You need a pirate
Good at piracy
Who'll bust you out of savagery
And put you, once again,
In front of the world
Woman.

Note

Translation previously published in *Antipode* 53 (2021). This poem was originally published with the title "Sonho" (1989) and is dedicated "to all the Black women scattered across the world. To all the other women, and to Isabel Nascimento, Regina Timbo and Marlene Cunha."

Toward Racial Consciousness

AROUND THE END of the 1950s, there was a lively debate about black people and racial relations in Brazil. Because of the specific conditions of the time, it was not as broad as the debate today, but it was similarly intense. The periodic emergence of discussions about the racial problem is, I think, driven less by the specific stance of black people as a race than by a moral shift in the general values of society. This is driven by sections of society that, necessarily, do not include black people. It is less a qualitative change in the racial comportment of society, than the sophistry and dishonesty of small groups who skirt the debate at the political level and raise problems that, though also political, are not in their power to resolve. (If it is the case that all problems need solutions.) Then, as now, the racial debate centered on the relevance of the role of black culture, the black cultural contribution, and, more recently, the denial of western culture by Brazilian black people, who have lived for so long under conditions that differ little from those under slavery.

Although black people are present in the debate, and in some cases black individuals or small groups appear to be in the vanguard of these conversations, up to now there has in fact been a lack of free and expressive presence of black people in all this. They are not present to ask fundamental questions, open up new fronts toward likely solutions, or even help effectively contest the idea that we could change, if not the relations themselves, then at least the dishonesty. Thanks to the stigma of racial prejudice, this dishonesty obfuscates the ways in which black people and their intrinsic culture are obliged to *be* in the world. It confuses their *being* with their immiseration and poverty. It fails to see the obscurantism that stops them, as a racial group, from realizing their potential in the society in which they inhabit one of the extremes.

This state of affairs, in which the overwhelming majority of black people still find themselves, lends itself in the current moment to feeding the countercultural current of *tupiniquim*. The exaltation of a supposed "culture" of the black race is taken as the true measure of the consciousness, or otherwise, of black Brazilians. In order to address the way of being in the world, and the consciousness of this world, which are two different things, I want to briefly relate an encounter I had. It is worth adding that at that time, at the end of the 1950s, racial relations and prejudice were also the topic of the debates directed by Abdias do Nascimento and his Black Experimental Theater.

She looked like me, physically. We were both slim, and the same height, though she was two years older than me. I met her while returning from secondary school, where I was in the second year. She was wearing a dirty, threadbare dress, and she had a child in her arms. It was dirty too, and she was heavily pregnant. At first, she smiled shyly at me, and studied her feet. Then she approached me very strangely, as if she was afraid of sullying me. She asked which class I was in. I said to her, also awkwardly, as if I ought to apologize to her for something, that I was in the second year of secondary school. Breaking the initial frostiness, we had a brief, unsettling conversation; she gave me advice about how to be an adult, though she was only fourteen. She kept repeating "keep studying" and said something that has lodged clearly in my memory: "Don't let them do this to you." She confused me, then and now, by saying that. She was always aggressive, and in that moment I was confronted with her aggression in full. What shocked me, from then on, was that in her presence I was always overwhelmed by the feeling of being with my double. It was as if she was another me. Of all our peers I only felt that with her.

I saw her a few more times after that meeting. Once, with her brother, she was trying to carry her drunk father. He had fallen over in the station, next to his basket of fish. He had a knife that always scared me. I saw the knife for the first time in her hand on the day when she swore to stab a white boy who had "snitched" on her in the classroom.

When I went to school, having recently arrived from Aracaju, she was in the year above me. Her name was Jurema. Her brother, Tião, was in my class. When I reached the fourth year of primary school, she joined my class. Although I was studying in a public school in a poor neighborhood, it was the first time that I had a classmate the same color as me. But there was an abyss between us. As a recently arrived Northeastern immigrant, I was introspective and frightened. She seemed to be scared of nothing and confronted everything and everyone aggressively, using language full of swear words and slang that condemned her to be the "*neguinha-de-morro*" [little favela pickaninny]—which is what everyone called her. For my part, I tried desperately to escape that nickname "*neguinha-de-morro*," so commonly used among children at the time. But though I was not like Jurema, the punishments, the contempt, the neglect, and even the name reached me too—constantly, indeed! I remember that in that period I wore my hair in a short afro and, like hers, it was the target of jokes in the neighborhood: "a jacket without sleeves is a vest, a black woman with no hair is a João." Groups of boys would follow us, yelling, while their parents and other adults stood by, or joined in. Once a girl lifted my dress "to see if I was a boy or a girl." It was deeply humiliating! That sort of thing happened a lot to us.

I found refuge from those street battles at home, in books. In the classroom I realized that Jurema had no way of escaping and she fought with everyone, defending herself or being disobedient. I was one of the top in the class; she was inevitably last. And with the uproar of the non-black children all around us. As if that was not enough there was the whole apparatus of indifference and disguised neglect of the whole institution of the school. The teachers, without exception, were women, white, antiseptic, pudic, indifferent, and pretty. Almost all of them came from a different world, far from the suburbs,[1] far from the favela. Their relationship with us was either cold empathy or total aversion. Like the teacher in the fourth year who deliberately confused us with one another. In a catechism class, dramatizing the bad angel and the good angel, she called Jurema to the blackboard and compared her to the bad angel, and a blonde girl, Rosa, to the good angel. That day, faced with the ululations and jokes of the class, Jurema, as she sometimes did, pretended not to understand the clear allusion that was being made to her color, and burst out laughing. She also pretended not to understand when, in October of that year, they refused to put our work in the annual exhibition because "that's how we are, sloppy." She pretended not to understand even when I, who was always in the top three, came first in that same month, but was not, as per the normal practice, called upon to be part of the guard of honor for the Brazilian flag, "because I didn't have decent clothes" and wasn't wearing uniform. By the beginning of November, she had disappeared from school.

In the middle of that year, something happened that marked my relationship with her, and my whole life from then on. As I said, an abyss separated us. On the day I saw her, fish knife in hand, a hundred meters from school, calling for the snitch, and threatening to stab him, I hid behind a wall and fled. I was filled with confusion, fear, and that sensation of being her, of being always by her side.

Up to that time she seemed not to recognize me. At times she joined in with the other children, assailing me for speaking differently. She openly disliked my quiet demeanor, and the fact that I was one of the best students. She didn't approach me directly, nor did I approach her, until the day in which I found out that she had made a joke about my brother's name. I felt I had the right to shout at her, even though I knew that the whole school had said it long before she had. When I let out what I thought was righteous indignation, she came right up to me, into my face, and told me we should settle it "outside." I was so scared that I said nothing. However, the other children split into two groups, one for her, one for me. I had no choice.

After class the stage was set. The whole class surrounded us, the two of us and in the middle with those who were egging us on. I was dying of fright not only because she was tough, but even more because I was ashamed to be fighting her, the "*neguinha-de-morro*." That made me exactly what I had always defended myself against. We got to the agreed spot. Jurema started to trash-talk, as was customary, saying what she would do to me. While she was speaking, I lunged at her, and scratched her face. Taken by surprise, she didn't react, she just looked at me, stunned. It seemed that two worlds existed in that place, in that moment: a great uproar that surrounded us, and the silence between us. It was the other children, more than anything, who forced her to continue. I felt a cry spread through my chest, and across my face, while Jurema looked at me, stunned. I do not know how long that went on, perhaps it was only a few seconds. I heard the voice of a man calling us his *"neguinhos-de-morro,"* asking if we were ashamed, and so on. He yanked me out of the circle. While everyone else surrounded Jurema, I snuck off, crying with fear and pity the whole way home.

From that day on, her behavior toward me changed. The class decided to raise me to the status of heroine and made me their new idol. As far as I was concerned, I had been saved by the man's hand and by that nickname, *"neguinha-do-morro."* I did not understand what was happening with her; she started trying to be always close to me. During tests she would stick by my side, asking me for the answers. I gave them to her with pleasure. I started to identify more and more with her, no longer as if I were just alongside her but as if she were my very image. I started to neglect my work. When her work and mine were rejected for the annual class exhibition, my identification with her reached a new height. When December came around, our teacher was shocked to see me, in my poor clothes, receiving a diploma from the authorities. I came first in the class. Jurema had disappeared from school.

Two years later I met her again. She told me that she had gotten "lost" and that the man whose child she was nursing had abandoned her. She had gone with another guy who had also gotten her pregnant, and he'd left her too. She was desperate to tell me that I must continue studying, as if that was absolutely vital for her. Again, a form of communication was established between us in which "everything" was not said, as if we each knew one another based on a fact that we were hiding. I guessed rightly that such a dialogue was impossible between her and any of our white peers. They did not know what only we two, by our lived experience, knew, and that became part of our personalities. That fact meant that she and I, each in our own ways, faced the prejudiced world with aggression, or in flight, with teeth and nails bared. The prejudiced and hostile world closed around her own world; it penned her life in with irremovable obstacles. She fell down before them, prematurely, defeated.

Today, I know nothing about her or her children. I went on. I don't know if it was through circumstances or desire. What is certain is that the drive to continue was fed by the desire to get out of that childish universe, which we two shared and which she fell victim to. Another thing that is certain is that today's external world is similar. Recently, I was refused entry to a building and forced to use the service entrance. The doorman justified his actions by saying that he couldn't work out whether I was a domestic worker or a friend of the person I was visiting. In the same way that when I was a child, the person who lifted my dress justified it because they couldn't "work out" if I was a boy or a girl, because of my frizzy hair. In the same way that the teacher couldn't guess that I was one of the best students in school, and that I had the same rights as the white children in the same conditions.

No one can really "guess" if black people do not raise their voices and say to the world exactly what it means to live everyday under the tyranny of the racial prejudice that dominates relations in Brazil. No one can guess, but we know that the negation of social values is not as real as it seems; we do not choose this negation. The apparent "contestation," which the majority of black people, like Jurema, seem to carry with them, is no more than the corrosive action of racial and social oppression on a particular group within Brazilian society. When she was fourteen, she knew that she was the product of an unjust order, and not only her but the whole race. Hence our concern for each other. It was this she was referring to when she whispered to me, "Continue!"

When I observe the fuss, and fashions, around black racial consciousness, I ask the Juremas within me, and those I pass in the streets, what this "racial consciousness" represents, for us. Does it revolve around protecting and preserving the folkloric culture of black people? Or rather protecting the naivety, despoliation, unpretentiousness, pre-given absence of good and bad, happiness, and other things that they say belong intrinsically to black people.

I observe, too, with some suspicion, the "strategies" rapidly put together so that we can overcome immiseration, poverty, and personal annihilation. These strategies offer us an absurd segregationism. They question, stupidly, if our struggle should or should not be undertaken

alongside white people. They blaspheme against us under the justification that we should take up our "cultural values," after four centuries of
systematic oppression and our lack of organization as a people. They
deliberately forget that those "cultural values" are nothing more than
the formula that we were forced to resort to, to defend ourselves from that
same oppression. Those values are charged with, impregnated with,
the stain of racism, so they are socially ineffectual.

I would like to ask Jurema, now, what she thinks, for example, of
praising the anarchic aggression that led to her marginalization. She
must know that that aggression was a response to her impoverished
material life. That it was a response to the uncountable and uncontrol-
lable demonstrations of racial prejudice that dominate the environment
we live in. In everything that we learned in our schoolbooks, our race
and its achievements are forgotten, hidden, and distorted. It was the
feeling of not *being,* though we *were* present in the world, that made us
into two automatons, bitter and dissimulated, not identifying with our
teachers, our peers, or with what we read in our books. I would like to
ask her if, after that experience led her to abandon school in the last
year—I would like to ask her, I repeat, if she would be really grateful to
know how many white Brazilians are proud of having in their social
composition "an element as important as the black person, just at this
moment when relations between Brazil and Africa are intensifying."

Would you be grateful, Jurema? If you did manage to survive, which
favela do you live in? What do you do to get your daily bread? I found
out, a long time after, that that drunk of a father of yours was murdered
by another fishmonger. At least I know that you might not eat fish so
easily now. I found out, too, that your brother, my classmate, was arrested for being a pothead and a menace to society. And you and your
children? How many more men have you had children with? Do they
think that this is life, Jurema? Because this is the only way for you to
understand the world and still be black, "within your culture." Isn't that
right, Jurema? The two of us know what it is to be black, and how many
things you haven't learned because you are black. And how much you
wanted to learn! Jurema, there are so many things they did not teach us.
But I learned. I do not know if that is why I continued.

In this instant I address myself to you, wherever and however you are. It is messed up that they mocked your suffering with so much comfort. Look, Jurema, precisely because things were the way they were with you, it was vital that you replied to me. Remembering our childhood, our adolescence, I cannot accept without revulsion what they want to give us as an alternative: our "culture" and our way of *being* in the world. I do not accept it, because it is prejudice. Those who offer us this are the same white people. They do not know that one day you said to me, "Continue." I continued, but I can tell you that it wasn't much use. The prejudice is the same, although today I may be more "alive." I don't let it destroy me as it destroyed part of you. Wherever you are, I am making your words my own: "Don't let them do this to us!"

Notes

The original title of this essay is "Acerca da consciência racial." Unpublished, undated, Fundo MBN, 21.1.1.

1. In Brazil, the suburbs are often poor, outlying neighborhoods surrounding city centers.

The Black Woman
in the Labor Market

TO UNDERSTAND the situation of the black woman in the labor market, we have to go back in time and lay out a brief history of the structure of Brazilian society. During the colonial period this society was profoundly hierarchical. We can understand it as a caste-based society, in which different groups played rigidly differentiated roles.

At one pole of this social hierarchy was the land-owning elite, in whose hands political and economic power was concentrated. At the other pole were enslaved people, the real labor force of society. Between the two was a layer of free men and women, living in precarious conditions, without livelihoods. The patriarchal character of colonial society permeated its entire structure, with extreme effects upon women.

Thanks to the patriarchal and paternalistic character of society, white women are endowed with the role of wife to the white man and mother to his children; her life is dedicated to them. In this way, her role is defined by leisure: being loved, respected, and idealized. This leisure is an ideological support for a society built on the labor exploitation of a large swath of the population.

Contrary to the white woman, at the other pole is her correspondent, the black woman, who is considered essentially productive. She occupies a role similar to that of the black man; that is, endowed with an active role. Above all, as an enslaved woman, she is a worker, not only doing chores[1] in the master's house (satisfying the desires of the Master, Mistress, and

their children, and making food for the enslaved workers), but also working in the fields and engaging in secondary activities during cutting and
milling. Yet, in addition to her capacity for productive work, she also
had the reproductive capacity of a potential supplier of new *merchandise*
for the domestic labor market: her condition as a woman made her the
potential mother of new enslaved people. That is, the black woman is the
supplier of a potential workforce, competing with the slave trade.

I do not wish to say, by making this previous observation, that the
slow growth of the population of enslaved people in Brazil was positive.
Compared to the United States, where the enslaved population saw significant growth, the balance between births and deaths of people of
African descent born in Brazil was markedly unfavorable. It is enough
to note that after the end of the slave trade in the United States in 1808,
until the US Civil War (1861–1865), the enslaved African population in
North America almost tripled.[2] Meanwhile in Brazil, where the slave
trade was still in effect, there was no increase in the number of enslaved
people, which remained stable at approximately 1.5 million in the same
period. Nevertheless, it is important to call attention to this "reproductive capacity" of black women, which gave her a traditional *productive*[3]
role in the colonial period of Brazilian history, alongside her masculine
counterpart. It should be noted, therefore, that it is precisely because of
this productive burden that the weight of the master's domination fell
on the black woman.

Thanks to the process of industrialization established in the 1930s, modern Brazilian society is now more dynamic with regard to production.
With the expansion of industry and services, social stratification, which
was previously profoundly polarized, became more flexible and gra-
dated. However, this greater flexibility remains deeply marked by the
different roles attributed to various groups in society. Multiple factors
perpetuate these differences. Inevitably, in a society made up of different ethnic groups, one of these was the factor of race.

In a society like ours, in which the dynamic of the economic system
creates gaps in the class hierarchy, there are mechanisms in place to
select the people who will fill these gaps.

The criteria of race constitute one of these mechanisms of selection that, through discrimination, relegates black people to the lowest places in the social hierarchy. The continuous effect of white discrimination also causes black people to internalize the inferior positions that have been attributed to them. Thus, black people occupy the bottom of the social hierarchy, and cannot access those spaces in the hierarchy that are designated for lighter-skinned people. Thus dialectically perpetuating processes of social domination and racial privilege.

The black woman—the element in which the structure of domination is most profoundly crystallized, as black and as woman—thus finds herself occupying the spaces and roles that have been attributed to her since slavery. The *slavocratic inheritance* continues for black women. Her role as a worker, in general terms, has not changed. The patriarchal holdovers in Brazilian society ensure that she is recruited to and assumes domestic service, and to a lesser extent manufacturing employment, in urban areas, and maintains her traditional labor roles in rural areas. We might add to the above, however, that contemporary mechanisms for the maintenance of privilege by the dominant group are superimposed onto these cultural survivals or residues of slavery. These mechanisms are essentially ideological, and have discriminatory effects as they unfold in the objective conditions of society. If black women today continue to do jobs similar to those they occupied in colonial society, that has as much to do with the fact of being a black woman as to do with having ancestors who were enslaved.

In a society like ours, in which archaic elements coexist with the process of modernization, education is a lever subordinated groups deploy to envisage better conditions of life and social advancement. However, precisely because of the archaic elements of society, educational advances, though much needed, have been limited and recent. A large part of the population has had little effective access to education. However, recent studies, based on the censuses of 1940, 1950, and 1970, have noted that white women have had greater access to higher education, reducing, in relative terms, the inequality between white women and white men. The same was not true in relation to the black and *mestiço* population, and much less in relation to black women.

As education is a requirement for accessing the best jobs in the labor hierarchy, it would seem that *populations of color* and white women would not be capable of taking on higher-status jobs and, consequently, securing better wages. Black women have fewer opportunities than any of the other groups. Here, it is important to establish a comparison between black women and white women. From 1930, with the decline of rural areas and consequent rise of urban areas, the way of life in urban areas meant that the economic power of men, as heads of families, declined a little. To maintain a stable family income, and indeed to survive, children and women were obliged to enter the labor market. On the other hand, an external factor meant that these groups, who had been previously excluded from the occupational hierarchy, had to engage in it: the need for industrial labor and other services are competing phenomena.

Those with the lowest income level are the first to be recruited. White women become part of the workforce in this way. Nevertheless, given that they are part of a subordinated group, they still take on "feminine occupations." In the first phase of industrialization, white women participate centrally in the labor force. With the decline of traditional industries, principally textiles, she finds herself expelled from this central industrial sector and ends up working in low-level bureaucratic jobs that, though badly remunerated, require some educational qualifications. As a result of this displacement, middle-class men rise to higher-level bureaucratic occupations.

The same does not happen to black women, for two basic reasons. First, because black women still do not have adequate education to qualify themselves for these bureaucratic jobs. Second, because these jobs imply public relations, or relations with the public. For example: sales. In this context, the racial factor becomes even more selective, keeping black women in traditional jobs as industrial workers.

Through this analysis of the situation of black women in the labor market, we have seen how this element of the population finds itself in the lowest position in the social hierarchy. However, it is not only through reflecting on the labor market that we can evaluate the subordinate situation in which the black woman finds herself. The mere fact of being a woman attracts a kind of sexual domination by men, a domination that originates in the early days of colonization.

The sexual exploitation to which black women were subject by colonial masters was determined principally by Portuguese Christian morals. These attributed to upper-class white women the role of spouse or "spinster," economically dependent on the man. And in the case of the wife, she is assigned the role of procreator. In other words, their sexual lives were merely maternal. Male sexual freedom, therefore, rebounded upon black and *mestiça* women.

In this way, the ideological mechanisms have played a key role in perpetuating the legitimization of sexual exploitation through time. Representations based on stereotypes of black women assume that black women's sexual capacity surpasses that of other women; that her color functions as erotic attractiveness; and, finally, that the fact that she is poor, and belongs to a "primitive" race, makes her more sexually unrepressed. This facilitates the man's task of exercising his domination free of any censure. The dominant morality does not bother establishing rules for those who lack economic power.

Notes

Originally published as "A mulher negra no mercado do trabalho." *Última Hora*, July 1976. Alex Ratts, in *Eu sou Atlântica*, notes some small differences between the archive copy and published copy. We have used the published version as the basis for this text.

1. There is a lot of controversy in African American history around the use of the word *chores* to describe forced slave labor. This controversy can also be applied to the Portuguese term *tarefa*, which has the same connotation. It is worth noting the common dictionary definition of the term *chore*: the unpleasant but necessary domestic tasks. Chores in this sense are not simply the light domestic tasks that one does to support a home or a household but indicate the domestic aspects of forced and coerced slave labor.

2. At the 1787 Constitutional Convention (United States), delegates agreed to include language in the US Constitution that would prohibit engagement in the international slave trade after 1808, and impose strict penalties on slave ship trafficking: The Act Prohibiting the Importation of Slaves. The 1808 prohibition also reverberated in Brazil. Upon Brazil's independence in 1822, the new nation began to try to curry favor with the United States by outwardly committing to ending the slave trade. This position was concretized by the 1830 treaty Brazil signed with the

United States, committing to ending slavery. However, while the declaration of Brazilian political discourse was one thing, the nation's practice was quite another. Historian Leslie Bethell has estimated that between 1822 and 1888 (the date of the legal abolition of slavery in Brazil), five hundred thousand enslaved Africans were trafficked to Brazil—an astronomical number given the US and British prohibition of the international trade. Indeed, the duplicitous dichotomy between Brazil's lip service to abolition and its continued practice of illegal slave importation gave rise to the popular colloquialism "para o inglês ver," which translates into "for the English to see" and refers to an act you do just to please someone when you have no intentions of following their wishes. See, for example, Michael George Hanchard, ed., *Racial Politics in Contemporary Brazil* (Durham, NC: Duke University Press, 1999); Leslie Bethell, *The Abolition of the Brazilian Slave Trade: Britain, Brazil and the Slave Trade Question, 1807–1869* (Cambridge: Cambridge University Press, 1970).

3. Translator's emphasis.

Maria Beatriz Nascimento:
Researcher

DOUBTLESS, EVERYONE REMEMBERS the hits that played on the radio all day in the early 1950s. The samba "Nega do Cabelo Duro" [Black girl with the nappy hair], whose lyrics went: "A jacket with no sleeves is a vest, a black woman with short hair is a João."[1] Another was called "Nega Maluca" [Mad black woman],[2] and there was one whose name I can't remember, but with a chorus that went over and over: "Mad black woman, let me be / go run to the cops and file a complaint." After we arrived from Aracaju, my parents, my brothers and sisters and I all lived in Cordovil. I was the youngest, and I had a short afro. Because of that, the kids in the street all called me João. They teased me every time I passed; on the way to school, or on some errand in the area. It was awful. For me, going out into the street was torture. My other brothers and sisters, perhaps because they were older, didn't have to go through this shame, but I never escaped it. One day, when I came home from school—this was in 1954, when I was finishing primary school—some teenagers and grown men were playing soccer. When I passed by, they surrounded me and lifted up my skirt to see if I was a girl or a boy. I arrived home speechless, practically unable to speak. With great difficulty I managed to tell my father what had happened. He was livid and he grabbed a knife to go out and get revenge on the people who had humiliated me. My mother persuaded him to leave the knife at home, but even so he went back to the spot and ran the group off.

I have never been ashamed to be black, or to have hair like a João. What does make me ashamed is to think that we are helpless in the face of reality, in the face of the world. That's why I keep fighting, struggling, believing in the values I learned as a child in the bosom of my family. This has not been without sacrifice. As is common in poor, black families, when I went to university my contact with black people reduced greatly. I shared my life mostly with white people. This became even more pronounced when I moved to the South Zone of Rio de Janeiro—that was, for me, a true migration: I had to adapt to a new world that was not the suburban one I was used to. In fact, the change that I observed in that movement was much more pronounced, in terms of behavior, than when I moved from Aracaju to Rio. Brás de Pina, where we first lived, looked like Aracaju. There we were always around the many black families of dockers and workers. When I moved to Zona Sul—this was ten, eleven years ago, when my daughter was born—I began to see another Brazil. The fact that I was studying history woke me up to the need to see black people in all their particularity and significance in the formation of Brazil. I confess that there were moments in my life when I hid, scurrying through the streets, clinging to the gutters; without the courage to face people, and afraid that they would confront me. I was always on the defensive, ashamed, and I don't know for sure if it was the shame of being black, the shame of being poor, or both . . .

I recently finished my master's degree in history at the Fluminense Federal University, completing my training as a researcher. I am very proud of this, not only because I have really tried to do it properly but also because I organized a group there, named after André Rebouças,[3] in which I found emotional and intellectual support. Today, the group's members are professionals in other disciplines; not only the humanities but also technology, chemistry, and physics. We know each other from when they were students; my students, those of Eduardo de Oliveira e Oliveira, Maria Berriel, Carlos Hasenbalg, and Yvonne Maggie. Our work started at a truly hostile time: 1974, at the height of Institutional Act Number 5,[4] when bringing people together to discuss these issues was difficult and dangerous. The group, which initially consisted of twelve students, now has more than twenty people, black and white, who are interested in changing the discourse that the official history of Brazil has imposed on us for many, many years. But the Brazilian state is very authoritarian, and Brazilian society is very compliant, especially the Brazilian society that is currently in Power, and those who are in Power isolate us within the sphere of our own undertakings ... For example, we are seeing a great revival of black culture, but—make no mistake—however paradoxical it might seem, this revival is a defense of white society. And those who do not realize it get right on board, thinking that it demonstrates a positive stance toward black people.

Many people are profiting from the racial question. They are gaining power and prestige, but to maintain their place they have to keep up the same discourse and the same dialectic. Any change could be fatal ...

Looking closely, we come to the conclusion that we live in a dual, or triple, society. Society imposes the idea that it is a white society, and that your behavior has to be standardized according to white dictates. To that extent, as a black person you cancel yourself out and start to live another life, floating with nowhere to land, without references and without parameters for what your peculiar shape should be. I am currently seeing three psychoanalysts. Many people are surprised when I say that, because it is rare to see black people in psychoanalysis. Economic conditions do not allow it. But we cannot forget that a large part of the black community is in a mental hospital or in prison. I'm not getting psychoanalysis as a hobby, or because I'm going mad, perhaps not even to fix anything in myself. It might be to help me to adapt to the duality that society forces me to accept. Because it stops me from being as I am, in the same way it does with many black people. From the moment we live in a dual society, we try to adapt, and in desperation we can end up in prison or in a mental hospital. The people who are meant to treat us do not know us, even if they think they do. It is something that I discuss a lot with my analyst. He always tells me that he likes black people a lot, that he goes to eat *angu*[5] in the suburbs, and that this business of thinking that black people are inferior comes from inside me. I tell him, no, the inferiorization of black people is something that I am forced to live with constantly, and that this has driven me to fight with people, to attack them, or to withdraw into my own shell. The black person who rises up through the class system might lose a bit of this thing that I have never lost. I am a nonconformist person. I don't like this kind of system at all. Though there are parts that I like, I don't like the whole. Because they have divided us, culturally, we live in search of cultural emancipation. They try to confine us to being *sambistas*, but we want something else, we have other ambitions, other projects. The black struggle is not easy in Brazil. It is driving many people into psychological institutions—I know. In the past year I have had to take more than one person from the Black Movement to the mental hospital. Eduardo de Oliveira e Oliveira is a good example. An incredible person, who knows how to put everything in its right place with great precision and clarity. He was one of those torn between a comfortable life as a university professor, and being a full time *militant*. He ended up isolated for ten days at home, no one went looking for him, he already had mental health problems, and there he was, he had died of hunger, abandoned. We should call this cultural assassination. It happens in a society that is culturally divided. This process tends to take a long time, it is insidious. It starts in primary school. As a concrete example, back in Sergipe, I studied in a school built on land leased from my grandmother, in front of her house. When I was there, I often invented a stomachache and fled from class. Why? Because there were so few black children like me at school. And this still happens to me today. I feel ill at ease and isolated when I'm in a group where there aren't many black people. I felt it in Angola when I was there during a conference of the Organization of Angolan Women, in 1979, in the month that President Agostinho Neto died. I was there to do research on Quilombos, as I have been for many years. In the hotel where I was staying, there were only white people serving. I felt sick, I had a feeling of nausea and almost vomited.

I think that a lot of black children have this problem, and as a consequence they don't study. I think this type of isolation, which is not easily perceived, is often why they fail to be promoted to the next grade and have difficulties in school. It's a mechanism of education that has nothing to do with how you are raised, and just teaches a technical approach to reading in which you don't know who you are, because you are not in the books. When I started to dive deeply into my own psyche, as a black woman, I understood that it was at school that I experienced pure, direct aggression: isolation, the erroneous and stupid interpretations of teachers; the absence of people of my color in the classroom; no points of reference. In my specific case, the way to break free from this situation of adversity that I was living was by studying and getting perfect grades. I was an extremely well-behaved child in primary school, I was often praised by teachers because I was the politest, I never even asked to go to the bathroom during class. I was very repressed. Imagine a child who doesn't even ask to go to the bathroom . . .

Being black is an identity attributed to us by those who oppressed us. To ensure that our future will be different, and better, we must think of ourselves as human beings, and believe that the world is there for all human beings to live in. There is still so much life and culture for us to give. We should not be afraid to show anyone that we were able to live for four centuries beneath the whip, and that we want to project our experience into the future, for new generations, so that we can contribute to making the world a place of respect, free from the exploitation of man by man, without oppressed and oppressors. Let all these things that we have suffered become lessons for life, an exercising of our capacities. Because the capacity of black people is unlimited and is not yet fully awoken. Because we have been suffocated by poverty, work, and immiseration. But our strength is emerging, and the legacy of suffering makes black people strong, which is necessary for society to be strong. Society may be dire, but it will only improve through our contribution as people, without alliances with anyone, not with the church, not with a party, not with anyone. We know that there is a space for struggle, the so-called ethnic struggle, that is our space, where we can project who we are, in the way that only we know how. We don't need fancy footwork or trickery; that might be clever, but we don't need it. We can enter society with strength because it has no way to deny our capacity to be human.

Notes

Originally published as "Maria Beatriz Nascimento: Pesquisadora." Haroldo Costa, ed., *Fala, Crioulo* (Rio de Janeiro: Editora Record, 1982).

1. A common man's name in Brazil. See the introduction.

2. Nega Maluca is a folkloric caricature in Brazilian culture. The story goes that there is a Black woman who has a child and comes looking for the father. When she approaches the man she identifies as the father, he says she's crazy and denies it, calling her "Nega Maluca" (Mad black woman). The story reiterates anti-Black and misogynistic stereotypes rooted in the history of the racialized, sexual abuse of Black women in Brazilian culture, specifically in the legacy of slavery and the perception that Black women are always sexually available/violable but their children have no father.

3. André Rebouças (1838–1898) was a Black Brazilian engineer and abolitionist. See "Letter from Santa Catarina."

4. This was the most notorious of the military dictatorship's (1964–1985) legal declarations, ushering in a brutal period of censorship, torture, and repression. See the introduction.

5. A typical Afro-Brazilian dish similar to polenta.

The Black Woman and Love

IT MIGHT SEEM odd that I have chosen the question of love, not sex, to refer to the state of being black and a woman, in my country. This choice is based on lived experience, and on observing the affective dimensions of being a woman faced with the complexity of heterosexual relations.

The theme of sexuality in relationships between men and women today is increasingly viewed from a sociological or political standpoint. The question of power pervades these discussions: the dominant status of the masculine, to the detriment of the other element, the feminine. Social and political economic explanations are used, emphasizing the role of work as a factor in resolving inequality and as the driving force of equality between the two sexes.

In principle, the political rhetoric of the modern world is rooted in the liberalism of Enlightenment Europe of the eighteenth century, and the pursuit of the ideal of equality between social actors in human society. It is the fruit of Economics, which invaded Philosophy and privileged the individual over the group. Enlightenment thought imbues the idea of the Human Universal with the masculine and overdetermined notion of the producer, who is rewarded for his efforts by becoming the boss.

In the West, a society of men was created, which came to be identified not only with the masculine gender but with the species as a whole. This perspective possesses a utopian drive; it foresees a world without differences. But, directly in opposition to Enlightenment thought, in the same moment that it emerged, the colonial project was annexing societies and cultures that were vastly distinct from European societies in political, social, and individual terms.

We know that the power of reason imposed this historical contradiction in the realm of ideas and reality. To see the mechanics of this ideology in the practice of western thought, in which affirmation corresponds to negation, we can reflect on Martin Luther's sixteenth-century phrase: "reason is a cunning woman." We would object: ergo, she must be imprisoned by a man and expressed as a male tribute. Only then can she be dominant.

According to this way of thinking, a woman is a man, but incomplete. She can be a man cyclically, according to her natural cycle (puberty and motherhood). Outside of these states, her ability to work responds to the needs of economic development (called upon or excluded as labor depending on economic fluctuations). Beyond these spaces, and even in them, she *is not*. She will be reason out of place, or she will exercise reason outside of the productive field.

Totalizing morality will blanket the woman, whether she be agential or submissive. It will dress her up in fantasies, dreams, utopias, and unsatisfied eroticism, while she is stagnated by the conditions of her psychosocial and physical architecture.

Within this framework, any kind of feminine expression is covered over by the institution of morality that represents, in itself, the inequality characterized by the conflicts between submission x domination; activity x passivity; infantilization x maturity. The counterpart to this state of things is to put the woman in a role that diverges from the social process in which violence acts as the negation of her self-esteem.

The black woman, in her daily struggle, both during and after slavery in Brazil, was seen as a workhand, typically unqualified. In a country in which it is only in the last decades of this century that work has become associated with dignity in a way that it was not before thanks to the stigma of slavery, a "historic destiny" is reproduced in the black woman.

It is she who largely does domestic service and provides the lowest paid services in public and private companies. These are jobs whose labor relations evoke Slavery.

The profound disadvantage of the majority of the female population reverberates through her relationships with the opposite sex. There is no concept of sexual parity between her and members of the masculine sex. These relations are marked more by masculine desire for exploitation than by a loving desire to share affection and material things. As a rule, in the poorer section of the population, it falls to the black woman to be the true economic axis around which the black family revolves. This family, in general, does not adhere to patriarchal norms, much less to modern norms of the nuclear family. The family is everyone (children, couples, parents) who lives with the difficulties of extreme poverty.

As for the black man (who is generally professionally under-prepared, because of historical and racial contingencies), he has the economically active black woman as a means of survival: since the woman, as we know, is subjected to a double shift.

However, not all black women are in this situation. When the black woman escapes to other kinds of work, she turns either to professions that require formal education, or to art (dance). In these roles, black women become true social exceptions. Even here, they continue to be providers, insofar as there are few individuals who cross the barriers to social advancement in a black family. When they do make that crossing, various dimensions of racial discrimination make it difficult for black women to meet black men, or indeed men of other ethnicities.

For example, a black woman who reaches a certain social level, in today's world, increasingly needs partnerships, even though these can exacerbate discrimination against her. This is because a society organically based on individualism tends to homogenize and stratify people, estranging those who are discriminated against from sources of desire and pleasure.

Partnership, the complementary force in all relationships, including material relationships, is obstructed and restrained in women's loving relationships.

In a society of this kind, the more a black woman specializes professionally, the more she is encouraged to individualize herself. Her network of relationships is also increasingly specialized. Her psychic construction, forged in the battle between her individuality and the pressures of racial discrimination, often emerges as an impediment to attracting the other. The other, accustomed to the formal norms of a dual relationship, fears the power of this woman. She, in turn, ends up rejecting these others: men, masculine types, and machos. She will not accept the proposition of unilateral domination.

In this way, either she remains alone, or she connects herself to alternatives in which the relations of domination can be loosened. Given that she lives in a pluriracial society that privileges ideal feminine aesthetic standards like whitening (from the *mestiça* woman to the white woman), her affective journey is extremely limited.

As a representative of the most subordinated ethnicity, there is little chance for her in a society where sexual attraction is impregnated by racial models. When she is chosen by a man, the choice emerges out of the belief that she is more erotic, or more sexually fiery, than others. These often beliefs are related to the exuberant characteristics of her physique. However, when it is a question of an institutional relationship, ethnic discrimination works as a barrier that is reinforced when she takes on a position of social prominence, as discussed above.

In the context in which she finds herself, the demystification of the concept of love falls to this woman. She must transform it into a culturally and socially dynamic force (by involvement in political activity for example), more often seeking greater parity between the sexes than "enlightenment equality." In rejecting the fantasy of loving submission, a participant black woman who does not reproduce masculine authoritarian behavior can emerge. She finds herself in an opposite position that allows her to assume a critical stance that intermediates between her own history and her ethos. She would offer partnership in sexual relations, which, in the end, would be replicated in broader social relations.

Note

Originally published as "A mulher negra e o amor." *Maioria Falante* (February/March 1990): 3. A slightly different, earlier version of the text exists in her archive, under the title "A mulher negra no Brasil e o amor" (The black woman in Brazil and love).

An Aside to Feminism

I FOUND MYSELF arriving at the resolution to the conflict. Two women vehemently agreed, nodding. I surprised myself, saying, loudly:

> Don't even think about a Third World War. We went through a First, and in the Second, I was born. My mother gave birth in spite of Hitler. We should all give birth and give birth plenty to husbands, brothers, to all men. Or if not, fight so that laboratories can intensify the production of semen right now, as soon as possible.

I looked at the women. They were smiling and nodding affirmatively, and for the rest of the night they stuck close to me. Oh! The solidarity of one member of a species to another.

I wish for a world of equals. A world of bees.

Birth, birth, birth. They will say it's promiscuity, but who can be against the self-preservation of the species? It's the other way up.

I want a world of uteruses, ah, if I could write it in ink. The History that I dream of is a continental history, like the walls of a uterus; only shedding and scraping the walls can destroy its contents.

Now I want to speak of the moon. It is crescent, and the Earth was given a new cycle of life, because the moon exists. I feel in me a great explosion of love that I contemplate from the "window facing the Corcovado." I would like to write a song about the power of giving life. Silent like the crescent moon, that is not silver, like in Gil's music, but indefinably gold, like bread, just toasted. I want to speak of my happiness of being the mother of a little woman. The ideal complement of a being. I look at this little human animal, that like the crescent moon makes me think about the certainty of continuity, and I rejoice in being able to be.

When I said that the solution was that women should give birth more, I was not thinking of myself, and perhaps now I can't. But I looked at all of them all like crescent moons, like flooded oceans, like continents of the purity of man and I believed that I had discovered the principle-of-pleasure.

And I wanted to speak of the moon, but I am not silent and full of light, like only she knows how to be. Woman of a planet-woman. Atomic-Earth-mother of a celestial body that drives my cycle, my hemorrhaging burst, that allows me to represent the power of mankind. Not in my words, not in my rights, not in my knowledge, but in my liquid, in the alcove of my truth.

But I want to speak of Light. And who am I to speak of the Moon? I have always seen her as an announcement of what is to come, a mute announcement, but in slow motion, like the dialectic that I understand of what lies there. I would like to be mute like the Moon that would announce my cycle, with a subtle shift—the moon that people quickly forget. But I cannot say that its influence has waned, because for me to forget is always out of reach.

Note

The original title of this essay is "Um aparte ao feminismo." Unpublished, undated, Fundo MBN, 23.4.5. As with other documents in the same file, this title is handwritten on a typed text, indicating that it was added later.

PART III

Quilombo: Thoughts on Black Freedom and Liberation

On Quilombo

Christen A. Smith

BEATRIZ NASCIMENTO'S DREAM of a History of Black People concretized in her research on quilombos—the focus of her academic production during her lifetime. Her theorization of quilombos was revolutionary. She made three key assertions: 1) that quilombos are evidence of the diachronic nature of Black identity in Brazil; 2) that quilombos reflect continuity between African (particularly Angolan) culture and Black Brazilian cultural forms; and 3) that quilombos are evidence of the deliberate, calculated, defiant, and political nature of the Black struggle against colonialism/slavery and patriarchal white supremacy in Brazil. In making these arguments, she asserts that the practice of quilombo was not isolated to the slavery era, but rather has been a continuous sociopolitical practice that has persisted from the sixteenth century onward. She also argues that the practice of quilombo remains in the contemporary creation of autonomous Black cultural spaces: Black dance parties (baile Blacks), samba schools, candomblé houses, and favelas. Nascimento provided important ethnographic and historical evidence to corroborate her claims. Through her research in places like Carmo da Mata, she reveals that quilombos did not disappear. Instead, they were maintained over generations by the descendants of their original inhabitants and continued to exist. Her research provided the factual data necessary to corroborate the Black Movement's exaltation of quilombos as an organic Black Brazilian cultural form and the oldest successful anti-colonial, anti–white supremacist political formation in the nation. This claim led the Black Movement to make the preservation of quilombo lands and land rights one of its primary demands during the negotiation of the new constitution between 1985 and 1988.

In the late 1970s and early 1980s, Beatriz Nascimento traveled across Angola, Brazil, and Portugal to conduct ethnographic and archival research on the history and contemporaneous existence of quilombos. Alongside her colleague, anthropologist Marlene de Oliveira Cunha and their research team, Nascimento used money from the Ford Foundation and the Brazil House of the Léopold Sédar Senghor Foundation to gather oral histories, engage in participatory mapping and participant observation, conduct surveys, and delve into the archives. In 1979 Nascimento traveled to Angola at the official invitation from the Intellectual Exchange Section of the Federal Council of Culture of Angola, Department of Luanda. During this time, she researched the origins of the practice of quilombo in Angola and witnessed one of the critical moments in Angolan history: the grief of the new nation in the wake of the death of its first president, Dr. António Agostinho Neto. She later completed her thesis on quilombos in 1981 during her postgraduate studies at UFRJ. The essays in this section represent her academic writing during this time, including excerpts from her master's thesis—her lengthiest academic piece.

Nascimento's thesis argued that quilombos have historically served as alternative social systems organized by Black people not only in resistance to colonialism and slavery but also as deliberately constructed spaces of peace (*quilombola peace*) amid the violence of this patriarchal white supremacist habitus. She deconstructed respected scholarship on quilombos of the time, including the work of Edison Carneiro, one of the earliest Black intellectuals to explore quilombos as a historical phenomenon in *O Quilombo dos Palmares* (1958).[1] One of her contentious arguments was that quilombos were neither "spontaneous flight in the sense of anarchy and disorganization" nor a "frustrated attempt to take power" nor "negative reaction of flight and defense." Rather, she saw quilombo as "a posture black people adopt to sustain themselves in both a historical sense and in the sense of group survival. This emerges as a form of social settlement and organization with a new internal and structural order." She goes on to say that "flight, far from being spontaneous, or motivated by an incapacity to struggle, is . . . the consequence of a whole process of reorganization and contestation against the established order." In other words, "flight" was the "manifest . . . desire for self-liberation"—a "new social nucleus"—an expression of Black freedom and a desire to shape a new, autonomous Black existence in freedom.[2] In other words, Nascimento disagrees with the dominant academic narrative that reduces quilombos to reactionary forms of resistance, evacuating the practice of its political meaning and complex social structure.

Nascimento backed up her critiques with field and archival research. She notes how both Portuguese colonizers and historians oversimplified quilombos, repeatedly citing a 1740 report of the Overseas Council of Portugal, which defined the word *quilombo* (or *mocambo*) as, "all habitations of black fugitives in groups of more than five, even if destitute or lacking buildings, tools or cultivation." She draws attention to the vast difference in the scale of quilombos in slavery-era Brazil—from just a handful of people to over twenty-thousand-person settlements—and argues that the colonial strategy was (and continues to be under the Brazilian nationalist project) reducing quilombos to mere groups of escaped slaves, downplaying them as a significant political and militaristic threat to the Portuguese colony and the Brazilian state. As Nascimento observes, "the quilombo and its associations are successful attempts at ideological, social, politico-military reactions, free of irresponsible romanticism."

Nascimento critiques two received ideas about quilombos. First, that quilombos were bands of runaways impulsively fleeing the cruelty of slavery without social organization. The second was the utopic vision of quilombos as laboratories of resistance and revolution. She upturns this second reductionist perspective by decentering Palmares as the idyllic representation of the quilombo in the Brazilian popular imagination. Palmares's size and structure made it fit with Marxist theses of embryonic revolution and large-scale resistance movements. Departing from this, Nascimento instead reclaims quilombos as tactical responses to the conditions of war that colonialism and slavery produced. She reinscribes the practice of quilombo as a calculated, effective form of Black confrontation against the social order.

Beatriz Nascimento's insights about quilombos were intellectually important and politically significant. Although her work was nascent in its historical analysis (historians now have access to more sources and details about the history of quilombos and might disagree with some of Nascimento's conclusions), her observations still resonate. She demonstrated that quilombos reflect Black culture and social organization and manifest a historical and cultural flow between Africa and Brazil. Notably, she traced the practice of quilombo back to Angolan culture, revealing it to be an assemblage of African military defense practices used in the context of war. She connects the practice of quilombo to the Imbangala nomadic people—a deeply problematic connection given the Imbangala role in "slave catching," but also a connection that reflects the often-contradictory history of slavery in Africa. To the Imbangala, *kilombo* had multiple meanings (see her essay "Kilombo").[3] In tracing this genealogy, she returns full circle to her principal intellectual project: insisting on the existence of a diachronic Black Brazilian identity that is not folkloric, but political and evolving, and that undergirds a Black Brazilian culture anchored in lived Black experience.

Marronage: A Hemispheric View

English speakers traditionally translate the word *quilombo* as runaway slave encampments or maroon communities—organized communes of runaway enslaved Africans typically located on the outskirts of colonial settlements away from plantations and city centers.[4] The term *quilombo* in the context of the Americas specifically refers to this practice in colonial Brazil. However, the practice of marronage writ large—escape from slavery, resistance, and the establishment of autonomous, relatively free spaces—occurred throughout the Americas among the enslaved. From the *cimarrones* of Panama and Peru, to the *palenques* of Colombia and Cuba and the maroons of Jamaica and the United States, enslaved Africans established a pattern and practice of flight, fight, and autonomous community-building in response to the injustices of slavery across the hemisphere from the moment that they stepped foot on these shores. Quilombos in Brazil have a unique historiography in this wider landscape. Brazil was home to Palmares: arguably the largest and best-known maroon community in hemispheric history. What's more, the practice of quilombo was widespread and multifaceted in the territory of Brazil for approximately three hundred years, and as mentioned previously, quilombo communities still exist.[5]

Quilombos in Brazil varied in kind, size, and duration. Yet, while quilombos were clandestine forms of resistance, their existence was widely known and their presence was obvious.[6] Regardless of their form, they represented Black people's insatiable desire to flee slavery and create autonomous communities. The practice of quilombo should be read in conversation with the history of Black revolt in Brazil. Between 1807 and 1835, Black resistance in the form of quilombo (*aquilombagem*) and planned and executed insurrection intensified. The zenith of this moment was, without a doubt, the Revolta dos Malês in January 1835, which we also discuss in the introduction. From the night of January 24 through the morning of January 25, a conglomerate of enslaved and freed Africans occupied the streets of Bahia and confronted armed soldiers and civilians. The revolt was led by a group of Muslim Africans called Malês, most of whom were from the Hausa nation in what is now Nigeria. Despite the relatively short duration of this armed struggle, this would be one of the most successful slave insurrections in the history of the Americas, and it would have a lasting impact on the Brazilian social order for centuries to come.

Although most revolts were never fully realized, the mere planning and elaboration of insurrection underscores the fact that Black resistance to white supremacy was a constant political reality in Brazil during slavery. Thus, when Nascimento argues that Black dance parties, favelas, and candomblé houses are quilombos, she is also arguing that quilombos are sustained practices that are part of the Black radical tradition of confrontation and refusal of white supremacy in Brazil. Historically, there has been a palpable tension between Black cultural spaces and the coloniality of patriarchal white supremacy in Brazil, as evidenced by the criminalization of Black cultural forms like candomblé, capoeira, and samba up until the 1930s. This tension historically corre-sponded to anti-colonial revolt and insurrections by enslaved people. This is the political understanding of the meaning of quilombo that inspired Beatriz Nascimento.

The volume of Black uprisings, and their resilient grinding away at the colonial/slavery structure, pushes us to consider the contemporary legacies of quilombos and the structures of violence that created them. In many ways Black Brazilians have been at war with the Brazilian state apparatus for generations, at times directly and at times indirectly. This war has been fomented by the state's incessant desire to violently intimi-date, repress, capture, and isolate Black people deemed to be a threat or out of place—like Black radical intellectuals.[7] This was at the forefront of Black intellectuals' minds during the military dictatorship, and it is the backdrop for Beatriz Nascimento's thinking. Quilombo was and is a practice of war encampment.

Continuity

> The quilombo, for us, is not a subordinated fact, but a *continuous* process in the total History of the country.
>
> —"ALTERNATIVE SOCIAL MOVEMENTS" (1981)

Historical continuity is a major theme in Beatriz Nascimento's thoughts on quilombo. Her master's thesis clearly argues for a recognition of the historical continuity between the practice of quilombo in Angola, the practice of quilombo by enslaved Africans and *crioulos* (people of African descent born on Brazilian soil) during slavery, and remnant practices of quilombo in urban and rural spaces in Brazil today. This latter idea—the historical continuity between the colonial-era practice of quilombo and the contemporary practice of quilombo in urban spaces (not just rural ones)—was controversial.

As Nascimento notes in the introduction to her thesis, the Ford Foundation agreed to fund her work on remnants of quilombos in rural Brazilian communities but not her research on the connection between quilombos and urban spaces (favelas). From this, we might infer that the Ford Foundation felt that her investigation of favelas as contemporary quilombos was either too far-fetched or too politically dicey. Yet, Nascimento found ways to make her argument. In chapter 2 of her thesis, she examines the Antônio Conselheiro movement (Canudos) and its relationship to race and abolition. The reader who is unfamiliar with the nuances of Brazilian social history may not fully grasp the depth of her analysis. Here, she revisits the Canudos massacre of 1897 by looking back at the messianic movement of Antônio Conselheiro, the charismatic leader who established an autonomous settlement of Black and mestiço people in the backlands of Bahia in the late nineteenth century. Situating this movement, and the subsequent state-sponsored massacre of the people of Conselheiro's settlement in 1897, within the broader history of abolition in Brazil, Nascimento argues that Conselheiro was not an eccentric leader of rogue and disillusioned poor non-white people, as the Brazilian government argued at the time; rather, Conselheiro was a quilombo leader, and his settlement was an extension of the practice of quilombo spilling over from the social fallout of the legal abolition of slavery in 1888.

Nascimento's discussion of the Antônio Conselheiro movement prefaces her presentation of her research in Angola in the fourth chapter of her thesis. Here, again, the theme is historical continuity. She outlines each aspect of her trip to Angola, as well as its political stakes—a diplomatic visit organized by the Angolan government shortly after Angolan independence. Here, she contends that quilombos "are, and have always been, characteristic of the social organization of Angolans." She also notes that the practices of quilombo are decidedly militaristic in nature. "They are both territorial and frontier areas, and strategic zones, whose occupation is oriented toward the defense of the territory itself and of the Angolan subsoil." It is perhaps partly for this reason that she left her field notes in Angola in government archives—to avoid revealing militaristic secrets that could compromise the fragile political infrastructure of the newly independent nation.

Continuity is also a salient element of the essay "Kilombo and Community Memory: A Case Study." Here she writes, "Historical continuity—that is why I refer to a dream. . . . Continuity would be the life of man—and of men—going on apparently without ruptures, though flattened by various processes and forms of subjugation, subordination, domination, and subservience. A process that took place, across many years, among those who, through our own abstractions, we include in the category of black people." She arrives at this understanding of continuity by gathering oral histories of the quilombo Carmo da Mata. She and her research assistants spoke with residents there to make connections between the slavery-era practice of quilombo and that community at that time. She writes, "we clarified a great deal about the connection of the history of Kilombo, in Carmo da Mata, to mystical apparitions and revelations, through trance and otherwise." This discussion of spirituality foreshadows discussions we take up in part IV, and specifically the practice of candomblé as a medium for understanding the historical continuities between the African cultural practices on the continent of Africa and the re-creation of those practices by enslaved Africans and their descendants in the Americas.

Continuity emerges again in "Kilombo," one of the most developed reflections on her theorizations of quilombo. Here, she clearly connects the contemporary practice of quilombo and the practice of quilombo during slavery to Angolan cultural practices of military training. Specifically, she notes that kilombo simultaneously means circumcision, the initiation space for young warriors, the camp for commercial exchanges, and the "act of moving as a fighting force." Language here becomes an important marker of continuity and again returns us to the theme of legitimating the idea of a diachronic Black identity tied to lived Black experience through a demonstration of the movement of the word *kilombo* across Angola and Brazil.

Flight

There is a relationship between the genealogy of quilombos in Brazil and the practice of Black flight and autonomy in contemporary Brazilian society. I define *flight* following Nascimento's thinking in terms of *fuga* (flight/escape). Linguistically and historically, the practice of flight (*fuga,* and the verb *fugir*) is deeply embroiled with slavery and the enslaved African desire to escape the institution of slavery physically, emotionally, psychologically, spiritually, and culturally.[8] *Lugares de fuga* (places of escape) are literal and figurative zones of flight that are both spaces of transit and movement and also *encampments in opposition to bondage.* Thus, fugitivity/escape/fuga is flight and settlement. Settlement in this sense is not a colonial, extractive, patriarchal, white supremacist practice but rather an attempt to create spaces of Black autonomy, home, and peace in opposition to the colonial state.

Sidestepping the narrow, traditional definitions of marronage suggested by most historians, Beatriz Nascimento argues that quilombos are not only places or community settlements but also a practice of freedom seeking—*quilombola peace.* Indeed, quilombola peace is a concept that emerges repeatedly in her theorizations as we see in part I. In "'Quilombos': Social Change or Conservativism?," she defines *quilombola peace* as the space "between one attack and the next by the official forces of repression." She goes on to say it is a moment when "it maintains itself, either in its withdrawal, or its own reproduction." For Nascimento, "if black Brazilian people had been able to leave a written record, we would certainly have more sources for quilombola 'peace' than war."

Nascimento elaborates on both *grand marronage* and *petit marronage.* Petit marronage is roughly defined as running away either permanently or temporarily from slavery. Grand marronage—the rarer form—is the establishment of independent societies as a result of running away.[9] As she notes, the word *quilombo* comes from the Kimbundu (also spelled *quimbundu*)[10] word *kilombo* and might literally be translated as *war encampment* but also signifies a series of spiritual and ritual processes of fortification for war and defense that constitute an autonomous commune and/or state.[11] In "Kilombo," Nascimento notes that "quilombo names a process of action, activity, and conduct within the three principles mentioned above. Therein lies its historical trajectory and its significance: the qualities of process, of continuum. However, we should not think of this continuum as static, but as dynamic."

By thinking of quilombo as fluidity, continuum, and the active practice of insurgence against the state, we can reframe quilombos as a political template for Black rebellion and refusal, as Beatriz Nascimento did. Brazil's identity as a colony, and the colonial state itself, were intermeshed with the conditions of slavery and the racial antagonisms that slavery produced. The colony was diametrically opposed to Blackness and indigeneity. Therefore, Black and Indigenous insurrections and acts of refusal, particularly slave insurrections and practices of quilombo, were anti-colonial manifestations. This anti-colonial practice becomes the precedent for Black organizing even after the legal end of the Portuguese colony and the establishment of Brazil as an independent nation. Black Brazilians argued throughout the 1970s that whereas the legal framework of colonialism ends in Brazil in 1822, the realities of colonialism persist for Black and Indigenous people. Thus, the Black radical movement that Beatriz Nascimento helped construct continues the legacy of decoloniality initiated by enslaved Africans fleeing plantations beginning in the sixteenth century. The symbolic place of quilombos in the Black radical tradition therefore indicts the true enemy of Black radical organizing in Brazil at this time: colonial, patriarchal white supremacy (symbolized by the state, the church, and the elite class). Beatriz Nascimento's analyses clarify this connection between contemporary Black struggle and decolonial and anti-colonial struggle.

Quilombo: An Enduring Symbol of Black Freedom

> The importance of "quilombos" for black people today can be explained by their historical emergence within a symbolic universe in which their liberatory character was an ideological driving force in the racial and cultural affirmation of black people.
>
> —"ALTERNATIVE SOCIAL SYSTEMS ORGANIZED BY
> BLACK PEOPLE: FROM QUILOMBOS TO FAVELAS" (1981A)

Quilombos were the Black Movement's battle cry against authoritarianism. Nascimento's theorization of quilombos as diachronic Black cultural forms—evidence of a Black past, present, and future—helped shift the national discourse on Blackness in Brazil. Her public scholarship, including venues like *Manchete* and *IstoÉ*, and her participation in public debates like the Quinzena do Negro, placed the topic of quilombos front and center on the national stage and accomplished several key political goals. To return to the conversation on racial democracy from the introduction to part I, insisting on a History of Black People allowed the Black Movement to argue for the existence of an identifiable Black identity anchored in lived Black Brazilian experience. This assertion was a key oppositional political move; for if Black history and distinct Black cultural practices existed, Black people were living Black political subjects. By extension, Black claims denouncing racism in Brazil could not be denied on the presumption that Blackness is not a real identity. The claim that anti-Black racism exists in Brazil, is and was socially significant. Despite stark racial inequalities, Brazil still maintained that racism did not exist within its borders.[12] Hence, quilombos were not only evidence of a practice of Black political possibility, but also of the existence of racism. This bold push back against racial democracy positioned the Black Movement to play a key role in the articulation of the new democracy after the end of the authoritarian regime.

The focus on quilombos as a Black Movement political platform gained momentum in the 1970s and peaked during three key political junctures in the 1980s and 2000s: the establishment of the territory of União dos Palmares as a cultural heritage site (*tombamento*) in Serra da Barriga in the state of Alagoas in 1986; the passage of Article 68 of the Brazilian 1988 constitution, legally recognizing, for the first time, the "Indigenous" rights of "remaining quilombo communities" (*comunidades remanescentes de quilombos*); and the establishment of November 20, the anniversary of the execution the last leader of the great quilombo nation of Palmares, Zumbi, as National Black Consciousness Day in 2011. These three victories were the culmination of three decades of debate between activists, historians, and anthropologists over the meaning of quilombo, its relationship to Indigenous territorial rights, and its cultural significance for Black Brazilians. At stake were questions of land rights, cultural and historical acknowledgment, and the viability of a legal path to reparations. Today, there are hundreds of "remnant" quilombo communities that have been officially recognized by the state, and hundreds more vying for recognition.[13] In addition, quilombo has also become a symbolic reference, inspiring young people to engage in the cultural practice of creating independent, safe Black spaces in opposition to heteropatriarchal white supremacy: *aquilombar-se*.[14] Beatriz Nascimento contributed to each of these political and cultural advances.

Ôrí

Missing from this collection is the theorization on quilombos that Beatriz Nascimento elaborates in the film *Ôrí*—perhaps Nascimento's most impactful and conceptually generative work. While there are boxes of Beatriz Nascimento's notes, papers, articles, miscellanea, and thoughts housed in the National Archives in Rio de Janeiro, a great portion of her intellectual legacy is archived in the documentary film *Ôrí*, which she produced over ten years with filmmaker and director Raquel Gerber. Released in 1989, the film is a distinctive, dreamlike rumination on the Brazilian Black Atlantic. The hauntingly beautiful film, which Nascimento narrates, relies heavily on her master's thesis on quilombos, her autobiography, and her philosophical musings. Her voice is both pedagogical and reflective, weaving historical analysis in and out with laughter and poetry. It cuts a path through samba, the slave trade, Atlantic landscapes, African-Brazilian religiosity, dress, African religions, Brazilian urban space, and more. *Ôrí* is also a formative archiving of Brazil's radical Black Movement, and a theoretical tour de force that uses sound, image, and word to tie together a vision of liberation. The sensibility that Nascimento displays in *Ôrí*, and the artistic practice that it emerges from, imbue her poetry across her life.

Nascimento's praxis beyond the writing was just as or perhaps more significant than her textual production. This is particularly true in relation to her work on Black women. Her status as a figure in the Brazilian Black radical scene comes across clearly in *Ôrí*, in which her charisma matches her intellectual fleetness. This is an important dimension of her legacy, which contributes to the diverse ways in which her work can be put toward intellectual and political work. Leading Afro-Brazilian feminist theorist Sueli Carneiro testifies to the impact of Nascimento as a young scholar-activist:

I had the privilege of attending Beatriz' famous presentation in the Quinzena do Negro at the University of Sao Paulo, in 1977. . . . There she was, dressed head to foot in gold, looking like a manifestation of Oxum on earth. Her ideas were audacious, she was beautiful, she was haughty when questioned. It was a magical moment that affirmed the black woman as the bearer of knowledge about her people. A magical moment of knowledge and seduction, of elegance and perspicacity. It was as if we were in a Yoruba ritual of feminine power.[15]

Nascimento was in her midthirties and had been a figure in the Black activist circles in Rio de Janeiro, particularly in its universities, since the beginning of the decade. Around that time, Nascimento was making important interventions about gender and Blackness in her writing and her public persona.

In Ôrí, Nascimento makes pivotal interventions to thinking Black transatlantic space. She argues that the quilombo was a historical, physical space (the site to where escaped Africans fled and established autonomous communities during slavery), a social model, and a terrain of political potentiality. Her arguments hinge on her unique conceptualization of quilombo as a dynamic, spatial, political field, rather than a static political institution located in the past. In this way, her theorization of quilombo moves away from an understanding of territoriality as fixity toward a framing of territoriality as becoming. Nascimento's ideas about the spatialization of Blackness—as it is defined and redefined through the experience of transcendental spirituality, diaspora, transmigration, rootedness, and imagination—motivate us to consider the geographic-ness of Blackness without anchoring it in fixed times and places.[16] Nascimento offers the possibility of a Black transatlantic space that flows across and with the Atlantic, back and forth, permeating, buoying, and carrying, like water.

Much of the work to build the concept of quilombos as favelas and autonomous Black cultural spaces like samba schools, candomblé houses, and Black Soul parties, emerges in Ôrí in ways that she was unable to do in her thesis. Recall that the Ford Foundation did not allow her to elaborate this part of her work as part of her research fellowship.

This may be why she decided to turn to film to develop her theoretical insights. In film she saw the possibility of freedom outside the confines of the stringent, hegemonic, Eurocentric academic written form. Regardless, the concepts she was able to develop in *Ôrí* are also present—albeit at times just under the surface—in her writings on quilombo.

An Academic Voice

This section on quilombo distinguishes itself from the other sections in this book in content and form. The essays here are a mix between excerpted chapters from her master's thesis and published academic essays. Much of this work is based on collective research, and she often uses the plural first person "we" and references to her research team, funders, and university professors. This, of course, shapes the tone of the work. For example, "Post-revolutionary Angolan Nativism" seems to be (from the context clues of the writing) a research report and a paper used to complete the requirements of a class with professor José Calasans. We make this assumption because of the way she situates here work as "the data that I secured while I was absent from the course for forty days." One can assume that she included this in the report in part to justify her absence. It is also clear that the questions she answers here are ones her professor posed to her. Her response mixes a tone of academic objectivity with diplomatic retrospective. Here, she also speaks to the audience of the Angolan officials who invited her to travel.

The fact that Nascimento went to Angola just after António Agostinho Neto's funeral reinforces the delicate political nature of her trip. She was building diplomatic relationships while also conducting field research. This detail merits special attention because it also locates this work within the context of the shifting political landscape of Black internationalism in Brazil at this time. The wave of successful African independence movements in the 1960s and 1970s led to the first Black diplomats being sent to Brazil.[17] This also opened opportunities for Brazilians, particularly Black Movement organizers, to travel to the continent of Africa. Nascimento's trip to Angola reflects the Pan-Africanism of Black Movement politics in Brazil during this period. Not only were Black Movement intellectuals looking to Brazil's Black history to make arguments about diachronic Black identity; they were also looking to the newly independent African nations, whose revolutionary struggles were also waged against the Portuguese, like in the case of Angola. Nascimento does a great deal of careful tightrope walking in this chapter as she explains the political landscape in Angola during the time of her visit. She wants to be deferential to the government officials who invited her. Yet, she has critiques of Angolan society, as is evidenced by her argument regarding the ingenuity of Angolan nativism.

Peeking through the blinds of her intellectual armor, is the familiar and keen voice of Nascimento's critique; admiration for Black communities and Black cultures; and deep understanding of the paradox of using the very rigid, formal, and European-inspired research methods that have been used to subjugate Black people for generations. Throughout the work, she insists on uncertainty rather than certainty; refuses oversimplified conclusions; questions stereotypical tropes of traditional scientific analyses of Black culture and history; and insists on the rationality of her interlocutors: rural, Black descendants of enslaved Africans who fled captivity to create community, carve out spaces of autonomy, and archive memory orally and intergenerationally. Here, Nascimento lays the groundwork for her pathfinding theorizations of quilombo as autonomous Black counter-state zones within the Brazilian nation-state. Beneath the formal, report-like assessments of the research she performed, lie gestures toward her more complex thinking on quilombos as repositories of Black memory.

Notes

1. Edison Carneiro, *O quilombo dos Palmares*, 2nd ed. (São Paulo: Companhia Editora Nacional, 1958).

2. All quotations are from "'Quilombos': Social Change or Conservatism?"

3. For more on the Imbangala history of quilombos, see Kabengele Munanga, "Origem e histórico do quilombo na África," *Revista USP* 28 (December/February 1996): 56–63.

4. See, for example, Richard Price, *Maroon Societies: Rebel Slave Communities in the Americas* (Baltimore: Johns Hopkins University Press, 1979); João José Reis, *Slave Rebellion in Brazil: The*

Muslim Uprising of 1835 in Bahia, trans. Arthur Brakel (Baltimore: Johns Hopkins University Press, 1995).

5. For a more robust discussion of the struggles of contemporary quilombo communities, see, for example, Davi Pereira Júnior, *Quilombos de Alcântara: Território e conflito: o intrusamento do território das comunidades quilombolas de Alcântara pela Empresa Binacional Alcântara Cyclone Space* (Manaus: PNCSA, 2009).

6. João José Reis and Flávio dos Santos Gomes, *Freedom by a Thread: The History of Quilombos in Brazil,* 1st ed. (Diasporic Africa Press, 2016); Reis, *Slave Rebellion in Brazil.*

7. See this argument in Christen A. Smith, *Afro-Paradise: Blackness, Violence, and Performance in Brazil* (Urbana: University of Illinois Press, 2016). We would also be remiss to not mention the recent assassination of Councilwoman Marielle Franco in Rio de Janeiro in 2018—yet another instance in this long history of the assassination and persecution of radical Black intellectuals in Brazil. See Caldwell et al., "On the Imperative of Transnational Solidarity: A U.S. Black Feminist Statement on the Assassination of Marielle Franco," *The Black Scholar,* March 23, 2018, https://theblackscholar.org/on-the-imperative-of-transnational-solidarity-a-u -s-black-feminist-statement-on-the-assassination-of-marielle-franco/.

8. There is a strong linguistic correlation between the verb *fugir*—as well as its derivatives in Brazilian Portuguese—and the history of slavery. Thus, the very term immediately invokes concepts of bondage and carcerality in Brazil. This has a great influence on the epistemological implications of the term *fuga* and distinguishes the Brazilian concept of fugitive/fugitivity/ flight. The discourse on fugitivity in North American Black studies is diverse and expansive, and also distinct from how this term and concept are understood in Brazil. For example, Stefano Harney and Fred Moten define *fugitivity* as a form of escape in opposition to the political and the organizational in terms of its relationship to Black sociality. This notion of fugitivity focuses on the philosophical impetus of perpetual flight. Here, I take a different approach grounded in Beatriz Nascimento's thinking that defines *fugitivity* in terms of *fuga* (flight/escape) and implies a relationship between flight from captivity/slavery/repression toward peace and liberation (if only temporarily) rather than escape as perpetual motion. This idea of fugitivity is grounded in the practice of quilombo as the deliberate seeking and creation of social alternatives to slavery. Stefano Harney and Fred Moten, *The Undercommons: Fugitive Planning & Black Study* (Wivenhoe: Minor Compositions, 2013); Damien M. Sojoyner, "Another Life Is Possible: Black Fugitivity and Enclosed Places," *Cultural Anthropology* 32, no. 4 (2017): 514–36.

9. Richard Price's 1979 collection *Maroon Societies* is widely referenced as a key text in defining maroon communities in the Americas. In Brazil, published research on quilombos extends back to the early twentieth century. See also Greg Thomas, "Marronnons / Let's Maroon: Sylvia Wynter's 'Black Metamorphosis' As a Species of Marronage," *Small Axe: A Caribbean Journal of Criticism* 20.1, no. 49 (2016): 62–78. For more on the political philosophy of the concept of marronage in the Black radical tradition, particularly in the anglophone world, see, for example, Neil Roberts, *Freedom as Marronage* (Chicago: University of Chicago Press, 2015).

10. Kimbundu is a Bantu language from the Congo-Angola region of Africa.

11. Beatriz Nascimento writes about the origins of the term in the texts included here. She also narrates this history in the film *Ôrí.* For additional sources on this etymology, see, for example, Nei Lopes, *Dicionário banto do Brasil* (Rio de Janeiro: Prefeitura da Cidade do Rio de Janeiro, Centro Cultural José Bonifácio, 1995).

12. See, for example, Alexandre Emboaba Da Costa, *Reimagining Black Difference and Politics in Brazil: From Racial Democracy to Multiculturalism* (New York: Palgrave Macmillan, 2014); Michael George Hanchard, *Racial Politics in Contemporary Brazil*, ed. Michael Hanchard (Durham, NC: Duke University Press, 1999); Rebecca L. Reichmann, ed., *Race in Contemporary Brazil: From Indifference to Inequality* (University Park: Penn State University Press, 2010); France Winddance Twine, *Racism in a Racial Democracy: The Maintenance of White Supremacy in Brazil* (New Brunswick, NJ: Rutgers University Press, 1998).

13. Article 68 opened a legal path for descendants of quilombolas (quilombo settlers) to demand rights to land and resources from the Brazilian government, extending indigenous land rights to Black people in the country.

14. Throughout Brazilian society today we see Black youth making references to the practice of creating autonomous, counterhegemonic Black spaces as aquilombar-se or practicing quilombo. Examples of this are the proliferation of cultural groups using the word *quilombo* to describe themselves as alternative spaces of Black cultural expression. One example is the Black queer dance, music, community, and cultural space Aparelha Luzia in São Paulo, which refers to itself as an urban quilombo. See https://brasil.elpais.com/brasil/2017/11/01/cultura/1509557481_659286.html.

15. Sueli Carneiro in Alex Ratts, ed., *Eu sou Atlântica: sobre a trajetória de Beatriz Nascimento* (São Paulo: Imprensa Oficial [SP] e Instituto Kuanza, 2006), 11.

16. This point on Black geographies invokes the work of Katherine McKittrick in particular. See Katherine McKittrick, *Demonic Grounds: Black Women and the Cartographies of Struggle* (Minneapolis: University of Minnesota Press, 2006); Katherine McKittrick and Clyde Woods, ed., *Black Geographies and the Politics of Place* (Toronto: Between the Lines, 2007).

17. Pierre-Michel Fontaine, ed., *Race, Class, and Power in Brazil* (Los Angeles: Center for Afro-American Studies, University of California, 1985).

Urgency (Zumbi)

[To the power Z]
Paths open to the heavy force
The oscillating movement of the known, in torn veins,
Irresolute and precipitant
Like a false backdrop.
In the mirror veils juxtaposed
Hide the gaze like metallic webs
Making the being diffuse.
Separating definitively the exterior from the interior
They knock each other and pierce old fantasies
Who do not look at each other like at one who belongs.
And then who surges into the arena
Flaming dancer of intentions
List like something descended in an occupied territory
Mysterious as an enchanted gift
From distant places
Propitiator who ignored chapters of his own doctrine
Raptured, like the first light of dawn.
Between darkness and twilight
No one would know to say his "Eternity."
What material is it made of
What mission is its destiny.
In the colors that squander
The perplexity of the combinations

It suffocated the cries of pain
It inhibited the screeches of happiness.
Flaming like spicy whips
The luminous voluptuousness blocked out the sounds.
Who was that traveler from such confines?
Confined in his own gases?

Note

The original title of this poem was "Urgência (Zumbi)." Written 1984/85.

"Quilombos": Social Change
or Conservatism?

Introduction

In 1974, I published an article in the *Revista de Cultura Vozes*, called "Black People and Racism." Among other things, I discussed my proposition to write a History of Black People. I wrote about the methodological difficulties involved, particularly in relation to the concepts of acceptance, integration, and equality. I argued that, in practice, racial prejudice was represented within the official ideology of oppression through this conceptual language itself. It attested to actually existing conditions of racism and discrimination. I wrote, specifically, that "'acceptance' and 'equality' are 'dominant' perspectives" (dominant, here, in the sense of the ideology of the dominant classes—particularly the intellectual class—including the concept of the dominant race, which has made us see a white ideology as a national ideology).

In the same article I concluded that the three concepts cited above, like everything attributed to black people, including "black culture," must be reexamined from the point of view of the dominant ideology, and its aspirations and desires. This is only possible in the context of faithfulness to (the) History (of Brazil). Only a historical survey of the experience of black people in Brazil, conducted by their descendants—that is, those who experience today, in practice, this lived inheritance—will be able to eradicate both black people's complexes, and white people's racial prejudice.

Adopting this intellectual position, I have set out to write a revisionist study of the History of Brazil. I was drawn to an examination of stereotypes applied to the descendants of Africans brought to Brazil. However, I then abandoned the methodological approach of studying the descendants of enslaved people, to turn to the study of black Brazilians, and their historical inheritance based not on captivity but on freedom. I immediately abandoned the study of racial relations and began to focus on historical centers of the black population which were, in general, free from official power. That is, those social settlements known generically by the name of *quilombos*.

In this present study I will undertake a critique of the existing bibliography on quilombos, in which an idealistic vision has proliferated; beyond that critique, my interpretation is based on those of the most lucid and clear-sighted scholars, who saw in the quilombo an attempt, though frustrated, to change the *status* of formerly enslaved people, and create social change in the slavocratic regime implanted in Brazil during the three centuries of colonial domination.

To begin this study, I seek a definition of *quilombo* that is closer to historical reality. I ask what *quilombo* was, and is, and what its implications are in Brazilian History, and in the historical trajectory of black people's lives in Brazil.

Quilombos as Social Settlements

A report of the Overseas Council, dated the 2nd of December 1740, defined the *quilombo* or *mocambo* as follows: "all habitations of black fugitives in groups of more than five, even if destitute or lacking buildings, tools or cultivation."

The contemporary entry in the Portuguese dictionary by Aurélio Buarque de Holanda Ferreira has the following: *Quilombos*, masculine noun. Brazilian. "Shelter of escaped slaves."

I see both the Conselho Ultramarinho and the entry in the most complete Portuguese dictionary as stereotypes of what quilombos were, and what a "quilombo" is in reality. Aurélio Buarque de Holanda Ferreira writes in the entry in his huge dictionary: "Quilombo of the quimbundo Union." Indeed, it is this that I want to turn to: Union of what? Union between what?

Herein is an omission in Brazilians' knowledge of their history, an unknown in the History of Brazil. No one has yet been able to clarify this historical lacuna that risks creating a rupture between black people and their past and aggravating ignorance of their current condition.

The specialized literature emphasizes black people's need to create quilombos as refuges from slavery. But there were other, much more striking ways for formerly enslaved people to act against the oppressive regime. There was abortion, suicide, and the murder of masters and their whole families. The flight from the ill treatment of slavery was not itself a strong enough motive to lead large numbers of black people to opt for a parallel life, community, and sociality. That is, ill treatment and corporal punishment would not lead thousands of people to create settlements, or societies.

There is still, in the literature on quilombos, a fact that is taken as a cause. Based principally on the documentation around the Quilombo of Palmares, some eminent historians see in quilombo a return to "tribal life" as a function of an imminent return to African origins. They even see the coronation of an innate ideal of liberty among the groups who made up the quilombo. It is reasonable that we might think that one of the aspirations of enslaved people should be liberty, but not in the sense in which the literature has interpreted it. This interpretation is definitively based on an understanding impregnated with bourgeois liberal ideology dating back to the utopians, to Rousseau, and to the thinkers of the eighteenth century. The same ideal is assumed to have led to the French Revolution. Recently, however, based on Marxist principles, historians see the quilombo as a frustrated attempt to take power. In this view the enslaved person is seen as having an "inadequate" awareness to ultimately achieve victory. In this way, Edison Carneiro himself, in *O Quilombo dos Palmares* (1958) does not hesitate to establish a hierarchy of three main moments of black people's reaction against slavery:

1. Organized revolt aiming to take power (uprising of black *malês* in Bahia in the nineteenth century);

2. Armed insurrections (the case of Manuel Balaio, 1839, in Maranhão);
3. Escape to the forest, resulting in quilombos (e.g., Palmares).

Following this same scale, the sage sociologist reinforces this position even further, calling the "Quilombos" a "negative reaction of flight and defense."

It is starting from Edison Carneiro that I question the idea of seeing quilombos as embryos of social change. We will see below how quilombo may be a posture black people adopt to sustain themselves in both a historical sense and in the sense of group survival. This emerges as a form of social settlement and organization with a new internal and structural order.

From Consciousness to Resistance

I understand the methodological and interpretative difficulty that studying "quilombo" throws up. It necessarily leads to a multitude of errors. I understand that the quilombo is formed more thanks to the human necessity to self-organize in a particular way, other than in the arbitrary form established by the colonizer. One person, or various people, in normal physical and psychological conditions, though living under a system of deeply oppressive institutions, could voluntarily imagine for themselves conditions more in line with their own potential and aptitudes. But these conditions were—it is universally and historically recognized—impossible to create under the slavocratic social order.

I will now, therefore, offer my own perspective on what determines the establishment of "quilombo" as a social structure. Let's take a cliché as an example, one among the many descriptions by travelers who visited the slave market of Valongo in Rio de Janeiro in the last century. Let's imagine a trafficked African man, from one of the more developed of the innumerable African social organizations. He is a black man of a higher ranking in the hierarchy of a particular African group (primitive society, state, empire, or unspecified social group). Let's imagine, even, that he is a potentate who, by the dividing force of the labor market here in Brazil, becomes separated from his subjects, or the large part of them, and even from his family. We could argue that this man, thanks to his experience of command or his place in the social hierarchy, is unlikely to rationally and consciously accept the new condition he finds himself in Brazil.

This man may be able, in the *senzala*, and in the plantation during working hours, to organize a group, whether in the form he knew previously, or otherwise. This could be done through rendering favors, the continuity of vassalage of his former subjects, or new relations, etc. . . . The continuity of vassalage was observed by Maria Graham in her Diary, which is cited by José Honório Rodrigues in his *Revolução e Contra-Revolução: Economia e Sociedade—Volume II*. We can assume that this is what took place in the accumulation of wealth by Chico Rei, in Vila Rica, in the eighteenth century. Beyond these African men, however, it is possible that (Brazilians) of mixed heritage might have had opportunities to establish new groups based on new relations. It is possible, given how slavery was organized, that groups could be formed in a way that was totally incomprehensible and opaque to those outside (whites, the overseer, the master, other black people, etc.). It is undeniable that black people were socially organized in relation to work without apparent fragmentation. Whatever change took place within the nucleus of work would therefore be imperceptible. This provided a marginal advantage to the initial nucleus of a quilombo that could develop without the intrusion of elements in opposition to it, or from outside it.

That group within the larger group therefore already had a leader. These could be organic leaders, as in the example above, or they could come from religious practices, a healer, a sorcerer, or, in some cases, a midwife. People who, thanks to their importance within the group, gathered it around them. Once this embryo of organization was established, it started to feel necessary to get away from the official order.

At this stage, the group had to undergo a profound crisis. Committed men and women went through a chaotic phase in which the various stages and situations that the embryonic organization has lived through up to then reach their limit, and come to require a more concrete, real body. This crisis takes a form that reflects the group's psychology. Perhaps it is this psychological chaos that establishes, at this moment, a strong ideological edifice that justifies taking a position against the established political, social, and legal order. This posture, however, can turn in on itself, and risks the disaggregation of the group as it is in formation. Reinvigorated by this, and by ties with their regions of origin, these connections are translated through the intensification of ludic (constant festivities, drumming, etc.), religious, and "philosophical" practices. These practices manifest the desire for self-liberation.

In terms of individual behavior (I put it in this way to differentiate it from group-psychology and ideology), we see an anarchic attitude toward abandoning productive practices. These fundamentally amount to the rejection of a continuing compromise with the dominant social order. The marginalization of the practices and customs of black people, promoted by that social order, is the reason for this contrarian posture, which is often reflected in vicious and criminal practices of banditry. Though these have a contrarian character, they could also be called pathological. Below we will discuss the relation between quilombos and criminality. It is at this moment that an exogenous factor comes to have greater significance. The momentary disequilibrium of the group in formation can be articulated with the disequilibrium of society as a whole. It is influenced by events such as the disorganization of economic life (the crisis of labor that came with the abolitionist process), war, or invasion (the wars of Independence, the relation between Palmares and the Dutch War). These factors, however, were never determinant.

After this internal crisis, while the group is still on the plantation, the next step is conspiracy against the official regime. Thanks to its historical and institutional conditions, the official regime can only offer one alternative: flight. What determines this flight is the poverty of resources endured by any group of enslaved people. This means that they lack the conditions by which to arm themselves adequately to undertake an open war between their new, insurgent order and the ruling order. Choosing flight takes into account, too, the geographical conditions of the forests as spaces of obscurity. Flight, therefore, is the chosen form of reaction, and it initiates a new, truly autonomous order.

Fleeing to Struggle

The designation *negro fujão* (black runaway), used in the official documentation to refer to quilombolas, has not been subject to critique in the literature on quilombos. The term has been perpetuated, not least by Edison Carneiro who, as already noted, passed on these prejudicial designations, and suggested that the quilombo was a negative form of struggle because it involves flight. Doubtless, such prejudice continues today. This makes it impossible to achieve a clear and precise vision of what a quilombo and its associations are. It is common in the official documentation to call any grouping of black people "quilombo," including communities which are clearly religious in constitution. This is the case with the quilombo of Nossa Senhora dos Mares e do Cabula, in the outskirts of Salvador, discovered in 1807. The report of the Overseas Council, of December 2, 1740, defines as quilombos or mocambos "all habitations of black fugitives in groups of more than five." However, Palmares and many other quilombos, from Sergipe to Minas Gerais, contained up to twenty thousand people. As social groups, we cannot understand five runaways and twenty thousand in the same frame. But the difficulties and indifference of the literature on quilombos allows this misunderstanding to remain sunk in obscurantism and prejudice.

This small study proposes, in a simplified form, to demonstrate that flight, far from being spontaneous, or motivated by an incapacity to struggle, is, before anything else, the consequence of a whole process of reorganization and contestation against the established order. It is the conclusion of a series of situations and stages in which various factors are in play: physical, material, socio-psychological, ideological, and historical.

If we take it as a viable hypothesis that organization on the plantations, in the heart of slavery, was prior to the establishment of a form known as quilombo in the geographical space of the forests, we will conclude, certainly, that the exodus and subsequent establishment of the group follows military necessity. The characteristic peculiar to Palmares and the majority of the large quilombos is that it is the men who flee first. When the quilombo emerges in its final form these men are the leaders in the field. They are leaders of the various mocambos, ranked according to importance and the military aptitudes of their leaders. Thus we can take it that flight is motivated by the need to resist and not by a desire for accommodation. Quilombo, therefore, cannot be reduced to flight. That is a stage of the struggle, even if official society has not yet organized repression. This diminishes the weight of the expression *negro fujão*. It is not spontaneous flight, in the sense of anarchy and disorganization. On the contrary, the fact that it is the men who flee first proves that the quilombo is oriented toward combat with a society that they have rejected. Assuming, that is, that it follows a standard process. This process happens when the black people involved feel adequately prepared to launch a new social nucleus, having previously chosen an area in which they can confront repression with some probability of success.

Thus, we can conclude that, under the official slavocratic regime, the quilombo and its associations are successful attempts at ideological, social, politico-military reactions, free of irresponsible romanticism. Much less is the flight to the forest a life of leisure in contact with nature. It is not underpinned by idealized freedom or nostalgia for the former homeland. Perhaps this is why, though the quilombo was one of the central features of the social formation of subjugated Brazilians, it was not picked up by the literary romantic movement of the last century, as forms of Indigenous resistance were. Liberty as an ideal, as noted above, is an interpretative obsession of scholars and writers who endlessly seek historical correlations between Brazilian and European realities. In quilombo, the ideal of liberty and the return to Africa can only be taken as determining factors if we honestly establish the individual and psychosocial problematics at stake. If not, the appeal to these factors will be mystifying. It will obscure the reality of quilombo within the History of Brazil.

Shedding flight of its negative, picturesque, and mystifying character, it emerges as the development of a process begun in the plantation, or in places where groups of people worked under the regime of slavery.

They flee, conscious that the rupture with society can only be achieved through struggle. This becomes obvious in the case of Palmares, when men left first to organize the resistance and took government in their own hands. Edison Carneiro, citing Nina Rodrigues, writes that leadership was in the hands of "those who showed the greatest valour and intelligence." That is, in the hands of those most capable of struggle. However, the literature about Palmares is concentrated on its repression during the period of the Dutch War and what immediately followed. There is no doubt that (citing Hélio Vianna) *Sertanismo de Contrato*[1] as an economic cycle, and as national integration, organized the decadent areas of the south of the country (São Vicente) around the capture of Indigenous people and quilombolas. We need to emphasize the official recognition of armed struggle and military organization as fundamental moments in the internal organization of quilombo.

The stage that follows the departure from the official order by those who establish themselves as leaders of the movement is characterized by the indoctrination and coercion of other men. This is done by agents of the quilombo working through networks of refuge that extended to the plantations. Everyone who writes about Palmares and other large quilombos insists on this. From my perspective, an indoctrination seeking new male members only makes sense in relation to the military and defensive setup of the new organization. Only after "arming" themselves did men rejoin their other social practices, seek "their" women and, if they were with them, their children.

It is possible that all of this was done significantly before the masters, overseers, and others with concrete access to official society knew about it. From this moment on we can assume that external knowledge of quilombola organization was possible.

The Quilombola Peace

Up to now, both the official and bibliographical literature on quilombos, from Nina Rodrigues to Clóvis Moura—even though they have totally opposite approaches—have been predominantly concerned with its rebellious and insurrectionary character. What the official documents give us is precisely a register of these moments when the quilombo waged war against the official order. What came before, during, or after is largely evaded. But even in these records, like in the secondary literature, the story emerges of the quilombo as an organized nucleus that develops internal social relations, as well as economic and social relations with neighboring regions. Obviously, a large part of the literature is concerned with raids, physical attacks, the burning of plantations, cattle rustling, etc., that the quilombolas undertook in the areas around the quilombos. But there are other references from neighbors of quilombo, stating that there are fields there where a variety of products are cultivated, which are exchanged for neighbors' products, including from plantations; in the quilombo domestic animals are reared and tools are made (means of production) to produce products that enable economic relations with their neighbors.

We can see, therefore, that established in a geographic space, presumably in the woods, the quilombo begins to organize its internal social structure as autonomous and articulated with the world outside. Between one attack and the next by the official forces of repression, it maintains itself, either in its withdrawal, or its own reproduction. We will call this moment the *quilombola peace*, for the productive character that the quilombo assumed as a nucleus of free men, though liable to enslavement. Both for its duration and its expansion across Brazilian geographical space, we can see that quilombo is an extended Brazilian historical moment. We can see this thanks, not least, to the space of time that I am calling "peace," which rarely appears in the existing literature. I believe that if black Brazilian people had been able to leave a written record, we would certainly have more sources for quilombola "peace" than war. This peace is precisely at the interstices of the quilombola organization. We need a more concerted interpretative effort to approach it. It surpasses the vision of quilombo as the history of attacks by official forces of repression against some other organization. Perhaps "peace" threatened the slavocratic regime more than war did. We need to understand the before and after of the war of the quilombos. The stronghold of free men, relating with other men, free or not, in Brazilian society, merits the effort of interpretation that I would like to undertake: the ties of solidarity with the small landowner, for example; the involvement of plantation owners who helped shelter people; and the relations between black people and non-black people within the quilombo. Edison Carneiro speaks of some "black settlers" who were white men who raised their cattle in the area of the Quilombo dos Palmares and were friendly with the quilombolas. Finally, the black State that was, for a long while at least, victorious.

It is well known and well documented that the quilombo was often based on enslaved labor. These enslaved people, according to the historians, were brought to the settlement against their will. Beyond this, we should ask what systems of production the economy of the quilombo was based on. In my view, the recourse to enslaved labor is much more a reproduction of forms people were exposed to in the colonial regime than a reinstantiation of African social organizations. Or rather, the "ruling class" of the quilombo recruited labor power according to patterns recognized at the time, and not, as some historians want to believe, through deliberately trying to reproduce analogous conditions to those that existed in the African systems they came from. Though the latter hypothesis cannot be totally ruled out, I believe that colonial society was much more influential in the establishment of the quilombola labor system.

We can approach the relations between sexes in the quilombo in a similar way. Edison Carneiro and Nina Rodrigues write that the first wife of Zumbi (Zambi) was white, and that the rest, in order of importance and leadership from the highest to the lowest, were *mulattas* and black, respectively. We can see that hierarchies based on race or on skin color reflected the colonial model of society, which influenced the internal structure of the quilombo more than the African origin of its members.

It is important to study the presence of other races, including white people, but above all Indigenous people. I want to observe and clarify the significance of this phenomenon and its implications for the success of the structure of the quilombo as a group aimed at the cultural and racial resistance of black people. In what ways does the integration of other people who were oppressed within colonial society help, or frustrate, the quilombo project?

Based on these different approaches, it seems possible to find in the structure of quilombo the model of the racial relations that have always existed in Brazil and that, in my view, endure after the Abolition of Slavery. Though the quilombo as a group subject to repression appears only to exist during the slavocratic system of production, it cannot have simply disappeared as an organization in which various social groups were involved, just because the slavocratic regime died out. It seems that it endured as much as a model as a part of the social structure. It absorbed new elements that appeared with the dismantling of enslaved labor. That is, it absorbed formerly enslaved people, as well as people from other racial groups who in some way remained outside the restructuring of the dominant economy. It is true that after abolition we don't see the quilombo as subject to repression. But if we consider the history of the repression of black people after abolition, perhaps we can identify this new repression with what happened historically to the quilombo. We propose that while the quilombo officially came to an end with Abolition, no longer had the same name, and did not suffer the same type of repression, it persisted as a resource for resistance and confrontation with official, established society. Black people and others continue to be oppressed in favelas and in the urban peripheries, thanks to the marginalization of labor and racial marginalization. Quilombo, transformed, endures. One proof is that in Rio de Janeiro the geographical areas of former quilombos, such as Catumbi (one of the largest), Lebron, Corcovado, and others, have transformed into favelas. They survive, though physically transformed, into our own time. At the beginning of the century, in the first decades in particular, the repression of *capoeira*, and black people who maintained their cultural, festive, and religious customs, was as forceful as the repression of quilombo in the previous century. This repression took the most complex and varied forms.

We have laid out the principal points that we want to clarify about quilombo. We are seeking a paradigm for Brazilian racial relations. These relations have been insufficiently studied, precisely because quilombo has been relegated to a secondary level and understood as a source of rebellion and insurrection. But this is the exception in the life of quilombo. Its key features are those that we have tried to account for in a straightforward way, which can be placed in the time referred to here as the "quilombola peace." Although it may coincide with war, it is within the "quilombola peace" that this model of social structure persists in the history of Brazil and the history of black people in Brazil.

Notes

The original title of this text is "'Quilombos'—Mudança Social ou Conservantismo?" Unpublished, February 6, 1976, Fundo MBN, 23.4.5. There are different versions of this text in Beatriz Nascimento's archive. This 1976 text is based on the original typed and hand-edited document at the location cited.

1. Expeditions to capture and recapture Indigenous people and escaped formerly enslaved people. These raids were largely carried out by the archetypal figures of Brazilian inland expansionism, the *bandeirantes* (literally *flag bearers*). Mostly based in the state of São Paulo, bandeirantes were adventurers and colonialists who violently expanded white domination across the South American continent, and were also key to expanding the mineral frontier in central and southern Brazil.

Alternative Social Systems Organized by Black People: From Quilombos to Favelas (a)

THIS PROPOSAL aims to establish a line of historical continuity between quilombos as a form of resistance organized by black people during the centuries of slavocracy, and their contemporary existence as a form of resistance today.

The importance of "quilombos" for black people today can be explained by their historical emergence within a symbolic universe in which their liberatory character was an ideological driving force in the racial and cultural affirmation of black people.

However, there are gaps in the analysis of the quilombo in Brazilian historiography as a whole. This gap in our understanding of black people in Brazil, and of Brazil itself, provokes a rupture with their past for black people. This aggravates a lack of understanding about their contemporary situation.

Thanks to the lack of deep research to orient them, educational texts reproduce a vision of quilombo based on prejudiced concepts from outdated books on the subject. In the historical literature, the importance given to quilombos is determined by the extent of their involvement in events of major significance for official historiography. Two examples of this are the quilombo of Palmares, which was a backdrop to the Dutch invasion of Brazil (in the seventeenth century), and the quilombo of Cosme, which played the same role in the episode of the Balaiada in Maranhão[1] (in the first half of the nineteenth century).

Alongside limited descriptions of the authorities' repression, we find a stereotypical interpretation of how "quilombos" were constituted. These descriptions reinforce the idea that black people are primitive, malign, and irresponsible, and that quilombos were groups with no political character. On the other hand, this literature identifies quilombos as refuges or hideouts of black people in an openly derogatory manner: "The rebel slaves, who did not want to accept their enslavement, fled to the virgin forest, where they formed villages of the type they had left behind in Africa. They chose chiefs and 'lived in a more or less primitive way.' These settlements . . . , in the 17th century, were called quilombos."[2] Yet the black people who made up the "quilombos" were from different ethnic groups and different geographical origins in Africa, and in many cases they included *crioulos* (black people born in Brazil). So perhaps they were not as primitive as all that, and nor, perhaps, did they hold on to the idea of those villages "left behind in Africa." Furthermore, throughout the whole period of slavocracy quilombos did not correspond to the type of organization found in the seventeenth century.

The specialized secondary literature is limited and dominated by a descriptive form of analysis. It refers, mainly, to the quilombos of Palmares. It generalizes the concept of "quilombo" based on the large semistates of the seventeenth century. Beginning from there, Edison Carneiro, for example, established a hierarchical scale to name three principal moments in the reaction of black people to slavery: "a) organized revolt aimed at taking power, for instance in the risings of the black *malês* (Muslims), in Bahia, between 1807 and 1835; b) armed insurrection— especially in the case of Manuel Balaio (1839) in Maranhão; and c) flight to the forest, from which resulted quilombos, best exemplified in Palmares."[3] Similarly, again based on studies of Palmares, the secondary literature sees the general causes for the establishment of "quilombos" as the following: a) rejection by black people of the ill treatment imposed by slavery; b) an innate quest for freedom by primitive man; c) crisis in the economic system and its political implications, reflected in a loosening of control by the slavocratic institutions over the labor force; d) the need for a return to a tribal context, or rather, a reaction to the detribalization caused by the process of the traffic and enslavement of black Africans.

While these overarching analyses of quilombos do have some evidence to underpin them, they cannot get us to a total understanding of the phenomena. Two characteristics can be seen in quilombos: their persistence throughout the slavocratic regime; and their generalized quality.[4] They occurred, if not quite in all the regions of Brazil, then at least in the majority of them, even where the slavocratic regime was less powerful. How are we to explain such a process, historically, if we do not attend to its own dynamics, and to its differentiation across time?

The fact that the secondary literature on the "quilombo" from the early decades of this century repeats these generalizations is, in part, down to the fact that black people, as a subordinated group, were not able to write. The Brazilian educational system has not historically benefited enslaved and formerly enslaved people. It is also down to the inability of the metropolitan and colonial authorities themselves to understand these human formations.

The terms *mocambo* and *quilombo* originate in *quimbundu*. Ignorance of their true meaning on the part of the Portuguese authorities made them into synonyms. Yet, after the wars in the Northeast in the seventeenth century, these authorities' fear of the reemergence of nuclei of black populations free of colonial rule forced them to define the object of their repression. They named as quilombos "all habitations of black fugitives in groups of more than five, even if destitute or lacking buildings, tools or cultivation."[5]

This definition, from the Portuguese Overseas Council on the 2nd of December 1740, has overwhelmingly influenced knowledge of quilombos right to today, notwithstanding that one of the fundamental characteristics of these human groupings were the very size of the settlements: estimates for the populations of "quilombos" in Palmares and Sergipe in the seventeenth century, and in Minas Gerais in the eighteenth century, are in the order of twenty thousand. Another characteristic was the specificity of quilombos' political organization. Palmares, which really was a State, had—during the peace of Ganga-Zumba—diplomatic relations at State-to-State level with the colonial authorities and the crown itself. Production is another important question. The economic activity of quilombos was often of significant scale, and resulted in a surplus that could be sold and exchanged with the inhabitants of the Captaincies and, later, the provinces.[6]

It is important, too, to highlight that in certain places called, vaguely, "quilombos" in the nineteenth century, there were not only so-called escapees but also people who had been freed through manumission or some other process.[7]

This specialized secondary literature is responsible for how these human settlements known as "quilombos" have been interpreted. Based on the oppressor's official documents, studies of "quilombos" always fall into an analysis of the moment when the dominant social order attacked black settlements.

They are, therefore, always analyzed from the perspective of armed conflict against the regime. There are no profound studies of periods of peace, in which society in a general sense, and slave owners in particular, tolerated one another, and economic and consumer relations with the "quilombolas" were maintained.

Interpretations of "quilombos" based on official documentation and on descriptive historiography bring us back to two principles embedded in the training of historians. On the one hand, classical liberalism, emerging from the ideas of the French Revolution, has influenced how authors conduct their interpretations based on principles of equality, without attending to the internal structures of quilombos, which maintained social inequalities within themselves, albeit not identical to the inequalities of a modern system. On the other hand, some authors are more explicit: based on Marxist-Leninist principles of social change, and on the basis of the intensification of armed struggle against the oppressive order, they search in the "quilombos" for embryonic revolution. They even interpret the motives for establishing the "quilombo" from this perspective.

It is undeniable that part of the character of black "quilombolas" emerged from a reaction to the slavocratic regime, the system that dominated all the productive activity of Brazilian society at that time. Freedom was one of the things enslaved people sought in "quilombos." But we have to understand another long-lasting historical dynamic of the "quilombos," by seeing the complexity of their institutions and the evolution of society as a whole as interacting processes. In this way we can understand their particularity as autonomous social systems in relation to society as a whole. The existing historiography contents itself merely with remarking on the capacity for struggle and resistance of black people involved in these systems and, by extension, the resistance of black people in general, across time. Hence the generalization of the term "quilombo" to come to indicate various manifestations of resistance. This mode of generalization is permeated by the ideological posture of the researchers themselves. So we have to ask: thought of as a form of black people's resistance to the regime of oppression, does the quilombo constitute an effective instrument for confronting the social order, with the capacity to change it in their favor? If not, it cannot be understood through an interpretation based on theories of social change.

We cannot analyze "quilombos" using the socialist interpretative framework developed for so-called modern social movements in Western Europe since the eighteenth century. Even less can we use a framework drawn from analysis of workers and socialist movements of the twentieth century. "Quilombos" are internal to the dynamics of Brazilian colonial society, and the subsequent pre-capitalist and pre-industrialist society of the nineteenth century. They can therefore be bracketed with so-called "archaic," or "primitive" social movements. Interpretations connected to theories of social change, notably Marxist theories, sound somewhat exotic in this context. They are removed from the reality that Edison Carneiro identifies: that quilombos are a negative reaction of flight and defense—unlike the movements to "take power" of the black malês of Bahia.[8]

In the twentieth century, the absence of insurrectionary black movements in Brazil, and the weakness of the rare protest movements, created the idea that black Brazilians have a docile spirit. The tradition of social movements in previous centuries seems to support this assertion. Some say that the rebellious and politically conscious black person disappeared along with the quilombos after the abolition of enslaved labor.

Meanwhile, social inequalities based on ethnic differences have intensified during this century.

If we are to understand the quilombos' apparent disappearance from the history of Brazil after the end of the nineteenth century, as well as how it has influenced, and survived in, the history of black people in the twentieth century, we have to understand its trajectory and historical meaning as an alternative social system.

The existence of populations constituting "quilombos" today, in territories laid out in previous centuries, raises the question of quilombos' physical continuity. We can find, in nineteenth-century correspondence between the chief of police of Rio de Janeiro and the Ministry of Justice and Internal Trade, various territories referred to as "quilombos" that are now favelas or ex-favelas with large black populations (with low disposable incomes), and populations of other ethnic origins with the same background and class position.[9] This population composition is very similar to that of former quilombos. The same situation pertains in Bahia, Minas Gerais, Pernambuco, and São Paulo, not only in urban areas but also in the decaying rural economy. There, black people retain two defining characteristics of quilombos: isolation from wider society and forms of production characteristic of "quilombos" prior to abolition.

The historical transformation of these settlements owes a great deal to the fall of the slavocratic system. With the domination of the modern economy and social system of the twentieth century, they acquired new relations with society as a whole. But we can find a line of continuity up to today in terms of their "pre-political" character of racial and cultural resistance, and, up to a certain point, in terms of their autonomy in periods of "peace."

The line of continuity to be established therefore discards the conceptualization of the quilombo as an insurrectionary project and contestation of the social order, while retaining the sense of it as a social system based on self-defense and resistance as a political form. Eric Hobsbawm shows how subordinated groups act within a modern social system: within their respective archaic social movements they manifest either a process of adaptation, or a failure to adapt, to the societies to which they coercively belong. However, these movements evolve historically; they belong to the world that oppresses them; they understand the principally repressive institutions of the modern societies with which they are involved. Their historical evolution is characterized by two phases: one, in which the subordinated groups' own institutions enable an autonomy in relation to the dominant society; another, when these same institutions no longer represent an efficient form of defense against the external world. Hobsbawm writes: "The ties of kinship or tribal solidarity that, combined or not with territorial connections, are the key to what today . . . are considered primitive societies, persist. However . . . they cannot constitute an effective defense of the human against the caprices of the social environment."[10] The first historical phase can be identified with social systems that were in the past generically called quilombos. Those favelas and areas of economic decline with large contingents of black people, which are on the sites of former quilombos, can be identified with the later phase of archaic social movements.

Further to the above, the following hypotheses guide the research:

1. What have come to be known in the historiographical literature as quilombos were archaic social movements in reaction to the slavocratic regime. Their particularity lay in establishing various kinds of social systems with communitarian bases.
2. Though encompassed by the single concept of the quilombo, this variety of social systems emerged out of institutional differences.
3. The greater or lesser success of social systems known as quilombos can be attributed to the strength of the dominant social system and its evolution through time.
4. The historical territorial areas of quilombos produce a physical and spatial continuity that preserves and/or attracts black populations in the twentieth century.
5. Certain institutional characteristics of archaic social movements are found in these territories. This suggests a line of historical continuity between the social systems organized by black quilombolas and social settlements in urban favelas, as well as in areas of decaying rural economies with significant black populations and other ethnic groups with low disposable income.

Nature of the Sources

1. Primary sources: Official documentation; reports from residents of the provinces; correspondence between legal representatives and the Ministry of Justice and Internal Trade; legal acts; newspapers. These sources are found in the National Archive, state archives, municipal archives, the National Library and specialized libraries, and the National Museum of History.
2. Secondary sources: National, international, specialized, and general secondary literature on the history of Brazil, social movements, and the history and sociology of black people.
3. Field research based on participant observation and interviews in areas of former quilombos.

Methodology

The methodology to be employed:

1. Documentary analysis and historical critique;
2. Ethnography and oral history fieldwork.

Notes

The original title of this text is "Sistemas sociais alternativas organizados pelos negros: dos quilombos às favelas." Unpublished, 1981, Fundo MBN, 13.1. This is the introduction to a research project of the same name funded by Casa do Brasil Léopold Sédar Senghor Foundation and the Ford Foundation. It is a project proposal, undertaken before the research was completed.

1. The Balaiada was an uprising in the state of Maranhão between 1838 and 1841. Many escaped, formerly enslaved people fought against the conservative regime. The revolt was put down violently by 1841.

2. Vicente Tapajós, *Manual de história do Brasil* (Primeiro Grau, Rio de Janeiro: Elos, 1970).

3. Edison Carneiro, *O Quilombo dos Palmares* (Rio de Janeiro: Civilização Brasileira, 1958 [1947]), 31.

4. Clóvis Moura, *Rebeliões da senzala* (São Paulo: Zumbi, 1959), 79.

5. Pedro Tomás Pedreira, *Os quilombos brasileiros* (Salvador: SMEC; Departamento de Cultura, 1973), 7.

6. Captaincies were the Portuguese imperial administrative divisions for governing Brazil. They were large, hereditary land grants from the crown.

7. Eric Hobsbawm, *Rebeldes Primitivos: Estudo sobre as formas arcaicas dos movimentos sociais dos séculos XIX e XX* (Rio de Janeiro: Zahar, 1970), 14.

8. Edison Carneiro, *O Quilombo dos Palmares*, 2nd ed. (São Paulo: Companhia Editora Nacional, 1966 [1947]), 3.

9. Arquivo Nacional (Rio de Janeiro), correspondence between the chief of policy and the ministry of justice, 1808–1835.

10. Hobsbawm, *Rebeldes Primitivos*, 14.

Alternative Social Systems Organized by Black People: From Quilombos to Favelas (b)

To the André Rebouças Working Group
To my sister Rosa V. Nascimento
To my teachers and advisors.
For
Francisco Xavier do Nascimento, and for
Prof. Dr. José Honório Rodrigues
I have relied on the help of the following friends and research
   assistants
Marlene de Oliveira Cunha
Laura Ramos Bezerra
Roberto Serfaty Rosemberg
Luis Antonio Vieira de Castro
Álvaro Pianno
Josef Waldemar Rösner
My thanks to the Ford Foundation and the Brazil House of the
   Léopold Sédar Senghor Foundation

As we begin the final stage of this work, we need, first, to evaluate our progress and clarify the concepts laid out in the initial plan for the project. Second, we want to reduce the five hypotheses previously laid out to a single principal hypothesis. We need to do so in line with the collection of material, the progress of the research, our analysis of the secondary literature, and the fieldwork. The interaction between theory and data has naturally led us to re-evaluate our hypotheses. Indeed, some of the premises of the project have in fact been totally abandoned.

Another key point is the connection between the quilombos already discussed (which we have named as social movements of formerly enslaved people) and the quilombos visited for the fieldwork, notably Carmo da Mata.

This evaluation and clarification of concepts must begin with the title "Alternative Social Systems Organized by Black People: From Quilombos to Favelas." This choice of title suggested that there were noteworthy differences between the various social movements that had been broadly referred to as quilombos. In outlining the project, we made five explicit hypotheses. However, the category of "social system," the reference point from which we began, came to serve, up to a point, as an a priori notion, because not all quilombos had the necessary elements to become social systems. Therefore, the new concept, proposed as the title of the work, came in practical terms to be part of the question analyzed by the project itself, in relation to how the concept of the quilombo was generalized.

On this basis we will establish a typology of quilombos between the seventeenth and nineteenth centuries. This will include those named in official documentation and in secondary sources, and will enable us both to make the concept of quilombo as objective as possible, and to redefine it, with hindsight, through the concept of the "social system."

Another clarification is needed, in relation to the path that the research itself took. When we submitted the project to the Social Science Committee of the Ford Foundation, the second part of the project on favelas was not approved. Only the initial part remained, covering the work on hypotheses around the persistence of black populations in decaying rural areas where quilombos had existed in the past. It would, therefore, be more accurate to change the project's title to: "Alternative Social Systems Organized by Black People: Historical Quilombos and Their Continuity."

To clarify this further, we can restate one of the project's hypotheses. The second hypothesis suggested that "there were institutional differences among historical quilombos." In the project we critiqued primary and secondary documents over the generalized use of the concept of quilombo. We noted:

> A report of the Overseas Council, dated the 2nd of December 1740, defined the *quilombo* or *mocambo* as follows: "all habitations of black fugitives in groups of more than five, even if destitute or lacking buildings, tools, or cultivation."

And:

> The entry in the Dicionário da Língua Portuguesa by Aurélio Buarque de Holanda Ferreira (Editora Nova Fronteira, p.1173) states: *Quilombos*, from *quimbundo*, capital, settlement, union. Masc. Noun. Brazilian: Shelter of escaped slaves.

We should take into account that both the report of the Portuguese Overseas Council, and this entry in the most complete Portuguese dictionary available give us a simplifying, stereotyped, and contradictory vision of the concept of quilombo. For example, we can see that in a single entry the term has a double meaning: one, vulgate (from the people) that was consecrated by official historiography and by common sense—Brazilian: Shelter of escaped slaves; and another, that tries to approximate its original meaning—*quimbundo*: capital, settlement, union.

The definition by the Portuguese Overseas Council dates from a period in which the proliferation of quilombos fundamentally threatened the colonial economy. The year 1740, in the Pombaline Era, marks an important moment in the General History of Colonial Brazil. Between 1694 and 1750, Brazilian quilombos were one of the biggest problems that the colonial and metropolitan authorities faced. Between these dates the largest quilombos in the colony were created: with the fall of

Palmares, the quilombos of Papa-méis, Camoanga, and Sergipe emerged, and, in 1750, the quilombo of Comarca do Rio das Mortes was destroyed. That quilombo was also known as "Quilombo Grande," not only because of its territorial proportions, but above all because it controlled the mining and economic frontier between the captaincies of Minas Gerais and Goiás.

The way in which the concept of quilombo was fixed in legislation in Brazilian captaincies, through the Portuguese Overseas Council, demonstrates above all that quilombos, or, more accurately, black people—whether enslaved, escaped, or free—constituted a concrete danger to the maintenance of control over the Colony by metropolitan interests.

The metropolitan and colonial authorities dealt with quilombos in a different way to how they dealt with the various African ethnic groups who came here enslaved. The latter they divided, in order to govern them. The quilombos, on the contrary, they gathered together under a single category in order to repress them more effectively, and to protect themselves from danger. To clarify further: a group of five black individuals cannot mean the same thing as the twenty thousand individuals[1] who, in the eighteenth century, controlled a key mining area.

The historiographical tradition, and common sense, has only served to repeat what was established in that remote moment. Our first task in this study is to better explain the concept of quilombo in accordance with its distinctiveness in particular historical moments, and with its regional specificities. Yet, we do not want to undertake only a descriptive study. Our interest goes further than this: to remove from the concept the marque that has crystallized on it through an aprioristic vision (as a moment, or, better, as episodic, spontaneous, and autonomous events separated from the general politics of the dominant forces of colonization in the Empire of Brazil). The quilombo, for us, is not a subordinated fact, but a *continuous* process in the total History of the country.

This task returns us to historical method itself. How can we explain this process of continuity in the past, and its projection in the present? Let us say that in the first phase we will take a critical look at the facts written into the History of Brazil. Strangely, certain ethnic groups who participated in that history are ignored.

We will then look at the Antônio Conselheiro movement and its insertion in the general movement of History at that time: the Abolition of captivity and the fall of the Old Regime, in 1888 and 1889 respectively.

How the research itself has developed influences how we will proceed here. We will necessarily have to use secondary sources, including the national literature, to understand quilombos. Or rather, to understand, in the first place, what has come to be called the History of the Losers, the history, we might say, of those who do not *write* History, but confect it, dialectically, with other segments of society, including the so-called dominant segment.[2]

We will then put the Antônio Conselheiro movement in the broader context of the history of his followers.

Notes

The original title of this text is "Sistemas sociais alternativas organizados pelos negros: dos quilombos às favelas (b)." Unpublished, 1981, Fundo MBN, 21.1. This is an introduction to the version of Nascimento's thesis held in Box 21, Folder 1 of the Arquivo Nacional. This text and the three that follow ("The Antônio Conselheiro Movement and Abolitionism: A Vision of Regional History," "Post-revolutionary Angolan Nativism," and "Kilombo and Community Memory: A Case Study") constitute Nascimento's thesis gathered together under the title "Alternative Social Systems Organized by Black People: From Quilombos to Favelas."

1. The best estimate for the population of Quilombo Grande.

2. The final section of this text in the archive is handwritten and unfinished.

The Antônio Conselheiro Movement and Abolitionism: A Vision of Regional History

THE HISTORY of subordinated groups is always told as a kind of exotic event, a sub-history beneath official history. These events, though, seen from the perspective of other disciplines such as sociology and anthropology, can be included in the category of social movements. History does not analyze them according to their synchronic and diachronic variables. The vision of official history is that these are atemporal facts that have no continuity within the space of a particular historical structure.

Official history, written from the perspective of the victors, is based on sources and documents collected when the institutions of the State were repressing these social movements. In general terms, these sources are made up of correspondence between members of the dominant classes, reports by local civic and religious authorities, and reports of military expeditions. Other sources, therefore, such as oral sources—even if they do exist—and documents of the oppressed themselves, are not used to write this history. Subordinated groups in Brazil have their own incomplete and badly interpreted history. It lacks a perspective that matches their true experience of life.

In the case of the Conselheiristo movement, the events of the repression and extermination of the settlement of Canudos were inscribed in the history of Brazil. Yet, history excluded them from the historical movements and dynamics of the socioeconomic, political, and ideological structure of the country. They were always seen as isolated facts that merely mobilized the center's repression or functioned as a reaction to something "bigger": the proclamation of the Republic. Canudos is studied as the sudden reaction of fanatics and bandits, a reaction that halted in 1897. It is treated as an appendix to victorious republicanism and juridical-political rupture in the administrative system of the country. The Conselheiro movement is disconnected from the temporal dynamics and structural and conjunctural conditions of the region where it erupted.

The present study is a modest attempt to analyze the Conselheiro movement within its broader space, as a set of historical events in a particular region of the country, and in interaction with the total history of Brazil.

We will use the terms "Conselheiristo movement," or "the movement of Antônio Conselheiro," rather than "War of Canudos" (as it is traditionally referred to in the history of Brazil). This is to deepen the synchronic and diachronic dimensions of the study, which aims at inserting the movement into the history of Brazil.

In line with this, we will begin by situating ourselves a little earlier in time. We will accompany Conselheiro from 1874, when he is in Jeremoabo, considering in historical terms what was unfolding in that region (the Northeast), and its articulations with the other regions of the country, with centralized power, and with political projects emerging from the centers of decision-making. We will, therefore, situate this study between 1850–1888, the period of the abolition of slavery. This is to draw out the connections between Conselheiro's movement and this crucial period of social change. We aim to articulate his movement with others that took the form of quilombos, the flight of formerly enslaved people, seasonal migration (the drought of 1877), and the final abolition of captivity.

Brazil: The Project of the Nation State

The internal differences and regional inequalities that characterized the Portuguese colony installed on this side of America still create a sort of blockage in terms of our economic, social, and political formation.

When approaching this question, traditional historiography always deals in terms of so-called cycles of economic development. Thus, we are still accustomed to seeing Brazil through instances of the economic hegemony of one region over another. The Northeast imposed itself on the other regions during the sugar, cotton, and cocoa cycles. The Southeast, in the mineral cycle, imposed itself for a period on the Northeast. Finally, the Southeast imposed itself on the North, the Northeast and other regions during the coffee cycle. Currently, with the development of the industrial sector in the Southeast and the South, these two regions are imposing themselves on the others, in a hegemony that has lasted more than a century.

These differences and inequalities always provoke attempts at solutions at juridical-political and ideological levels, seeking a unity that has always been difficult to establish.

For nearly a century leading up to the proclamation of the Republic, ever since the transposition of the administration of the Portuguese Empire to Brazil (1808), a project for the formation of a nation state in the model of European nation States had been laid out by the dominant classes. This project was not attentive to regional differences. It sought, in very aggressive ways (forced adhesion to independence), and through the hegemony of one region over the others, to unite the regions of the Brazil in a single State.

For most of the nineteenth century through campaigns and counter-campaigns, this political project of strengthening the state apparatus led to alternating moments of national unity (centralization) and regional autonomism (federalism). From the *Segundo Reinado*[1] onward, the process of the formation of the State in Brazil is characterized by its basis in the interests of the dominant classes of the Southeast, to the detriment of elements of the same classes in other regions, such as the Northeast.

Between 1840 and 1870—corresponding at the juridical-political level to the consolidation of the unitary monarchy and to centralism over autonomism (international Law of 1840, restricting the Additional Act of 1834)—the system of coffee slavery was dominant. Today we can see that the notion of decadence, notably in relation to the sugar- and cotton-based Northeast, was really more a vision of a proprietary class trapped by an agro-exporting outlook, than it was directly a decline. What seems to have happened is that transformations in the international market led to a transfer of the dominant pole. According to Manoel Maurício de Albuquerque, certain sectors of the slavocratic class of the Northeast continued to be influential. In spite of the economic crisis in their region they were able to adjust their productive activity within the transition that was taking place in capitalism. A typical example would be the transformation of the traditional manufacturing mill into a centralized mill and then into a factory. At the juridical-political level various slavocratic sectors moved into the structures of power. While the Southeast was riven by competition and division between different areas of coffee exploitation (for example, they were timid when it came to abolitionist proposals), the other regions, principally the Northeast, but others too, who were previously slavocratic, opted for abolitionism.[2]

This framework of different conjunctures across Brazilian regions can, in our opinion, explain social movements that, in the final instance, were in opposition to this state of things. The movement of Antônio Conselheiro was the most significant of the epoch. It emerged in a much larger framework in which pillaging, migration and other forms of opposition also occurred:

> The first and probably the most important source of bandits is in those forms of rural economy or rural environment which have relatively small labor demands, or which are too poor to employ all their able-bodied men; in other words, in the rural surplus population. Pastoral economies and areas of mountain and poor soil, which often go together, provide a permanent surplus of this kind, which tends to develop its own institutionalized outlets in traditional societies: seasonal emigration . . . raiding or banditry.[3]

Between 1850 and 1880 the production of coffee continued to reproduce labor based on slavery. But the agro-exporting regions it incorporated did not have the means to maintain enslaved people in the same situation as before (the emergence of the centralized mill and of the factory was an adjustment of productive activity in the Northeastern provinces). The factories freed up enslaved labor, which was then sold to the provinces of the Southeast, which was dependent on the external market and maintained a conjunctural supremacy though without being able to pursue activities other than agro-exportation in the form of coffee.

Meanwhile, the problem of the concentration of lands in the Northeast, alongside new relations of production, led to the dislocation of impoverished populations, creating a potentially changing scenario: "Socially, [banditry] seems to occur in all types of human society [which are in . . .] transition to agrarian capitalism [. . . and] for even more obvious reasons [as the effect of] landlessness."[4]

In the backlands of the Northeast, the concentration of lands had become fraught. The centralized mill and factory emerged as more advanced capitalist forms of production than the traditional activity of the old *engenho* mill, known as the *banguê*. The Baron of Jeremoabo and some of the other major landowners in the region, owned a large part of the municipality of the same name. Canudos, where Conselheiro would later settle with his people in 1854, was the only cattle ranch owned by the Baroness of São Francisco.[5] The problem of land continued to be an essential factor in the emergence of these types of social movements until the first decades of the twentieth century. From the socioeconomic and politico-institutional perspectives the problem of land was a constant risk for the decision-making forces of the hegemonic center and the interests of the dominant classes of the Southeast with their project of creating a centralized nation State.

The Beginning of the Process of Abolition: The End of the African Slave Trade

The year 1850 marked the end of the African slave trade in Brazil. This came about more through English pressure—and the increase in the price of enslaved people caused by policing—than because of the attitude of the dominant classes in Brazil toward removing enslaved labor from production.

One of the main problems that Brazilian agriculture has always confronted is the scarcity of labor. The end of the international trade was only one of the causes of this scarcity in the second half of the nineteenth century. The most important was the reduction in the rate of growth of the enslaved population, alongside a rising rate of mortality. As we indicated above, before this the solution to the problem was the movement of enslaved populations from the North and the Northeast to the coffee-growing Southeast, where labor was most needed.

The Interprovincial Traffic within the Origins of Social Movements in the Northeast in the Second Half of the Nineteenth Century

According to José Calasans, in his pamphlet *Antônio Conselheiro and Slavery* [*Antônio Conselheiro e o escravidão*], the problem of servitude was entirely ignored by Euclides da Cunha in his essay on the war of Canudos. Calasans asks: "Could the historic episode of Belo Monte . . . have occurred without the participation of formerly enslaved people, or men who achieved their liberty shortly before the great migration to the Northeast? [Was Conselheiro not] the bearer of a message about slavery and the monarchy, the two great problems of his time?"[6] Starting from this we will sketch out an analysis that can respond to these questions, and use the first part as the basis for an extended exegesis.

1. The first explanation refers to the moment when formerly enslaved people participated in the Antônio Conselheiro movement. When we analyze demographic data from the General Census of Brazil of 1872, we find that in the 11 municipalities of Bahia where, from 1874, Antônio Conselheiro recruited his followers, there was a population of 102,789 free black and *pardo* people to 36,118 white people. That means around 60 percent of men and women were either black, or pardo, with their ties to slavery severed. On the other hand, the enslaved population of these same municipalities was approximately 17,000 black and pardo

men and women. This gives us a vision of a majority black population that was as much free as it was enslaved.

In the period in which Conselheiro began his journey from Ceará to the interior of the states of Sergipe and Bahia, the Northeast yielded enslaved populations to the Southeast through the interprovincial traffic.

The forced migration of enslaved Brazilians that followed the suppression of the African slave trade began with the plantations, estates and cities of the North, and this movement went from 1851 to its virtual abolition by provincial legislatures in 1881 . . .

The Northeastern provinces sold free-born *ingenuos* (enslaved people who benefited from the Law of the Free Womb) whose plantation owners had fallen into poverty or who had changed their productive activities. . . . This trade in brutality and suffering was similar to the African trade . . .

The enslaved people came in chains, often overland, from the backlands of Pernambuco, Paraíba, Bahia and Minas Gerais to be sold in Rio de Janeiro and in São Paulo. There are indications that many of these unfortunate people tried and succeeded to escape on the way. Nineteenth-century newspapers from Bahia tell us that domestic enslaved people lived in a state of constant terror of being sold to plantations in the south.

The compensation offered for the return of escaped enslaved people in 1878 and 1879, in newspapers in Ceará indicates that prices in the interprovincial slave trade were higher than the economic conditions in Ceará could sustain.[7]

It is well known that freed black people, Indigenous people, and *caboclos* were not spared during these movements of populations from one province to another in the period of slavery. We can also infer that free populations, even white ones, were not able to find work even in the contractual labor market, which in any case was not much different from the slavocratic regime.

The reference in the citations above to those who escaped during the interprovincial trade offers a hypothesis, which is not completely unfounded, that this trade, as much as the concentration of land, led to an excess of free and enslaved labor looking for alternative means of survival. On the one hand, this excess of labor, fearing re-enslavement (given that in some provinces the ties of slavery had loosened), abandoned their homes and wandered into the backlands. On the other hand, impoverished free populations—even small landowners who were unable to find profitable occupations—also sought alternatives in different places where they might be better able to survive. Many of these struggling landowners abandoned their old properties along with their slaves.

This transformation of the Northeastern economy led to a form of social disorganization and marginalization of these populations, and a climate rich with the potential for social conflict.

We have already shown that social movements like Antônio Conselheiro's found fertile terrain to develop in these conditions. Conselheiro himself, though he was not originally from the strata of society which felt the pressures described above, could not escape becoming a reflection of the chaotic situation in which people from various classes of the Northeast of Brazil found themselves. A significant feature of Antônio Conselheiro's involvement with the problems of these populations was the allusion that he made, through his clothing, to the notion of pilgrimage. He wore a sweater made of "azulão," apparently a kind of American denim that was used to wrap bales. Conrad, citing a traveler who observed enslaved people arriving from the Northeast to be sold in Valongo, writes that:

> The enslaved were all dressed in blue cotton. . . . These enslaved people were generally put on ships in Ceará. That province was the principal embarkation point of the interprovincial slave trade.
>
> In 1880, Ceará was an emporium for the Northeast slave trade. It was a province in which free labor had existed since 1845. . . . In 1883, it was a refuge for those who escaped neighboring provinces. Complaints against those who protected fugitives (*cupins*) came from Pernambuco, Piauí and Rio Grande do Norte.[8]

The fact that Antônio Conselheiro came from the province of Ceará is another very significant point. That province was the main source not only of the movement of enslaved populations, but also the movement of free, impoverished people. The effects of this traffic in the provinces of the Northeast made the regrowth of quilombos possible.

The formation and establishment of quilombos has been a phenomenon throughout the history of Brazil, and across its whole geographical space.

The general causes for the establishment of quilombos considered by scholars are: a) rejection of the maltreatment of slavery; b) crisis in the economic system and its political implications, reflected in the loosening of control exercised by the slavocratic institutions over the labor force.

The period studied here offers a good example of these two causes in action. However, running contrary to this, at the same time as there was a loosening in relation to the labor force, there was also a pressure on populations in terms of re-enslavement. These phenomena, working simultaneously, provoked individuals to react, and to seek alternative means of economic, political, and social survival. In that moment in the history of the Northeast, quilombos proliferated above all in the backlands of Pernambuco, Bahia, Alagoas, and Sergipe.

Manuel Benício, cited by Calasans, justifying the fact that the only reform of the institutions that Antônio Conselheiro accepted was slavery, suggested: "Perhaps because a large part of the quilombos and *macumbeiros* [the correct term should be *mocambeiros*, from *Mocambos*, which is the same as quilombos] joined his errant crusade."

Manuel Benício does not say from what point these quilombolas and mocambeiros joined the Conselheiristo movement. In a general way, the secondary literature allows us to understand the eve of Abolition. But Conselheiro began his activities at the beginning of the 1870s, and already at that time, the social problems caused by the interprovincial slave trade were felt in a blunt way by the black and *preto* population of the Northeast. We can hypothesize that groups of fugitives or free black people who had joined quilombos already accompanied Conselheiro when he was based in Geremoabo and Mocambo, what is today Olindina.

Based on documents in the Public Archive of Salvador, Pedro Tomás Pedreira names Geremoabo and Monte Santo as quilombos in Bahia.

However, we cannot identify the date of either the inauguration or destruction of either of these places.

José Aras tells us that Canudos was, at the beginning, a "redoubt of outlaws": "Formerly enslaved outlaws from the factories of Sergipe and Alagoas (Palmares) came up by the channel of the Rio Tapiranga (Irapirange was the former name of Vaza-Barris) to find refuge in Canudos."[9] These people threw themselves into being blacksmiths and carpenters and "when people living in the area needed weapons, they went to Canudos, and so did people looking for revenge."

The general idea that the population of quilombos was made up of villains and avengers can be understood through this quotation from Hobsbawm: "Otherwise social banditry is universally found wherever societies are based on agriculture (including pastoral economies), and consist largely of peasants and landless labourers ruled, oppressed and exploited by someone else."[10] Through what has already been explained we can see how in the Brazilian Northeast there were fertile historical conditions not only for quilombo-style movements, but also for political movements like that of Antônio Conselheiro. That movement intensified after the Abolition of Slavery. It is at that point that we need to add to our analytical framework the millions of unemployed, formerly enslaved people who had previously been legally maintained by their masters.

2. The second explanation for the question we are analyzing here emerges from establishing the crucial moment at which the so-called "great Northeast migration" took place. The drought of 1877, which took place during the period when the interprovincial traffic was still legal, dislocated people from the affected provinces. There was, indeed, a significant expansion of the slave trade thanks to the drought:

> Prices fell drastically in the North, especially in the impoverished province of Ceará, and the slave owners ... accepted anything that they were offered. An indication of the scale of the export of enslaved people in Ceará during the drought can be seen by the large tribute that the provincial Governor received in 1879 from the taxes paid on

the enslaved people who were embarked. In that year the province received four times as much in those taxes than it did the year before. This rapid expansion put the equilibrium of the system of slavery in danger."

The equilibrium of the economic system as a whole in Brazil was in profound crisis thanks to regional differences. An example of this is that Ceará and Amazonas abolished the status of servility before the rest of the provinces. Meanwhile, the Southeast had still not completed its immigration project of bringing Europeans to work in the coffee industry, and the Northeast, partially liberated from enslavement and a surplus of free labor, moved ahead, in some areas, with the project of wiping out the slavocratic regime. This put at risk the unitarist, monarchical project, which always sought to find a legal and political balance between regional differences and conflicts and put them in the context of the National State. Added to these factors was the pressure of the mass migration from the rural and urban Northeast caused by the 1877 drought.

Although a large part of these Northeastern populations migrated to the frontiers of rubber expansion in Amazônia, quite a few went to the Southeast. This process of internal immigration ran in parallel to external immigration. It requires further study, in relation to its social and ideological implications at the end of the nineteenth century. External immigration was what the dominant classes most wanted, as much in the Southeast (the region most prominently involved) as in the Northeast. European immigrants were preferred to Northeast immigrants not only to resolve the question of the transformation into free and waged labor, but, more importantly, because there was a consensus among the powerful classes that Europeans were better workers than black or white Brazilians, and their European origins contributed to "civilizing" and "whitening" Brazil.

We know, therefore, that the Northeastern worker was not considered to be the best worker for the plantations in the Southeast, or elsewhere, for fundamentally ideological reasons: a belief in their inertia, inaptitude, and biological inferiority. This abandonment of the immigrant populations of the Northeast in the final instance would destabilize the very meaning of national unity. It can also be considered as a factor in the emergence of Conselheiro. He gathered together suffering people who only found one form of escape: the establishment of a society based on a traditional system. This system was incompatible with the capitalism that part of Brazil—principally the Southeast—was entering into. The ties of solidarity, comradeship, family, and more typical in a non-capitalist, peasant society, were the institutions that these immigrants built up around Conselheiro in the settlement of Canudos. Hence the repression of the movement by the central powers. This repression was launched out of a fear that the Northeast would demand a form of separatism, breaking with the alliance between the dominant political classes in the North and the South. Through this alliance the Abolition of slavery was hurriedly concluded and, soon after, the Republic. The Republic had federalist dimensions and greater regional autonomy, but was not in the end finalized before the repression of movements such as those in Rio Grande do Sul (1893), and, above all, the extermination of Conselheiro and his people.

In terms of the Abolition of slavery, which was enacted only at the legislative level, the process of change outlined here continued in the heart of the dominant classes. In this way the Conselheiro movement intensified, first of all with the expansion of formerly enslaved populations who benefited from the Law of 13th May 1888. These formerly enslaved people were known, in the period, as "the people of 13th May." Letters from the Barão de Geremoaba of 4th March 1897, and José Américo of 28th February 1894 refer to the demographic reinforcement of the movement of Antônio Conselheiro. They call attention to the danger of this phenomenon for the established order.

Conclusion

The silence over the ethnic composition of Conselheiro's followers reflects a stubborn viewpoint in the History of Brazil. In a general sense, this official history seeks to deny the existence of these elements in all social and political movements of the past, with the exception of the revolutions in Bahia at the end of the eighteenth century and the first decades of the nineteenth century, the Balaiada in Maranhão, and the Cabanagem in Pará.[11] With these exceptions, the impression from official history is that black people and Indigenous people did not revolt against the established order. However, it is difficult to accept, in a country in which the majority of the population are non-white and suffer enormous misfortune, that these people would not be present in some way in large-scale social movements.

In this work we have laid out the free and enslaved ethnic composition of the eleven municipalities that fell within the sphere of Antônio Conselheiro. Annexed to this text is a sample of how many black people were living in these areas. The General Census of Brazil in 1872 provides us with data about race, sex, and profession for parishes and municipalities. Among the races we find: whites, pardos, pretos, and caboclos.[12] Among the enslaved people we find pardos and pretos. We have thus put together the four tables in the annex.

From this data we can infer that, for as long as it lasted, the Conselheiristo Movement relied not only on the presence of formerly enslaved people, but also on free pardo and black populations. We can therefore show that the excerpt of Conselheiro's manuscript "Tempestades que se levantem no Coração de Maria" [Rising storms in the heart of Maria], in which he writes about Abolition, emerged, not least, out of his deep contact with these groups.

All the municipalities under his influence had a greater quantity of pardos and pretos than whites or caboclos: Conde, Abadia, Inhambupe, Entre-Rios, Alagoinhas, Itapicuru, Soure, Pombal, Tucano, Monte Santo, and Geremoaba always had a higher proportion of free pardos and pretos and enslaved pretos than other ethnic groups.

This work requires revision and extension in terms of the role of quilombos in the movement of Antônio Conselheiro. In the future we will try to expand it further, with greater scientific rigor.

TABLE 1.1. Population of Enslaved People in Relation to Sex, Civil Status, Race, and Nationality in the Municipalities and Parishes under the Influence of António Conselheiro, 1872

Municipio	Freguesia	Sex		Civil Status						Race				Nationality			
				Men			Women			Men		Women		Men		Women	
		Men	Women	Single	Married	Widow	Single	Married	Widow	Pardo	Preto	Pardo	Preto	Brz	Foreign	Brz	Foreign
Conde	N.S. das Mortes do Itapicuru da Praia	711	466	533	155	23	280	167	19	269	443	192	274	700	11	450	16
Abadia	N.S. da Abadia	363	306	306	246	98	186	95	25	149	214	127	179	344	19	288	18
Inhambupe	Div. Esp. Sta. de Inh	813	646	692	98	23	564	65	17	259	552	227	419	758	55	627	19
	N.S. da Condeição de Apará	674	532	596	69	9	474	48	10	195	479	177	355	647	27	52	6
Entre-Rios	N.S. dos Prazeres	1,335	1,270	1,096	207	32	1,051	191	34	345	990	406	870	1,233	102	1,234	42
Alagoinhas	Jesus N.S. e José da Igreja Nova	121	1,285	1,163	45	4	1,244	38	3	600	612	622	663	1,202	10	1,277	8
	Sr. Deus Menino de Araças	220	203	209	8	3	188	12	3	74	146	70	133	218	2	201	2
	Sto. De Alagoinhas	455	388	399	53	9	316	63	9	175	280	209	179	436	19	363	25
Itapicuru	N.S. de Saúde da Missão	619	533	430	155	34	383	121	29	246	373	220	313	592	27	514	19
	N.S. de Livramento do Barracão	91	81	51	32	8	44	32	5	35	56	41	40	91	—	81	—

TABLE 1.1. (*continued*)

Soure	N.S. da Conceição de Soure	272	113	209	53	10	66	40	7	111	161	45	68	265	7	103	10
Pombal	Sta. Teresa de Pombal	179	131	163	14	2	119	9	3	79	100	63	68	179	—	131	—
	N.S. do Amparo da Ribeira de Pau Grande	190	124	175	13	2	117	6	1	59	131	52	72	190	—	124	—
Tucano	Santana de Tucano	377	393	365	12	—	385	8	—	109	268	124	269	376	1	390	3
Monte Santo	N.S. Conc. E Sagr. Coração de Jesus do Monte Santo	753	685	725	22	6	654	24	7	310	443	280	405	745	8	681	4
	Sto. Sacramento de Massacará	186	163	177	7	2	156	5	2	80	100	173	90	181	5	160	3
Geremoabo	São João Batista de Geremoabo	228	154	225	2	1	149	4	1	96	132	57	97	221	7	145	9
	Santo Antonio da Glória e a Curral dos Beis	60	53	25	24	11	25	16	12	29	31	23	30	60	—	53	—
	N.S. do Bom Conselho do Mts. Boqueirão	154	128	137	15	2	107	16	5	52	102	42	86	147	119	9	
	N.S. do Patrocínio de Coité	364	319	353	9	2	309	7	3	156	208	142	355	9	313	6	
Total		9,256	7,979	7,969	1,091	1,96	6,817	967	195								

TABLE 1.1. (*continued*)

| Municipality | Parish | Sex | | Race | | | | | |
| | | | | Men | | | Women | | |
		Men	Women	White	Black	Pardo	White	Black	Pardo
Conde	N.S. das Mortes De Itapicuru de Praia	5,482	5,103	1,921	2,286	1,118	1,799	2,127	1,049
Abadia	N.S. da Abadia	2,900	2,020	1,063	1,248	494	710	848	384
Inhambupe	Divino Esp. Sto. De Inhambupe	5,219	4,214	1,152	3,527	436	951	2,852	340
	N.S. da Condeição de Aperá	4,815	3,927	2,168	3,262	289	901	2,662	300
Entre-Rios	N.S. dos Prazeres	4,186	4,587	884	2,724	481	757	3,025	515
Alagoinhas	Jesus, Maria e José da Igreja Nova	4,342	4,424	642	2,774	859	745	2,802	818
	Senhor Deus Menino de Araças	1,601	1,742	214	1,040	335	234	1,075	418
	Sto. Antonio Alagoinhas	3,038	2,829	774	1,767	470	592	1,173	1,023
Itapicuru	N.S. da Sáude da Missão	5,131	4,963	1,164	1,181	1,101	1,638	1,913	1,087
	N.S. Livramento de Barracão	3,851	2,236	881	1,001	1,909	503	1,000	680
Soure	N.S. da Conceição de Soure	3,048	2,541	1,057	1,293	559	983	1,137	300
Pombal	Sta. Teresa do Pombal	1,731	1,649	517	948	255	612	781	243
	N.S. do Amparo da Ribeira de Pau Grande	1,831	1,571	592	1,018	201	547	810	204
Tucano	Santana de Tucano	3,288	3,155	1,111	2,024	151	1,005	1,996	146
Monte Santo	N.S. Conc. E Sagr. Coração de Jesus do Monte Santo	3,874	3,727	420	2,617	820	278	2,538	889
	Sant. Sacramento de Massacará	1,320	1,064	85	890	324	83	730	230
Geremoabo	S. João Batista de Geremoabo	5,923	5,632	1,693	2,755	1,314	1,544	2,673	1,264
	Santo Antonio da Glória de Curral dos Reis								
	N.S. de Bom Conselho do Monte Boqueirão	3,412	3,310	242	2,424	721	230	2,332	730
	N.S. do Patrocínio de Caité	6,127	6,032	1,724	2,793	1,265	1,695	2,734	1,352
Total		74,127	67,635	19,306	39,777	13,793	16,812	36,422	12,797

Note: the incorrect totals in the columns and the missing totals are an accurate reflection of the source document for this translation

Notes

The original title of this text is "O Movimento de Antônio Conselheiro: uma visão de história regional." Unpublished, 1981, thesis draft, Fundo MBN, 21.1. Different versions of this text exist. This translation is based on the archival draft version of Nascimento's thesis.

1. Spanning 1840–1889, this refers to a period of Brazilian history marked by regional uprisings and the rule of Pedro II.

2. In reprinting this piece, Ratts (*História feita por mãos negras*) cites this paragraph as an interview with the historian Manoel Maurício de Albuquerque, but we are using the draft version of the thesis, which embeds the citation.

3. Eric Hobsbawm, *Bandits* (London: Weidenfeld & Nicolson, 2010).

4. Hobsbawm, *Bandits*.

5. José Aras, *Sangue de Irmãos* (n.p., n.d.), 5.

6. José Calasans, *Antônio Conselheiro e a escravidão* (Salvador: Artes Gráficas, n.d.), 1.

7. Robert Conrad, *Os últimos anos da escravatura no Brazil* (Rio de Janeiro: Civilização Brasileira, 1975), 64.

8. Conrad, *Os últimos*, 213.

9. Aras, *Sangue de Irmãos*.

10. Hobsbawm, *Bandits*.

11. The Cabanagem was a violent uprising by a coalition of peasants, escaped slaves, and small landowners in what was then Grão-Pará, in the North of Brazil, between 1835 and 1840. The rebels controlled the provincial government for a year. Tens of thousands of people died in the course of the rebellion.

12. See the introduction for the translations of these terms.

Post-revolutionary Angolan Nativism

Contents:

"This work was done after a visit to Angola between September 18 and October 18, 1979. In this work I use the method of participant observation, historical orality, and oral History, as well as the official documents supplied by the Federal Council of Culture of the People's Republic of Angola."

Introduction

My trip to Angola in September/October 1979 came about thanks to an invitation from the Intellectual Exchange Section of the Federal Council of Culture of Angola, in the Department of Luanda. The trip coincided with the beginning of the second term of my graduate studies at the Federal University of Fluminense, where I was taking courses in my area of concentration, the History of Brazil.

This work owes a great deal to Professor José Calasans, Chair in the History Department, and his course in Oral History. He suggested that I develop this area of interest, and approved my trip to the People's Republic of Angola to study the social conditions in which the populations of that country found themselves, as they adapted to the new post-Independence and post-Social Revolution reality.

I will attempt to outline the data that I secured while I was absent from the course for forty days. I will do so according to the points laid out by the Professor:

The points surveyed were as follows:

1. To identify Angolan nativism before, during and after Independence from Portugal, and after the Socialist Revolution and identify points in common with what happened in Brazil in the pre- and post-Independence period before and after 1822;
   a. To identify whether there was a flourishing of nativism on both the Angolan and Portuguese sides; and
   b. If social movements existed that were equivalent to the Mata-Maroto movements in Rio de Janeiro and Bahia after 1822;[1]
   c. If there were, within the nativist process, changes of names of localities, of families, of establishments or monuments. For example like the Brazilian politician Francisco de Acabaya Motezuma, who took an indigenous name to replace his Portuguese surname; if there was a reaction to Portuguese vocabulary in official and popular language use; and if there were changes of names of clubs and societies.
2. To identify firsthand divergences or convergences between the roles of the politician, the intellectual, and the poet;
   a. Whether politicians, intellectuals and poets struggled on separate fronts.
   b. How poetry and literature were involved in the struggle for liberation.
   c. If, like in Brazil in 1822, political struggle took place through verse.

I developed this approach alongside the personal research with which I arrived in Angola: "Alternative Societies Organized by Black People: From Quilombos to Favelas" (*mussekes* in Angola). It was the interest sparked by this research that led to the invitation from the Angolan authorities to visit their country.

I did my survey in small fishing villages in the urban zone of the Ilha de Cabo facing the Bay of Luanda, in the Province of São Paulo of Luanda. In this phase I undertook not only participant observation, but also consulted secondary documents such as maps, official documents, books, and more. Based on these, I drew up tables of African populations of historical kingdoms (from the thirteenth century to the nineteenth century), existing and former provinces, neo-colonial states, and recently independent states. These surveys were done using ethnolinguistic categories that persist from the thirteenth century to today.

I laid out twelve tables, four of which correspond to quilombos, or as I conceptualize them, "alternative societies." These quilombos, sometimes called *quimbos*, are today municipal stewardships, and deserve a special study. We have not been able to do this, as it would require extensive fieldwork.

The work for this statistical survey took seventeen days. It culminated in a population census, which established a baseline of refugees, prisoners, and deaths across various provinces and quilombos in the People's Republic of Angola. In this period of statistical research I worked with the National History Museum, the Cultural Exchange sector of the Federal Council of Culture, Luanda Section. I organized the survey jointly with the Center of Historical Documentation. I will explain, below, the role of that center. Angolan History is in a precarious position in relation to primary sources. The majority of the material is in Portugal and Brazil, and much was destroyed during the country's successive wars of liberation.

Nevertheless, I was in constant contact with the government authorities, and with elements of a determinedly active economic class in the urban, rural, and suburban zones of Luanda and in other provinces such as Lubango, Moçamedes, Luanda, Kwanzaa Norte, Kwanza Sul, Malanje, and elsewhere. There were also delegations present in Angola from other African countries including Equatorial Guinea, the Sahara,

Namibia, Zambia, Somalia, Mozambique, Cabo Verde, Timor, São Tomé and Príncipe, Palestine, and even other eastern and western countries such as Japan, USSR, Bulgaria, Yugoslavia, Australia, Portugal, and Italy, as well some delegations of economic and technical cooperation from Brazil, the Arab countries, North Korea, and others.

I was in close contact with the delegations from these countries, not least because they were staying in the same hotel as I was. This was productive in terms of the results of the survey in question.

The presence of these delegations in Luandan territory owes, in part, to the agreements that the People's Republic of Angola (PRA) has maintained between its provinces and African and non-African countries. This has led to an increase in cooperation at economic, technical, cultural, and intellectual levels, as well as the opening of new diplomatic missions that have allowed the PRA to rapidly integrate itself among the developing nations of the Third World. This includes its own task of National Reconstruction through the preparation and development of its human resources. This is happening notwithstanding the great trauma suffered by the Angolan nation with the death of Dr. António Agostinho Neto, the President, the Leader of the Revolution, and perhaps the most important leader of all the liberation movements now on African soil. He died on the 10th of September this year. Many of the delegations of the countries listed above were headed by ministers and Heads of governments. They came to demonstrate their solidarity to the Angolan people for the loss of their leader and to engage in negotiations to reinforce the theme of National Reconstruction. "The struggle continues, and victory is certain," has been the watchword of all of us foreigners whenever we meet Angolans.

We witnessed the whole phase after the funeral of António Agostinho Neto. We arrived in Luanda on the 18th of September, one day after the government delegations had arrived for the funeral ceremonies, and we stayed in the city until the 18th of October. During that time, we also undertook a journey to the north of the country. During this period— or, more specifically, until the 4th of October—Angola closed its borders because a civil war was unfolding against internal factions in the Movimento Popular de Libertação de Angola (MPLA). The fighting was with factions who were against the long-desired opening to the West that Agostinho Neto had begun, and remnants of former guerrilla fighters who were supported by foreign powers and sought to keep power in strategically and economically important territories. The city of Lubango and the region of Cabinda found themselves in the hands of extremist factions of the União Nacional para a Independência Total de Angola (Unita) led by Jonas Savimbi and supported by the nuclear-armed capitalist powers and the Union of South Africa. We were told in Portugal that these areas were recaptured by troops from the pro-western factions of the MPLA.[2]

After the capture of these politically and economically strategic regions, the war encroached on the borders of Luanda. Regime buildings were bombarded only five kilometers or so from Luanda, in Kakwako.

From the 4th of October the situation began to settle down and we were able to leave Luanda and travel to Kwanza Norte, in order to undertake a field survey of quilombos in that Province. We turned back at the edge of the quilombo of Kua Putu, as we found that the whole region was in an outright state of war, and there was the risk of an accident or an attack on our little caravan by the competing forces.

I left Luanda for Kwanza Norte in the company of the Director of the Cultural Exchange Secretariat and a representative of the National Museum. Later the group was joined by the Commissariat officer of Ndalatando and their aide, and a representative of the People's Armed Forces for the Liberation of Angola from the Organization of Angolan Women (OMA) of Ndalatando. We visited Nova Oeiras, Ndalatando, Msasangano (of huge historical value because it was the main gateway for embarking enslaved people on the Rio Kwanza, and the ruins of its Fort, built in Portuguese and Dutch styles of the fifteenth, sixteenth, and seventeenth centuries are perfectly maintained), and Kabango. We visited quilombos inhabited in traditional ways at Kua Putu and Dembo. These quilombos would remain legally and administratively as they were in the past, if they weren't in open conflict with occupying troops. The head of Kua Putu is to this day a Soba, and *dembos* are led by a Dembo, a chief who takes on the form of a demon, wearing from three to eight horns, made of their own hair, and communicating through animal horns.

We arrived back from this short excursion on the 7th of October in Luanda. There we continued the work of analyzing the data, which we finished around the 10th. On the 18th of October we left Luanda via Portugal and arrived in Brazil on the 24th October 1979.

For reasons that we will explain below, we left all the results of this survey on "alternative societies . . ." in the Museum of Natural History, in the Secretariat of Culture of Luando, Sector of Exchanges, in the Commissariat of Luanda/Coordinator of Kakwako. Beyond the documentation of the research project presented here, the material consisted of the data that have already been mentioned and of tape recordings outlining how the rest of the research would develop. We did not, therefore, bring any documentation back to Brazil, a fact that we are trying to overcome in part through this summary report.

We chose to leave the documents of the survey on "alternative societies . . . ," under seal, in the hands of the Angolan authorities, for two reasons:

1. The People's Republic of Angola, a country that is only recently independent of the Portuguese metropole (1975), is in a phase of economic, cultural, and technical reconstruction. Indeed, it is in a phase of reconstruction of the entire psychological life of its people, traumatized and battered by a war that has lasted at least thirteen years. At the same time, seemingly paradoxically, it is entering a phase of counterrevolution (according to the idea that all revolutions have a counterrevolution, as developed in the thesis on the history of Brazil by José Honório Rodrigues). Angola's internal situation is critical. There is no political unity, though there is a party in the Marxist-Leninist lineage that is imposing a dictatorship of the proletariat. There is no cultural or behavioral unity. Thanks to the guerrilla wars that continue (ethnic group against ethnic group), there is little prospect of an enduring peace. There is no linguistic unity in the interior. It is a country, therefore, under serious risk of failing to achieve national unity, and under serious threat of attack. Even so, and after such a short period of independence, it seeks cooperation at all levels with the western powers, including Portugal and the United States of America. Furthermore:

2. Professional ethics have obliged me to take this attitude. To the extent that we were acting as intellectual collaborators in a different country, as foreign scientists, we faced serious moral problems in taking the documents referred to in this work with us. They remain in the hands of their rightful owners. This decision was further reinforced by the fact that we were able to verify theoretically that "alternative societies . . ." (quilombos) are, and have always been, characteristic of the social organization of Angolans. They are both territorial and frontier areas, and strategic zones, whose occupation is oriented toward the defense of the territory itself and of the Angolan subsoil. For strategic reasons, therefore, the documents that confirm this cannot be removed to another country, least of all in the critical situation in which Angola finds itself.

The short preamble below further justifies these points. It then remains to present the survey carried out for the course PHT 02017 under the supervision of Professor José Calasans.

Short Preamble

Portuguese colonialism in Africa created a society with many characteristics similar to Brazilian society.

Angola, more than any other former colony, developed in many ways like Brazil. According to David Birmingham, the initial colonial occupation of a region in Africa by the Portuguese, in the fifteenth century, took place because Portugal saw the chance to establish, in Angola, a colony populated in a similar way to that established in South America for the production of sugar. Furthermore, Angola possessed vast mineral wealth, notably in Cabinda, and Portugal planned and initiated a mercantile process of extracting the riches of the Angolan soil and subsoil from the sources of the Rio Senegal right to the Congo River Basin.

In this process, soon after the fall of the Kingdom of Ndongo (whose N'gola kings lent their name to the region), Angola became the preferred zone of action for the Portuguese policy of mercantile domination (seventeenth to twentieth centuries). Unlike other mercantile powers, the

Portuguese metropole sought to occupy, and indeed ended up by occupy-ing (after the war with the Dutch in Angola and Brazil), vast territories of the African interior, reaching the so-called Guinea Coast, regions that right up to today suffer from some form of cultural and historical domi-nation by that mercantile power.

The Portuguese colonial process, often without the means to take the concrete measures of classical colonialism, enabled almost direct con-tact between Angola and Brazil. There were moments when Portugal—because of war between western powers, for instance in the case of the unification of the Iberian crown—neglected its dominance in Africa, and the Americas. In these moments Brazil and Angola maintained mer-cantile and other forms of relations between themselves without the intermediation of the Metropole.

There is proof of this, for instance, in documents belonging to A. Abreu, a Jewish merchant who traded various products, including enslaved people, between Pernambuco and Bahia and Angola in the sixteenth century.

This was a persistent reality, though there were various periods of interruption and repression, when the metropole was strong enough to inhibit these activities. They persisted, however, until the end of the eighteenth century. Then there were the slaving interests: a large con-tingent of Angolans were taken to Brazil as enslaved people, which meant that relations between Brazil and Angola continued until around 1850 and the end of the trade in enslaved Africans.

As this brief sketch shows, Angola's destiny has always been con-nected to Brazil's. José Honório Rodrigues, in an interview with the *Jornal do Brasil* in September 1979, speaks of the affinities between our peoples. He shows that, Rio de Janeiro above all (and we would add Minas Gerais, Pernambuco, and Sergipe), was created by Portuguese from the Minho and by enslaved Angolans, who imprinted a very spe-cial character on these states.

Furthermore, the most widely spoken languages in Angola—Kimbumdu, Kikongo, and others—have made a major contribution to the Portuguese spoken in Brazil. A significant proportion of the Afri-cans in Brazil, in the states of Maranhão, Pernambuco, Rio de Janeiro,

Minas Gerais, and Sergipe, and even in Bahia, are from the so-called *nagô* group, a branch of the *Banto* group. Angola, therefore, contributed, above all, through its people to the formation of the Brazilian population today.

We will move on, now, to discuss our report of conditions in post-revolutionary Angola. We would like to clarify that, thanks to the restricted time period and the precarious conditions that we worked under, this survey perhaps does not meet expectations, but we have tried to draw some conclusions from our period of participant observation.

Beyond the data from participant observation, we used recently produced official documents such as that produced by the National Institute of Languages, "Reflections on the Study of National Languages" and the "Notebook on National Culture, no. 15," published by Lavra & Oficinas, by António Agostinho Neto. We also used poetic and literary works by authors who are now Angolan municipal politicians.

Origins of Angolan Nativism

Response 1.

As far as we know, in comparison with nativism in other former Portuguese colonies, before independence Angolan nativism was the fiercest. The very fact of being the most important colony of the Overseas Portuguese Empire created the most promising political/intellectual class among the "ancien regimes."

Like Brazil, which in its time was the most important western colony, not only for its own Metropole but also for other colonial powers such as England, France, and Holland, Angola was always the object of envy for the traditional powers. Portugal saw this, and recruited jurists and public figures in general from among Angolan natives. They often used Angolans as important government functionaries not only in their own territory, but also in Mozambique, Guinea-Bissau, and so on—and even in the heart of the Overseas Empire.

Current Angolan class composition is difficult to appreciate, thanks to the socialist regime installed there. But before Independence there was a large, engaged, literary and poetic production in which nativism and the search for national identity flourished. We could compare it to Brazil in the period before 1822, in the apogee of Minas Gerais that led to the Inconfidência Mineira. We could cite Luandino Vieira, Armindo Francisco (the latter educated by evangelical missionaries), and António Agostinho Neto himself, the revolutionary leader and first President of the Angolan state.

RESPONSE 1.1

Nativism flourished on both sides. I met many young Portuguese students who escaped the war in the period of liberation and identified with the national feeling of the colonized people. Many of them fled to Brazil in the pre-Independence period. Among those Angolans descended in the first generation from Portuguese and with a deeply nativist element, is the current Director of the Federal Council of Culture of the People's Republic of Angola, Antonio Jacinto. On the Angolan side, there is Agostinho Neto. We understand, too, that many of the Portuguese who left Angola and now live in their country feel that they not only want to assess their assets in Angola, but to participate in the task of national reconstruction, accepting the Socialist Revolution as a "necessary evil" for development that was stalled by the bureaucratic machine of the old Portuguese Overseas Council. The nativism of the authorities was intensified by the experience of long years in the prisons of the Portuguese secret police. The Portuguese were extremely repressive to autonomist movements, and long periods of banishment made many exiles' nativist tendencies extremely radical. On the other hand, both before and after Independence, what we could call a neocolonial process saw the USA, the USSR, England, France, Israel, and others, involving themselves in Angola and seeking to divide it along international lines. This made the country almost occupied, and certainly the stage for very diverse interests. The revolutionary phase and the struggle between, on the one hand, the socialist systems of the USSR, and on the other that of Continental China, intensified the national feelings of Angolans such that in the current phase of national reconstruction "original" (black) Angolans, mixed Portuguese/African Angolans, and those descended from Portuguese people and other Europeans all demonstrate a xenophobia that seems to us to be deeply ingenuous and idealist. They consider Angola to be the most important country in the world, capable of competing with, and beating, any foreign power or any developing country.

Normal Angolans, today, are seeking to free themselves from an influence (or, better, various influences) that they consider pernicious. This significant presence of elements from eastern countries distorts not only traditional African culture, but also cultures from overseas. Nevertheless, this does not mean that among the class in power a sectarian belief in Marxism-Leninism has disappeared. They pretend, however, that this Marxism-Leninism has an Angolan character and, in a broader sense, an African and internationalist character.

It is here that we see the strong sense of Angolan nativism that, to us, looks like the various phases of nativism in Brazil after 1822, or rather, an attempt to align themselves with the Third World, but with specific characteristics, refusing interference in its internal business by whichever power, whether from the West or the East. It seems very brave to us, in a way, to refuse interference in the face of Cuban and Soviet influence.

For a visitor, it is moving and fascinating to see the affection and respect with which Angolans, not only from the classes in power, but also from the country's diverse ethnic groups, are dedicated to their traditions and to the rich soil of Angola.

RESPONSE 1.2

It was not possible to know, in situ, what the reaction had been to Portuguese people during the war of Angolan liberation. From previous reports, we know that it was very strong, but we cannot leave aside the fact that, precisely thanks to the modern context in which the social movements of liberation developed, some of their principal drivers included the pressure on the Portuguese from Global Organizations such as the UN and UNESCO, as well as Soviet action and propaganda against them.

We already know, and it is confirmed in the Museum of Slavery in Luanda, that until the first months of 1975, black Angolans, for example, were still beaten by whites for any kind of mistake. Many were essentially enslaved and sent handcuffed and beaten to the mines and plantations of São Tomé and Principé, Mozambique, Timor, and even to the Metropole.

However, we do have information that in the first case the initiative came less from Portugal than from the infiltration of forces struggling over interests in Angolan territory. They acted within white society, through agents, and intensified the antagonisms between Angolans from Angola, and those descended from the Portuguese, between Christians and non-Christians in the face of the colonial authorities. This was a typical policy of revolutionary movements of this century, using the new techniques of economic neo-colonialism. And the guerrilla motive to loot the so-called bourgeois population still exists.

Indeed, often when we referred to the Angolan past, citing Portuguese colonialism as the cause of the contemporary *state of things*, average Angolans responded by saying: "It was not the Portuguese who created this situation"; and when we retort that it was those from the metropole who were responsible, they tell us: "these thugs who took power in 1975 . . ."

We see, therefore, that the relationship between Angolan nativism and the former colonizers is very complex. Certainly, at some moments, informants told us that the armed struggle and the expulsion of the Portuguese and Angolan interests aligned with the old regime were important for the new face of an independent Angola. However, they themselves demonstrate in everyday practice a certain nostalgia for the capitalist period that does not match with an apparent adhesion to the Marxism-Leninism that sought, and seeks, to impose itself on most of the country. The yearning for the epoch in which Luanda was the major metropole of the colonial Portuguese Empire was visible among fallen capitalists and both new and old communists. It seemed to us, though, that if there was a phase of antagonism to the former colonizers—like with movements such as the "matamorotos"—this did not emerge from an organic opposition between Angolans and Portuguese. Variously we heard: "there were Portuguese and *Portuguese*." It seems to us, even, that the antagonism emerged from young people, and from certain ethnic groups who were disadvantaged and kept away from power during the colonial period. In the case of the former, the antagonism was not between Angolans and Portuguese, but, with the influence of new western social movements, it was more black vs. white. Those ethnic groups who lived closer to Portuguese culture maintain still a kind of respect and equilibrium in relation to "metropolitan" culture and display. Specifically, we did not identify xenophobia toward the descendants of Europeans we met among the ethnic groups of the N'gangala ethnicity (from the Northeast), the Ienenes (from the South), and the M'bundos (one of the largest ethnic groups in Angola).

Our contact with exiles in Portugal showed us the *exotic* face of Angolan nativism. The exiles prefer, even when they are antagonistic to the metropole, to say that they are the descendants of a culture and a common past with Portugal. Their great hope is to develop a harmonic form of cultural contact with Portugal, according to what they see as a Luso-Brazilian pattern.

RESPONSE 1.3

Portuguese colonial policy in Angola was very specific. It was different from the pattern of metropole-colony of the other Portuguese protectorates. Angola, like Cabo Verde, was, for Portugal, a true laboratory for a type of administrative policy using native frameworks. For various reasons that we cannot explain in this short work, languages that were considered to be national were maintained, and so were the ways of life of the various tribes and ethnic groups who made up the Angolan people.

Within this colonial policy of "divide to govern," Portugal, along with the other powers committed to ethno-colonialism, shored up local hostilities and maintained traditional regional divisions for their own ends.

In this sense, regional denominations were broadly maintained and regional names retained, such as Malanje, Luando, Calhamboloca, Moçamedes, Cunene, Kassanje, Cabinda, Kwanza, Luanda, Bengo,

Catete, Canga-Zuze, Cassoneka, Ikolo, just to name some of the geographical names that were never changed during the domination of the old regime and which still remain. In this way, too, family names, or rather ethno-linguistic names, were retained by individuals, even if they also received a Christian name imposed by the secular and religious authorities of Portugal and the other powers who took part in the colonial formation. We could cite as an example the native names of contemporary figures: the Provincial Commissary of Luanda, Agostinho Mendes de Carvalho did not lose his ethnic name of Kimbumdu origin: he was called Unhanhenga Xitu. Or the poet and General-Coordinator of the Municipal Commissariat of Kakwako, Armindo Francisco (Francisco is his last name, and the Christian names that are last names come from the first name of the grandmother, the oldest uncle, or the father, and are added to the native name). He never lost his original name, Kianda (in the kioco language), which is his ethnic name. Both were educated by missionaries.

There are still institutions with local names, such as the main government building, the Palácio de Mutamba, the Portuguese fort that defended the bay of São Paulo de Luanda, the Fort of São Marcos, though its official name is the Museum of the Armed Forces.

However, there were changes and reversions to names that in particular periods had been given to Portuguese heroes, like the Secondary School Salvador Correia de Sá, considered by the new regime to be one of the foremost aggressors against Angola. The city of Salazar, in Ndalatando, lost its name for obvious reasons and Lobita became Moçamedes, among others. The province of Cunene changed its name back to the native name, today correctly written as Ienene.

To explain the official policy about retaining or changing toponyms in the People's Republic of Angola, and the reaction to Portuguese vocabulary, we would rather cite sections of the two documents referred to in the preamble, about the linguistic and cultural policy to be adopted in this phase of National Reconstruction.

Angola, as we have already said, is seeking national unity. As the country is divided into tribes and ethnic groups before it is divided into classes, one of the means to minimize this dangerous disaggregation is a national language. This is an essential means for communication between the various peoples and provinces, and therefore for national integration.

Response 2

As we have already outlined above, the active political class is made up of politicians and intellectuals. The majority of this class were young people coming out of evangelical or Catholic missions. The poet and the writer dominate. Poetry was one of the most incisive forms for diffusing the political thought of economic and political Independence and the ideal of racial, cultural, and social autonomy.

This work took up a very vigorous ideological line, crossing the frontiers of the colony and the Metropole and reaching toward other countries. The poetic form was the strongest arm for contesting the regime, defending the interests of the oppressed and exalting Angolan nativism. What surprised us during our stay in Angola was that this movement gained its greatest strength after the Socialist revolution. Angolan political thought is translated into poetry (in epic style, but more strongly translating essentially existential, biographical, and tribal sentiments), which compete with the exhortatory and doctrinal discourses of the MPLA authorities who speak in caustic, primal, Marxist-Leninist terms. The poetry, however, is rich in imagery, and among the best of modern poetic production. It is a better expression and vehicle for Angolan revolutionary and liberatory thought than political discourse.

The interest and practice of poetry, along with the composition of popular music, does not only emerge from the celebrated poets, but from the population in general.

We believe that this phenomenon is thanks in part to a feeling, which is expressed better in lyrics, of nativist exaltation. In spite of the broad diffusion of poetic culture, most Angolans lack any formal or academic instruction. Having been a Portuguese colony, and, more recently, a culturally isolated Dictatorship of the Proletariat (which has enabled a massive influx of cultural production from the Soviet world and impeded fertile contact with the traditional cultural centers of the world, and especially with Brazil), and given with the limited diffusion of mass communication and the press, Angola has transformed into a society ruptured from the means to develop its own culture as a western culture. In this way, the free and spontaneous production of human feeling, and not only political but existential feeling, has had only one, or, better, two, channels of diffusion: literary and social fiction, and, above all, poetry.

RESPONSE 2.1

The politician, as a fighter in the phase of liberation which Angola is still going through, had to practice through verse in order to communicate their feelings and their thought, thanks, as we have already noted, to the lack of other means of communication. The writer, and above all the poet, had the most important political role in the struggle, all of them, without exception, having lived through many years of repression in Portuguese dungeons and prisons. On the other hand, many of them were guerrillas who carried arms, as well as working in western and eastern countries when they were temporarily able to escape from their prisons, clandestinely struggling, in exile, for the liberation of their country through poetry.

The main leader of the Revolution, and the first President of the People's Republic of Angola, Agostinho Neto, was one of the best of the new generation of poets in the Portuguese language and, after his death, he was given the title of Immortal Guide of the Revolution in Africa. In the model of Lenin and Mao Tse Tung his poetry is a true measure of Angolan Revolutionary thought.

RESPONSE 2.2

One of the measures to nationalize knowledge, or, better, Angolan intellectual production, was the creation of the Union of Angolan Writers. Through its colloquia it sought to print the political-humanist face of the Revolution.

Though only an impressionistic vision on our part, this entity, whose members are nearly all connected to the Federal Council of Culture, seems at the moment to be trying to enact a lurch Westwards, seeking to fill the cultural gaps of the ethnic groups of the country. Through this they are entering into a clash with the faction of the Party that maintains an extremely Soviet tenor within the MPLA. Contrary to the other branch, this faction seeks to centralize Angolan culture and impose an eastern mentality. The Union of Angolan Writers comes with its own ideas, seeing the possibility of maintaining the ethnic-linguistic and cultural-behavioral differences of the various provinces. As demonstrated in the documents attached here, the new political mentality of Angolan humanists seeks a less traumatizing form for the people, in the sense of both a unity of communication and the much desired national unity.

RESPONSE 2.3

This final response can, we believe, be seen in those that come before. To conclude we want to transcribe sections of a poem by Armindo Francisco.

A Luta Continua [The struggle goes on]

The struggle goes on because I am tired of hunger
The struggle goes on because I am tired of poverty
The struggle goes on because I am tired of calumny
The struggle goes on because I am tired of being stupid

For 500 years I've been illiterate
I am no one
I am not hungry
For five hundred years I've been a boy
Even when I'm a hundred years old

For 500 years I've been beaten
For 500 years I've been squashed

My father was called boy
My mother "Oi, Maria"
The name of my sister is girl

The struggles goes on because I am tired of faith and the Empire
Of western civilizations
Of hypocritical religions
I am tired of being sub-human
I am tired of being ignorant and ignored

The struggle goes on because I am tired of waiting
I am tired of crumbs
My land has manna, honey and milk and I do not eat
I have been hungry for centuries

I no longer bear the theft of my bread
I no longer bear the theft of my power
I no longer bear the theft of my wealth

Just yesterday someone on my street begged for alms

The struggle goes on because from the ocean to the east
The grocer still cries oranges, oranges madam

The washerwoman still says: good day madam
The struggle goes on . . .

Notes

The original title of this text is "O nativismo angolano pós-revolução." Unpublished, December 14, 1979, Fundo MBN, 23.4.3. This text was written as a course paper in Beatriz Nascimento's studies at UFF for a course led by professor José Calasans Brandão, a historian of the sertão from Sergipe. Her trip was funded by the Ford Foundation and the Léopold Sédar Senghor Foundation and with an official invitation from the Angolan National Council of Culture. The work was later incorporated into her thesis, hence the date given here.

1. *Mata-Maroto* (kill-the-sailor) refers to conflicts that took place in the 1820s and 1830s in Bahia in the Regency period, between Brazilians and Portuguese. They were in essence struggles between separatists and loyalists.

2. The Angolan civil war lasted in different forms into the twenty-first century. The period Nascimento is describing was marked by Cold War tensions, and a territorial struggle between the MPLA, the main anti-colonial independence movement and first government of independent Angola, the FNLA (the National Liberation Front of Angola), initially led by Holden Roberto, and Unita, founded by Jonas Savimbi, a former FNLA member. Each group had different territorial strongholds and international backers.

Kilombo and Community Memory: A Case Study

I WOULD LIKE to call this essay "Memory or Oral History as Tools for Group Cohesion." Or even "Memory and the Hope of Recovering Usurped Power." Perhaps the malleability of this work's title is because it is unfinished. It is a prolonged and exhaustive study.

In saying this, I am trying to express my experience of studying Brazilian quilombos in a project called "Alternative Black Social Systems: From Quilombos to Favelas." This project is, also, a great dream. Scientifically speaking, we seek to demonstrate that people and groups that created what we conventionally called "quilombos" in the past can, and still do, seek to create them today.

In my understanding, this is not a question, precisely, of survival or cultural resistance, though we will use those terms, at times, as scientific points of reference. What we seek in this study is Historical continuity—that is why I refer to a dream. Every historian is a talker, and a dreamer, in search of *continuity*. We could even say that that is our goal as students of the human process on the planet. Historical continuity is an even more abstract term than the anthropologists' "survival" or "cultural resistance." Continuity would be the life of man—and of men—going on apparently without ruptures, though flattened by various processes and forms of subjugation, subordination, domination, and subservience.

A process that took place, across many years, among those who, through our own abstractions, we include in the category of black people.

The work presented here is nothing more than a partial research report. It does not pretend to be truth nor to define a thesis. I am merely saying: this is what I found.

This research, for reasons that we do not include here, took place in rural Minas Gerais, in communities that were not particularly isolated but that were in a former quilombo.

The first stage of the work involved surveying areas with the names of former quilombos, in the Brazilian Institute of Geography and Statistics list of municipalities, settlements, and localities, as well as the areas of ex-quilombos discovered through bibliographical and documentary sources in the National Archives and the Public Archives of Minas Gerais. During this first stage we also visited three of these places in Minas and established initial contact with the inhabitants. We then chose a case study, even though we did not lose sight of the comparison between the three former quilombos.

The second stage of the research was dedicated to fieldwork, using the methodologies of oral history, ethnography, and participant observation. The quilombo of Carmo da Mata was our field site for studying the conditions of the black people who live there.

We took this approach because of how the research developed. This quilombo, out of the three studied, was the one that contained the highest proportion of Afro-Brazilians (black and *mestiço*). We identified it, though, without the support of primary or secondary documents. In the first stage, during the survey, we found a growing, latent, class and race conflict that would come to fruition later (as we will describe below).

In Kilombo, in the municipality of Carmo da Mata, we found a particularity that we did not observe elsewhere: there was a family there in which the mother—who, according to the information we were given, was 110 years old—was a direct descendent of the quilombolas who had lived in the region for many years, since 1888.

We contacted this woman in the first phase of the research. She did indeed seem to be as old as they said. She had a large family, some of whom still lived in the region, and some of whom had migrated to São Paulo, Paraná, Mato Grosso, and other regions with better employment prospects. When we met, we asked her why that region had been named Quilombo (Kilombo). She told us that it was because of the appearance of a miraculous saint some years before in a cave above the village. The area was high and rocky, and contained a small valley with a river called Calhambola. *Calhambola* is a substitute term for *quilombola*. When we asked the same question of white people—owners of businesses and relatives of farmers in the region—they responded initially that they did not know, but soon after, someone having consulted a young relative in Belo Horizonte, they told us that the name of the village was Kilombo, because black people who had fled slavery settled there.

The two versions intrigued us, because whenever we asked black people, they repeated the explanation that attributed the origin of the local name to a miraculous saint, telling us that the saint was to be found in the local Catholic chapel. During the Reinado—a street festival that commemorates the trilogy of Saint Benedict, Our Lady of the Rosary, and Saint Ephigenia—very special things took place and, along with other black people, mestiços, and white people, the children and grandchildren of D. Idalina—the last quilombola—returned to the village.

In the second stage of the research we decided to follow the whole process leading up to the festival of the Reinado. We did not come to this decision by chance. We thought that the Reinado, like any event deeply imbued with symbolic content on the level of Afro-Brazilian myths, could represent historical continuity. We saw that not only did these celebrations have very direct connections to what we were seeking in the quilombo (with the capacity to be both a dramatization of the conditions of life of the black inhabitants and, possibly, the translation of memories into cultural codes), but that they also represented the particular dynamics of race relations in the village.

The most typical example of this was how black informants insisted on relating the origin of Kilombo to a miraculous or legendary event. We heard this not only in the quilombo of Carmo da Mata, but in others that we visited.

During the first stage of the research, we clarified a great deal about the connection of the history of Kilombo, in Carmo da Mata, to mystical apparitions and revelations, through trance and otherwise. The most revealing account came from Sr. Neca, the youngest son of D. Idalina, the elderly descendent of the quilombolas of the region. Before him, some black people had implied a similar story, but when we asked him who the saint belonged to, he responded: "To us." When we inquired further: "Us who?"—he replied: "To us, the Kilombo."

One of our hypotheses is precisely that the areas in which "quilombos" were located in the past assume a spatial continuity, preserving or attracting black populations in the twentieth century.

Of the three quilombos studied—Carmo da Mata, Comarca do Rio das Mortes and Alagoas—for the first and last it was impossible to find any primary or secondary documentation other than the IBGE list already referenced. We therefore had to do oral history research to reconstruct their trajectories. We began with interviews, participant observation, and photographs. For Comarca do Rio das Mortes—one of the largest in the history of Minas, also called Quilombo Grande—we employed the same methods, but we also found many bibliographical references and primary documents.

We learned of the quilombo of Carmo da Mata in September 1976, when we were staying in a small farm in the village of Riacho in the municipality of Carmo da Mata, fourteen kilometers from the region that we later went to study. On asking our hostess who the patron saint of the small Catholic church of Riacho was, she told us that it was the church of Our Lady of the Rosary. In Christianity this Virgin is the protector of slaves, and of black people in general. We asked whether black people often visited the church. The farmer gave us, in a very precise form, the initial outline of the research that we would later develop.

We were told that, from a historical point of view, black people and white people went to that church, but that the former's "Christian" practices intensified during the festival of the trilogy of Saint Benedict, Our Lady of the Rosary, and Saint Ephigenia. On that occasion, they held street festivals "that only they knew how to lead." The name given to this tripartite festival by black people in the region was the Reinado. It consists of four bands—little armies or battalions, each led by a commander, always black or mestiço: Congada, Moçambique, Catupé, and Vilão.[1]

Returning to Rio de Janeiro, we looked for the origin of this "revelry" in Luis da Câmara Cascudo, but found little to help us. We returned later to the region of Carmo da Mata and proceeded to survey in more detail the ideas of the black and the white inhabitants.

From various accounts we were led to believe that these were not simply folkloric-religious festivities. There was a whole historical density at stake. The costumes had names and specific meanings. The first referred to an African patriarchy that gathered political and administrative power in the Kingdom of the Congo in the thirteenth to fifteenth centuries. The second, also referencing the African past, represented a matriarch, or, at the least, a powerful, decentralized, female political force in Africa in the same period. "The difference between Congada and Moçambique is that in the Congada, it is the king, and in Moçambique, it is the queens, but the differences that black people identify are in the drum beat and box rhythms."[2] The third band, Catupé, represents the indigenous Brazilian, and the last band, the Vilão, represents the Portuguese.

It was September, and we were trying to find out if there was a Reinado near the farm. We were told that on that Sunday afternoon there would be a performance, considered the most authentic around, in the nearby village, whose name was Kilombo.

The reference to the name interested us, to the extent that we wanted to start our research from the historical-cultural concepts of quilombo, and the reinado. It was from this perspective that we engaged the hypothesis of a historical continuity between the quilombo and its representations and redefinitions in the contemporary world. Hypotheses 1, 2, and 3 of the work refer to this.[3]

Later, we sought to find this quilombo in the historical sources referring to quilombos from the eighteenth and nineteenth century in Minas Gerais. We found nothing in the National Archive in Rio de Janeiro, nor in the Public Archive in Minas Gerais, in Belo Horizonte. We looked in the Bishopric of Carmo da Mata in Divinópolis in the same type of documents, but without success. We necessarily opted for oral research.

Through oral accounts, we learned that the quilombo of Carmo da Mata organized itself through contact between black "corumbas" and indigenous Purí, who lived in that region. The black people were bantu, of Mbunda ethnicity. They lived by hunting, and small crops of pineapples, beans, and bananas, and harvested palm hearts. For a long period, not a single attack on the community was registered.

Around 1888, according to these accounts, white foresters from São João d'El Rei, came looking for land for coffee and cattle. They seized the area and expelled the black people and the Purí, its original inhabitants. Massacres and re-enslavement followed. It was after the battle between the white foresters and the quilombolas that the miraculous saint, Senhora Santana, was found.

One of the farm workers found her in a cave, after following a cow that had strayed from the herd. The steer had a broken horn and the man wanted to know where it had been hurt. Following the trail of blood left by the animal, he found, in one of the caves around Calhambola, what seemed to him to be the image of a woman with a broken hand. Later, accompanied by other black people, he confirmed that this was an icon of Senhora Santana. Everyone believed that she wounded the steer because it belonged to one of the cruelest farmers of the region, who most mistreated black people and their workers.

The image received a "spiritual cleansing" before being brought to the camp and enthroned in the Catholic church, whose patron saint was Our Lady of the Rosary. It is an icon made of ebony, a dark wood, in a baroque style. The black people attribute its origin to a quilombola in the region. They later sought to verify this in a Kimbanda spiritual center. Asserting, around the middle of this century, that the saint belongs to the quilombo, the leaders of the Reinado built a new chapel on the site where the image was found. Up to the moment of this research they have been trying to transfer the icon to this small chapel.

This process, driven by the leaders of the Reinado, all black people, has led them into a conflict with the Catholic Church and the white people of the region.

Around 1910, one of the sons of one of the six white families started to live as a married couple with D. Idalena, the descendent of the quilombolas. Among the various black children of this woman there is, therefore, one mestiço, the son of this white man, a descendent of the white farmers. This son of D. Idalina has a significant role in the community. As well as being a good farmer, he is blessed as the principal captain of the Reinado. Acting as the key leader of the community, it is he who leads the struggle against the regional powers. This struggle extends from the recuperation of the Mutual Aid Box of the Reinado, that was in the hands of white friends of the parish priest of Carmo da Mata, to the reclamation of the statue, that he considers to belong to all the black people, along with the alms promised to him. Alongside this process, he has tried to have his white ancestry legally recognized, with the goal of recovering the lands lost by his black ancestors. That is, because he is the biological son of white farmers, he is trying, through notarized documents, to inherit the lands that, according to the "law of the whites," belong to his father.

After a year of research, this mestiço man revealed to us the latent conflict that we had noted. The conflict revolved around the possession of the miraculous saint by the black community—aspects of the Reinado. Through this, they sought to control the income from the festivals and the alms given during pilgrimages made to the saint, and ultimately to take the land. Through the leadership of Sr. Neca, son of D. Idalina, the group built the chapel of the Reinado beyond the jurisdiction of the parish of Carmo da Mata. The chapel was built in the heights of calhambola, with money from the Reinado, near the cave where the saint was found. In 1979 they intended to take the saint there and organize the Reinado there autonomously.

As we have already said, the Reinado dramatizes a conflict, but with the corroborating information of the various accounts, it was possible for us to ascertain that the Reinado also aimed to express the conflict itself. In it were demonstrated the conditions of a community that, in other times, distant from the Reinado, had been invisible.

We developed the key phase of this research between August to September, during the period of the Reinado. We took part as participant observers, interviewers, and photographers, pursuing not only the dramatization, but also the symbolic contents of the Reinado. Through interviews we documented the inter-racial and inter-class conflicts of the community with society in general. In this period the metal workers were on strike in Minas, and many black people returned to the area of the kilombo, fleeing the strike or unemployment. We observed, too, the temporary solutions to the conflict, at the level of solidarity, friendship, and other forms of group cohesion, enacted in the festivities of the Reinado itself.

Difficulties and Claims of Research

Among the difficulties encountered in this stage of the work, we would like to emphasize the absence of specialists within the team, not only in terms of the human sciences, but also technical specialists. A geographer and an anthropologist, or a linguist, would be important contributors.

We are interested in amplifying the concept of the quilombo, in order to extrapolate its purely historical characteristics, in the sense that one of the principal hypotheses of the research refers to the fixity of populations in geographical terms. The places where quilombos were formed, in the past, have relatively similar climates and topographies. We are investigating up to what point these characteristics function as a pole of attraction for the population of particular regions, or if these characteristics encourage, or not, the expansion of the economic frontier, thus preventing them from remaining empty, while accommodating smallholdings, whether of white people or black people. We also continue to ask if it was precisely this feature of being a frontier region that led to attacks on, and destruction of quilombos in the past. To what extent, even today, is this problem repeating itself? All of these are questions that return us to the concept of historical continuity.

It is very common in Brazil—but we see it too in Angola—to find quilombos that are located on plateaus or hills, near rivers or other natural routes, possessing quite specific climates, where the conditions of the Sun and other stars give a sensation of open space, of the oceanic and the infinite. Hence these organizations possess not only the characteristic of geographical frontiers, but also demographic, economic, and cultural frontiers.

In Angola, this stood out in the survey that we undertook. We brought this observation forward with the intention of verifying if the same was true in Brazil. We know that, in the past, this may have happened, and the economic importance of quilombos is part of our findings. Such findings bring us to the hypothesis that quilombos were historically subject to harassment because they were found in lands suited to various types of economic exploitation by the dominant economic system. This is the reason for the attacks and destruction.

In terms of the study of the contemporary mentality and symbolic world of the community studied, and its history, we would have to turn to other scientists who could help us clarify these questions and apply a theoretical basis to our impressions, which are based only on historical knowledge.

Our other problem was the ambitious extent of the original project, according to which we were to undertake research in four States. Up to now, we have only been able to undertake fieldwork and related archival research in Minas Gerais, and even so, we were unable to get to the quilombo of Serro.

Although our conception of the study of quilombos does not take into account the preservation of linguistic components, or of specifically African culture and ethnicity, we are considering studying and doing field research in this quilombo, which was one of the most important in the country, and which was made up of only one ethnic group. In the period of the destruction of Serro, its leader, the quilombola Isidoro, walked to Minas Gerais searching for Ambrósio and his quilombo, Comarca do Rio das Mortes. We would like to know why he undertook this journey, and what inter-relations these leaders had. Was it customary for quilombolas to look to reorganize themselves with others, or even to seek refuge with quilombolas who had not yet been repressed? We would like to know if this approach involved a kind of national sentiment on the part of quilombolas.

Of the other states, we surveyed quilombos in the area of influence of Antônio Conselheiro, in the interior of Bahia. We used secondary documents and the demographic census of 1872. We included eleven municipalities where there were quilombos which were attacked, and whose members joined the ranks of the leader of the Northeasterners at the end of the last century.

Overall, three states are missing from our research, as is fieldwork in Bahian quilombos such as Orobó, Nossa Senhora dos Mares e Cabula, and Buraco do Tatu.

For this research we have relied on the financial support of the Ford Foundation. We would also like to profoundly thank Marlene de Oliveira Cunha for her research assistance.

Notes

Originally published as "Kilombo e memória comunitária: um estudo de caso." *Estudos Afro-Asiáticos* 6, no. 7 (1982): 259–65. Note that a version of this text is also part of her master's dissertation, from which other texts in this section are taken. In this case the later, published version has been used as the source text.

1. The fact that Black people organized these bands according to ethnic and historical differences led us to the hypotheses of a conflict whose historical continuity would be revealed during the religious trilogy.

2. Testimony of the farmer we stayed with in 1976, before the research.

3. Hypothesis 1: What are known in the historiography as quilombos are archaic social movements in reaction against the slavocratic system, whose particularity was to inaugurate various social systems with communitarian foundations. Hypothesis 2: The variety of social systems covered by the singular concept of quilombo emerges due to the institutional differences between these systems. Hypothesis 3: The greater or lesser success in the organization of social systems known as quilombos emerges in relation to the strengthening of the dominant social system and its evolution across time.

The Concept of Quilombo and Black Cultural Resistance

Objectives

1) To outline the pre-diasporic history of quilombo as an African institution of Angolan origin.
2) To describe the connotations of this institution in the colonial and imperial periods in Brazil.
3) To delineate the role of the institution of quilombo in how ideological principles become cultural resistance.
4) To historicize that ideology within the black consciousness movement and Brazilian society in the twentieth century.

Introduction

The western world constructed an image of Africa as an isolated and strange continent, where History began with the arrival of Europeans. The History of black people, like that of the territory they came from, is only allowed to exist in the context of the major events of western civilization. This is a serious failing: historians risk rupturing the identity of black people and their descendants both in relation to their African past, and to their historical role in the countries they were forcibly relocated to in the slave trade.

In the long, hard struggle to defend personal and historical identities, black people's resistance has taken many forms. We could make a long list of such social and political movements in Brazil. One, the Quilombo (or Kilombo), is the object of my study. It is a key milestone in the history of our people's capacity for resistance and organization. All these forms of resistance can be understood as the history of black people in Brazil.

Quilombo as an African Institution

Unlike other Europeans, the Portuguese settled on the African continent and established a colony in Angola. Two initial incentives led them to do so: the first was to repeat what they had done in Brazil, to acquire lands and establish a colony. The second, soon frustrated, was to find precious minerals.

As early as the fifteenth century, the Europeans discovered that the slave trade was the true source of wealth. Brazil became the major recipient of such "merchandise" in the middle of the sixteenth century. As demand grew, penetration into the African interior intensified, often coordinated by the king of the Congo, who aided and abetted the Portuguese attacks.

The preferred "hunting ground" was the ethnic region of Mbundu, in the south of Angola. It was in the seventeenth century that the Portuguese definitively settled on the trade in humans, more than any other activity, as the best way to serve colonial interests. Three principal methods proved effective. The first was using traffickers, who purchased slaves in far-flung markets along the borders of Congo and Angola. The Mbundu people, located near Lake Stanley, famously called these traffickers *pombeiros*. The second method was to impose tribute on conquered Mbundu chiefs, to be paid in young adult slaves known as *peça da Índia* [a piece of India]. The third method was to take slaves directly through war. For the Portuguese governors this last method was most appealing; many had interests in Brazil and needed to supply slaves for their own lands there.

When they arrived on the African continent, the Europeans found many forms of societies. Indeed, in that period these societies were undergoing processes of redefinition, with the emergence of state forms in some places. As in the Kingdom of the Congo, these clashed with traditional structures such as the lineage-based mode of production of the Mbundu.

David Birmingham (1973) gives a full account of the conflicts within the bantu societies of Central-West Africa at the moment of the Portuguese incursion. Many ethnic groups overlapped in the same spaces, and came into conflict with one another, whether while succumbing to the new conjuncture, or resisting European invasion. Among these were the Imbangalas (also known as the Jagas). They were hunter-gatherers who came from the east. Around 1560, they invaded the Kingdom of the Congo, and by 1569 had succeeded in expelling the king and the Portuguese from the capital, forcing them to hide on an island in the river. Between 1571 and 1574, thanks to their access to firearms, the Europeans managed to force this belligerent people to retreat.

Ten years later, the Imbangalas fought alongside the Mbundu against Portuguese incursion. Their entry into Mbundu territory, however, had been preceded by a fierce struggle between the Mbundu leader, Ngola, and Kingui, leader of the Imbangala.

The Imbangala who dominated Angola were considered to be particularly fearsome. Living entirely from pillage, they did not raise livestock or plant crops. Unlike other ethnic groups, they did not raise children, to avoid disruption to their lifestyle of continuous movement. They killed their children at birth and adopted the youth of the groups that they defeated. They were anthropophagic, and ornaments, tattooing and palm wine held special cultural significance for them.

The Imbangala's nomadic character, and the specificities of their social formation, can be seen in the institution of the Kilombo. The warlike Imbangala society was open to foreigners, once they were initiated. Initiation replaced the rites of passage of lineage-based systems. Partly because they did not live with their children, but adopted youth from other groups, the Imbangalas had an important role in this period of Angolan history, often resisting the Portuguese and controlling the vast regions that supplied slaves. The Kilombo disrupted lineage structures and, in the face of other institutions in Angola, established a new centrality of power.

Initiation rites were based on the practice of circumcision, by which young people of different lineages were incorporated into one warrior society. Here is where the Kilombo got its meaning. Individuals would become Kilombo once they incorporated themselves into Imbangala society.

Kilombo also meant the territory or field of struggle, the *jaga* and the sacred place where initiation rites took place. When some Imbangalas were involved in the slave trade with the Portuguese, the encampment of escaped slaves was referred to as Kilombo, and so were nineteenth-century Angolan trading caravans.

The slave trade brought Brazil and Angola into close interrelation, so it is not hard to connect the history of this institution in Africa (Angola) and Brazil. The difficulty is to establish direct lines of contact, such as quilombos in Brazil that had territorial or ethnic origins in Angola, members of quilombos in Brazil who were direct descendants of members of Kilombos in Africa, or direct links between the struggles of quilombos in Brazil and those on the other side of the Atlantic.

Quilombo as an Institution in the Colonial and Imperial Periods in Brazil

The first reference to a quilombo in an official Portuguese document appears in 1559. After the wars in the Northeast of Brazil in the seventeenth century—including the destruction of the *Quilombo* of Palmares, and its consequences—pockets of black populations re-emerged living free from colonial rule. This reemergence frightened the Portuguese authorities. In a document of the 2nd of December 1740, they gave their own definition of what quilombo meant: "all habitations of black fugitives in groups of more than five, even if destitute or lacking buildings, tools or cultivation."

Among the Brazilian quilombos in the seventeenth century, the great state of Palmares was beyond compare. Its dismantling was a seminal moment in the History of Brazil. The historical evidence suggests that the spread of quilombos at the time was directly related to it.

The dates of these events are noteworthy. The Quilombo of Palmares paralleled what was taking place in Angola in the late sixteenth and early seventeenth centuries. Indeed, Palmares is perhaps the only quilombo through which we can directly associate the Kilombo as an Angolan institution with the quilombo of colonial Brazil.

Jaga resistance peaked between 1584 and the middle of the next century, after which, the group allied itself with the Portuguese slave trade. At that very moment, Angola-Janga was being built: the quilombo known as Palmares in Brazil.

Palmares is linked to Angola in other ways. Firstly, the name of its African leader Ganga Zumba recalls the similar title of the king of the Imbangala, "Gaga." Secondly, the records of the hair-piece that Ganga Zumba wore in Recife during the Palmarino truce, recall the Imbangala king Calando, who wore his hair in long braids adorned with shells as a sign of authority. Third, the mode of warfare based on opposing probable enemies on multiple fronts. Just as the Angolan kilombo cut through the vertical power-structures of the lineage-based system and established a new center of power in relation to other institutions. Palmares, too, made a horizontal cut through the colonial regime, and confronted it too with a new kind of centrality. In Brazil Palmares was, after all, also known as Angola-Janga.

The name of the colonial territory "Angola" is derived from the bundu king N'gola, who passed it on to his many descendants and successors. It is very possible that some members of this African dynasty were transported to Brazil during the slave trade, and indeed may have become leaders of the resistance movement. The surname Janga is a variation of *jaga*, and probably demonstrates that these two lineages—the Ngola and the Jaga—were linked in the leadership of the Quilombo of Palmares. Both names connect Palmares to Mbundu territories in Angola.

Thinking about this Quilombo in Brazil allows us to assess the extent of interaction between Brazil and Angola at that time. Other quilombos, though, distanced themselves from the African model. They adapted to their needs inside Brazilian territory. But the historiographical task of studying quilombos in Brazil, and analyzing them according to their form and structure across time remains unfulfilled. In general, quilombos are described as if throughout history they were African villages where the black population took refuge to pine after their motherland.

In the colonial period, quilombos were characterized by the formation of large States, such as that of Comarca in the Rio das Mortes in Minas Gerais, dismantled in 1750. Like Palmares, this quilombo responded to the structural and economic conditions of Brazilian economic "cycles" in Brazil: from sugar in Pernambuco to gold in Minas Gerais.

It is possible, from this perspective, to describe quilombos as alternative social systems, or, in the words of Ciro Flamarion: breaches in the slavocratic system.

An important, and controversial, element, is to account for the position of large quilombos precisely in relation to the regime of slavery. The African is no more a "good savage" than Africa is a strange paradise.

The institution of slavery was known and used since African antiquity. What it lacked was colonial slavery's *proprietary* quality. A free person could end up in the condition of slavery in many ways, whether through war, political instability, being the child of an enslaved person, as a punishment for breaking group norms, or in response to internal threats that could lead individuals to seek protection from other lineages (so-called "voluntary slavery").

This final factor is relevant to quilombo as an institution formed by people who had either been subject to, or threatened with, colonial slavery. Quilombo, as a social group founded in extraordinary conditions, bore these traditional forms and practices of slavery within it.

The great quilombos were spatially and temporally linked to the social system of slavery. They could not be entirely economically isolated from it. Their interaction with the slavocratic system can be seen, for instance, in Ganga-Zumba's willingness at the treaty of Recife to allow unincorporated Palmarinos to become colonial slaves.

It's important to remember that when joining the quilombo, people who had been enslaved under the colonial system often put themselves in the position of voluntary slavery. That this practice was widely used in Africa makes this easier to understand.

Nevertheless, the quilombos of the seventeenth century were distinctive as groups and ethnicities in particular territories and economies that posed a threat to the colonial system. We can argue that it was faced with these quilombos that Brazil identified itself for the first time as a centralized State.

With the dismantling of the quilombos of Tijuco and Comarco do Rio das Mortes in the eighteenth century, the geographical area, official repression, and ethnic diversity of quilombo all changed. Ethnic diversity became more and more common thanks to colonial slavery's policy of mixing people of diverse origins.

In the eighteenth century, quilombos proliferated across the territory of the colonial captaincies. Unlike the large quilombos of the previous century each institution could not itself be said to have been a threat to the system. If the seventeenth-century quilombo was a wholescale breach in the slavocratic system, these were cracks. Seen as a whole across territorial space and historical time, while they often co-existed peacefully with it, the institution of quilombo produced an inherent instability in the system of slavery. Changing economic activities in different regions often led to loosening ties between slaves and masters. This colonial fragility led to the growth of the practice of escape. It became integral to the structure of quilombo. Looting, plundering and banditry were key to the survival of these agglomerations.

The Penal Code of 1835 defined quilombo as a refuge for bandits and distinguished it from other forms of resistance by enslaved people. But it was, nevertheless, a threat to the stability and integrity of the Empire. The punishment for being a member of a quilombo was the same as for being part of an insurrection: beheading.

In this period quilombo became wrapped up with the so-called "black danger" of the wars in Bahia and Maranhão. Police suspicions increased. Powerful religious practices developed in some quilombos in this period, for example in Nossa Senhora dos Mares e Cabula in Salvador.

Significantly, at that time large quilombos were founded on the slopes and peripheries of important urban centers. In imperial Rio de Janeiro, for instance, there were quilombos in Catumbi, Corcovado and Manuoel

Congo. Many of these organized themselves within a single ideological framework: flight as a reaction to colonialism. We can see this not only in literary references, but also in the oral tradition that sprang up at this time.

The Quilombo as a Guide
toward Ideological Principles

By the end of the nineteenth century, quilombo had come to be an ideological instrument against oppression. Often through abolitionist discourse, its magic nourished the dreams of freedom of thousands of enslaved people on the plantations of São Paulo.

Quilombo's transition from institution as such to symbol of resistance transformed it once again. The emergence of the quilombo of Jabaquara is the best example. Black fugitives from the plantations of São Paulo migrated to Santos and founded a quilombo that was declared by the followers of Antonio Bento. This quilombo became a huge favela. It both frustrated the ideal of a free territory dedicated to African cultural practices and, at the same time, enacted armed resistance to the slavocratic regime.

However, it is principally as an ideological form that quilombo enters the twentieth century. The old slavocratic regime having come to an end, with it went quilombo as an institutional resistance to slavery. However, precisely because it had been, for three centuries, a concrete, free institution existing in parallel to the dominant system, its aura continued to nourish yearnings for freedom in the national conscience. In the wake of the São Paulo Modern Art Week of 1922, the Brazilian publisher Editora Nacional published three books on quilombo, by Nina Rodrigues, Ernesto Enne, and Edison Carneiro. It's also worth referencing the work of Artur Ramos and Guerreiro Ramos, as well as Felício dos Santos's slightly earlier novels.

This key moment in Brazilian national identity elicited intellectual production on quilombo. It sought to emphasize quilombo's positive aspects in order to reinforce a historical Brazilian identity. Quilombo is remembered as a form of utopian desire. In this period, works on quilombo, including in samba lyrics and academic contexts, showed varying levels of familiarity with theories of popular resistance. Up to 1964, it was common to find the official historical narrative of quilombos in school textbooks. Even into the 1970s quilombo played an ideological role of threading popular resistance to oppression into narratives of Brazilian nationality. It provided material for participative fiction, such as in the theatrical work of Arena Contra Zumbi. The territory of Palmares came to signify the hope of a fairer Brazil; of liberty, unity, and equality.

In analyzing the meanings of quilombo, we cannot overlook the question of heroism, which is intrinsically connected to the history of quilombo. The hero figure, particularly Zumbi, is inescapably central. More than any other element in the history of quilombos, the image of Zumbi retains representational force as part of a new national soul.

Between 1888 and 1970, in the struggle for recognition of their role in Brazilian society, black Brazilians could not, with few exceptions, express themselves in their own voices. It is remarkable, therefore, that just when the country was suffocating under a profound repression of freedom of thought and freedom of assembly, such an expression became possible. The 1970s were that moment of possibility.

Perhaps by virtue of being an extremely oppressed group that did not pose an immediate threat to institutional power, black people were able to inaugurate a social movement founded on a discourse of self-affirmation and the recovery of cultural identity.

It was the rhetoric of quilombo, and the analysis of this alternative system, that served as the principal symbol for the trajectory of this movement. We could call this a correction of nationality. The absence of full citizenship and effective means of reparation, and the fragility of a popular Brazilian consciousness, led to a rejection of the national, and within the movement, to the identification of a heroic past.

Just as before it had served as a reaction to actually existing colonialism, in the 1970s quilombo returned as a form of reaction to cultural colonialism. It reaffirmed African heritage and sought a Brazilian model that fortified ethnic identity.

All the literary and oral history of quilombos helped drive this movement to overhaul hackneyed historical concepts.

In November 1974, Palmares do Rio Grande do Sul, a group that included the poet Oliveira Silveira, suggested in the *Jornal do Brasil* that celebrations should mark the date of the 20th of November, to commemorate the murder of Zumbi and the fall of the Quilombo of Palmares, rather than the 13th of May, the date of the abolition of slavery. Memorializing an event that emphasized the capacity of our ancestors to resist had a greater positive significance, they argued, than abolition, often characterized as handed down from above by the slavocratic and imperial system.

Their suggestion was immediately well received. The search for greater clarity about the history of resistance led to workshops, debates, research, and projects that fed young people's longing for liberty through institutions, schools, universities, and the media. Quilombo came to be synonymous with black people, their conduct, and the hope for a better society. It became an internal and external crux for all forms of cultural resistance. In the search for greater recognition of black inheritance, everything, from attitude to association, became quilombo. Today the 20th of November is enshrined in the national calendar as Black Consciousness Day.

Final Considerations

This brief study has sought to put quilombo into a singular temporal framework. Because the diversity of quilombo has previously been underplayed, this has necessarily been descriptive. An analytical project is needed to understand the persistence of quilombo in Brazilian thought and in the collective unconscious of black people.

During its existence, the quilombo has served as a symbol for ethnic and political resistance. As an institution it retains unique characteristics from its African model. As political practice it proclaims liberal, emancipatory ideas that resist the distortions imposed by hegemony at moments of national crisis. For black people, often figured as docile and subservient, the figure of heroism fortifies everyday struggles against oppression and social inequality.

Quilombo is a powerful tool in the process of recognizing a black Brazilian identity, and moving toward deeper self-affirmation as black and Brazilian. Alongside other practices that strengthen cultural identity, the history of quilombo as an actually existing breach in the system of oppression of black people offers hope that similar institutions can have the same effect today.

Note

Originally published as "O conceito de quilombo e a resistência cultural negra," in *Afrodiáspora* 3, nos. 6–7 (1985): 41–49. This translation previously appeared in *Antipode* 53, no. 1 (2021). Nascimento published two versions of this essay. The text here is the earlier, shorter version. A second, expanded text appeared in 1994 as "O conceito de quilombo e a resistência afrobrasileira," in *Sankofa: Resgate da cultura afro-brasileira*, vol 1, ed. Elisa Larkin Nascimento (Rio de Janeiro: SEAFRO/Governo do Estado, 1994). There are two main additions in the later text: first, an extended discussion of the political and territorial disposition of West and Central Africa during the slave trade; second, a section entitled "Brazilian Quilombos and the Revolutions of the Nineteenth Century," which expands on the history of quilombos in Brazil. That version adds historical depth, but does not fundamentally alter Nascimento's argument.

Bibliography

Birmingham, David. *A conquista Portuguesa de Angola*. a Regra do Jogo, Lisboa, 1973.

Carneiro, Edison. *O Quilombo dos Palmares*. Rio Civilização Brasileira, 1965.

Conrad, Robert. *Os últimos anos da escravatura no Brasil*. Rio: Civilização Brasileira/MEC, 1975.

Freitas, Décio. *Palmares, a guerra dos escravos*. Porto Alegre: Editora Movimento, 1971.

Nascimento, Abdias do. *O Quilombismo*. Rio/Petrópolis: Editora Vozes, 1980.

Nascimento, Maria Beatriz. "O quilombo do Jabaquara." *Revista de Cultura Vozes* (maio-junho), 1978.

Rodrigues, José Honório. "A rebeldia negra e a abolição." *História e Historiografia*. Petrópolis: Vozes, 1970.

Serrano Carlos. "História e antropologia na pesquisa do mesmo espaço: a Afro-América." *África—Revista do Centro de Estudos Africanos da USP* (no. 5), 1982.

The Role of Women in Brazilian Quilombos: Resistance and Life [Project]

1. Scientific Significance of the Project

This project will produce primary and secondary outputs on the presence of women in Brazilian quilombos. It will attempt to demystify the historical role of *the feminine*, generally considered as secondary to male quilombolas. Though they are occasionally mentioned in the secondary literature, they are anonymous in the primary sources. They are absent characters in the project of freedom that quilombos are understood to be today.

The intended outputs that will emerge are:

a) Articles and texts in academic journals and collections.
b) Contributions to education, presentations, and conferences on the historical role of women.
c) Publication of a book containing the final results of the research.

The project aims to contribute to historiography on the conditions of women in the organization of quilombos. It will fill in gaps in the historical study of quilombos, which is characterized by a deficiency of information. It will aim to serve as a reference point for subsequent research.

2. Justification

As we enter the second century after the Abolition of Slavery, Historians need to encourage research into sources which contain new knowledge about the history of Afro-Brazilian people. These sources can be building blocks for recovering the mosaic of experience of men and women brought by force from Africa to America, and who, under particular conditions, contributed to the effort of economic, social, and memorial production of our people.

While the phenomenon of the quilombo has been exhaustively discussed by black militants at an ideological level, intellectual work continues to suffer from a lack of the historical information that would be needed to transform quilombo into a new theoretical framework. Quilombo continues to be associated with negative connotations of banditry and flight, seen as less important parts of social reality, and associated with the phenomenon of historical defeat. If we begin by approaching it as a broader theoretical question involving inter-related disciplines, we can identify quilombo, in a macropolitical sense, as temporally and spatially lived in both Brazil and other parts of America. Its significance emerges from micropolitics, which are so often derided by the Social Sciences. We need to insert women into this framework.

Accompanying the limiting tendencies of official historiography, in relation to subordinated peoples, and thanks to the generally military character of quilombos, women are an absent element in the social (everyday) and political context of these communities. This obscurantism of the feminine role is not only something that emerges in relation to quilombos, but is a pattern in the study of history and historiography in general.

However, even in the scanty bibliography and the few primary sources by a few authors, including myself (that are available), every now and then references emerge to the names of women in quilombos; whether among the masses, or as chiefs, warriors, miners, or political advisors in war. Generally they stand out because they are the mothers or sisters of male chiefs (Alcatune or Alcotirene in Palmares) and workers (the women of Quilombo Grande).

If the men in quilombos practiced war and constant territorial displacement, as much in Africa as in America (Brazil, the Guyanas, Cuba, Haiti, Jamaica), the women, the few who are referenced, took part as members of these efforts. If the quilombo gained historical saliency through the official documents of the sixteenth, seventeenth, etc. centuries, the question of the absence of sources, rather than constituting an obstacle, allows the student of History to trace back the story in the most detailed way possible in the sources that are still not opened or critiqued.

The study of the quilombo as a surviving community is being undertaken in various Brazilian states. The role of the woman, for the reasons presented here, must be part of attempts to reconstitute, historically, the process of the development of black resistance.

3. Outline of the Project

3a. Objectives

The basic objective of the project is to examine the role of the various women who stand out in the liberation effort that the quilombo represents. It is to bring out the female sex as an active force in the creation of alternative to black enslavement. In this sense, it is of interest to confirm the manifestations of the feminine sex, even in a traditional way, as a political form of *being in History*. To know up to what point their contribution enabled the organization of a social formation that was considered deviant. To know up to what point, considered as belonging to the oppressed sex, women functioned within that structure of power that was considered marginal in relation to the dominant system. The intention is to observe their degree of autonomy in influencing the system itself. It is necessary to ascertain the power relations between them, and the male chiefs of their community, as well as their power relations with external colonial forces.

Thus, counterposing the result of this research framework with the ideas of established historiography (banditry, fugitivity, and rebellion) that are so ingrained in historical sciences, ideas that reinforce prejudices that become reflected in the memory of the student.

In this sense, the survey of the data will lead to the publication of a monography that will critically reinterpret the concepts attached to the quilombo and, principally, the role of women, in a broad sense, that is absent and anonymous in the historiographical literature, even though they were a social group who were extremely active in traditional agrarian societies.

3b. Organization of the Research

Doing this research requires dividing the project into three inter-related approaches and distinct stages:

i. Survey of primary and bibliographical sources on quilombos in three Brazilian states: Bahia, Pará, and Minas Gerais, according to their productive characters;

ii. Photographic registry of sites, and mapping of areas that were quilombos in these states;

iii. Critical monograph on the role of women in a traditional society and the dynamic of opposition to the modern system.

Note

The original title of this essay is "O papel da mulher nos quilombos brasileiros—resistência e vida—Projeto." Unpublished, Fundo MBN, 14.2.9. This document exists in various draft forms in the archive, none of them complete.

Kilombo

DURING YEARS of research on quilombos in Brazil, one of the things that has most intrigued me has been the tendency, in official and historical literature, and in oral memory, for the phenomenon to be forgotten. Paradoxically, however, its memory sporadically recurs, and, occasionally, quilombo bursts through into national consciousness. In the twentieth century, this has happened specifically when political relations are in profound crisis.

It was only recently, on reading the work of Thomas Kuhn (Scientific Revolution, Vth Text), that I finally understood that the quilombo is a paradigm, though it has not been interpreted as such. Faced with other models of a vision of the world, it breaks through and imposes the power of its significance onto the world's African descendants.

As an (intensely) lived history, its trajectory is unbroken, and deeply ingrained in the minds of Brazilian people.

What Would Quilombo Be?
(*Kilombo, from Quimbundu*)

In Brazil, words of African origin never have a singular meaning. This is partly thanks to the structure of African languages themselves, and partly thanks to their history in the national context (the same word can be pronounced in a range of languages, not necessarily that of its ethnic origin). What is enunciated is generally just an expression, independent of the signifier. The word summons things up as an instrument of invo-cation/evocation/revelation.

In this sense, quilombo names a process of action, activity, and conduct within the three principles mentioned above. Therein lies its histori-cal trajectory and its significance: the qualities of process, of contin-uum. However, we should not think of this continuum as static, but as dynamic.

When the Portuguese conquered the ancient kingdom of Ndongo in the Congo basin, there was an ethnic group called Jaga or Imbangala. Warrior-hunters, originally from East Africa, they had arrived in succes-sive waves since 2000 BC, since the Bantu had crossed the equatorial forest, desertifying it, and transforming it into the Sahara. By around 1569 they had managed to expel the king of Congo and the Portuguese from the capital, forcing them into exile on an island in the river. The Jaga de-stroyed the Portuguese sense of security in Central-West Africa. This ethnic group was atypical because, beyond being nomadic, they did not possess lineage. They did not include women, in the sense that other peoples did, nor did they raise children or form States. They constituted themselves as a transversal power in relation to the governments of the territories they came into contact with. They recruited male adolescents from other lineages, who, after undergoing a circumcision ritual, were adopted by the ethnic group in order to increase their fighting force.

The act of circumcision transformed the young men into kilombo. The sacred house and the territory where the initiation of the warrior took place was also called kilombo. The camp where they undertook com-mercial exchanges was also called kilombo. And, finally, the act of moving as a fighting force was the movement of the kilombo.

The young man initiated into the kilombo was prepared to receive and develop the vital force. Or rather, his body would become a solid and healthy thing, with which to confront any and all exertions, any and all adversity. He was prepared not only for war but also to take and found territories. His destiny as an adult would be to practice nomadism and create territorial settlements.

In this way the kilombo was transferred to América. From the six-teenth century onward, across the whole American territory, settlements

were founded by these individuals: quilombos in Brazil and the Southern Cone, *cimarróns* in the north of South America, *apalancados* (in
Cuba and Haiti), and *maroons* (in the rest of the Caribbean islands).

We can understand the history of the Quilombo of Palmares in this
way. Its founder and civilizing force was Zumbi de Angola Janga.

As an African system in colonial América, quilombos were often constituted as States, capable of putting the stability of trade and prices of
the merchants of metropolitan Europe at risk. Whenever one of these
settlements was organized, it affected the colonial system:

1. It withdrew a significant part of the enslaved labor force, who
   abandoned the plantations and mines to live alongside their
   equals and strengthen the insurgency against the regime.
2. Because the quilombo was based on the power of war and pillage,
   it reduced the areas available for the production of raw materials
   for export.
3. It obliged the colonial and metropolitan powers to maintain
   soldiers and troops in a permanent state of readiness, prepared
   to attack Afro-American establishments.

This whole process caused prices in the international market to fall,
and forced the metropole to spend their efforts in replacing the labor
force, which increased the price of enslaved people in Africa.

This movement continued across centuries of colonization in all
parts of Central and Southern America. After the abolition of slavery,
the process of the quilombo is no longer documented. However, research has shown that it was internalized in the practices and conduct
of the free descendants of Africans. It runs through collective black
memory and the collective national memory as an inspiration, no longer as a declared, violent war, but as a force of struggle for life.

Kilombo Today: Force of Singularization

The bantu philosophy of the *vital force* persists today in the Brazilian
way of being. What seems to be the acceptance of difficulties is based in
this philosophy, which insists that life must be performed, strengthening

it as an instrument of struggle in the physical body and the mind. Thus, Afro-Brazilian religions of bantu and nagô (a West African ethnicity) origin, became syncretic to furnish their believers with the principle of this force, which serves as the mechanism of existential and physical war. As in the ancestral quilombo and in initiation rites, it is marked by the strengthening of the individual as a territory dislocated in geographic space. Founded by enslaved and quilombola predecessors, it remains a living, active paradigm in American territory.

Through their action in their own localities, whether in the spiritual "terreiro," in family communities, in favelas or in recreational spaces (manifested in music of African, Afro-American, or Afro-Brazilian origin), the African peoples of América stimulate change in social and racial relations.

Occupying space with their physical body (existential territory), they can seize hold of the city, reproducing the means of ancient quilombolas, making themselves, like them, visible to the regime. They make this into a discontinuous space in time, in which the "slits" provoke lines of flight and are elements of a dynamization that generates a specific social environment.

So it was with quilombos and their cognates throughout the history of América. So it is with black or Afro-American groups today.

Note

The original title of this essay is "Kilombo." It was written in the early 1990s. Unpublished, Fundo MBN, 2D.CX 22. DOC4. Ratts notes that this text was written for the journal *Nommo* of the Instituto dos Povos Negros de Burkina Faso, but that he has not been able to identify whether it was published.

PART IV

Black Aesthetics, Spirituality, Subjectivity, and the Cosmic

The Body, Territory, the Spiritual, Immaterial, and the Ancestral

Christen A. Smith

Goodbye my love
I am leaving
And I already miss you

"Body-map of a distant country that seeks other frontiers that
limit the conquest of me."

—"study in e major, opus 10 no. 3"

WRITING CAN BE a profoundly intimate act. It picks up the lint of our thoughts, feelings, and political surroundings and morphs along with us as we travel life's roads. This is particularly the case with Beatriz Nascimento, who evolved her writing creatively over time, following the rhythms and tempos of her internal and external worlds. In this final section, we present a miscellany of Nascimento's written thoughts, all of which engage in some way with her reflections on art, identity, the symbolic, the psychological, the aspirational, the philosophical, and the introspective. The papers we present here are bits and pieces of ideas and feelings that she collected. They poetically and powerfully provide us with a glimpse into the internal workings of her mind.[1]

Beatriz Nascimento believed that culture, aesthetics, representation, and self-awareness were key elements of the project of constructing a History of Black People. She recognized that one of the primary ways that the slavery/colonialism project waged war on Black people was through cultural appropriation and misrepresentation. By denying Black people a diachronic identity (a present, a past, and a future), mainstream Brazilian society recast this population as morally bereft, void of culture, apolitical, and primitive. Stereotypes and grotesque imaginaries came to be commonplace ways to dehumanize and erase Black people from the national story in the media, literature, and film. For this reason, Nascimento spent a great deal of intellectual time critiquing Brazilian popular culture. She deconstructed the myths of Blackness alive in the white imaginary, mapping intellectual paths of Black resistance and refusal, imagining the possibilities of new Black worlds, and reflecting on the spiritual and philosophical meanings of life and death.

Blackness in the White Imaginary

In 1976 filmmaker Carlos Diegues produced the film *Xica da Silva* in Brazil, starring renowned Black actor Zezé Motta. *Xica da Silva* was an instant national hit, becoming one of the most watched and discussed films in Brazilian history. However, while the film won widespread critical acclaim in the Brazilian media and in mainstream Brazilian society writ large, Black Movement intellectuals vehemently critiqued the film for its gross stereotyping and negative portrayal of Black people. Beatriz Nascimento was one outspoken critic. In 1976 she published "The Slave Quarters Seen from the Big House" in *Opinião*. Here, she bitingly reviews the film, railing against the director and carefully and thoughtfully picking apart the details of the film's racist frame. The politics of this piece are in its tone and in its attention to detail, which clearly demonstrate her intent to censure the film and condemn the film industry that allowed its production. However, in addition to deconstructing the film itself, this essay returns us to her thesis: rewriting the History of Black People. Here, she uses *Xica da Silva* to point out how anti-Black racism in Brazil operates. Instead of Black people writing their own stories, white people narrate Black people's lives, ignoring and erasing Black lived experience. This theme is one that came up repeatedly in essays in previous sections and one that resonates across her writing from the 1970s and early 1980s.

Nascimento takes up a similar charge in the 1981 essay "The Slaves Seen by the Masters." There, she again critiques the Brazilian film industry, setting her sights on Carlos Diegues (whom she refers to as Cacá Diegues—a twisting of his name into the Brazilian word for *poop*). She takes on the director's pushback against the "ideological patrols" that critiqued *Xica da Silva*, which we can assume include Black radical intellectuals. This essay expands on the previous one, outlining more clearly some of her more sociological critiques of the film's racial politics. For example, she talks of the "know-your-place" aggression of the film. She also reminds us of the political tension of the time, by mentioning the director's overreaction to criticism, stating that Diegues interests were defended in ways "even more authoritarian than the Censors, even in a politically closed country, like Brazil in 1976 under the regime of Institutional Act Number 5."

The next two essays, "What They Call Culture" and "Literature and Identity," both take up the question of identity and the stakes of myth making for marginalized people. "What They Call Culture" was published in the journal of the Brazilian Psychoanalysts' Society. Here we return to the theme of mental health by way of an engagement with Freud. The focus of the essay is on the hero myth and its psycho-symbolic significance. Nascimento writes, "people in need, who are discriminated against, and who have limited educational resources, often seek intermediation through historical myth and critiques of the system and its relations." Zumbi is the figure she considers here. "The myth of the promised land—the Quilombo of Palmares—and the edification of the hero Zumbi, civilizer of black culture, accrue meanings beyond the stereotypes of history and tradition." She continues, "The myth, therefore, emerges out of the real and into the symbolic." Again, we return to the question of History, but this time Nascimento takes us on a different path, considering how the search for History also maps onto hidden psychological desires for meaning, belonging, and continuity. We cannot help but think here that she is also reflecting on her own psychological investment in quilombo as a symbolic myth, and what it means that Zumbi and Palmares became the symbols of the Black Movement.

"Literature and Identity" brings us back to the question of representation. She is concerned with the representation of Black people in Brazilian literature and the lack of Black protagonism among Brazilian literary authors. She argues, "identity is formed not through single elements of character, but the social inter-relations in which they originate. These social relations are the formative context in which aspirations and frustrations combine." White authors "repeat and reproduce stereotypes" of Black people in their writing by individuating Black stories rather than seeing Black people as interconnected—the possibility of Black organized societies. Consequently, white authors erase the possibility of Black continuity—connections between people, Black love, the collective history of discrimination and dispossession: in sum, the cumulative impact of racism on Black people over space and time. "Literature behaves as if it were just a reflection, placing fictional black people in confrontation with the real, based on what is seen as the product of his labor, the progress of his life, and his relationship with the world."

Teaching as Movement Building

One of the key roles that Beatriz Nascimento played in the Black Movement was helping to establish Black student nuclei in universities across the country. We have spoken previously about the GTAR. Her work advising this group led to several moments when she was called on to advise other Black student and academic groups at universities across Brazil. The pieces "Letter from Santa Catarina" and "Aruanda!" reflect on these conversations and outline Nascimento's vision for Black-led study groups inside universities. The questions that she raises and the outlines she presents are not just road maps for organization building but also her vision mapping of what Black Studies can and should be in Brazilian universities. "Letter from Santa Catarina" explains her role in supporting the founding of the Centro de Estudos Afro-Asiáticos (CEAA), and "Aruanda!" is an outline of her suggestions for the budding Centro da Referência Negromestiça (CERNE) in Bahia. The latter is particularly informative given its clear and direct listing of key actions that she believed CERNE could take to create a vibrant Black Studies project.

An Existential and Metaphysical Territory

Black women's imaginative and material lives unsettle the rendering of the Black body as ahistorical and recall that the production of space is uneven and intellectually unresolved. Black women's relationship to diaspora is, by definition, both here and there, then and now, simultaneously and contiguously—redefining the relationship between space, time, territory, and identity by the very nature by which we move through and experience the world—those who are uprooted and replanted, violently and freely, through time.

"For a (New) Existential and Physical Territory" is an entangled, complex text that represents the multiple voices of Beatriz Nascimento. A term paper written for a class titled "Urban Space-Time: Cities, Territory and Conduct," it represents Nascimento's intellectual largesse in motion through its rumination on Félix Guattari and Gilles Deleuze's work *Kafka: Towards a Minor Literature* (1975). The book was written in the years following Guattari's influential trip to Brazil, and the publication of *Molecular Revolution in Brazil* (1981), a selection of texts and interviews from that trip (including, famously, a lengthy exchange between Guattari and Lula Inácio da Silva). Nascimento picks up key concepts from these French theorists and brings them to bear in a reflection on becoming Black and processes of territorialization. It is a paper that is unfinished and experimental. It also represents the range of her reading and her penchant for cultural critique. It is a window into her mind at work that is at times frustratingly unfinished and at other times excitingly filled with possibility. This possibility becomes particularly salient toward the end of the text when she brings Guattari and Deleuze into a new set of dialogues as she begins to unpack intricate, cosmological reflections on the relationship between white, black, and red blood in the spiritual traditions of candomblé. Her discussion of Vital Force, and Guattari's ecosophy, here gestures toward a much bigger and more elaborate, nascent theoretical frame of which Nascimento seems to have been on the brink. It is as if the essay begins at the end.

Throughout we see, yet again, Nascimento's abstract and speculative thoughts on life, death, subjectivity, and emotion through a poetic and biographical voice. The same themes haunt her here as they do in previous sections: embodiment, transcendence, materiality, and spirituality, and the intersections between the metaphysical realm and the material experience of the social world.

Poetics

In the 1990s Beatriz Nascimento's voice changes in tone. Whereas her 1970s and early 1980s writing is didactic, pedagogical, and politically firm in its engagement with the national debates, her voice in the 1990s is decidedly poetic. We feel this turn in "For a (New) Existential and Physical Territory" and in other essays from this period, included in previous sections. She is reflexive, philosophical, and flowing in her analysis. Her prose has a poetic pitch to it that changes the intonation of her written voice. She feels more confident, surer of her ideas, and firmer in her refusal to mimic the western tropes of elite writing. Indeed, in the essay that closes this section, she moves seamlessly between poetry and prose in both cadence and form.

From the archives, "Cultures in Dialogue" appears to be notes for an event (the original title in the archives is "Evento Culturas em Dialogo"). This piece is most likely an outline of a talk that she was to give, as it has bullet points and key ideas mapped out. One of those key ideas is one of her primary theoretical contributions: transatlanticity (*transatlanti-cidade*). She notes that she first coined this term during the making of the film *Ôrí*. Again, she returns to the theme of historical continuity: "within all the discontinuity, there is a discernible continuity in History for peoples who have been dominated and subordinated." The Atlantic is a primary space for the mediation of this continuity: "Only the

Atlantic as a free and physical territory made meetings and unmeetings of disparate Cultures possible." The film *Ôrí* is the primary focus of this piece, and cinema is a key theme. Nascimento invokes the question of psychology again, this time talking about the "phenomenology" of vision as it relates to the cinema and the social imagination.

"Portugal" is a poem/essay that she recites in *Ôrí* as a voice-over to a series of visual shots of the water and Brazilian nature. This is one of the only poetic renderings of her thesis on quilombos. Here, she takes her research and rephrases it, discussing the Middle Passage, quilombo, and the Atlantic as a space of transition.

"Angola" also includes poetry but is a more straightforward reflection on her time in Angola in 1979. This piece connects to the chapter in her master's thesis on Angolan nativism. She chronicles a brief meeting that she had with Angolan revolutionary soldiers while she was on her trip. The focus of the essay is not the political landscape of the country, however, as it was in her thesis chapter. Here she presents a personal reflection on what it meant to sit and talk to young men who introduced themselves as people going off to die. This is the first of a series of conversations about death that close out this section. "It was difficult to explain to those who were going to die how absurd it was, how uncomfortable I was to be drinking with the dying."

Dying is a key theme in the final three essays as well. "Study in E Major, Opus 10 No. 3," "Zumbi of Palmares," and "The First Great Loss: Grandma's Death" are all deeply personal, moving, and at times chilling reflections on death and loss. The first essay begins with Nascimento's vulnerable discussion of her grief at the loss of her friend Raquel and the ways that this loss intensified her psychological condition (mania). She then carefully and artistically weaves that conversation back to Angola along the Cuanza (or Kwanzaa) River, the sea, and her grief and euphoria upon physically being in the land of her ancestors. She also recalls the meaning of her arrival in Angola on the day of Agostinho Neto's funeral. "Death has the power to level, and to spread its impression uniformly, especially when you mourn an individual with implications like Neto's."

"Zumbi of Palmares" is a another profoundly intimate text, which has never before been published. This essay/story/reflection is Nascimento's recollection of a powerful dream in which she saw the warriors of Palmares and at the same time saw death. The warriors that she saw reminded her of the book that her grandmother once had which illustrated warriors in the forest—a book that the next essay, "The First Great Loss," also revisits.

We end this section with "The First Great Loss" both for its breathtaking beauty and its emotional weight. Beatriz Nascimento's death still haunts those she left behind. It felt fitting, then, for us to end with her own reflections on losing one of the most important people in her life: her grandmother. "Even today I am appalled and perplexed in front of death. I cannot cry. I do not know if I feel sadness." Yet in this loss there is the irony of hope as well. When she lost her grandmother, she also lost her grandmother's book, but in that she found the desire to write a book herself.

The Vision

Presenting Nascimento's work on aesthetics, the cosmic, and the spiritual in this way perhaps suggests a more polished body of work than exists. In fact, not least because of the conditions of her access to academic institutions and the racist structures of Brazilian intellectual life, her work remained fragmentary. The case for reading fragments and traces of archives holistically, whether along the grain or against the grain, is well established, particularly in relation to recovering the theoretical productions of Black women.[2] So too the importance of opening our conception of what counts as intellectual work when writing Black women's intellectual history. We hope, however, that these pieces are also read as traces of praxis that went through and beyond writing. That is to say that they are records and archives of Nascimento's radical praxis of artistic creation, political organizing, and intellectual debate all aimed at the creation of materially, aesthetically, and psychologically liberated spaces for Black people in Brazil.

The pieces here also take the reader deep into Nascimento's psyche, as she writes about questions of memory, dream, family, and love. Though many of these archival fragments (such as "Zumbi of Palmares") were unpublished in her lifetime, their archival form, as typeset documents, strongly suggests that they were not only meant as personal reflections but that she was gathering them together with the view to some form of publication. Nevertheless, they are deeply personal reflections. We end with them not only because they are among her latest work (though their dates are unknown) but because they gesture toward a new creative agenda and a new kind of writing that was maturing and developing when her life was violently cut short.

Notes

1. Portions of this essay come from our previously published essay on Beatriz Nascimento, "In Front of the World."

2. M. Fuentes, *Dispossessed Lives: Enslaved Women, Violence, and the Archive* (Philadelphia: University of Pennsylvania Press, 2016); S. Hartman, *Wayward Lives, Beautiful Experiments: Intimate Histories of Social Upheaval* (New York: W. W. Norton, 2019).

Femme Erecta

To how long do I belong?
Only these years? Impossible
So many chronologies mark my body.
Infinite . . .
If not, why such expression
Such unforeseeable sensation. Exploding atoms
Surely I would not know, how do I know to identify
They were necessary to feel a lot
To acquire arms, to put yourself on your feet.

Note

The original title of this poem is "Femme Erecta." February 10, 1990.

The Slave Quarters Seen
from the Big House

SOMEONE ONCE said that art does not need to be ahead, because it is already the vanguard. Like all axioms, this one needs to be rethought. Sometimes, art can be deeply conservative. So it is with the cinematographic art of *Xica da Silva*. This is not just a question of aesthetics. In art, form is content. As discourse, as communication, the film would be better off languishing on the Censor's *index* of forbidden works. It is disrespectful to an episode in the history of a people, disrespectful to a whole people's history, disrespectful in its vilification of that people, and disrespectful in reproducing precisely the stereotypes from which that people are, right now, trying to free themselves, through their own cultural autonomy.

Xica da Silva is a total mistake from first principles. I will try to analyze it in detail. It is an impoverished projection of Gilberto Freyre's *The Masters and the Slaves*, without the empirical depth of the eminent sociologist's work, and without the critical possibilities that literary work opens up. In the critique of racial relations in Brazil it sends us back to the Stone Age.

Let's think through why *Xica da Silva* is a mistake. The director purposely backs away from historical fidelity. Perhaps this is justified by the idea that works of art do not presuppose scientific rigor. Fantasy is the raw material for a good work of cinema. I agree. I do not agree, however, with the absence, in every single moment of the film, of the knowledge of a people who created the Brazilian nation alongside white people. And I do not agree with the film's cheap and vulgar humor, laid on top of the most vulgar stereotypes about that people. No. It is unforgivable that a filmmaker who declares himself full of "love for the people" should fail to know the people. Love presupposes knowledge.

Carlos Diegues's masterpiece is senile. (I dearly hope that he is not making another film, and has already accepted the end of his cinematic career.) As I have already noted, in general terms, he has reiterated *The Masters and the Slaves*. The Portuguese characters in the film, from João Fernandes to the intendant and the loose-tongued "inconfidante," are oppressors and exploiters, but they are indulgent with the black enslaved characters. They are sentimental (the father of the *Inconfidante* and João Fernandes) and, above all, admirers of a good love story. The black people, both enslaved and the quilombolas, are passive. They are inconsequential rebels (robber bandits) and merely appreciate the kindness and generosity of the Masters (for example, the scene in which Teodoro agrees to form an army to save João Fernandes). Racial conflict (which does not really materialize) is only advanced by less gifted people: the unsatisfied wife of the intendant, the stupid priest, the impotent city guard, and the children, clearly just out of an English boarding school, trained in stone throwing. But all of this is in spite of any concrete motivation.

In sum, the *ethos* of the Portuguese colonizer is one of humanity and recognition toward black people. A pleasant slavery, a jolly slavery!

Carlos Diegues begins his film with João Fernandes in the virtuous posture of a flautist. That is an inconceivable position for a contractor, a pariah class of functionaries sent by the Portuguese Crown to Brazil. Surprisingly, as the action unfolds, the contractor—Walmor Chagas— transforms into the image of a bourgeois intellectual, torn between love, the people, and the Crown. He is compassionate and is forced to be an oppressor (Teodoro, Xica, Cabeça, etc.). Could it possibly be the eighteenth-century image of our filmmaker?

The film, to be fair, does offer some potentially rich moments. It sees the quilombo as an alternative to the bipolar relation between the masters and the enslaved. And it is here that Diegues, even in a light-hearted and ironic way, could pass on vital information, if he named the true conflict: the quilombola against the masters and Xica da Silva, as representatives of another class. But to show that the Portuguese Crown depended on another social structure to exploit the wealth of the Gerais, he is happy to reinforce the myth of the kind Master, emphasizing that the colonizer, far from exploiting black people, was kind enough to buy Teodoro's diamonds. And not that the social organization directed by Teodoro was autonomous to the extent that it could impose its own rules while maintaining its structure (at least at that moment) on a solid economic base. Diegues extends his ignorance to its final consequences, by deconstructing the film itself in the episode when Xica da Silva resorts to Teodoro to save João Fernandes. The quilombola denies his position up until the pivotal point of the film when he goes along with the "banter" of the contractor's wife.

At that moment, I confess that I lost hope that white Brazilian intellectuals could ever understand the real history of black people. Diegues, and whoever else, can claim that the film isn't serious. I agree, but then the parrot's last anecdote comes onto screen.

Perhaps there is an explanation for what happens. If, before making the film, Carlos Diegues came down a little from the heights of his omnipotence and reflected on himself, and the implications of the history of his own people, I would think that, thanks to social and cultural relations, he, as a white Brazilian man, might have been able to introduce the black Brazilian, and his human and racial counterpart, in a specific way. But by repressing this within himself and relating an episode from his own history, he makes black people (Xica da Silva, Teodoro) his heroes only in order to gloat over them.

The director's identification with his hero is not affectionate enough to save him. I am not saying that he treats his hero in an idealist manner, or as a victor. But any author, in creating their hero, has to ensure that, at the level of the unconscious, their understanding of them forecloses any alternative.

But can we hope for this from our filmmaker? Here I am not talking about what he does with Xica da Silva, which we will come back to below, but to this: Diegues destroys Teodoro. From the beginning,

Teodoro, like the rest of the characters, meanders through the film like a "zombie." Though Diegues does not know him at all, Teodoro correctly moves around the edges of the grotesque scenes of Xica de Silva and her ululating *entourage*.

In "assaulting" the contractor on his arrival, Teodoro sets up the historical and (if it were not for Diegues) artistic impact. He establishes his autonomy and makes João Fernandes see that he is not part of his "troop." He marks out the limits between him and the contractor. Teodoro institutes the economic relation between quilombola freedom and the dominant economic system.

Further on, in the only beautiful moment in the film, Teodoro separates himself totally from the order within which he meets the contractor, Xica da Silva and Cabeça, when he buys his wife for a fair market price. Through saving his son he ensures his own survival, and that of his social organization, throughout the story of the film.

Diegues, up to then, had not understood Teodoro. I think he glimpsed his own "internal blackness" when he saw the crux of what a hero would be. It would have been better if he had left Teodoro to one side, as he was beginning to do, and concern himself only with his picturesque Xica. Were it not for the director's treatment, the quilombola could have held onto an alternative that rose above the rest's mediocrity. But the moment Diegues turns his attention to him, that possibility is utterly destroyed. Only then, strangely, does the director resort to historical fidelity, which up to that point he has ignored.

If a positive version of the director's fantasy about black people were possible, he would have held onto Teodoro symbolically until the end. But Diegues destroys the climax of his own work, as, without doubt, he destroys his own "internal blackness." Perhaps in a reflection of his understanding of sexuality as destructive and devouring, the early death of Teodoro, in the director's hands, is directly linked to his sexual intercourse with Xica da Silva.

Analyzing the scene in which the wife of the quilombola appears in tears (?) and the shadow is projected onto Teodoro and Xica da Silva, we see, perhaps, the unconscious attitude of the filmmaker: sex is aggression and destruction. And so the film dies!

It is not strange, therefore, that the villain João Fernandes de Oliveira is the one Diegues truly identifies with. It is he who is distressed at the very moment of departure (though from atop his horse) and who speaks about life and love. Fernandes leaves Tijuco immaculately, nothing touches him, not even the dubious sexuality of Xica da Silva (which is only suggested).

This impasse for the director was the same that we saw in Antunes, the director of *Compasso de Espera*. Antunes is better, though, perhaps thanks to his experience living with black people. He seeks to hold onto his hero, though he does not do so for the same motives as Diegues. Jorge, in *Compasso de Espera*, is also slowly and gradually destroyed. But he reflects the internal anguish of the director at not recognizing himself in his principal character. Teodoro dies abruptly without the audience seeing. This reveals, again, Diegues's irresponsibility.

It is disrespectful to the History of Brazil itself to use an unstudied, unelaborated episode, and treat it without the discussion and dramatic quality that the circumstances require.

What is there to say about the treatment of black women? The Xica da Silva of History is not present in a single moment of the film. Again, the filmmaker could argue that a work of art for a general public does not require rigor or fidelity. Again, I would agree. It does not require rigor, but it does demand respect, because art is symbolic, and because that symbol has to be in human form, it is tied up with the person, with whom the audience has to emotionally identify.

Xica da Silva is not a person. She does not even love the contractor. Diegues succeeds in belittling her even more than the prejudices of literature do. Diegues could have made his film based on the plot of the samba by the Samba School *Acadêmicos do Salgueiro*. In that case he would not have run the risk of making a serious film, or a "samba of the silly creole," but he would also not have destroyed a symbol—a debatable symbol, evidently—of the black race.

Diegues's Xica da Silva is abnormal. She is not even the mad woman of the secondary literature. She is intellectually disabled, stripped of thought, incapable of asserting herself at a personal level. I am not referring to the political level of race, but the level of personal affirmation as a woman who could have in her hands the money that her exploiter gives her.

Once she is free, when she is blocked from entering the Church her reaction is infantile and ridiculous. The person who suggests recompense and reparation for that humiliation is the white man, João Fernandes, who promises her a chapel. When it is impossible to get to the sea (not, as the filmmaker suggests, because she was tired from the journey, but because prejudice and the racial complex blocked her from going beyond the limits of Tijuco), the person who suggests that they build the galley and the artificial lake is the musical white man.

Xica da Silva reinforces the stereotype of passive, docile, intellectually incapacitated black people, dependent on white people to think. Her behavior with the contractor is that of a coddled child who cannot conceive of what they want. The Xica da Silva of history is a powerful, dynamic woman, conscious of her surroundings, like women in African social structures that were, in part, transferred to Brazil. Diegues could have verified this by looking at the role of black women in Afro-Brazilian religions. Or by turning to the myths of our race: the mother-Goddesses like Nanã, Iansã, and Oxum.

But no, it is easier to deal with her through the myth of aberrant sexuality developed across four centuries of the domination and exploitation of black women. Xica da Silva is transformed into a brutish animal, weak and irrational. Her eroticism does not truly legitimize her power. Even that is inconsequential. When, for a fleeting moment in the film (at the "African banquet"), she thinks for herself, Diegues fixes her up in a sterile and banal scene. The single moment in which he concedes to the audience to present a sexual scene of Xica da Silva, it is not a woman who is presented, but a metallic and bestial image; a western understanding of Africa and Africans, as primitive, *wild*. Someone needs to tell Diegues that Africa is just a few hours' flight from Brazil.

One of the points at which the filmmaker shows a profound ignorance of the race of his heroine is when he manages to make Xica da Silva seem to be a woman. But he makes her into a mockery of white women. If we were to invert the roles of Xica da Silva and Hortência, the wife of the intendant, we would have the same result. A capricious woman, always having tantrums and hysterics, the precise opposite of a black, formerly enslaved woman. Simply inconceivable!

So, we have to reflect in the face of all of this. Why does young Diegues put this exhibition on for us? Does he think popular culture is debauched? Or is the question different: why does he debauch popular culture? What cultural impasse is the Brazilian intellectual class stuck in?

He takes an episode from the History of Brazil and puts it on screen so uncritically that it merely reinforces every prejudice and dumps them in front of the wider public. Is this his understanding of how to make popular "culture"? It is taken from the tradition and understanding of the phenomenon by the people. But, Diegues, is the tradition and interpretation of this phenomenon by the so-called people just, honest, or unprejudiced? Are the people a monolith? Are they intrinsically good?

With the justification of making a work to entertain and reach a greater number of people and redeem *cinema novo* from the shipwreck of creative nullity that it has become, Diegues lurches in the opposite direction. He forgets that creation needs critique—the critique of Carlos Diegues. Diegues leaves me thinking that his class, and its traditions, are stuck in the Big House throwing scraps to the Slave Quarters. It was what their predecessors always wanted to do to us.

If the man has not forgotten that past, or cannot critique it through his interpretation of our reality, please leave us black people out of it. Watching the scene of the seduction of the factotum of the Court reminded me of another scene, in *Satyricon*, by Fellini. A black vestal virgin seeks to restore the sexual potency of Encólpio, the hero. It is a scene of great symbolic power and beauty. But, dear readers, it is a warning. Does Diegues understand that between him and Fellini there lies a great expanse of Dark Ocean?

Note

Originally published as "Senzala vista da Casa Grande," in *Opinião*, October 5, 1976, Rio de Janeiro, 20–21.

The Slaves Seen by the Masters: Merchandise and Counterculture in National Cinema

IN THE TRAJECTORY of Brazilian National Cinema, *Cinema Novo* is undoubtedly a key moment. In the 1960s, it was an offshoot of the *Nouvelle Vague,* and it addressed itself to a nationalism characterized at the time by the ideological dominance of the "National Bourgeoisie." At the beginning of the 1960s, elitist intellectual thought about social origins and social crisis flourished, running counter to the developmentalist sentiments of the Kubitschek era.[1] *Cinema Novo,* full of the drama of the lives of Northeasterners and *favelados,* was bound up with the thinking of the former Institute Superior de Estudos Brasileiros (ISEB) [the Superior Institute of Brazilian Studies] and the Centro Popular de Cultura (CPC) [Popular Culture Center] of the União Nacional dos Estudantes (UNE) [National Union of Students].[2] At the time, we were leaving *Bossa Nova* behind as a lyrical and naïve music (*João da Silva, the simple citizen*), and turning to a new music of protest and denunciation (progressive music). There was at once a whole proud delirium, and a denunciation—based on the work of Josué de Castro—of economic scarcity in particular Brazilian Regions, and of the ghettoized population of the favelas. Cinema could not long remain behind. Films began to portray a search for national identity that is still the object and expectation of "the Brazilian petty bourgeoisie" today.

Glauber Rocha's work is pioneering in its questioning of the differences and inequalities in the bosom of the national community. Glauber's metaphorical themes make a polemic out of the nativist sentiments within the dramas of the Northeast. He, and other directors, also glimpses the problematic of black people. Yet, even in Glauber—in *Deus e o Diabo na Terra do Sol* and in *Dragão da Maldade contra o Santo Guerreiro*—there is prejudice and ignorance about black people. In these films there are no real rural black people, only fantasies of them.

On the other hand, Nelson Pereira dos Santos does bring forward the question of black people. Without a doubt, though his cinema is more documentary and urban, Nelson is prepared to look directly at the troubled lives of the needy in Brazil, as Glauber is in the Northeast. (I would put these two filmmakers on the same plane.) *Cinema Novo* disdained producers. At the crux of the relationship between director/producer is the fact that the director must prostitute themselves—and this they refused. Thus, the director-producer emerged, as in the case of these two geniuses of National Cinema. It was all part of a posture of denying the capitalist relation, and its means of attracting financing. Everyone should remember dos Santos's celebrated aphorism: "A CAMERA IN YOUR HANDS AND AN IDEA IN YOUR HEAD." This, therefore, was an ideologically produced cinema. It took a vow of poverty, and was incompatible with the fat-cat style of financing overproduction. Today Nelson Pereira dos Santos's aphorism has become a parody: "A CAMERA IN YOUR HANDS AND A THESIS IN YOUR HEAD."

3. From Engaged Cinema to Cinema Financed by the State and Private Funding: From *Deus e o Diabo na Terra do Sol* and *Vidas Secas* to the Delirium of Funding; Compromised Cinema

In the 1970s, many of Nelson and Glauber's disciples tried to navigate overproduction financed by the Bourgeoisie. Cacá Diegues, whose directing career began in the 1960s, addressed the question of black people. However, it is a thread that he exploits but cannot fully realize.

His cinema is neither metaphorical nor documentary. It is based in black legends from romantic literature and not in historical facts. It explores the possibility of inserting the black problem into the ideology of the ISEB and the CPC of the UNE; the ideology of the petty bourgeoisie. "Ganga Zumba," for example, in the film of the same name (in which he explores Augusto Boal's idea from *Arena conta Zumbi*), shows the weakness of his proposition. But Cacá Diegues was *most* unsuccessful in *Xica da Silva*, a deeply compromised and weak film.

What I have called the delirium of funding happens not only in the arena of the arts, but above all in academic production . . . It is a new slave market.

4. Counterculture or Subculture: The White View of Black People

In 1975, the institutions of SECNEB in Bahia, SINBA and IPCN in Rio de Janeiro, CECAM in São Paulo, CEBA and GTAR in Niterói,[3] sought to affirm Afro-Brazilian culture in the conjuncture of national culture— or rather, counterculture. They did not have a very clear idea of the mass process that had begun in 1974, under the stamp of the CEAA[4] in the Cândido Mendes Faculty in Ipanema. Much less did they foresee the scale that this project of affirmation would take on, to the extent that it influenced parts of *Cinema Novo*, which has now abandoned engaged cinema for cinema compromised by private funding and government bodies. In 1976, *Xica da Silva* came out.

We did not know that, while black people in these institutions struggled against difficulties of all kinds, from confrontation with National Security organs to financial shortages, the black man once again became a saleable commodity. This time through the "media."

Xica da Silva shows this most violently. It marked a regression for our projects of cultural affirmation. It was traumatic for all of us. Unlike *Amuleto de Ogum*, *Xica da Silva* reflected the racist postures not only of the director but of the producers and financiers. The conversion of its director to large, *Hollywood-style* productions was also a conversion to a compromised cinema of spectacle and an abandonment of Nelson Pereira's aphorism. This new type of cinema was just *bread and circuses for the people*. It reiterated the racist ideology of its director. For us—as the director of the Unidos de Lucas Carnival Samba School, and Candeia Filho put it—"*Xica da Silva* was a total nightmare," because it finished with the apotheosis of the race. *Xica da Silva* made the people smile at their own image, and fed a dangerous conformism.

Xica da Silva cost us a lot. All the more so since it is now two years since the filmmaker proclaimed against "ideological patrols." I would respond to the interview given to an Italian newspaper by Mr. Diegues, by asking if the national intellect wanted, really, to put it this way: "MONEY MARKETS: COUNTERCULTURE OR SUBCULTURE OF NATIONAL CINEMA?"

I would ask: was it really an "ideological patrol," or was it the defense of the right to be a new black person, a new person? The refusal to accept a stigma created by the national collective. Once and for all: *stop using us as a commodity to be sold in a new Valongo*. We assert that, for us, Cacá Diegues's career stopped then. Our response was a cry that rose above the clamor of all the different black entities of that period, from the recreational to the political. It was a huge ENOUGH to the racists, and to the users of our image, our identity.

Before that film, the critique of art and national cinema had proceeded, in general, complacently. The rupture happened when I spoke in the name of those institutions cited above—they asked me to write an article on the film and it was published in this spirit in the weekly alternative paper *Opinião*. The first question that I asked of the national intellect was: what was going on in the minds of those old intellectuals of ISEB when they were gloating over and vilifying black people, just when black people were seeking their identity and affirming their self-image? It was at this crucial moment that that figure of the "slave-as-negation-of-this-new-image" emerged. They suggested to us that we did not have the right to a History, only to entirely biased retellings.

However, the director himself could not understand. When a critic, rather than a Censor, blacklists a work, the author's interests suddenly come to the fore in a way that is even more authoritarian than the

Censors, even in a politically closed country, like Brazil in 1976 under the regime of Institutional Act Number 5.

The other question that I asked in the article—"The Slaves Seen by the Masters"—was posed to intellectuals in general: why do we represent ourselves to ourselves in such a distorted way? Not an image of capable men and women, but one in which we can see all our stigmas. And why did it come out in precisely that moment when groups were searching for ways to be free of racial stigmas?

So I wrote in the article that the path that the *people* must follow to implement a new vision, or, better, a new ideology of the people itself, will be winding. We still affirm: who said to the director of *Xica da Silva* that the people of "Madureira" are good, and pure, in their poverty? When racism exists in the minds and hearts of the people, why show the internal poverty of the group of black people that he (the filmmaker) tried to represent in this film? What can we say of a people that "laughs at itself," as seems to be the intention of the film? I would say that the humor of *Xica da Silva*, the humor that it puts forward, is impregnated with the repression that black people, as an integral part of the people as a whole, suffered at that time. Black people thus lived again in their own individual experience the idea that "black people should know their place." This was a dictum that in the 1960s was critiqued by Millor Fernandes, but in the 1970s came to be conformist and escapist. It was this message that the film ended up passing on. It demonstrated more the ideology of petty bourgeois directors who saw the people as a simple confirmation of *ethos*, than seeing what Afro-Brazilian culture and ideology really is, or seeing the representations that Afro-Brazilians make of themselves.

Alongside this was the *know-your-place* by which this work of art undermined the resistances of a stigmatized and repressed people. This "repression," or, rather, the super ego or the social ego, returned to provoke the demobilization of that expectation of cultural freedom that black entities and institutions had been organizing in that period.

Xica da Silva came out at a moment when a whole generation of young black people were protesting against racial discrimination through the sound and dance of *Black Soul* in the great cities of Brazil.

Theirs was a new identity from Shaft, Muhammad Ali, James Brown, Malcolm X, and other leaders who, in representation or otherwise, struggled for an end to the American racial crisis.

We experienced the artistic and cinematographic production that emerged after *Xica da Silva* as a cold shower for a potentially productive population. While young (and not-so-young) people sought a positive racial identity, works of art were made that reinvoked the "slave woman" who accepts an alliance with the colonial and slavocratic powers, thinking only of her class advancement. The individualization of *"know your place": get in or get out.*

That was the message of the film: a prejudiced and racist vision. Could we call this counterculture or subculture? Yes, the film is expensive, but culturally it is null, in my perspective.

So, we can move onto the next debate: Culturalism, counterculture, or subculture in the contemporary production of feature films?

Notes

The original title of this essay is "A senzala vista da Casa Grande: Merchandise e a Contra-cultura no Cinema Nacional." Salvador, January 12, 1981. Unpublished, Fundo MBN, 25.4.81.

1. Juscelino Kubitschek de Oliveira was president of Brazil between 1956 and 1961. His government was marked by a push for grand reformist and developmentalist projects such as the building of Brasília, under his slogan of "fifty years progress in five years."

2. ISEB was a powerful think-tank founded in 1955. It was a hotbed of leftist debate and national developmentalist thought, including scholars such as Hélio Jaguaribe, Nelson Werneck Sodré, and Alberto Guerreiro Ramos. The CPC of the UNE was founded in 1962 in Rio de Janeiro and brought together leftist intellectuals, artists, and writers. Its first director was Carlos Estevam Martins. It promoted a vision of a politicized popular art. Both institutions were shut down after the military coup in 1964.

3. SECNAB: The Society for the Study of Black Culture in Brazil (Sociedade de Estudos de Cultura Negra do Brasil); SINBA: The Society for Brazil-Africa Exchanges (Sociedade de Intercâmbio Brasil-África); IPCN: The Institute for Research on Black Cultures (Instituto de Pesquisas das Culturas Negras); CEBA: Centre for Brazil-Africa Studies (Centro de Estudos Brasil-África); GTAR: André Rebouças Working Group (Grupo de Trabalhos André Rebouças).

4. CEAA: Center for Afro-Asiatic Studies (Centro de Estudos Afro-Asiáticos).

What They Call Culture

IN HIS ESSAY *Moses and Monotheism*, Freud moves into risky terrain. It is strange, even surprising. In the course of reading the essay, from a lay perspective, it struck me that a psychoanalyst who is normally understood as morally concerned with the individual, launches himself into the mythical-religious trajectory of his community. I was curious to find an illustrious Jewish writer trying to explain, psychoanalytically, the origins and foundation of the myth of the hero, precisely while under the shadow of the Nazi threat. I was surprised not only by the theme—the myth of the hero—but also by the historical moment in which Freud wrote. I want to investigate the connection between these things.

I aim to clarify to what extent *Moses and Monotheism* emerges from the author's critique of personal and cultural identity. How should we understand his interest in analyzing the civilizing hero as a psychosocial component of a contested and persecuted group? What moved Freud to investigate the roots of the sentiments that connect a people with their hero?

I ask this question because people in need, who are discriminated against, and who have limited educational resources, often seek intermediation through historical myth and critiques of the system and its relations. What kind of symbolism does this lead us to? Would it be wrong to suggest that the drive to recover historical figures emerges from a guilt complex, analogous to Freud's analysis of Moses? In any case, it is in order to resolve a "complex" that groups transform myths that had previously been associated with banditry into positive images. Perhaps this is how we can nurture a positive self-image ourselves. Even if there is no guilt associated with the past of enslavement, an interpretative complex remains, in which total identification with the weak, the defeated, and the inhuman is insufficient, at the level of daily struggle, for us to oppose forms of discrimination. In the end, this confrontation requires the reinforcement of the ego.

The myth of the promised land—the Quilombo of Palmares—and the edification of the hero Zumbi, civilizer of black culture, accrue meanings beyond the stereotypes of history and tradition. The shadow of this refashioned myth has circulated in manifestations that have been hidden up to now, including in Afro-Brazilian religions, revealing a temporal continuity between our ancestors and our lived history. Consequently, we encounter the enormous importance of proving the territorial and historical existence of the chosen one as the civilizing hero of black Brazilian culture. He is a hero who can be shared among those born here: black people, Indigenous people, and White people, too. The myth, therefore, emerges out of the real and into the symbolic. The hero becomes a morally conciliatory figure, banished from the History of Brazil itself. It would fill the gap for those who, over twenty years (1964–1985), have been stripped of their individual and private rights to collective symbols. We can blame this parricide on a specific sector: those who represent the legacies of the colonial morality that banished and murdered "Zumbi de Palmares."

We should recall Bertolt Brecht: "unhappy the people that needs heroes."[1] While we still need to create and recreate heroes, and to codify and recodify symbols, we are, still, deeply unhappy.

Notes

The original title of this essay is "Daquilo que se chama cultura." *Revista IDE*, Número 12. Sociedade Brasileira de Psicanálise. São Paulo. Dezembro 1986, 8.

1. Beatriz Nascimento writes "infeliz o povo que necessita de heróis," although this line from Brecht's play *The Life of Gallileo*, "unglücklich das Land, das Helden nötig hat," is more commonly translated in English as "unhappy the land that needs heroes." The shift from the land to the people is interesting, as Brecht is broadly referring to an elision between a nation and a people, an elision that Nascimento consistently complicates across her work. However, the lack of citation suggests that she is quoting from memory, which may also explain the shift.

Literature and Identity

BLACK PEOPLE in Brazilian literature can be seen in two ways. Both are difficult to relate to the question of identity. Identity has a number of meanings. Whether at the level of the individual, or the set of individuals belonging to the same ethnicity, family, or nation, identity is determined by many factors. I want to suggest that identity is formed not through singular elements of character, but the social inter-relations in which they originate. These social relations are the formative context in which aspirations and frustrations combine.

We can use two statements to help us situate black people in literature, and articulate how, in general terms, literature and black people interact.

1. "With few exceptions, this literature is conceived and written by white authors from the socially and economically dominant group—intellectuals who repeat and reproduce stereotypes both in fiction and memoirs. This form of literary production is achieved by introducing black people into narratives, and above all into memoirs, as figures for the prevailing relations between white and black. The black man is given subaltern roles, whether figured within the system of slavery, or in the modern system of the allocation of labor. In the former case, we see extremely submissive enslaved people like Bertoleza in *O Cortiço* by Aluísio Azevedo. In the latter case, we see working men and women, or people living marginal lives in regional settings. And there is

another, very common, instance: black people are always placed ambiguously between racism and processes of social advancement" (in Josué Montello, *Tambores de São Luís*).

In this literature, black people do not talk about their intimate anxieties as people, their true vision of the world, or the broad scope of their psychology, as discriminated against and as dispossessed. They do not address the wider political dynamics of this state of things. In the face of this framework, it is hardly even possible to wish that they would.

In the literature in question, black struggles to remove themselves from this condition are always idealized. They border on an exaggerated romanticism and tend to present fragile, infantile behavior that leads to frustration and perplexity.

This literature attends a historical model of black people in which their cry of pain—suffocated by the avalanche of contradictions within a Brazilian culture and society largely built by those that still live as if enslaved—sometimes functions as an impediment to their own quest for emancipation and modernization. In this representation black people never achieve anything apart from indignation and a vague searching for change, because they act as a shield for the struggles of the rest of the oppressed. They are more the standard bearers than the agents of change, and the specificity of their problems remains unclear.

Literature behaves as if it were just a reflection, placing fictional black people in a confrontation with the real, based on what is seen as the product of his labor, the progress of his life, and his relationship with the world. So, the descendants of Africans remain imprisoned in a singular cultural model, reeducating themselves, fictionally.

It is a bumbling and stereotyping literary psychology. It was black authors, principally Lima Barreto, who were driven to address racial prejudice not as an isolated characteristic but as a dynamic and who made an analysis of their own psychology possible. Other great literary figures who deploy the question of black people do not do so in this way. It is as if the character, whether dispossessed or highly qualified, has no psyche of their own that can actually manifest itself—they are either endowed with magical musings, or are passive victims of fatalism.

Love, in this literature, is always interracial. Few works refer to love between a black man and a black woman. When they do, it is a love devoid of pleasure, in which feelings are restricted to the needs of material survival. With rare exceptions, the tendency, rather than to represent two beings who desire one another, is to represent two characters brought together by the most basic contingencies of existence: food, work (generally the woman), providing for other ambitionless beings, and death.

I cannot think of an author who addresses the history of the black family as a literary theme. Black men's affection always manifests in sexual desire for white women, and white men's for black women (enslaved, nanny, pregnant), or for *mestiças* (the *mulatta* as the measure of eroticism), outside institutional structures. In both cases this literature of stimulation represents more the *challenge* of the other than the complete encounter with the other. And the relationship is always submissive.

In truth, this reflects an ideology/myth based on the fantasy that intersexual desire has another national-fantasy as its objective. This necessarily drifts into an unresolved frustration: the quest to break out of social hierarchy, to enter the forbidden world of the other, who occupies a forbidden social space.

This ideology was, until recently, grounded in an aspiration that is not always confessed, though some authors are explicit: that the resolution of racial inequalities and social status should come through intercourse between the sexes and the human product of these relations. That is, through the *mestiço* children unleashed by the whitening ideology of Brazilian society. This whitening is idealized in concepts like *morenice* and racial democracy.

Do not think that this analysis is a partisan trial with a prejudiced conclusion. The role of miscegenation is undeniable in pluri-ethnic countries, including Brazil. It is important not to see them from a eugenicist perspective. They are not the positive endpoint of inter-ethnic relations. These relations transcend any dangerous extrapolations, above all when they are faced with the real individual, political, and social conflicts entailed by our country's ethnic inequalities.

We can assert at least one broadly positive thing to emerge from these exchanges: in my view the politics of any organized society must be based on an acquired individual right to respect the freedom that is embedded in the desire of one human being for another. However, contrary to the "good will" of some writers, this cannot itself be seen as the root of national self-esteem. That is too broad a simplification of the social totality. In fact, this ideology covers up the vastness of prejudice and racial discrimination.

1. A different approach is to discuss the absence of writing in the life of the majority of black people in Brazil. This absence emerges from the impoverishment and illiteracy, that the majority of the Brazilian population is mired in, or the delay in establishing an educational philosophy in Brazilian schools that embraces the elements of black culture that return to African origins.

It is necessary, first of all, to analyze the possible role of African orality. According to some studies this remains current in black people's modes of communication. We should see orality not only as a tradition to be preserved or rescued, but as a variation of the processes of domination that determine racial and social inequality. The profound impoverishment of this part of the population after the Abolition of Slavery was driven by factors including the economic crisis in the first decades of the century, the non-settlement of formerly enslaved people on the land (they were substituted by immigrants), the rise of prejudice and racial discrimination in the emerging labor market, the centralizing politics of the State, urban growth, mortality, and the exclusion of descendants of Africans from education and therefore from access to writing. In this context orality is compromised: it tends toward the imaginary and loses its own objectivity.

As a complement to this oral literature we can appeal to the lyrics of compositions, whether in artistic forms like Congada, Folia de Reis, Boi Bumbá,[1] etc. . . . or in the compositions of *sambistas* in the urban centers. This musical literature, whose themes vary from political critique to everyday life and lyric, compensate in many ways for the majority of the population's lack of command over language. In many compositions the verbal fluency and literary skill verges on real poetry, and an almost formal erudition.

Its production, however, is seen as purely ludic, a-historical, and individual, and not as the manifestation of a socialized *logos* and the product of a collective *ethos*. It is seen not as a musicalized literature, but just rhyming music, and its words fall into the void.

But in the end, it is in this sphere that the voice of the silenced majority begins to emerge.

Notes

The original title of this essay is "Literatura e Identidade." Written for the II Perfil de Literatura Negra—Mostra Internacional de São Paulo, 1987, Unpublished, Fundo MBN, 4.2.46.

1. Congada is an Afro-Brazilian folk form that includes music, dance, and storytelling. It reaches back to the early eighteenth century. Folia de Reis is another popular cultural manifestation of religiosity with Catholic points of reference. Boi Bumbá, or Bumba Meu Boi, is a folkloric, popular form of drama, poetry, and performance with a long history in Brazil, going back to the eighteenth century. It often includes a satirical critique of social structures.

Letter from Santa Catarina

SINCE THE 1970S, various people in the Black Movement have been coming together to meet. These assemblies offer catharsis, and the opportunity for organic synthesis. They have served psychological, spiritual, generational, and intellectual-genealogical functions within groups and between groups. In March 1974 a collective desire emerged to hold these meetings in physical spaces that had, up to then, not been widely frequented by black men and women.

The first meetings of the Black Movement in Rio de Janeiro, therefore, took place in the Cândido Mendes University Building in Ipanema and in the Opinião Theater in Copacabana, in the South Zone of the city. At the Cândido Mendes College, students at the Fluminense Federal University gathered to discuss an article by Beatriz Nascimento ("For a History of Black People"). They came together to take the first steps toward the creation of the Center for Afro-Asiatic Studies (CEAA, Centro de Estudos Afro-Asiáticos). The group grew from about a dozen people at the first discussion to nearly two hundred people the following week. This revealed a latent desire, which in that moment was sparked and spread throughout the population in Rio de Janeiro, Niterói, and São Paulo.

A number of different tendencies quickly emerged, largely of a conflictual character. For the first time in the history of social movements, personal and existential interests were subsumed into collective political drives and a *hidden social* I (general, broad, and total). The interesting aspect of those first experiences (of the existential as an instrument of political action) was that they manifested themselves in verbal and oral expressions against domination. However, thanks to individual and social (class) differences, this discourse was very internally fragmented. Yet it had a "common objective": to rebel against the silence imposed by the regime of arbitrary power, and its ban on meetings that "risked" the whole ideology of the regime.

Let us imagine hundreds of people, men and women (young and old), of the most diverse origins and sexes, ages, social backgrounds (family, education), neighborhoods, regions. Some of these people (at the Opinião Theater, at least) were older, and associated with the Black Experimental Theater (Teatro Experimental do Negro [TEN]) that had in previous decades organized black and mulatto intellectuals in various areas.

The majority, however, were young people with access to information about African independences and the civil rights movement in North America (Social Integration and "Black Power," the Vietnam War and Soul Music). They watched the fall of colonialism in Portugal (and its Overseas Empire) and in the Lusophone African countries: Guinea-Bissau, Angola, and Mozambique. They were largely new students at the university who took part in Soul Music groups. They sought a Brazilian way of pushing back, internationally and intercontinentally, against the colonial dependency that has internally impregnated every citizen and every national institution (politics, literature, the press, the electronic media, and national conduct). Racial discrimination, color prejudice, latent and manifest violence against our black personhood became the rallying cry for liberation for this highly subordinated group, excluded from the basic rights of full citizenship.

Bringing together people with different social perspectives and expectations around a single racial identity—black—contradicted the political impulse of the Black Movement. As a concept, race is charged with unconscious and abstract attributes. It emerged from European biological science (e.g., Darwin, Humboldt, and other naturalists and scientists from the middle and end of the nineteenth century). It is marked by generalizing concepts, open and specific denials of African and American humanity. In those discussions, at the most fundamental level of the individual, race required profound revisions and refutation. The first meetings, therefore, took place in the frustrating and recalcitrant territories of the unconscious: the traumatic experiences of African transmigration (diaspora), enslavement (the old regime), persecution (against individual and collective processes of self-liberation and the self-determination of [African] fetishes stigmatized by Official History), anonymity (loss of family names, whitening of previous generations), pauperization (loss of property and all goods of value in the economic ruptures that emerged out of neocolonial economic dependency, and changes of policies according to the needs of the strongest national elites). In sum, the pursuit of leadership and communal militancy.

The article cited above, and "Black People and Racism," put forward a proposition and a question. Eighty-seven years after the Abolition of Slavery, and eighty-six years after the Proclamation of the Republic and the First Federal Republican Constitution, who are black people in Brazil? The implication was that it is those who have darker skin. And it was those people who came together in our first meetings. The interpretations of the question "Who are black people?" were varied, diverse, and disparate. Some responded that black people are all those who are oppressed, allies, militants of the "black cause."

The concept of race in the European scientific and biological imaginary again became the marker for differentiation and not collectivization or nationalization. Old concepts are secure in elite minds and institutions: whitening, resolution through miscegenation, the relative extermination of Black chromatization.

The various individuals and groups clashed on the terrain of the verbal-affective. The absence of a written or generalized historicity required a collective effort of repressed historical memory. The *I* will be the semantic figure that occurs and reoccurs. The *collective ego* flowers as if it is accepting and assuming itself in the declaration that "we are thus, just like this, we are black people." Meanwhile, the super ego and the realist view of the individual unconscious rejects this proposition and tries to impose it not in the plural but in the singular. That is, it prepares itself, in a modern sense, to accept the difference incorporated into ideas of human inequality, the power to participate in the national collective, the regional collective, in familial and geographic destiny, enthroning heroism across generations, in the spectrum of promotion, of well-being, of aesthetics, of visibility of the self, and visibility of the other (the axé), in opposition to the current regime, in the context of elections and the participation of political parties from 1978 to 1984, in the recovery of civil and human rights through political opening, in the search for disrepression.

In 1979 I enrolled in the postgraduate course at the Federal University of Fluminense, with a research project already underway, financed by the Ford Foundation. The project, *Alternative Black Social Systems: From Quilombos to Favelas*, was based on my militant experience, as well as research in lived and oral History. The hypothesis was to refocus away from enslaved life, toward the conservativism of quilombola life, and the certainty of historical continuity and discontinuity. Ninety years after the Abolition of Slavery, I insisted that though the History of Brazil had not yet reached all free people, it could not obscure the various expression of lived freedom that black people in the past and the present had attempted.

In 1978 I went out to prove this hypothesis in the *congadas* of Minas Gerais, to research how Brazilians expressed their repression and their frustrations not only as a group but as networks of individuals.

What new human being emerged from the struggle for freedom? How were they inserted into modernity? How were they overcoming the crisis of enslavement, impoverishment, and racial discrimination? How to escape from depersonalization and anonymity?

Two years into the research I met the sociologist Raquel Gerber once again. I had data from urban centers including Rio de Janeiro, São Paulo, Salvador, Belém, and Belo Horizonte, as well as the decaying rural areas of Minas Gerais, where I had met the living remainders of former quilombos. In 1980 Raquel and I began to make the first steps toward the narrated documentary *Ôrí*. Our reunion took place at a very special moment; in 1981 Glauber Rocha died. Raquel had written her master's thesis about him: "The Myth of Atlantic Civilization." His passing was the transmutation of a life dedicated to great, nationally unifying Brazilian themes. Our reunion had a cathartic quality, so we tried to confront the death of the Brazilian word and image and the end of a line of thought that, ever since Oswald de Andrade, has led us toward a national identity based on the ideas of the urban and rural intelligentsia. The strength of the Black Movement was focused in the two major urban centers of the country: Rio de Janeiro and São Paulo. I belonged to the first and Raquel to the second. We had both returned from research trips to Africa: me from Angola, and Raquel from West Africa (Mali, Senegal). We were both adherents of candomblé.

Mental Ecology, "the mental and affective reforestation,"[1] of our people, possessed infinite possibilities for the stimulation of their artistic, aesthetic, and poetic arteries, above all through Afro-religiosity.

In *Ôrí*, the director, the team, and I were conscious that instead of emphasizing the shared negative points of the current human condition, we would seek out, critically and analytically, those sanctuaries where people come together to intercede in their lives, where they look for mutual support in confronting their adversity and promoting the common good, independent of individual and group differences of politics and ideology.

Politics and ideology are historical instruments for people to move toward the union of greater tendencies. But, while these factors promote unity, the discontinuity present in the soul of history reverses this process in the search for individual self-determination and what we call historical continuity. There is, therefore, the micropolitical.

Faced with the Black Movement, I noticed early on that the processes of continuity and conservativism (what I call quilombo) are the strongest stages. In that moment, around 1975, I wrote an unpublished article, "Consciencia do Racismo" [Consciousness of racism], in which I introduced the concept of the *Quilombola Peace*.[2] This peace, and the concomitant, intermittent process of war, was maintained through the production of food and information by those not involved directly in defense: women, the old, children, and adolescents.

In 1982 the global pressures of IWC (Integrated World Capitalism)[3] brought a brutal economic recession to Brazil. At the international level, Islamic fundamentalism, the pressure of the Israeli state, the foreign policy of Lebanon and the crucial moment of Angolan Unification drove us, in the Black Movement, toward participation in party politics. It was a way for us to rebuild citizenship and guarantee our survival as a political force that had been, up to then, anarchic. We made and unmade pacts across national territory during the elections that year.

The text of Ôrí, which naturally tended toward the academic-descriptive, could not be constituted out of the visual reading we had acquired up to then. Far from the academic centers, black political life in Rio, São Paulo, Minas Gerais, and the Northeast (Recife, Maceió, and Salvador) offered us cultural preservation as mass reaction to discrimination and the regime of arbitrary power then in force. Surprisingly, even to myself, the text began to take on the form of unpublished aphorisms and poetry. An aesthetic language, apprehended through the visual.

My verbal and oral engagement with the narration, the interlocutors, and the images for the film were bound up with a personal transformation.

From 1982, in parallel with my militancy in the Black Movement, Ôrí was being made not only with the technicians but periodically with some militants, who at times made up most of the documentary team. When it was finished in 1989, in my opinion, Ôrí held various documents of an archaeological, archetypical, and historical character. The soundtrack, the music, and the soundscape took on a documentary form themselves, realizing a pathway toward their formal counterparts: poetry and music.

Launched at the Pan-African Festival of Cinema and Television (Fespaco), in Ouagadougou, Burkina Faso, Ôrí received the Paul Robeson Prize for the best African diaspora film, and later the Costa Azul prize, in the Man and Nature section in Troia, Portugal. In Brazil, almost all the screenings were followed by debates, which were generally quite unproductive. However, we did not want to allow what I had named from the start as "the obstacle" and principal contradiction of the Black Movement up to that point, to crystallize: the desire to be a racial movement, and not a historical movement. Cathartic events still take place in the Black Movement, as in any human coming together. But when catharsis impedes group dialogue, when aggression predominates instead of constructive and collegial dialogue, it is as if we are, in these very spaces, regressing, and reactivating the primitive attitudes of personal competitiveness and discrimination that, ironically, we struggle against. This generates merely a profound waste of productive energies for those who truly desire, through triumphs and slip-ups, to carve a path toward the future, and a more attuned, more dignified form of humanity. To be, in the end, a *better individual and collective subject*. I know that this is the true purpose of those who throw their efforts into combating racism, prejudice, and discrimination.

Notes

The original title of this essay is "Carta da Santa Catarina." Unpublished, November/December 1990, Fundo MBN, 3.2.69. Alex Ratts, in *História feita por mãos negras* (2021), notes that this text was prepared for the event Sou Negro, in Florianópolis, November 19–24, 1990, organized by the Fundação Cultural Prometheus Libertus.

1. Pedro Paulo Lomba, *Ypadê* (n.p., n.d.).

2. This article is not in the archive, but it is possible she is referring to the unpublished "Acerca da consciencia racial," translated here as "Toward Racial Consciousness," though she does not discuss quilombola peace there explicitly. There are sections on "quilombola peace" in Nascimento's thesis, and she refers to this concept in her 1990 article "A Esquerda que o Negro Quer."

3. Félix Guattari, *The Three Ecologies* (London: Bloomsbury, 2005).

For a (New) Existential
and Physical Territory

"Black Danger"
Miracle of nightfall
dark and invisible
myth, not glory.
No bats make history.

AUGUST 6, 1988, MB NASCIMENTO

RECENTLY, WHEN I RETURNED again to my studies, I found myself
on the familiar soil of an obsolete territory. Obsolete not because this
territory has ceased to exist, or has been surpassed—in truth it is con-
tinuously in flux—but because it has been reduced to a status of minority, with all that implies: the slight, the inferior, the preliminary, the
impotent and the infantile. This territory is both the path already taken,
and the one that lies ahead.[1]

Reading, analyzing, and interpreting certain authors—Gilles Deleuze and Félix Guattari's "minor literature"—has led me to a particular
turning on this path. At the beginning of the 1980s I began to sense
something, encoded in the little poem above. Would we get the "vampire's revenge" that Janice spoke of in class?[2] In 1988, three months after
the centenary of the Abolition of Slavery in Brazil I saw that for us to

survive this hostile world we would need—like animals need—to seek out more volatile, weightless, and mysterious routes through life. If we are to have an influence, our own "violence"—born of resentment, repression, and a fruitless desire for revenge—must not merely reproduce the processes that lead Humanity forward. It would be better, then and now, for us to be serious, grim, and nocturnal; to be sinister, to be vampire. Like them, we do not suck out the sap of power through confrontation, but by moving past the obstacles put in our way by the perverse visage and oppressive regime of Capital. It was like coming to a conclusion: What use do we have for History? If I am powerless, I have no need of it. History serves those who tell it. Over time, it becomes one with power. In this country, my life is not power, but that is not the end of it. A *Rock* cannot dismantle the structure of power. The task is not merely to exist but to make life more beautiful, and happier. History is the field and territory of the victors, but it would be futile to replace it with a history of the defeated—we have not yet been defeated. Those who have been called beaten are individuals, full of stories. Their stories may be small, but they are rich and captivating.

But yet we leave it to the *other* to tell the stories of our journeys. We are always lamenting that we are subjected to the *other*. Will it always be so? Is there no history of viruses, of birds, of bats, of insects? Are we merely putting on rituals without understanding their—our—true strength? Do these histories only need to be activated? Who were Zarathustra and Zumbi if not the same *Homo Sapiens*? Who were they if not, primordially, ourselves? *Sueka*, one of the names used by Zumbi and his followers in Palmares, came from an African language. It meant invisible, mysterious; what you become when war is waged. I believe that up to now we have not understood or practiced our difference. Worse, we have not respected it. Our discourse is replete with binaries, flowing in an interminable sequence: we are black / they are white (vice-versa) . . . we are poor / they are rich (vice-versa) . . . we are bad / they are good (vice-versa). . . . This endlessly sabotages our reality. It is repetitive, unsustainable, and unbearable. In *Words and Things*—"Man and his doubles"—Michel Foucault, referring to the disappearance of Discourse, writes at one point: "What is language, how can we find a way round it in order to make it appear in itself, in all its plenitude?"[3] Foucault's text glosses the poem that introduced this text; in what follows I will think through how.

Introduction as Justification

In getting this final piece of work onto the page I have come up against a series of obstacles. Some have come from outside, others from within. They are:

1. First, the return to University after ten years, and to the rhythm of academic life. My critical attitude to them led me to abandon the study of discourse and literature. I worked instead through cinema, poetry, prose, and the essay. I produced around a thousand poems and other unpublished extracts. A small part of this material went into the film *Ôrí*, directed by Raquel Gerber. The film emerged from my involvement in black political and cultural movements and my personal trajectory through the History of Brazil as a woman, and as a black woman. The film was shown internationally and received various global prizes, most recently the 33rd Golden Gate Award in San Francisco, USA. It is being distributed on video in Brazil.

Dedicating myself once again to academic work, I have felt trapped by the literary form necessary for this ritualization of knowledge. It has meant overturning my own mode of expression. It has provoked a physical repulsion to the written word.

2. The origin of this repulsion lies in a personal negation of the western rationalist thought that for so long has been part of my intellectual training. After years of research, and as an expression of twenty years of activism, I have come to a radical rejection of everything that could seem European or erudite. This has accompanied a desire for a rupture with strictly scientific thought. This puts me in an ambivalent position: even as this thought fascinates me (I have been socialized in it, I cannot escape it),

I reject it as being premised on colonization. I turn to Clarice Lispector's words—an author who has influenced me a great deal—"To write is my freedom."

3. The concepts of linguistics, well covered in the course, are unexpectedly new to me in the current context. As I have always been a repository for the Great History of the eighteenth and nineteenth centuries, I would require a greater familiarity with linguistics to write with perfection. This has paralyzed me with timidity.

4. The commitment to turn the text in on time and the need to do a great job have impeded the fruition of a dialogue between the paper and the pen and/or the professor. I understand, though, the urgency of discipline to do what is necessary. So I accept the challenge. I hope to deliver a text in a "minor tongue." I free myself from any blame for pretense that this could contain.

On this point I return to Foucault to respond to the question of language: "In a sense, this question takes up from those other questions that, in the 19th century, were concerned with life or labor. But the status of this inquiry and of all the questions into which it breaks down is not perfectly clear."[4]

I want to decipher Foucault's enigmatic words through the idea that language is the most technologically advanced instrument that human beings have for well-being. It is the key, even, to happiness.

Foucault continues:

Is it a sign of the approaching birth, or, even less than that, of the very first glow, low in the sky, of a day scarcely even heralded as yet, but in which we can already divine that thought—the thought that has been speaking for thousands of years without knowing what speaking is or even that it is speaking—is about to re-apprehend itself in its entirety, and to illumine itself once more in the lightning flash of being? Is that not what Nietzsche was paving the way for when, in the interior space of his language, he killed man and God both at the same time, and thereby promised with the Return the multiple and re-illuminated light of the Gods?[5]

I believe this is the best that has been thought in the West. I don't want to discuss it, because I am not concerned with merely opposing an opposition. On the contrary, I want to approach a black machine-of-thought, a minoritarian machine-of-thought.[6] I do not know if it will be possible here, but, for example, I would like to contribute with a vision of the minoritarian a little different from Félix Guattari's. I will come back to this. I will say, first, that I am speaking from my own location, within the exterior of my own ethnicity.

The Text

Although I don't want to dwell on History, I will return to a fact that is exactly twenty-four years old. In Rio in 1968 the moment was June, not May. June saw the great marches of the Student Movement, as well as the anti-racist mobilizations and anti-war movement in the United States of America. In August, a single moment at the Olympic games in Mexico captured the attention of the world's press. The gold medal winning athlete (American, black) and his teammate, the bronze medalist, took to the podium and raised their left fists, in the symbol of the Black Panthers. With this gesture they refused to receive their prizes. It was a negation of North American nationality. It was the most searing image I had ever seen. I stopped in the street when I saw it in my hands, on the cover of the magazine *Fatos e Fotos* [Facts and photos].

At that moment I abandoned all my bourgeois projects. It was as if I had found an imaginary *Exit*[7] from the March of the One Hundred Thousand.[8] At that moment I became conscious of my blackness and the extent to which I could really start all over again. My political activism began then, with the militancy of the Black Movement. In truth, these were the first stirrings toward a social change that was beginning to crystallize in every continent of the world, no longer in the *Imaginary*, but in the *Real*. There were other moments, such as in the film *Cry Freedom*, the history of South African militant leader Steve Biko's life. In one scene Biko is on the way to Johannesburg. He was under a banning order—a common tool used against leaders and intellectuals in the fight against apartheid—that confined him to his territory of ethnic origin.

In the film, the lights of the police cars fall on his dark face. The police officers don't recognize him, they see just another black man. They call out to him: "What is your name?" Biko responds, slowly, firmly, and calmly: "I am Bantu Stephen Biko." He declares his own death with extreme dignity.

These images can be placed alongside evolving conceptualizations of the territorialization/deterritorialization of the black minority, and its process of collective change. This collective change is set off by the individual as the protagonist of a technology exercised by thought and by the human mind: the actor offstage, with little knowledge of the script, that Walter Benjamin reminds us of. What Félix Guattari, and Deleuze and Guattari, demonstrate about the secondary characteristics of minor literature appeals to me here. It seems to offer a clear explanation. They write: In minor literatures, "everything is political . . . their cramped space forces each individual case [to be] immediately connected to politics."[9] It is this possibility of individuation that this text will seek to discuss.

My re-entry into the University is subsumed within an attempt to be minoritarian. If "everything takes on a collective value," to believe in language, and to speak, would be micropolitical actions. "The conditions are not there for an individuated enunciation that would belong to this or that 'master' and that could be separated from a collective enunciation."[10] I always feel that I am writing about myself, but that this *myself* contains many others. I write, therefore, from a collective, about and for collectivization. If I am left without someone else as an interlocutor, this desire sometimes paralyzes production. It is a moment of otherness, imbued with utter solidity. The solidity of the Black Panthers or of Biko. It is also like the tension described by Félix Guattari/Guattari and Deleuze: "to speak, and above all to write, is to fast."[11] All the difficulty of this text, like that of what came before, comes from an "overwhelming" desire to detach myself from the masters, to invent a language inside this one in which I write. "I want an invented truth" (Clarice Lispector in *Água Viva*). At times I feel in me the restlessness that unsettles Kafka in one of his Letters to Felice: "Fundamentally my life consists, and has always consisted, of attempts to write, and more often, of abandoned attempts."[12] He describes "the impossibility of not writing, the impossibility of writing in German; the impossibility of writing otherwise."[13] I remember that during the course, in a discussion on how to express yourself, the question arose of whether it would be different according to your background. This question crystallizes in how to write, and in how to write the becoming minoritarian of the minority.

The opposition of majority-minority was created by nineteenth-century European thought. It is part of a sequence that progresses toward the infinite. However, in the sociology of this century, which still dominates our own discourse, the opposition has been transformed into two apparently fixed blocks. Yet, to speak of minority as a monolithic block risks homogenizing different minorities (women, children, homosexuals, proletariat, and ethnicities) and not looking more closely for the differences that lie at the heart of each particular minority. This becomes even more misleading when you consider these questions from a material and economic perspective. Thus, all black people in Brazil are seen as poor, needy, wretched, incompetent, and so on, in an endless enunciation of stereotypes which serves to reinstate the domination and subordination of place and territory. I think, then, that the concept of minority needs further reflection. Guattari argues that a minority may definitively desire to be minoritarian. I would have my doubts about this perspective of becoming . . . "Marginality calls for recentring and recuperation."[14] (Here it has a conservative meaning, along the lines of the idea of "home"[15]: the return to tradition, to the point of departure, to the center, to control.)

The North American gay movement, for example, "are minoritarians who refuse to be marginalized."[16] This is a typically 1970s idea of American citizenship (North Americans do not encompass all homosexual people born in, or with citizenship of America). America is a name (an enunciation) of the geographical space in which these people exercise their conduct as homosexual. That is, the physical space of the individual: their sexuality. There are homosexual people in America of all variations and stripes of ethnicities and nationalities: Hispanics, whites, blacks. Multiple differences can occur within a single minority, so the space they occupy is much bigger than we might imagine. An enormous cartographic endeavor would be needed to understand the individuals within the great blocks referred to as minorities. Black women, for example, black homosexuals, and a great unfolding sequence of differences. Félix Guattari, in a passage of another book, reiterates what was affirmed above, "Minorities are something different; you can be in a minority because you *want* to be. For example, there are sexual minorities that champion their nonparticipation in the values and modes of expression of the majority."[17] The fundamental *difference* that I perceive emerges from the origin of the minority. Up to a certain point, sexuality and ethnic origin have a common characteristic: they are both biological. However, ethnicity has a territory, full of women, children, and so on. The case of the street children in big cities for example. They are, in general, black.

And Guattari continues: "We can imagine a minority being treated as marginal, or a marginal group wanting to have the subjective consistency and recognition of a minority. And there we would have a dialectical combination of minority and marginality."[18]

I do not understand this expression, *dialectical combination*. I imagine that to be marginal may be a circumstantial characterization, while to be minority is a permanent condition. The "consistency of subjectivities" can change as much in a minority group as in a marginal one. Transience is a constant (space/time relation) always producing deterritorialization, so there is an intra-minority singularity. I disagree that there is a *definitive desire* to *be* minoritarian. While North American homosexuals refuse to be marginalized within the minority, others are the majority. Or, better, they are in *the place of the majority*. This reveals an interaction across flows of chronological time that functions as a frequency and not as *a dialectical combination*. Minority is not harmony. It is constantly being dislocated, including for the majority. To be the majority is also a becoming. For some within minorities, being the majority would be a reterritorialization, emerging from impulses fomented in the discontent of being out of power, excluded, impoverished, and oppressed.

One of the black movements of the 1970s enacted this type of agency to the nth degree, based in the concept of black cultural and racial identity. Lévi-Strauss, at a UNESCO conference, announced that, unless we were careful, the concept of cultural identity could come to be a new racism. On the basis of a Marxist dialectic we believed for years that consciousness would lead to liberation. That this would result in a new conduct in relation to white people: "Cultural identity constitutes a level of subjectivity: the level of subjective territorialization. . . . It is a means of self-identification in a specific group that conjugates its modes of subjectivation in relations of social segmentarity. . . . The idea of 'cultural identity' has a coefficient of deterritorialization. The idea of 'cultural identity' has disastrous political and micropolitical implications, because what it fails to grasp is precisely the whole wealth of the semiotic production of an ethnic or social group, or a society."[19]

Black cultural identity would deny singularity and processes of singularization. It would impose a dictatorship of conducts and a fixed set of models. This would be impossible to achieve when dealing with differentiated and dissimilar individuals. It would—after Guattari, citing Rimbaud in *Illuminations*—get in the way of becoming black.

Could there be a black nature? A racial nature? Is there a nature that can adhere to the color of the skin, as it adheres to an idea, a political party, a union, or some apparatus of State? Could there be a space today for such aberration, for such repression of flows? . . . To think like this would be to deny the anthropological principle of cultural exchange. This brings me to Neusa Santos Souza, and her work *Tornar-se negro* [Becoming black]. It is a psychiatric study, whose central thesis points to the social ascension of black people, and the so-called whitening/loss of a black race, which were the results of an *ideal of the white ego*.[20] In the years 1980–1984 there was an idea that spread across the humanities of rejecting any thinking about the potential for social change that began from an analysis of the individual. This paradigm privileged the role of the colonized and dispossessed masses as the unique and only possible machine of change. The masses constituted the social.

This idea was theoretically backed up by both Marxist and non-Marxist intellectual heritages. There was a consensus in which the unconscious was only portrayed by art. Beyond this was the terrain of ghosts, inhabited by human fantasies. It could only be narrated as a pathological space. This idea was premised on the dislocation of the ideal ego. It began from the ideology of lack and not from the mapping of desire. George Groddeck writes: "I hold the view that man is animated by the Unknown, that there is within him an 'Es,' an 'It,' some wondrous force which directs both what he himself does, and what happens to him. The affirmation 'I live' is only conditionally correct, it expresses only a small and superficial part of the fundamental principle, 'Man is lived by the It.'"[21]

However, exterior/interior, minority/majority, white/Black are nothing more than contacts between the unconscious and the field of space/time that it creates. In this field there are various kinds of language, including the other's gaze on the body.

Hence this supposed ideal of the white ego, which is nothing more than a transference—through affect, through desire—between two or more individuals. Whitening was just an ideology captured by the apparatus of the State, institutions and groups of people committed to the maintenance of denomination. The ego does not accept limits. Can the ego not desire anything, not be anything? What is there that is pathological in desiring to be black, white, yellow, man, woman, child, gay, asexual . . . ?

In the mid-1980s a lightning bolt struck black consciousnesses. Michael Jackson began to appear with light skin and a "white" phenotype. As black people who wanted to deepen their identity, to become more and more black, how were we to deal with this phenomenon? The single most successful black person was "becoming white." Michael Jackson lived his talent, invention, happiness, and success without being imprisoned by his genealogy. Isn't it possible to explore a black becoming in this, too? Perhaps. In the lyrics of "Black or White" Jackson sang, "I am not going to spend my life being a color."[22]

This thought points toward a social "exit." Everyone was bound to their archaisms, standardized and dogmatized into a singular conduct: black conduct. To accept this, or not to, was a zero-sum game for affective human and social status. A unique, closed, and controlled territory was decreed for the individual by inverting a racial marking within the minority itself. Such conservatism requires a deterritorialization/reterritorialization if we are to avoid fixing a minoritarian hegemony based on an eternal relationship of oppressor and victim.

It occurs to me to illustrate what *becoming minoritarian* means, in my understanding. I want to do so through Dilma Lóes's audiovisual piece *Quando o crioulo dança* [When the creole dances]. In it, among other testimonies of betrayal and suffering, a militant declares: "I began to love myself when I became an adult." Knowing the speaker and their life's trajectory, I glimpsed for the first time the resolution of *racism* inside another individual. Political activism had led this person to value themselves and to effectively break with their external image. Announcing "love me," *amo-me*, molecularly, I am no longer divided between the desire of the other and my own desire. Here I want to open a parenthesis in the meaning of the micropolitical war-machine. The *racists* would never think that hidden in the occult, inside the black person, is affect. Though the world outside may be painful and set against them . . .

The effect of this affirmation quickly emerges: image, sound, color, and speech establish a collective enunciation. As singularized individuals, we can understand that it is the difference between lack and need that causes racism. In the same way, a deep unease is forced upon the individual by discrimination—*complicity* in the face of what *oppresses* in the relationship oppressor/oppressed. The autonomy of desire points toward black becoming, that is not restricted to "all those systems of punishment which develop as if they were chosen, profitable activities and attitudes of a particular system of social hierarchy . . . this way of trapping the processes of singularization by specialists who immediately categorize them within the affective and theoretical tools of the institutional equipment of segregation."[23]

Recently, during a formal discussion about demographic politics in government institutions, a black woman, a former student of mine, said to me: "Our task in the face of institutions is not to reinforce discriminatory types or models, but to make them more human. To recover the humanity lost in the years of colonization and discrimination. The postulates of social and political theories are simulacra, put forward by the petty bourgeoisie. I want to be something that is more human." This postulate in the voice of a black woman can be found translated in the poem below by Éle Semog,[24] dated June 1992, whose title is "It's Not Enough to Be Black":

Today my son dreamed
That the planet Earth
Wanted to come in at our window
And I kissed him and said:
Good morning little one
The bad world is not going to catch us
It's not enough to be black . . .
I want to impale the racist
And their harassed philosophers
At the end of nothing
After that, I could be happy
But today I am black
I am no utopia.

This becoming-utopian is the production of "territorialized subjectivities in myself, in the physical body."[25] It means being free of the ethics of production and accumulation that divide man up according to the order of Capital. This would be to build another system, based on an African territory understood no longer as a place of the past, but of the modern. No longer the slave, but the quilombola.

A new force for struggle and restructuring. In Muniz Sodré we can find a design for this becoming: "The black Arkhé is not the result of a 'telluric biologism', but is part of the everyday History of African descendants in the Americas as a 'counter-place' . . . a concrete construction of group identity, penetrating the interstices of the dominant bloc."[26]

Blackness, therefore, is not hegemonic in either space or time. It is not inside *To Be*, neither is it in the word *black*. Its realization takes place on many dynamic levels. In dealing with black Brazilians, there is also a becoming white and a becoming Amerindian and many inter-lacings in an endless process of serialization . . .

The principal of Vital Force, like *Axé*, has similar meanings. Vital Force is the bantu linguistic and philosophical principle contained in the phoneme *ntu*. The *ntu* refers to the individual themselves and the *muntu* to the other/other individuals.

The *muntu*, therefore, exists as a reflection, and in animals, minerals, plants, and human beings (both living and dead), but not as something immanent: the contact of two beings is needed to form it.[27]

The *ntu* is only complete and only acquires force by recognizing the other. For the bantus, the unity does not exist, because it recognizes itself in the presence of the other *ntu*. Like a mirror. It is not a principle of equality, but of self-recognition by that which is similar in form or being. For Muniz:

As force, it maintains, grows, diminishes, and is transmitted as a function of the (ontological) relation of the individual with cosmic principles (supernatural entities, ancestors and all invisible beings) and with the descendants.[28]

When, today, in some African ethnic groups the individual becomes weak, or dies, it does not simply mean illness, but the loss of the Vital Force. *The whole group* dedicates itself to the practice of care so that the collectivity itself does not weaken and die. This supposes a principle of complicity. If the individual dies, they come to their end in contact with the *Earth* such that it can be restored and reconstitute *Life*. The Vital Force, therefore, is not paralyzed. Muniz Sodré writes: "The Bantus consider the *muntu* to have '*the power of knowing.*'" The Vital Force is human genetics engendered in the physical architecture of the individual. It is a philosophical concept in an African scientific style. And it incorporates the principle dynamic of *Axé*. That which is structure, from which all departs or returns. The home of all *Knowledge*.

This Vital Force can be understood as a kind of vigor, or what in the West corresponds to physical health. We should, I think, put the ecosophical principle of Félix Guattari alongside a deeper study of the diverse substances that connect and combine in the chain of humanist forces.

Axé

This Vital Force, or *axé*, is contained and transmitted through substantial elements of matter. The elements that carry *axé* can be put into three categories:

1. "red blood"
2. "white blood"
3. "black blood"

The Red Blood Encompasses:

a) Of the animal kingdom: menstrual blood, human or animal blood;
b) Red blood of the vegetable kingdom: dendê oil, tree bark, honey, the blood of flowers.

The White Blood Encompasses:

a) Of the animal kingdom: semen, saliva, breath, secretions, plasma (of the snail);
b) Of the vegetable kingdom: sap, juice, alcohol, white drinks mainly from palm trees, the white powders of some vegetables, the *ori*,[29] vegetable butter;
c) Of the mineral kingdom: salts, chalk, silver, lead.

The Black Blood Encompasses:

a) Of the animal kingdom: ashes of animals;
b) Of the vegetable kingdom: the dark juice of some vegetables; the *ilú*,[30] indigo, the extract of some types of trees;
c) Of the mineral kingdom: coal, iron, etc.[31]

Notes

The original title of this essay is "Por um território (novo) existencial e físico." Unpublished, 1992, Fundo MBN, 21.3.4. Our translation here was previously published in *Antipode*.

1. This translation was previously published in *Antipode* 53 (2021). It was originally written as a course paper in 1992 for a class on *Urban Space-Time: Cities, Territory and Conduct* in the Department of Theory of Communication at the Federal University of Rio de Janeiro. The course appears to have been led by the anthropologist, and translator of Deleuze and Guattari, Janice Caiafa.

2. This reference to a class discussion during her course is also a reference to Deleuze and Guattari's essay "Kafka: Towards a Minor Literature" (1985) in which they refer to Kafka's writing, which "distinguishes two series of technical inventions: those which tend to restore 'natural

communication' . . . and those which represent the vampirelike revenge of the phantom or re-introduce 'the ghostly element between people' (post, telegraph, telephone, wireless)" (593).

3. Michel Foucault, *The Order of Things: An Archaeology of the Human Sciences* (New York: Vintage Books, 1970 [1994]).

4. Foucault, *The Order of Things*, 306.

5. Foucault, *The Order of Things*, 306.

6. Nascimento is here referring again to Deleuze and Guattari's essay on Kafka, in which they write of literary machines, machines of writing, and machines of expression.

7. "Exit" is in English in the original. We should note the implicit reference to Deleuze and Guattari's concept of "line of flight."

8. This is a reference to the Passeata dos Cem Mil, a march led by the Brazilian student movement that took place on June 26, 1968, and constituted an early high point of resistance to dictatorship in Brazil, shortly before the crackdown that began with Institutional Act Number 5 on December 13, 1968. That act increased the dictatorship's violent and repressive tenor, and limited freedom of association, press, and protest. Nascimento's reference to an "exit" from the March is an indication of the fractures between the radical Black Movement and the largely white student and leftist movements. This schism is played out on camera in Nascimento and Gerber's film *Ôrí*.

9. Gilles Deleuze and Félix Guattari, *Kafka: Towards a Minor Literature*, trans. Dana Polan (Minneapolis: University of Minnesota Press, 1986), 17.

10. Deleuze and Guattari, *Kafka*, 17.

11. Deleuze and Guattari, *Kafka*, 20.

12. Franz Kafka, *Letters to Felice*, 2nd ed. E. Heller and J. Born (London: Secker and Warburg, 1974).

13. Deleuze and Guattari, *Kafka*, 16.

14. Félix Guattari, "Gangs in New York," in *Chaosophy*, ed. Sylvère Lotringer (New York: MIT Press, 1995), 291.

15. In English in the original.

16. Guattari, "Gangs in New York," 291.

17. Nascimento cites "another" Guattari book here, and the quotation she gives is unreferenced. It is in fact a reference to *Molecular Revolution in Brazil* by Félix Guattari and Suely Rolnik, trans. Karel Clapshow and Brian Holmes (Los Angeles: Semiotext(e), 2008), 173 (originally published as *Micropolítica: Cartografias do desejo* [Petrópolis: Vozes, 1986]).

18. Guattari and Rolnik, *Molecular Revolution in Brazil*, 100.

19. Guattari and Rolnik, *Molecular Revolution in Brazil*, 173.

20. *Ideal Ego*. A phase used by Freud in the framework of his second great psychic theory: the instantiation of the personality resulting from the convergence of narcissism (the idealization of the ego) and identifications with the parents, with their substitutes, and with collective ideas. While instantiated differently, the ideal ego constitutes a model to which the individual seeks to conform. J. Laplanche and J. B. Pontalis, *Vocabulário de Psicanálise* (Lisboa: Martins Fontes, 1970), 298.

21. Nascimento does not give a page reference, and we have been unable to identify the original text in published translations of Groddeck.

22. Nascimento cites the line in English, but misquotes the end of the lyric as "being a colored."

23. George Groddeck, *ibid.*: Nascimento does not give a page reference, and we have been unable to identify the original text in published translations of Groddeck.

24. Editor of *Maioria Falante*, Rio de Janeiro, Brazil.

25. Nascimento does not give a citation for this reference.

26. Muniz Sodré, *O terreiro e a cidade* (Petrópolis: Vozes, 1988).

27. Muniz Sodré, *A verdade seduzida* (Rio de Janeiro: Codecri, 1983), 129–30.

28. Juana Elbein dos Santos, *Os nagô e a morte* (Petrópolis: Vozes, 1976).

29. Literally *head,* a Yoruba metaphysical concept relating to that which guides individual spirituality.

30. A Yoruba term for a wooden drum used in the northeast of Brazil.

31. Nascimento includes the following "observation" after her bibliography: "The word *sueka* was one of Sylvia's kindnesses which she used while speaking to us during the course. Various students of Black culture and linguistics helped clarify some of the reflections in this text."

Cultures in Dialogue

WITH THE SUPPORT of modern capitalism, mercantile colonialism endured until the 1970s and ended with African independences from the Portuguese Overseas Empire. That moment inevitably reformulated national borders across the World. It is interesting, and provocative, to note that the fall of the new empires (the Soviet Empire) in Europe began with their disaggregation/unification in the late 1980s and early 1990s. This prompts an optimistic contemplation of the future of the cultures and peoples of the Third World (both in the periphery and in the so-called First World—that is, both the fall of the geopolitical frontiers imposed by colonialism, and a new prospect of what the planet can, through man, bring to political, physical, existential, and imaginary perfection).

From this point of view, dialogue—even if it coexists with war—will be able to heal the pain of years of territorial domination over others.

2. Transatlanticidade

This is a concept coined in the making of the film *Ôrí*, directed by Raquel Gerber. The film puts forward Beatriz Nascimento's thesis that within all the discontinuity, there is a discernible continuity in History for peoples who have been dominated and subordinated. That always elevates dignity and human singularities, seeing, ecologically, the Atlantic Sea as a means, a medium, and a vector between the peoples of Europe, Africa, and America.

Only the Atlantic as a free and physical territory made meetings and unmeetings of disparate Cultures possible. Both genocides and genetic transformations. The Atlantic transported, and fed, peoples from here to there and from there to here. Even with new means of transport and communication, and perhaps because of them, the Atlantic, the disaggregating element, made men gregarious, imposing its mystique and its power of virtual communication. Its Oceanic meaning (infinite, limitless) makes these culturally differentiated peoples, up to a certain point, harmonious.

The Atlantic is considered by Afro-Brazilian peoples as a Goddess-mother (Iemanjá-Oxum feeds Brazilian existentialism). We surrender to it as it intervenes in our happiness. Through its mirror it can cure us of the deepest open wounds we have gathered across our whole history.

3. Film as an Instrument for Solidarity between Peoples

In critical theory, Walter Benjamin writes that we can infer a contemporary vision that is phenomenologically new, from the technics of reproduction. For him, photography freed the eye from the hand; for him, for the first time in the reproduction of images the hand was exempt from essential artistic tasks. Photography allows the work to approach the spectator. The multiplication of examples replaces a singular happening with a mass phenomenon.

Cinema is the hardening of this phenomenon through film. In the final instance, film is the most effective agent of transformation in overhauling tradition. The social significance of cinema derives from the end of the element of tradition in cultural inheritance.

Cinema enriched our concentration. Until the end of the nineteenth century no one paid any attention to unusual slips in conversation—Freud brought these into the light in *The Psychopathology of Everyday Life*. Expanding the world of objects, in the visual as well as in the auditory order, cinema has had profound consequences for perception. The discoveries triggered by spoken cinema enriched the qualities of expression and made power reinforce control over cinema and deploy it as a tool.

Television did not absorb cinema. It had to subject itself to film's formula. According to Félix Guattari, in "The Poor Man's Couch," in dire commercial conditions it is still possible to produce good films that modify the combinations of desire, destroy stereotypes, and open us up to the future.

Cinema, television, and film can play with the social imagination and they can serve to reinforce images and to change them, when they are seen as a form of collective communication. Film can be a way of molding opinion. It can not only change behavior but can incite collective movements that lead to action, that becomes change. Events like the Gulf War, the impeachment of the last Brazilian president, the beating of the African American Rodney King and the disturbances that followed in Los Angeles, are examples of how audiovisual vectors can configure action to promote solidarity between peoples.

Note

The original title of this essay is "Culturas em diálogo." Unpublished, March 1994, Fundo MBN, 26.1.11.

Portugal

THE EARTH IS ROUND; the sun is a disc.

Where is the dialectic?

In the sea.

When I returned to Angola, I spent ten days in Lisbon. What moved me most was crossing the Tejo. That river opening onto the Atlantic . . .

The Atlantic in Lisbon seems higher, and lesser, than in Brazil.

Inside the car I fell into an ecstasy about this side of my history. How could they have left from here for the unknown world? What greater force made them confront this Ocean and search for Africa and America? And I, this little being, am the result of that mad adventure. There, I cried with love for those navigators, my parents. I cried for having hated them, I cried for still regretting that history. But I cried, fundamentally, in front of the poetry of the Tejo and the Atlantic meeting, the poetry of that departure for conquest. They did it out of fear, too. Maybe they blushed in the face of all the beauty beyond the Atlantic sea.

This is the dialectic of my life:

Parents and parents,[1] Africa and America and Europe—Africa.
Parents and nations.
Angolas, Jagas, and the people of Benim, where my mother
    came from.
Parents and nations.
Palmares, Bahia, Sergipe—Brazil.

Parents and nations.
Atlantic—mother.

I am Atlantic. Now I have found a beautiful reference.

Some went through that ocean.
Others came from it.
And I am here, I went from it, and came from it.

Oh infinite peace to be able to make connecting links in a
    fragmented history.
All those national constructions are geopolitical outlines, they
were nothing until they had a name.
Only the ocean is real. Because it is the *m-a-r*.[2]
A primordial sound.
Shall we build a bridge from Gibraltar to Africa?

Notes

The original title of this essay is "Portugal." Unpublished, Fundo MBN, 23.4.5.

1. This line includes a pun that is hard to translate: she writes "pais e pais," which means *parents*, or *fathers*, but sounds very like *país* (country). In the typewritten original in her archive, neither word has an accent, so we have translated it here as "parents and parents."

2. *Mar* in Portuguese means *sea*. Here Nascimento writes it out letter by letter. Here she is referencing the word's sonic echoes with *mãe*, which means *mother* in Portuguese.

Angola

IT WAS A PHRASE I repeated often.

At first, we dazzled one another.

They called me Angolan, and I felt Angolan.

But gradually they came to themselves and remembered either with displeasure, or with admiration, that I was Brazilian.

I reminded those who despised me that I was enslaved, and now colonized, in a racist and autocratic-capitalist country.

In those moments I experienced an intolerable xenophobia, and I suffered deeply. I reacted by trying to explain the dynamics of Brazil and how, in this place in particular, I did not feel Brazilian. I explained that I hoped that they understood that it was their ancestors who were responsible for the enslavement of our people. They were surprised and apologized. Then I said, "Shall we build a bridge to Gibraltar?" They laughed.

One day I was in my hotel room, and I was summoned down to the lobby. Five members of FARPLA[1] were asking for me. They said that they had come to speak "to the Brazilian," to "have a drink" with me. I sat with them. They were young. The oldest was about twenty-four, and the youngest (a new recruit), was about seventeen. Handsome, strong, black. They told me that they were going to the front in Cubango, the frontier with South Africa, to attack positions there, in support of SWAPO.[2] I asked when they would return. "Never," they said. And they launched into a well-worn Leninist discourse. I asked them to stop, almost in tears. I told them that discourse was a myth, that it no longer justified anything. That I was seeing men in their prime of life telling me, as if it was natural, that they were heading off to die. The oldest replied, "Are you scared of death, Beti? I'm not. The instant of death is fear. If you don't have that anymore there's nothing left."

It was difficult to explain to those who were going to die how absurd it was, how uncomfortable I was to be drinking with the dying. But, at the same time, it was beautiful to see their faces and their determination. Only the youngest recruit bowed his head, remembering the naturalness of everything.

We spoke a lot about Brazil, and they asked me to recite some well-known poetry. I recited some fragments of Cecília Meireles and of Drummond, and some psalms that I had in my head. They repeated some with me and I saw tears in the eyes of the major. On saying goodbye, he told me that he was going to sabotage his car a little, so that they didn't have to go to Huambo tonight. We spoke until the early morning and he promised that he would return another day so that we could continue to talk about the meaning of death—and no more Leninism.

The next day I had an appointment and I arrived back late at the hotel. They were all there, but they were no longer the same as the day before. We drank almost in silence and said goodbye. A few days later, the name of the major, José, was at the top of the list of soldiers killed by the South Africans.

My god, war is absurd. I want to stop the war in Africa, and everywhere. I do not believe that the dream is dead. I cannot possibly accept anyone's death. That is written in all faiths.

Notes

The original title of this essay is "Angola." Unpublished, Fundo MBN, 23.4.5. The typed document in her archive is ambiguously titled. The word *Angola* is handwritten at the top, but this is common to other short pieces in the same file so it may not indicate a title. Under her name on the document, the word *gravado* (recorded) is noted, suggesting this may have been recorded, perhaps for *Ôrí*, after her return from Angola.

1. The People's Armed Forces for the Liberation of Angola, originally the armed wing of the Movement for the Liberation of Angola (the MPLA), and later the official Angolan armed forces.

2. The South West Africa People's Organization, the Namibian independence movement.

Aruanda!

THE HISTORY of peoples is recorded in the remnants that pass through human experience on the planet. The species itself is a journey inside the order of the Universe: other bodies, masses, matter, and invisible beings are in constant relation, sometimes coming together, sometimes falling apart. However, the fecund senses of Human History on Earth are the transitory and the transmissible.

When we resort to remnants, we constitute—in the present, instantly—the general principle of the cosmos and of sensual knowledge. These register in the brain, which distributes information about, or associated with, the physical body. From there it passes outside and reestablishes the principle of the Whole.

It is logical to vanquish the fear of death and to organize life as it is, uninterrupted. This mega-conflict inside the human soul—the rejection of finitude—marks out the human, among all living things, as a rich and singular animal.

These short paragraphs above constitute my first reflections on reading the outline of the project to establish CERNE.[1] Something comes into my memory: a primordial difference between the history of the human species and its disciplines: (universal and regional) History and Anthropology, which is a particular disciplinary current of History.

Why do I begin this text with the opposition between these two "subjects" of human knowledge? Because they both recur so often in the past of Africans and their descendants.

The living history of our people is written in pillage, cruelty, and death. The great drama of slavery and economic colonialism are the *original crime*. I'm not interested in going back again to the old colonialist. I want to relate *thought* to *adversity*. Millions of living beings and humans in the world pass through adversity—the black people of Brazil above all.

A crime in the origin of History establishes a triggering process that becomes repetitive, and which returns to death. Whether in life or [XXX],[2] throughout this millennium of American discovery, human effort has sought paths toward freedom, out of the loop that has been closed since 1492. Never so much as in the last three decades have the colonized people of the world sought to break this ancient deadlock—a deadlock that transforms itself into violence.

In the middle of the last century, during African and Asian neocolonialism, this effort produced a European counteroffer: the birth of anthropological science. In a moment of profound crisis in the center, while Africa continued to bleed her population to the Brazilian trade, it was occupied by predatory Northern European colonizers. Among them were students of *Anthropos*: scientists and naturalists who accompanied expeditions. The black response was the movements of *negritude*.

At the same time that they drained life from Africa, new raids were launched against our territories and against our family and ethnic archives (statuary and precious materials). The most serious event was the creation of reserves, delimited preservation areas where they infantilized Africans. In this violent and iniquitous context European science dissected the people of this other continent, divided them up like species, made generalizations about their *modus vivendi*, their vitality, their individual, social, and spiritual attributes, and turned them into forgotten beings.

This process continues. Irrevocably, it seems. The science of niches can be understood, in essence, as the knowledge of the relation between *totem and taboo*. Though it contributes to overcoming difficulties in understanding between one individual and another, it cannot but be based in domination and colonialism.

"African knowledge" is put in museums, libraries, and academic and religious temples. Our knowledge is canonized. What does this mean?

The protected archives of the West will guide our future, loaded with stigmas and preconceived marks. In the next generations we will have to live with this, and to live well with it. In the end, these are the true records of the inter-relations between Europeans, Africans, and Americans, and they are preserved by the hegemonic hemisphere.

I see in the CERNE proposals the positive side of this process. Preserving the records of individual and collective experience is a dignifying task. I see it as a center for the preservation of symbols, and of the black and *mestiça* humanities of Bahia and of Brazil. This task, in truth, was initiated in 1974 from within Brazilian universities.

The black students of the Federal University of Fluminense in Niterói, through their professors, the Director of the Institute of Human Sciences and Philosophy and the head of the Department of Anthropology, Maria Beniel, and a student, Marlene Cunha, organized the first Weeks for the Study of Black People. Behind these events there was the concrete objective of reformulating the Ministry of Cultural Anthropology that was full of concepts about the invisible "primitive."

Every year, Anthropology, History, and Sociology professors from across the country, as well as spiritual leaders of African religions, came together in a shared effort with these students. They would come to the University and, in 1978, to the MEC. Together, through their own skills and through group projects, they sought to restructure the concepts of the discipline. These professors, generally, came from disciplines inspired less by European and North American Anthropology from the period 1850–1930. In the end, thanks to their collective work they made advances on a number of fronts to return the Afro-Brazilian *being* to their place in various literatures. Alongside this project, at around the same time, the Black Movement organized political entities in various Brazilian universities and reinforced black cultural heritage.

I participated in various of these meetings in the 1970s as a teacher of history and as a participant organizer. Hence the CERNE proposals touch me deeply. The Center must be a radiating hub, and an attempt to *heal* the long process of adversity that the Afro-Brazilian community has been through. I would like to raise some points as suggestions:

1. Curing the Trauma of Slavery

I do not report on the work of the students at Fluminense in order to name them as some kind of vanguard, and even less to mark out the Black Movement in regional terms. I can say, as a historian, that there was a wider process in the country that quickly became a mass development among Brazilians. The black question and the question of slavery can only be resolved with the effort of every human on the planet today.

Rather, I refer to that work because we came together to seek to overcome and find an internal human cure for the people who find themselves to be the last of the oppressed. It falls to them to enter into liberation, to free themselves from enslavement, and from social discrimination based on the color of their skin.

In 1989, the nation shrugged off the yoke of totalitarianism and entered, through suffering, the era of full rights. However, the task of the Black Movement—whether we give the struggle of subalternized peoples this or another name—is not going to end. It deserves a deeper, more structural, and less emotional reflection.

The following tasks will fall to Afro-Brazilian institutions:

1.1. Move beyond a vision of the subject that continues to reinforce the intellectual hegemonies of the countries of the center and of the north. Both in terms of the handling and treatment of the Afro-Brazilian archive and above all in terms of individuals, and, yet more, of young people.

Look again, in this first phase, toward West and Central-West Africa, and understand the intercontinental relation with America (Brazil and the Antilles). In other words, recognize that the taboo that Africa became a hundred years ago is, for us, broken. And that we are approaching a new African who will come into the year 2000 a free man.

1.2. The African did not leave the continent. They are rooted. This is profoundly different for us, the *wretched of the earth*. The African sits among their national elites, their leaders at the center of their own compass. They are deeply cultivated and vigorous men and women because of this. They are concerned with establishing relations with other countries to benefit from formal education, erudition, and modern technologies, as well as the goods and the *fetishes* of the world of consumption. The meeting between them and us is marked by a difference of structural perspective.

While we reinforce the religious and political god (salvation, conservation, preservation, cultural reserves), they direct themselves toward the material gains of modernity. That is another cultural, historical, and actual concept.

1.3. Here we arrive at the most interesting point for CERNE, touching on its task of community education: As a national whole, the Black Movement took on, and is now passing along to society, the actual results of twenty-two years of national struggle and struggle of the descendants of Africans. In order to understand the Afro-Brazilian, it is necessary to learn from them the new generation that is emerging, the generation that is the true victory of those years of struggle. They are securing dominion over their own bodies. Let us look at the body of a black child. The struggle against racial discrimination in which we are involved brings, right up today, only one victory: our dominion over our *black body*, where freedom is exercised in fact. The only space we have truly conquered. And it had to be thus. This century, poverty shamed us. Although still not in a widespread form, that which was repressed—the freedom of gesture, the strengthening of our tone and our plasma—is now privileged in our economic and legal struggle for the will to power of our people. Taboos around exaggerated sex, laziness, trickery, and street-smarts are being kicked into the dust by these new generations of Brazilians.

1.4. This is when institutions like CERNE must intervene, and offer support, so that this Brazilian does not forget the direction that they must truly take. The black body is educated and strengthened by the dancing of the community—"Black Soul," samba schools, religious *terreiros*. For the freedom of a people that in the midst of its emancipatory process relied merely on its physical self (often ill fed), we must offer the weapons of the mind, of bodily memory, of deep love and respect for self, for others and for the nation. In this way we expelled the ancestral *slave*, recovered our vivacity, our gaze, and became different to that which monolithic ideology had built. To a certain extent, too, the *internal colonizer* was expelled. We came to know ourselves, to decolonize ourselves. This process is irreversible and must be felt more and more in the economic sphere. I believe that this is how we can see, in general, the contemporary Afro-Brazilian. When I speak of economics, I refer to the whole spectrum of economic philosophy. We must invest in time, because as I noted before, in the USA and in West Central Africa (principally places with a similar linguistic experience) the new "black" is emerging very vigorously. They will meet us—the others—who are profoundly unprepared for a free and full relationship without new "colonialisms." We have to invest in what pays.

The country has always been open to foreigners, and only recently exiled some of its children. But they were men of a higher social extraction, therefore better equipped for exile. The world that is unfolding will end up breaking through the last bastions of borders. The trend is toward the freedom of more and more territorial areas of conflict, and toward a liberation of human progress. The populations of vast areas of the world are growing, and ours is growing at a gallop. The discourses of the Black Movement in the 1970s called attention to unemployed men and women and those on low salaries. It called for the institutional protection and settlement of abandoned orphans and children, for respect for the life of black women, the protection of her children against family planning that went against the safe care of her body, her rights to choose and to sustain herself.

If we raised our voices in a discourse that was poorly articulated, this was due precisely to the total absence of economic and monetary support. Our speech necessarily either fell into the void or was institutionalized by leftist parties, creating factions and schisms. This is not, and was not, bad in itself. It was the most powerful instrument that the Black Movement had. We know what the external reality was: impoverishment, the absence of an elite, and a deinstitutionalization difficult to overcome without a politico-institutional solidification of associations, such as through CERNE.

2. Resources must be returned to education, reeducation and professional training of those able to enter the labor force.

It would be interesting to know, for example, how it came to be that a young student, debating with me and other professors in UERJ during a screening of *Ôrí* by Raquel Gerber, spoke of their rejection of being African, and affirmed himself as *Brazilian*. Yet his full professional realization today, in this country, is cast into doubt. Let us imagine that this young man, with little contact with the outside world, receives an offer to work outside Brazil.

Let us say that the average Brazilian, after crossing the border, has to live with Africans and Afro-descendants in any place that they go today in the world. Imagine that, suddenly, they are chosen for a job in West Africa. The feeling of the preservation of knowledge (of being Brazilian) and new experience (of being the stranger) can draw out of them the ambition to grow, to enrich themselves materially and internally. Or even to be the opposite of someone who had no intention of being "colonized" or exiled. Hence their initial resistance.

Part of CERNE's program, in my view, must be to disseminate information about this new migration route toward African markets. We need a little more fervor for exchange. This is a step that can create space in the medium and long term for a solution to the question of the labor market. Naturally, we will have, here, new areas in which to allocate labor, so this transfer must be temporary, dynamic, mutual, and secure.

2.1 In the CERNE proposal, only cultural products are listed under intercontinental knowledge. It is important to track other potentials for exchange of goods through establishing effective and secure networks with Angola, Guinea, Mozambique, Cape Verde, Nigeria, Ivory Coast, Ghana, Zimbabwe, Kenya, and the Congolese regions. This should be a systematic process of increasing reciprocal exchange.

It is important that the proposal valorizes production, as the descendants of enslaved people are themselves historically productive and entrepreneurial. The work must be part of a central strand: current, modern production. I see a good exit route in this. I remember, for example, when I was in Luanda in 1979, doing research. I had the opportunity to meet the directors of OMA,[3] a kind of utopia come true. One of them told me that the charge of Angolan national construction included the historic interruption of bantu kinship: "bantus raised here need to go there, and bantus raised there need to come here." I understood this not as a massive project of repatriation—that would be grotesque and, presumably, violent—but rather something molecular, like CERNE, that can begin to think seriously about the creation of effective cohorts through the promotion of work, leading, finally, to resolving the perversity caused by the crime discussed above. It is for this reason that I refer to a systematized exchange that is responsible, mutual, and secure.

2.2 Without a doubt, Africa is in our unconscious, and is our psychosocial *logos*. That interruption left us without names and without family pasts. At most we can record up to the first generations after abolition. Africa, as I mentioned, was a domestic, social and [XXX][4] taboo.

From the point of view of the historian, transmigratory people who return to their genetic origin without overcoming it experience a profoundly alienating process. Peace between peoples is a task for the world of the future. When I speak of peace, I mean knowledge, recognition, communication, and respectful conviviality with the other. We are no longer on the cusp of an apocalypse. Men and nations, good and bad, are resolving the questions of their borders. The Afro-Brazilian must be prepared for the future, because life is going to continue independently of them, and of the moment of historical and planetary transcription. Notwithstanding our differences, there is always much to learn from, and give to, other human beings.

CERNE should produce knowledge about the professions that can be reciprocally exchanged. Provide specialized training and shared human resources for the different parties involved. Beginning with training specialists in the area of International Relations, to be spokespeople for this initial political effort. This can be done alongside universities and technical training schools like SENAI and SENAC.[5]

2.3 Preliminary contacts with similar entities in the country and in the Antillean regions.

3. The Living Archive of Candomblé and Its Correlates

3.1 Medicine, health, food—urgent measures.

The various strands of candomblé can above all identify new knowledges for the healing process. The gathering of knowledge can be redistributed in commercial products and exchanges with the original continent, which is rich in organic materials, living beings, and minerals. Literary production, academic or otherwise, can offer studies on the conscious redistribution of the products of flora and fauna. I make this suggestion to CERNE as a contribution to the international relations network.

Popular knowledge would be key to this effort. At the minimum this project would benefit preventive medicine and the maintenance of human physical health.

Through these projects, work will be valued once more, and the relations between man and ecology will become less conflictual. This can be done immediately by turning to Central America and the Caribbean. It would require rebuilding and exchange among the various institutions of the Black Movement. Signatures of the entities should be organized by their styles and their types (logotypes) and distributed at first as informal proposals. We should locate an emblematic archive of the political movement of entities in Africa, here and in the Caribbean. It should be protected, and respect for blackness and spirituality transmitted in the goods exchanged, in the name of intercontinental associations working as a global organization. It would be for CERNE to do this work of restoration, and the initial assessment of the spiritual and political factors of this contemporary process, aiming toward a global exchange of information.

This would keep the spirit of the 1970s alive and active; that moment of the total collapse of old colonialisms, and which must be lived openly and serenely in the near future.

Notes

The original title of this essay is "Aruanda!" Unpublished, Fundo MBN, 2D.23.4.5.

1. The Centro da Referência Negromestiça, based in Salvador, Bahia, later directed by Antonio Risério. The organization published the magazine *Padê*.

2. Manuscript illegible.

3. The Organization of Angolan Women (Organização Mulher Angolana), founded in 1962, originally in support of the MPLA.

4. Manuscript illegible.

5. These national vocational training organizations still exist today: SENAI is the Brazilian National Service for Industrial Training, and SENAC is the Brazilian National Service for Professional Education.

Study in E Major, Opus 10 No. 3

Goodbye my love
I am leaving
And I already miss you

I made a song out of goodbye
My verses will say
From the heart
You too must sing
When I return
I will be happier

And in your voice
I will hear this song
That I made you

Study in E major by Chopin after talking about Angola. I never knew what to say I went to do in Angola. Sometimes I feel a very powerful blockage from others, thanks to Raquel's death and the intensity of my mania. And the mania was a form of saying goodbye to everything that came before Angola. I wanted to understand Angola as the moment of being there. As a return crossing. Breaking all my references that could connect me to the western part of the world. It was an equatorial-hemispheric cut. It was the explosion of repression.

Oh! How beautiful it was to see the territory-mother and live in it like a fetus in the uterus. At every instant I fell back into ecstasy in the

face of events. Kakwako, Funda, . . . Ndalatando, Luena, Dembo, Ma-
condo, Massangano.

The Cuanza in Massangano has the infinite dimensions of the sea,
the sea between the reefs, green, and shaded by acacias. It was where I
heard the word *quimbanda* [healing]. It was one afternoon and the river
passed by on its bed of stones, like an enormous liquid serpent, the
extremities that provoked friction were invisible. The calm of the cobra-
river, far from its estuary, far from its source. I looked at it without believing in such beauty. And I thought about André, as if he was right
there with me. And I looked at the fort as if I was a busy man of the
sixteenth century.

Terror, horror, ecstasy. How was it possible? How could they survive
in exile, leaving this vision behind. The people who accompanied me
stayed silent, respecting my wonder in front of the Cuanza in Massangano. It was different in other places. It was not like that in Ndalatando,
but the intensity of emotion was the same. In these moments they had the
sweetness of those who have suffering as an innate gift. Comprehension
changes for those who rediscovered the physical space left long ago. Mute
love that deepens even more the pleasure of remaking links lost long ago.

And the fish came, served like a millenary ritual, that transcended
dogmatic frontiers. Supper where the tensions slowly relax, giving
way to known situations, that can be shared. The absence of Agostinho
Neto, for example. Everyone seemed to suffer this loss in one way or
another. There were those who had for a long time been very intimately
connected to him and suffered from their experience. There were also
those who only mourned the loss of a leader who had a suffocating effect on everyone.

Death has the power to level, and to spread its impression uniformly,
especially when you mourn an individual with implications like
Neto's.

I arrived in Luanda on the day of his funeral. I saw many people crying in the plain, a restrained cry, but with many tears. They told me
when I arrived that people were entering a trance, thousands of people,
a kind of collective hysteria. They were beating their heads on the floor,
repeating the millenarian gesture for greeting kings.

Like my parents, hunters, I arrive in the game of seduction with the certainty of my conquest. (film the boy)

But where is the hurry, between lights and sound?

Between lights and sound I only find my old body. Old companion of illusions of hunting the beast. Body suddenly imprisoned by the destiny of men from outside. By the desire for a history, that today counts without blame as if I was inattentive in the moment of conquering.

Body-map of a distant country that seeks other frontiers that limit the conquest of me.

Mythical-quilombo that makes me content of the shades of the palm trees.

Like those of my parents, hunters.

Note

The original title of this essay is "Estudo em Mi maior, opus 10 no.3." Unpublished, undated, Fundo MBN, 14.2.9.

Zumbi of Palmares

ONE DAY, in my Grandma's house, in a chest with some other things, I saw a book. The book spoke of warriors and palm trees. I no longer remember the details. I know that I read it, and went to the edge of the plot, where it met the sea, and lay on my back, looking up at the palm trees. Lying in the thick vegetation, I imagined those warriors in battle.

Later, at school here in Rio, I read about Palmares and I remembered the story of my Grandma's book. I thought that it was the same, though now it is about slaves and bandits.

Today, after so much reading and reflection, I still yearn for those images of warriors fighting in the forest.

And I wanted to see them as I saw them in Aracaju. I wanted to see it the way I saw it in my dreams.

But what I saw in my dream was a shaded place, where various black men were to be found, all around forty years old. They were all agitated.

I could hear them talking among themselves. They said to the man who was with me that they were going to take me to a temple where they were celebrating an ancient rite.

In a hurry, we left by road. They were in cars, like taxis, and I was behind in another car with my companion. We went down a long road, and at dawn we arrived at the place. It was a temple like the Church of Santa Bárbara in Bahia.

The men went inside the temple, and I saw myself on the terrace in a group of people, all white and bald. It was a terrible, repugnant image, because they were all bumping into each other, trying to make contact with each other's mouths. They were somehow deformed and I understood that they were deaf and mute. They made a constant noise like the gnashing of teeth. I was very afraid and I tried to get out of there. At the same time, I felt great sadness for their condition.

Among all this, I saw him. He emerged out of the depths of the temple between two rows of young, black men. Thin, limping slightly. His face, though beautiful, was austere, and this terrified me, because it was an austerity that gave me something to fear. Then I recognized him, his face the one I saw between the palm trees at my grandma's plot. The strong shapes of the faces of the men in my house. The regular features of men from the Bantu world. My terror increased, as they slowly approached. I tried desperately to flee, and fell into a shallow ditch between the railing that separated me from those deaf-mute people.

He approached, and leaned over the railing, looking at me, fixedly. Without looking away he asked the young men who accompanied him: "Why did you bring her here?" The young men extended their hands, wanting to help me out of the ditch. I was still afraid of everything, and seeking some way out. Then I saw a spiral staircase that took me to an immense lawn, which I reached without difficulty.

On the floor I see my companion, flanked by two children, one black, my daughter, and the other white, wearing gypsy clothes.

I open my eyes. I am still trying to understand where I was. I stopped at two inverted triangles on the ceiling. I recognized immediately what the dream meant. At that time I was drowning in reading and reflections about him. That question he asked was at once a warning and a reproach. That's what I think. It is seven years now since I had that dream. Since then, at times, I have felt like an incarnation. I return, always, to my desire to rummage in Grandma's chest.

Note

The original title of this essay is "Zumbi de Palmares." Unpublished, undated, Fundo MBN, 14.2.9. This text has not, to our knowledge, been published in the Portuguese-language collections of Beatriz Nascimento's work.

The First Great Loss:
Grandma's Death

EVEN TODAY I am appalled and perplexed in front of death. I cannot cry. I do not know if I feel sadness. Like when I learned that Grandma died. Her death created a great silence inside me, as if it was me who had died. I waited for it over the long months that preceded. I wanted the book from her chest. Afterward I always believed my education to be incomplete for not having read that book again, for not having seen it again.

I dream that what I write will one day be the reconstitution of that beautiful story of people and palm trees, perhaps the story of my grandparents in that yearned-for Sergipe.

Grandma and the Book: My Two Aches

Right now, I have two joys. One that is in the past, the other that I may have in the future. How am I to write a book if there are so many rules? I would like to write about warriors and palm trees . . . but they demand a thesis from me, a truth to be defended.

How to defend a truth? It is, or it is not. And the truth is that I am a black girl from Sergipe, moved by so many transmigrations, so many uprootings. I am always seeking an ungrounded territory. A quilombo where I know some ancestor of mine lived.

That is a truth. I must be descended from them. If not, how could I explain all of my involvement, all these memories, all these dreams. All of this desire to say, "He existed, and he existed like this." This is an imagined truth. It is a sublime truth because it goes beyond my common condition—to be a descendant of the quilombos of Sergipe is to feel the tragic dimension of the loss of land while at the same time living surrounded by that land, in search of the point where this story was broken.

To which *he* am I referring? I know it is the strong Bantu mask, the mask that bears all the aches of muscles punished by work, the aches of an individual communized by the weight of slavery. The aches of not having wanted to leave Africa. The aches of not being able to return. So, flight and the dream of heroism, inevitable death, death as a return to your own humanity.

He gave his human saga to future generations, the myth of the hero of God.

Grandma's chest was thrown into the sea after she died.

I felt the loss of the chest as a second loss of my beloved. The angel of my infancy. I came into contact with the world through her and everything had her scent. That smell of coffee that was the flavor of the drink that she and only she made. That taste became smell, and everything I looked at with her: the banana trees, the papayas, the *araçás*, the coconut palms, the prawns, and the crabs smelled like the sweat of Madalena. The smell that I extracted from the taste of her coffee.

I wanted the book from the chest. A child's bequest that was denied me by the brutality of adults. It is only a few years ago that I was able to ask Mom for it and she said, "I threw it into the sea." I felt surprised, happy. I asked, "But why into the sea?"

It had to be into the sea, the living being that makes things perennial. One day I will dive to look for the book inside the chest.

The book inside the chest, the book that I have to write—two more aches.

Note

The original title of this essay is "A primeira grande perda—a morte de vovó." Unpublished, undated, Fundo MBN, 14.2.9.

Final Section

A Conversation between Bethânia N. F. Gomes, Archie Davies, and Christen A. Smith

Part I: The Woman

BETHÂNIA GOMES: When I talk about her, I always want to go right back to the first day I was with her, in her arms. First, I heard a voice. I was feeding; her body, her arms, and me.

Growing up, the first thing I thought was that she was really, really beautiful. Though people used to tell me I looked so much like my father, I always felt that actually I was just like her. And it was comforting to be like her. She was funny, she was bright, she used to play the acoustic guitar. Some of my first memories are of her playing the guitar and singing, singing, singing. Singing with my dad, or with friends. She made me into a strong girl, a strong woman, without losing my vulnerability or my femininity. The way she treated me, she wanted me to be able to face obstacles and overcome them.

I remember this bright, funny person, always with a lot of people around her. I have memories of childhood, of being at the beach, and at my grandmother's house. And Christmas was summertime, with whole families at the beach: my cousins, my mom, my uncles. I liked playing in the sand and making castles

FIGURE 5.1. Bethânia Gomes and Beatriz Nascimento,
private collection of Bethânia Gomes.

and digging and running around in the sand. And I remember
my mother coming over, and she picked me up and carried me
into the sea and threw me right in the water: no mercy! And I
remember wondering, *Why did she do that to me?* I remember
thinking it was mean, but then looking at her, and she was
smiling, a really peaceful smile, standing there and watching me
try and swim. And then she joined me in the water and swam
with me, and calmed me down. That is the type of mother she
was. She shaped me to be a warrior from the very beginning.

FIGURE 5.2. Beatriz Nascimento and her sisters, private collection of Bethânia Gomes.

Looking back, that was a gift. She taught me how to fight, she taught me how to overcome things that I didn't want to face. I wouldn't say fear, exactly, but there are things in life that you have to face, and things you have to overcome, every hour, every day.

She read a lot, played guitar, and there were lots of parties! Family parties, parties with friends. And I still love to go to parties!

She was a very exciting mom. She was just a very exciting woman, and I could tell she was admired, and she was loved.

I loved hanging out with my mom so much that I didn't like children's birthday parties. I always felt very awkward at children's birthday parties. I was always bored. I think it was because I was used to going to parties with my mom and seeing so much culture and music and people talking . . .

When she and my father separated, our family of three broke apart. I heard she was in a lot of pain, but she used to always say that I was a very supportive daughter and I was very caring. She was supportive, no matter what.

She was warm. Her body was my home. Even if sometimes she seemed to be broken, because she had bipolar disorder, and she went through mental health crises, but even in those moments it was like when she threw me in the water, and I had to just get it together. Our dynamic was really interesting . . . our body language . . . It was a really different kind of motherhood for that time. Sometimes she had to travel, and sometimes she had these crises, so I was also raised by my aunts. So, you know, I would get slapped around by these four big powerful Black women, you know! So I'm tough!

It was a matriarchal family. My mother was born into a matriarchal family. The biggest example was my grandmother, Rubina. She ruled the home. And she made the home a place of comfort for my grandfather and a place of growth for his children. I know from my own father that my grandfather used to treat Beatriz a little bit differently from the other girls. He would spoil her a little bit. She was a Daddy's girl. Her connection with her father was so strong, and the love her father had for her was so strong. It could have created a kind of jealousy in the family, but I could see that when she was around her father there were moments of great love and comfort for her. There was no judgment: I don't think my grandpa ever judged her as much as other people in the family did.

She was a really big source of beauty and intelligence, and I think for her it was very hard to balance all that, and accept that she had all of that in her. She started reading at the age of four, by herself. She had a lot of books around.

CHRISTEN SMITH: When you mention beauty, I cannot help but think of the gorgeous picture that you have of you and her on

FIGURE 5.3. Bethânia Gomes and Beatriz Nascimento, private collection of Bethânia Gomes.

the beach. Your mom is wearing a bikini and turned sideways looking at the camera with an elegant smirk on her face. You are in your bikini clinging on to her leg. One thing that I love about this picture is the way that your mother exudes sensuality in it! She is beautiful and sexy and she knows it! So often, we as Black women are taught to ignore our sexuality—or worse, abhor it. Yet we are enchanting, sexual beings who also think critically (not one thing at the expense of the other). We have to be careful not to fall into the trap of hiding/refusing our sexuality because it is also a part of who we are not only as people but also as intellectuals. I can't help but think about the conversations happening now in the Black community in Brazil regarding the loneliness of Black women (*solidão da mulher negra*).[1] Beatriz is one of the first to write about the challenges Black women face in love in Brazil—and she did so eloquently. However, we would be remiss not to recognize that she was definitely not a lonely Black woman. Despite all of the political and social challenges of racism and misogynoir that she faced and theorized, she also lived life fully with multiple rich and fulfilling relationships over her lifetime. She had fun and she was always flirting, dancing, writing poetry, playing—embodying her full self!

BETHÂNIA: My mother got lots of attention from men! I remember the last time that she visited New York and hung out with me at the company [Dance Theater of Harlem], I was so embarrassed! We were at a dinner and she caught the eye of a young man who was walking through. One of my French colleagues started to tease me and say "Look, Bethânia, your mom is just like you!" She was confident and got lots of attention from men!

There were lots of men at her funeral, all upset, calling from around the world in tears . . . calls from men in Germany, in Angola. I was like, "Wow! Who are all these people?" She was popular and had friends all around the world. There is joy in this. Our story is not only based in suffering—it is a story of joy. We, Black women, are not suffering. We may be in a struggle, but we are not suffering. There's a big difference! There's a joy that she has in her spirit that is very different from *o jeito amargo* [bitterness] of some people who take on that narrative of *solidão da mulher negra*.

The media, the system, white society itself, are really comfortable with the bitterness. It is OK for them. The angry Black woman is a welcome story. But the labels that are put on us are labels to help them feel better about us, not labels that are organic to our experience. No, no, I go against that. We don't have to be like that. My mom was *a mulher bem acompanhada* [well-accompanied woman]!

Mamãe was an amazing human being. She had a lot of qualities, and I think one of the reasons for her mental health situation was that it was *a lot*. God just poured so much on her, and then when she felt the weight of that, and the responsibility of that, that's when she would break down. And the responsibility of having a child was heavy too.

There were two pregnancies that were interrupted because of school, and then the third pregnancy was me . . . so I guess I tried to come three times, and then the third time I made it!

She was still at university. She was still going in, and my father was too, so the rest of the family were like, "Well, we're going to take care of this kid, we're going to help!" So, I came into this world like that, with the support of my aunts, with the big support of my oldest aunt, Carmen, who became my godmother, and the whole family. It was very quilombo-like for me! I was so outgoing, and I had my different relationships with each of my aunts, even when I was really tiny. Every aunt had a different name that I chose.

The men in the family were always very calm, and more like "Ooh! We're not going to mess with this."

So that's what my mother was. She was this beautiful force, a beautiful being, a beautiful force. Everywhere she walked in, it was like "Pffff" Oxunmaré!" She claimed her orixá was Oxumaré.[2] And it's funny because, you know how when the rainbow comes, everyone is like "The rainbow is here! The rainbow! The rainbow!" And that's how she was! When she showed up, it was like "Oh! Beatriz is here!"

CHRISTEN: You talked about your mother always playing music and playing acoustic guitar. Do you remember the music that she liked to play?

BETHÂNIA: Oh yes! A lot of the songs she played were northeastern: Luis Gonzaga, forró. Everything was very . . . in my house we didn't play Bossa Nova! You know what I'm talking about . . . white Bossa Nova! There was no Bossa Nova. I started listening to bossa nova when I got to New York! But at the house, Mamãe

FIGURE 5.4. Beatriz Nascimento and José
do Rosário Freitas Gomes, private collection
of Bethânia Gomes.

used to sing on the guitar . . . "Acorda Maria bonita, levanta vem
fazer o café . . ." She used to sing that. Sometimes I wake up in the
morning, and I hear that in my head . . . because I've got to wake
up and have my coffee, and the police is up!

   *A música é assim, Archie: [sings] Acorda Maria bonita, levanta
vem fazer o café, que o dia já vem raiando, E a policia já está do pé.*
Now that is *so* Black Lives Matter, isn't it!

CHRISTEN: It is the best song ever! It is so Black . . . it is the
   Blackest song!

BETHÂNIA: The fucking NYPD is up! Gotta get my coffee!
   Wherever you are, NYPD, Texas PD, Brazil PD, UK PD . . .

CHRISTEN: It's the diaspora! Black people around the world can
   relate to Maria having to get up early, get her coffee, and get to
   work because the police are already in the streets ready to terrorize
   us, just like the overseers whose job it was to police us to make
   sure we went to work during slavery. The history of morning

coffee for Black people in Brazil is very telling. During slavery, morning coffee was a part of enslaved people's rations. The idea was that it would help them wake up and get to work. The slavery exhibit at the Museu Afro-Brasil in São Paulo includes archives of a plantation owner's notes on "slave rations," and they include morning coffee! There are so many layers to that folk song!

BETHÂNIA: That was the music that Mamãe used to play . . . Sometimes it was my mother and my father both playing the guitar. My father would be playing the *morna*, the Cape Verdean "pom, pom pom" . . . and my mother would cut in, and start with the samba "ta ti ti ta ti ti . . ." He'd be like, "Beatriz, come on!" And she would say, "Come on, José! It's too melancholic!" They call the Cape Verdean *morna* melancholy. I understand it, it's in my blood, but my mother, it wasn't in her blood! When I listen to morna, I feel I'm there, it takes me there. the Cape Verdeans, they go with the sea. With the morna, you're going with the rhythm of the boat, or you're going with the rhythm of being on the sea, floating. But the samba is totally different. She used to play Pixinginha, everything Black. But don't get me wrong: she loved rock, she loved classical rock. She loved Pink Floyd, Cat Stevens. George Harrison, that was her crush! She *loved* that man! Ray Charles, but that was everybody in the family. So much music in the house. Music all day. My mother did not like Roberto Carlos . . . but Tim Maia forever! Jorge Ben! So much Jorge Ben, Jorge Ben all day!

———

BETHÂNIA: She grew into this amazing intellectual, but there was a moment in her life, in her late teens, that she kind of quit it. She finished high school and she went to work in a *fábrica de tecidos*, a textile factory. My family was very connected to textiles, and making . . . my grandmother wanted to be a seamstress but she wasn't able to because she had ten kids, as well as others, *agregados*, cousins, nephews, that would pass through. My grandmother took care of everybody. So she didn't have the time to pursue her dream, which was to be a *costureira*, a dressmaker. Some of her daughters pursued that dream. Ana Maria made clothes, my aunt Zélia was always knitting, making quilts. Grandma had a machine at home. I remember playing with it, and for me it was very easy. I think it's a talent that we all have. And when I had to sew my pointe shoes, *snap*. I always sew my pointe shoes nice and neat! And I always teach my students in Harlem how to sew . . . it's a talent that I have, and I know it comes from my grandma.

BETHÂNIA: One of the last places my mother went, before she passed, was a trip to Haiti, and to Martinique. That was her last trip. What came out of that, I always ask myself. I was in New York already. I got a beautiful postcard. Of course, in my life of movement and traveling the world I've lost the postcard, but if I saw it today I would know it. And it said something like "Look at these beautiful African colors, look at the colors of this place, it's just beautiful, these are our colors, and you know, *I love you, my queen.*" And I was like "Yay! I love you, Mamãe!" My mother used to send me postcards from everywhere she went. I have one from the first time we were separated physically and she sent me a postcard of an indigenous Brazilian boy with this arrow. He was so cute, and I was like "Oh, I have a little brother!" I thought he was my brother! And in the card she said, "To my queen, a picture of a king." So, I thought he was my brother. She used to call me *rainha da Mamãe* [Mom's queen].

Part II: Political Activism and the Dangers of Being a Black Intellectual

BETHÂNIA: Once, when I was about seven, we were taking the bus—I used to lie on her lap on the bus—and then this group of students gets on . . . and this is the thing about being an activist, it's *active*, all the time. You're active when you leave your house, you're active at home, with your child . . . there is no down time. And this group of students got on the bus, a group of teenagers. And there's a Black boy in the middle but they're mostly white Brazilians, and then this girl starts telling the Black boy, "Get away from me, you stink! *Preto! Macaco! Sai!*" and she goes on about how he's Black and stinky and she doesn't want to sit next to a Black person, and everybody's laughing, and he's kind of laughing but he's embarrassed.

My mother turns around to them and says, "Do not talk to him like that. You should be ashamed of yourself for talking to him like that. Don't talk to any other Black person like that ever again, do you understand? Educate yourself." And she turned to the young man and said, "Don't let anybody talk to you like that ever again." Silence in the bus! I remember, I was so freaking proud!

She'd be in the university, in a symposium, in the bus, talking to the kids, and she'd be like, "Shut the fuck up! Don't be reviving violence, don't do it!" I was so proud. And you know, that's probably one of the reasons she died. Somebody came and shut her down, because she'll tell you "Don't do that." She'd step up.

She was an activist, like her body was a quilombo, her body was Palmares itself: *pa! pa! pa!* Her body was like this walking quilombo. That's what she was, to me. And I'm not the only one. She was this really powerful, powerful person. Yet she was playful, she was funny, she liked to party, and she liked to love!

———

She was pretty much welcome at the Universidade Federal Fluminense. But it was during the dictatorship, and the student movement was the *click* to start her activist life. That was the key, the door.

She was arrested during the riots. They arrested a lot of people. Some people got hurt, some people were tortured. Some people died. I remember her talking about her friends who never showed up again, who never came back. And I remember her talking about her experience of being arrested. She was arrested and they didn't go further in abusing her, but they sexually harassed her: they lifted her skirt. I remember, at a very young age, hearing my mother telling this story, that was one of the details: "They lifted my skirt." And when she talks in *acerca da consciencia racial*, she talks about the guys lifting her skirt . . .

They did many things to many women. Stories that are way, way worse than my mother's story. And I remember my mother telling her story freely, because her story was not as bad as so many other people. I think that's why she could tell her story. Because her story in a way wasn't as bad. Nobody inserted anything into her vagina, nobody raped her . . . I know stories that are awful, awful, like what they did to Dilma Rouseff. She was tortured. My mother wasn't tortured. But she was abused.

She was held for about twenty-four hours. My grandmother was going nuts. At home in that time it was like the opposite of a carnival, but with a carnival feeling . . . a lot of movement. My grandmother wanted to throw all the books away in case the police raided and found them. But I think my mother was saved because my family lived in Brás de Pina and the police didn't think that in the *periferia* people were going to university. They wouldn't have imagined that you had an intellectual growing up there in the Black working class. So that's probably what saved her. That mentality that "those niggers ain't going nowhere." Finally she got home safe. And sometimes she would tell this story. But I know she wasn't allowed to tell this story in front of her grandma!

CHRISTEN: She probably didn't want to traumatize her. Parents suffer a lot. It's interesting to me the stark contrast between what you're describing, in terms of the carnivalesque feeling of this moment where everybody is in a frenzy, everybody's running around, and the silence of the archives around this moment. And you rarely hear stories from Black people about the military dictatorship and their experiences. You rarely get things written about it from Black people. But that moment was loud! So there's this tension, this contrast, between what was experienced and lived at that time, and how we talk about memory. Because even in *Ôrí*, you know, you have this whole narrative and there's no reference or mention to just how dangerous and crazy things were during the dictatorship.

BETHÂNIA: In the first takes of *Ôrí*, in the beginning, they're having a meeting. It's a lot of them. That's ten years later, but it's still kind of dangerous! They were very brave.

CHRISTEN: People tell me that right before the military dictatorship started to crumble was the most dangerous moment. Like 1974, 1976, around then. It always blows my mind, the difference between the silence in the archives and the relative occlusion of the Black experience with violence in the national narrative of the dictatorship—the institutionalized memory of the moment— and what the lived experience was really like for Black people: busy, loud, crazy . . . like carnival.

BETHÂNIA: Exactly. And you don't hear so much of stories told by Black people as much as you hear the white people. That bugs the shit out of me! For example, when I watch the Petra documentary— *On the Edge of Democracy*—it's so romanticized . . . I have a really big problem with that. Throughout that film, I was waiting to hear some of the narrative that *I* have.

CHRISTEN: Totally.

BETHÂNIA: Something like the narrative that I heard hearing from my mother: [*speaking fast, urgently*] "They did this to me, and they did this to me, and they put me in a room, and they were asking me all these questions! And they asked me what I was reading! And they asked me what I do, and who do I think I am! And then they lift my skirt! And then I was very agitated! And then ba ba ba . . ." That is the story that *I* heard. And I was just listening, as a child.

CHRISTEN: A lot of times these narratives are more about white folks' indignation about people not recognizing white folks' privilege. It's not really about the repression, it's about how dare you do this to *me*. And I think that is what makes them uncomfortable. I think it's important for us to talk about this. Part of the reason why I think Black folk don't talk about the dictatorship is because the dictatorship didn't end for Black people.

BETHÂNIA: Exactly.

CHRISTEN: And so folk are still scared, and people are still being repressed. And the police still raid our houses, and we never stopped living in the dictatorship. It only ended for white people.

BETHÂNIA: It did not end for us. So, when she was telling me what happened to her, the next day it could happen to her again.

CHRISTEN: And it could have happened in the 1970s, the 1980s, the 1990s, the 2000s, 2010, 2020 . . . and you know, that's the problem. We never stop being at risk. People don't talk about this kind of stuff because they're still scared.

BETHÂNIA: The dictatorship . . . was a big factor in her life. It was a turning point in her life, in university. . . . Then she graduated, then she became a mother, and then when I arrive she was still studying, she was doing *pos-graduação*, I breast-fed in the classroom. I guess that's why I don't like classrooms! [*laughs*] Because if you're born in the classroom, by the time you're like fifteen you're done with the classroom! You wanna dance, you wanna move—you don't wanna sit!

Once I started moving I think it was impossible to hold me, I think I was one of those crazy babies who always climb everything. I was never quiet, and I became a terrible toddler who used to throw the cats out the window! I was terrible. Wearing high heels, walking round the house in high heels. I was a terrible one. But both my parents made it. They both graduated. A lot of help from the family, *minhas tias*, a lot of help, a lot of support. There was a whole quilombo! I really wish I could find it, track my family and find out which quilombo we are from, because that's the way it was, and the way it is today, even though we're distanced from each other.

Part III: Black History and Culture

BETHÂNIA: I was probably ten years old when my mom came to my school to do a little seminar about Black history. I remember they invited her to come and do a little lecture. But it was just for the kids who were going into high school, and so I was about ten years old, and all the kids who were about to go to high school, about fifteen years old, came to me and were like "Oh my god, Bethânia! Your mother is so cool!" and I was like, "Damn! Cool! The big kids are talking to me! My mom was like my passport to talk to the older kids!" [*laughs*] I always wanted to be with the older kids anyway. I was so proud of her presence. She was like a queen, really, the way she presented herself.

I'll never forget when she first came to my ballet school. It was in my second year in ballet and I had this really good teacher, Judi. And my mother and her were talking and talking and talking . . . My teacher was a ballerina, a really beautiful dancer, and I saw her and my mother next to each other, and the two of them were so balanced. My mother's posture was so beautiful. She wasn't a dancer, but she had this noble way of being, such that *everybody* would just respect her. They could see, you know, in Brazil, that this was a different Black woman . . . but no, I don't want to say that she was a different Black woman, that's not fair because I know my country's situation. Black women, most Black women, in my country didn't have that choice, didn't grow up in an environment where a *father* says, "You are beautiful." I know that I come from a home, from a family, from *um berço rico, nao rico em dinheiro, mas rico em cultura, rico em historia, rico em identidade, negra, mesmo, entende?* So, no, I don't think it's fair to say she was a different Black woman. She wasn't different. Along with her sisters she just had an opportunity, which she fought for through her studies. My grandma was a woman who said, "None of my daughters are going to work in nobody's kitchen." And when my grandmother said that, I don't think she meant just *nobody's going to be a housekeeper*—she was also talking about marriage, and about society. And none of them did do that, and, thank God, she should be very proud today. None of her daughters did, none of her granddaughters did, none of her grandsons did. We're all good. We are still fighting. We are a family of working people, and some are artists today. And I say, thank God, I had the privilege of being able to become an artist. Actually, my grandfather, Francisco, was a musician, he played the *bandolin*. That's where Beatriz picked up the guitar. My grandfather never had the choice to be an artist. He couldn't even think about becoming a musician! No way! He had to become a stonemason. And eventually, he married a girl and had children, a family. But little did he know—well, maybe he knew!—that he was building a lot of strong-ass Brazilian motherfuckers that are still coming up today!

ARCHIE DAVIES: I wanted to ask you bout *acerca da consciencia racial*. I think that's one of her most powerful essays, and it is a very personal, urgent voice that she uses in the essay. How does her writing compare to how she spoke? Can you hear her speaking in her writing?

BETHÂNIA: That essay is one of my favorites . . . because I can hear her telling me that story. And I can hear her telling me and my cousins this story, and I can hear my aunts also telling us this story. It's a story that most of them went through.

It's all described in *acerca da consciencia racial*. It's exactly what me and my cousins used to sit and hear, listening to the stories, living in Sergipe, but also in Rio. The discrimination at school. The dangers and the struggles of going to school as a Black child in Brazil. What always amazed me was that she became so brilliant in school, while having to deal with this racist life . . . going to school, coming back from school . . . getting home. For a lot of us Black children . . . It was twenty something years later, but still I understand when my aunts and my mother talk about the struggle of going to school, and it's amazing how they had the resilience and the strength to grow and to get through and become successful, all of them, all of them.

My aunt Rosa was called a João as well, you know. My aunt Rosa and my mother, they were not androgynous, but they had this beauty that was like, they didn't need to add things to it. Of course they were girls, they were beautiful, they wore short hair most of the time, and grew up to be women who wore short hair their whole lives, and I think they always go back to that moment, "Hey! João!" . . . I heard that expression so many times out of my mother's mouth, and my aunts' mouths. And sometimes they would be together telling this story, and it was very intense, but it was very enriching. And now I look back and I'm like, "Oh my God, this is amazing." And it's amazing how . . . *como* . . . I don't know how to say it in English . . . *a oralidade é tao importante e sempre foi a nosso instrumento nas vidas das familias pretas brasileiras. Para saber da nossa história! Graças a deus houve aquelas momentos de contar histórias, para o dia, seja de noite, seja depois do almoço, e contar essas histórias. Que são histórias hoje já ancestrais para os jovens de nossas familias, da nossa famílias, para Luana saber, para Maria Clara saber, para Arjan saber, para George saber, para Michael saber, para João Pedro, para Perola saber, para Nana saber, nossas crianças crescem hoje também sabem dessa historia.* That's why I think *acerca da consciencia racial* is so important not just for our family but in terms of history, of how us children were treated back then, how racism can be so damaging, because that is not just her story in there, that is Jurema's story. And Jurema is another story. *A buraca é mais em baixo para Jurema.* The hole is deeper for Jurema. Jurema is totally a victim of the system, even more than Beatriz. So I do feel her voice very, very much. I feel her voice not just in terms of telling us her story, but of telling herself that story as a healing process, getting it out of her system. Because you can tell in that writing that she gets mad. In the end she's like, "How many Juremas are out there today?" I can go today, October 7, 2021, I can have the same question in Brazil. Even here, right here where I am in Harlem. How many Juremas do we have, still?

Acerca da consciencia racial means that you have got to be conscious of that shit to move on! And yes, you gotta fucking study, you gotta try your best no matter what—if you have dyslexia, if you have ADHD, keep pushing, go to school every day. Get an education, go to your ballet class. Become a prima ballerina. Yes! And that's what my mother says in *acerca da consciencia racial*. What did I do as a dancer? I had to be the best, to be able to graduate from Teatro Municipal do Rio de Janeiro, I had to be the best to become a ballerina that could have a professional life in Brazil. And I had to be the best when I got here, because I was an immigrant, because I was told I was a Latina at that point. People [in the United States] look at me like "What is she?" And I was like, "I'm Black!" and they're like, "No you're not!"

CHRISTEN: Which is ridiculous! For the record.

BETHÂNIA: That blew my mind! But what I'm saying is that, yes, I do hear her, and I hear her until today. Her questions in that essay are for today, still. She's still Afrofuturista to me, she's always the one that speaks ahead. She was Afrofuturista before she was born. When will the moment be when she can stay in the past? When is she going to be history?

Notes

1. See, for example, the special issue of *Women's Studies Quarterly* organized by Luciane Ramos Silva, Tanya Saunders, and Soanirina Ohmer, "Introduction: From Solidão, to Isolation, to Solidão-rity." *WSQ: Women's Studies Quarterly* 49 (2021): 16–49.

2. In Yoruba religious practices in Brazil, Oxumaré is the god of transitions, the spirit of the rainbow and the serpent.

Afterword, in the Guise
of a Postface

Muniz Sodré

TO BEGIN WITH, an exemplary story. Some time ago, during a ceremony I was taking part in, in a building of one of the headquarters of Afro-Brazilian religion in Salvador, there was a speech in memory of the founder, one of the great ancestral mothers of the candomblé initiates. The only person present who had known her personally was an old woman from the community. She, however, had no historical information to share. Yet after the speeches, an academic researcher who was seated at the table told us some more of her life story.

This apparently minor episode evokes the distance between historiographical accounts and people's narratives about their own existence and transformations. In the first, information is indispensable, as the unfolding written record of what is said, whether it is endorsed by more or less reliable sources. In the second case, orality predominates. Verbal discourse can seem foreshortened by gaps in memory, but it is almost always endorsed by familial relations and territorial references. Mário de Andrade has observed that "the people do not customarily date the commonplace actions of their lives." The dominant classes, meanwhile, are zealous in celebrating their trivialities as the feats of great men: the diarrhea of Don Pedro I on the banks of the Ipiranga eternalized as the cry of national independence.

This occurred to me when sketching out a commentary about this collection of texts and the historiographical details of Beatriz Nascimento's life. I knew her intimately, from the end of the 1970s. Over the years, I became her friend, her best man, and the supervisor of an unfinished master's thesis that was cut short by her brutal murder. I am, therefore, compelled to blend objective facts with personal reminiscences and what is inscribed emotionally in my mind.

For me, Beatriz represented, before anything else, a *contemporary* subjectivity, in the sense of the term used by Giorgio Agamben, of "a singular relationship with one's own time, which adheres to it and, at the same time, keeps a distance from it."[1] In other words, not in the current moment but in the untimeliness previously beckoned in by Nietzsche. Something, therefore, that implies a temporal fissure in objective, epochal terms, but also brings with it the possibility of disjuncture between the subject and their full psychic conformation, their immersion in suffering.

The social and cultural environment of this singular relationship can be described as an aggravation of the confrontation between the persistence of racial inequalities and the emergence, from the mid-1970s, of a generation of educated young Black people visibly influenced by African and North American counterinsurgencies. In a general way, the discourse of these movements is characterized by resentment and, particularly in Brazil, by frustration arising from active denialism by light-skinned citizens: no one admitted to being racist, nor even recognize this stain as a national question. Black people always bore with them the color of their skin, as well as the dregs of eugenic stigmatization and the effects of an ambiguous hierarchy, by which the fact of paleness manifested a patriarchal desire for fraternal relations while, depending on the circumstances, revealing itself to be unequivocally racist.

Personally, I had to listen, in newsrooms in Rio de Janeiro, to the argument that Brazilian racism was "invented by an American sociologist." It was a crime against the fatherland to place in doubt the hypocritical proposition that Brazil was an example for the world of racial harmony. This was not only a right-wing political position, as is often supposed today. The leftist and official search for national unity oriented itself around a knowledge of an abstract and indivisible people, indirectly modeled on European universalism.

The very idea of the nation was never disassociated from that of the homogenous and undifferentiated masses. It was a vision that differed little from the representations put forward by the Right. It was a vision that left aside the *plebs*, the *lumpenproletariat*—that is, the people outside the official organization of civil society, as well as culturally diverse peoples—Black people, *mamelucos*, *caboclos*, Indigenous peoples, *ribeirinhos*; those who, in practice, along with the *bandeirantes*, conquered Brazilian territory.[2] Whatever their European theoretical matrix (Leninist, Stalinist, Trotskyist) or doctrinal affiliation (Soviet, Albanian, Chinese, Castroian), the Brazilian Left was always within the limits of an abstract liberal republicanism, oblivious to concrete national contradictions like the continuance of slavocracy.

It is important to reiterate now (something that I have stressed in various texts) why Beatriz did not allow herself to become trapped in any political framework. She was only radically "contemporary": that is, she was an intellectual of the fracture. To compare her with others of her period is really to misunderstand the singularity of her intellectual position: averse to the seductions of party and immune to the distractions that the shady operatives of the system tried to put in the way of militants. What she really wanted was to unmask the farce of racial democracy and bring to light a counterinsurgent historiography, typified in the quilombos. She was a historian by vocation and training. She confronted the choice between the "Henrique Dias paradigm"[3]—that which, in the seventeenth century, was put at the service of the whites to govern Black and mixed-race people—and the "Zumbi dos Palmares paradigm," that which refused co-optation and surrender. Beatriz would have nothing to do with Henrique Dias, nor with Chica da Silva, nor with those of her peers whom, as is well known but often silenced, were "porous" to the intelligence services of the dictatorship.

This is not to say that she did not value conciliatory aspects of the movement organized by Black people, bearing in mind the example of the ideological offensive of the Black Front in São Paulo, when the militants demanded rigid discipline among themselves (with ambiguous and, sometimes, protofascist qualities) with the aim of gaining the trust of the white population and overcoming institutional barriers. According to the testimony of one of the survivors, in the Public Forces of São Paulo, that had as a rule the whitening of their rank and file, the Black Front succeeded in signing up more than four hundred Black people.

As with Chica da Silva: though she did not identify with this historical figure, Beatriz contested her characterization in the film by Cacá Diegues. Chica was known to be rich and to have owned enslaved people as a companion of an important Portuguese diamond merchant. In the film, otherwise magnificently interpreted by Zezé Motta, Chica stands out for the exuberance of the Black body, and for her sexual prowess, evident in the cries that burst from the private quarters of the Portuguese man. This bothered Beatriz's feminist consciousness, and set off a journalistic discussion about what she considered to be a white working-class vision of Blackness.

The quilombo was, however, for Beatriz, a great theoretical and empirical object, as well as an existential path. She knew, like Abdias do Nascimento, that the figure of Zumbi dos Palmares had Pan-Africanist potential due to his transnational, pioneering, inspirational character in the slave revolts in Santo Domingo, Cuba, Jamaica, Guyana, and Virginia (United States). Alongside that insurrectionary aspect, there was a formative one, as noted by D. José Maria Pires: "I think that we have still not dedicated ourselves to the study of quilombos and sought to learn the lessons that they left for us. Quilombos were true centres of education for life. Their organization was certainly much more human and more advanced than that of the Portuguese who enslaved us."[4]

But what would the quilombo be as an existential pathway? For me, in Beatriz, it means to have inscribed in the body the trance of a denunciation of the project of extermination of the Black condition, in which the State/Master's house and the members of the dominant patrimonialism were always accomplices. Foucault said, and it is true, that "racism is indispensable as a condition for taking someone's life." If this sword of Damocles has always been existentially difficult for all Black people, it was and remains more threatening in the condition of being a woman.

To be or "become" Black in Brazil in the middle of the last century left indelible marks on feminine corporeality—even more so if you made the quilombo your mythical home. Beatriz Nascimento was a distant daughter of Zumbi.

Notes

This essay was originally published in Portuguese in Ratts, Alex, 2022, *Beatriz Nascimento: O Negro Visto por Ele Mesmo*, Ubu Editora: São Paulo.

1. Giorgio Agamben, *What Is an Apparatus? And Other Essays*, trans. David Kishik and Stefan Pedatella (Stanford, CA: Stanford University Press, 2009), 41.

2. *Mameluco* and *caboclo* are terms denoting different kinds of racial mixture in Brazil. *Ribeirinhos* are communities, often majority indigenous and racialized, who live along rivers in various parts of the country. On *bandeirantes*, see the note in "'Quilombos': Social Change or Conservatism?"

3. Henrique Dias (d. 1662) was a Black military captain in the Brazilian army.

4. D. José Maria Pires, "O negro e a educacano," in *Perspectivas teológico-pastorais, Iter* (1982): 84–87.

BIOGRAPHICAL GLOSSARY

THIS HIGHLY SELECTIVE list introduces just a few of the intellectuals, activists, writers, and artists with whom Beatriz Nascimento was in dialogue (and at times disagreement) over the course of her writing and practice.

Hamilton Cardoso, born in Catanduva in 1953 and brought up in São Paulo, was an activist and intellectual involved in the Brazilian Black Movement from the 1970s to his death. He trained as a journalist and believed that the Black Movement needed to expand into new spaces in Brazilian society. He was a poet, writer, and reporter, and is featured alongside Beatriz Nascimento and Eduardo de Oliveira e Oliveira in the significant documentary on the Black Movement, *O negro da senzala ao soul* (Black people from the slave quarters to soul music) (1977). Having been involved in the *Convergencia Socialista* grouping and the journal *Versus* in São Paulo in the early 1970s, he was one of the founders of the MNU in 1978. In 1981 he helped found the magazine *Ébano*. His writing includes "Movimentos sociais na transição democrática" (Social movements in the democratic transition).

Sueli Carneiro was born in São Paulo in 1950 and is one of the leading Black feminists in Brazil today. She holds a doctorate in education from the University of São Paulo. She is a philosopher and has been an active figure in the Black Movement and Brazilian Black feminist politics since the 1970s. In 1988 she founded Geledés—Black Women's Institute. Her significant works include *Mulher Negra: Política governamental e a mulher* (Black woman: Government policy and women) (1985), with Thereza Santos and Albertina da Oliveira Costa, and *Racismo, Sexismo e Desigualdade no Brasil* (Racism, sexism, and inequality in Brazil) (2011).

Marlene Cunha was born in Rio de Janeiro in 1950. Cunha was a contemporary and collaborator, both intellectually and politically, of Beatriz Nascimento's. They worked together in the Grupo de Trabalho André Rebouças and did ethnographic work in Minas Gerais. Cunha trained in anthropology and studied Afro-Brazilian religions. Her 1986 dissertation from the University of São Paulo was called "Em busca de um espaço: a linguagem gestual no candomblé de Angola" (In search of a space: The gestural language of candomblé in Angola). She was the first president of the GTAR. She died in 1988.

Conceição Evaristo, born in 1946, is a leading Black Brazilian feminist and one of the most renowned contemporary writers in Brazil. She is an important voice on Black women's experiences in Brazil, as well as on Afro-Brazilian experience, politics, and identity. She is the author of several critically acclaimed novels, poems, and stories, many of which have been translated into English, including *Ponciá Vivencio* (2003) and *Becos da Memória* (2006). She won Brazil's most renowned literary prize, the Prêmio Jabuti, in 2015, and is also an important literary critic.

Lélia Gonzalez was one of the foremost thinkers of Black politics, identity, and anthropology in Brazil and one of the founding figures of Brazil's Black feminist movement. Born in 1935, and an anthropologist by training, she is widely recognized as one of the principle Black radical intellectuals of twentieth-century Brazil. She majored in history and geography in 1958, and in philosophy in 1962. She later took a master's in communication at UFRJ, and a PhD in social anthropology. In 1983 she founded the Nzinga Black Women's Collective in Rio de Janeiro and became a significant political figure including as a candidate for the Brazilian Worker's Party in various elections in the 1980s. When she died, she was head of the Department of Sociology and Politics at the Catholic University of Rio de Janeiro. Inspired by psychoanalysis as well as the Black Movement, she developed important concepts such as "Amefricanidade" (Amefricanity) and "Pretoguês" (Black-tuguese), among others. Her important works include *Lugar do Negro* (with Carlos Hasenbalg) published in 1982, and many essays. Beatriz Nascimento corresponded and worked with Gonzalez into the early 1990s. She died in 1994.

Clóvis Moura was a writer, historian, and sociologist, born in Piauí in 1925, in the northeast of Brazil. He was one of the most well-known and influential Black intellectuals in Brazil in his lifetime, and a longtime political activist. He wrote extensively about Black Brazilian history, including the history and political significance of quilombos, and made pathfinding critiques of anti-Black racism in Brazil. He was aligned with Brazilian communist parties in his youth and was a journalist for important leftist newspapers in Brazil, including *Última Hora* and *O Momento* (Salvador). He took a broadly Marxist approach to questions of race and class in Brazil. His important books include *Rebeliões da senzala: quilombos, insurreições, guerrilhas* (1959) and *Dicionário da escravidão negra no Brasil* (2004), among many others. He died in 2003.

Abdias do Nascimento was a prominent Afro-Brazilian writer, actor, intellectual, and politician. Born in 1914, he founded some of the most significant Black cultural and political organizations in Brazil, including the Teatro Experimental do Negro (Black Experimental Theater) in Rio de Janeiro and the Museu da Arte Negra (The Museum of Black Art). He edited and wrote many influential books on Black history in Brazil, including *O Genocídio do Negro Brasileiro* (1978) and *O Quilombismo* (1980). He edited the magazine *Quilombo* from 1948. He was also a significant politician, beginning with his involvement in the Frente Negra Brasileira (Brazilian Black Front) in the 1930s. He was forced into exile in 1968, returning to Brazil in 1983. He was a senator for the Partido Democrático Trabalhista (Democratic Labor Party) from 1994 to 1999. He died in 2011.

Eduardo de Oliveira e Oliveira, born in 1924, was a close colleague of Beatriz Nascimento, in the GTAR and in the MNU. Born in Rio de Janeiro, he was a sociologist and played a prominent role in the Quinzena do Negro at the University of São Paulo in 1977. His work helped lay the groundwork for the Black Movement in Brazil and São Paulo in the 1970s. He died in 1980.

Thereza Santos was born in 1938 in a Black, lower-middle-class family in Rio de Janeiro. She was an actor, communist activist, teacher, and writer. She worked for and produced theater with the Black Experimental Theater of Rio de Janeiro, and made many films. She was politically active both in Brazil and in Africa. In the early 1970s she worked with Eduardo de Oliveira e Oliveira in the incipient Black Movement in São Paulo. Invited to Guinea by the PAIGC, between 1974 and 1978 she took part in educational, cultural, and political work in the context of the anti-colonial struggle in Guinea, Angola, and Mozambique. She left Angola in 1978, having fallen out with the authoritarian tendencies of the postindependence regime. She died in 2012.

Sebastião Soares was an early member of the GTAR and was later president of the Instituto de Pesquisas das Culturas Negras (Institute of Research on Black Cultures).

Muniz Sodré is one of the foremost Black intellectuals in contemporary Brazil. He was supervising Beatriz Nascimento's master's dissertation in the early 1990s, at the time of her death. He is currently professor emeritus at the Federal University of Rio de Janeiro, and was formerly president of the National Library Foundation from 2005 to 2011. He has published thirty-four books on various topics, most of which have reflected on Black culture and communications. In 2019 he was named to the Literature Academy of Bahia.

CHRONOLOGY

1942—Maria Beatriz Nascimento is born on July 12 in Sergipe, Brazil, to Rubina Pereira Nascimento and Francisco Xavier do Nascimento. She is the eighth of ten children.

1950—The Nascimento family moves to Rio de Janeiro.

1964—The beginning of the military dictatorship in Brazil.

1967—Beatriz Nascimento and José do Rosário Freitas Gomes, an artist from Cape Verde, are married.

1968—Beatriz Nascimento begins her studies in history at the Federal University of Rio de Janeiro (UFRJ).

1968—Institutional Act Number 5 begins a period of harsh repression by the military dictatorship in Brazil.

1970—Beatriz Nascimento's daughter is born. Her father is José do Rosário Freitas Gomes.

1971—Beatriz Nascimento graduates with a bachelor's degree in history from the Universidade Federal do Rio de Janeiro (UFRJ).

1973—Independence of Guinea-Bissau.

1974—Beatriz Nascimento publishes her first essays in *Revista de Cultura Vozes*, including "For a History of Black People" and "Black People and Racism."

1975—The André Rebouças Working Group (GTAR) is founded by Black students, including Beatriz Nascimento

1975—Independence of Cape Verde, Angola, and Mozambique.

1976—Publishes "The Black Woman in the Labor Market" in the magazine *Última Hora* and other pieces. Her interview in the magazine *Manchete*, "Black People, Seen by Themselves," is noticed by military authorities.

1977—Beatriz Nascimento plays an important role in the *Quinzena do Negro* (Black Fortnight) at the University of São Paulo. Meets the filmmaker Raquel Gerber. Publishes "Our Racial Democracy" in the magazine *IstoÉ*.

1979—Begins a master's in history at UFF and later postgraduate studies at UFRJ. Travels to Angola.

1981—Completes her thesis on quilombos at UFRJ.

1982—Publishes "My Internal Blackness" in *Village Voice*. It is the only piece of writing she published in English in her lifetime.

1983—Francisco Xavier do Nascimento, Beatriz Nascimento's father, dies.

1984—Beatriz Nascimento appointed as a teacher in the public sector in Rio de Janeiro. Teaches history at the Colégio Estadual Roma in Copacabana.

1985—End of the military dictatorship. Publishes "The Concept of Quilombo and Black Cultural Resistance" in Afrodiáspora.

1987—The book *Negro e cultura no Brasil* (Black people and culture in Brazil), of which Beatriz Nascimento is coauthor with José Siqueira and Helena Theodora, is published by UNIBRADE in Brazil.

1987—Takes part in the Pan-African Festival of Arts and Culture (FESPAC) in Dakar, Senegal.

1988—Centenary of the abolition of slavery in Brazil.

1989—The film *Ôrí*, directed by Raquel Gerber, is released.

1991—Travels to Martinique and Haiti to take part in the International Festival of Culture.

1992—Begins master's in social communication at UFRJ, supervised by Muniz Sodré.

1994—Travels to Germany for a presentation of *Ôrí*.

1995–28 January—Beatriz Nascimento is murdered in Botafogo, Rio de Janeiro.

1999—Bethânia Gomes donates Beatriz Nascimento's archive to the Brazilian National Archives in Rio de Janeiro.

2007—Alex Ratts publishes *Eu sou Atlântica*, a biography and collection of her writing.

2015—*Todas [as] distâncias: poemas, aforismos e ensaios de Beatriz Nascimento* (All the distances: Poems, aphorisms and essays by Beatriz Nascimento), edited by Bethânia Gomes and Alex Ratts, published by Editora Ogun.

2016—The Library of the Brazilian National Archives is named after Beatriz Nascimento.

2018—*Beatriz Nascimento, quilombola e intelectual: possibilidade nos dias da destruição*, organized by the União dos Coletivos Pan Africanistas (The Union of Pan African Collectives), published by Editora Filhos da África.

2021—Beatriz Nascimento is posthumously awarded an honorary doctorate by the Federal University of Rio de Janeiro.

INDEX

Page numbers in italics refer to figures and tables. Page numbers in bold refer to original translated texts.

www.ingramcontent.com/pod-product-compliance
Ingram Content Group UK Ltd.
Pitfield, Milton Keynes, MK11 3LW, UK
UKHW030733060325
455883UK00003B/15